TPI New Testament Commentaries

General Editors
Howard Clark Kee   Dennis Nineham

Paul's Letter to the Romans

TPI New Testament Commentaries

These paragraph–by–paragraph commentaries have
been written by modern scholars who are in touch
with contemporary biblical study and also with the
interests of the general reader. They interpret the
words of the New Testament for the twentieth
century in the light of the latest archeological,
historical and linguistic research and are neither
over–simplified nor abstruse and academic.

TPI New Testament Commentaries

Paul's Letter to the Romans

JOHN ZIESLER

SCM PRESS
London
TRINITY PRESS INTERNATIONAL
Valley Forge

First published 1989
Third impression 1993

SCM Press   Trinity Press International
26-30 Tottenham Road   P.O. Box 851
London N1 4BZ   Valley Forge, PA

British Library Cataloguing in Publication Data

Ziesler, John
    Romans.
    1. Bible. N.T. Romans—Expositions
    I. Title
    227'.106

    ISBN 0-334-02297-5

Library of Congress Cataloging-in-Publication Data

    Ziesler, J. A.
        Paul's letter to the Romans/John Ziesler.
        p.   cm.—(TPI New Testament commentaries)
        Bibliography: p.
        Includes indexes.
        ISBN 0-334-02297-5 : $24.95
        1. Bible. N.T. Romans—Commentaries.   I. Title.   II. Series.
    BS2665.3.Z54   1989
    227'.107—dc20   89-35586

334 02297 5 (cased)
334 02296 7 (paper)

Typeset by Gloucester Typesetting Services
Printed and bound in Great Britain by
Biddles Ltd, Guildford and King's Lynn

Contents

CONTENTS

Acknowledgments

I am grateful to Dennis Nineham, editor of the series, for his invitation to write this commentary, for his constant encouragement, and for his constructive criticism. I also owe a considerable debt to the many students with whom I have worked on Romans, and especially to those who have made me see things in a new light. There is a special debt of gratitude to the late Marcus Ward, and to the now aged commentary by W. Sanday and A. C. Headlam, who in my student days jointly gave me a fascination with the letter which has never left me. That their reading of it was in important respects different from what mine now is, only goes to show that we are all engaged in a task of interpretation whose results are never more than provisional.

Lastly, to Sally I owe more than I can say here, or anywhere.

References, Abbreviations and Technical Terms

The biblical text used is the *Revised Standard Version*.

The titles of the books of the Bible receive their customary abbreviations. Biblical references are given by chapter and verse, and where necessary also by section of verse; thus I Cor. 6^{2b} means the second half of verse 2 of chapter 6 of Paul's First Letter to the Corinthians.

Articles in periodicals are cited by the abbreviated title of the periodical, followed by the volume number and/or its date, then the page number.

The ancient manuscripts of the letter are numerous, and no two agree exactly, because dissemination of such texts was entirely by laborious copying by hand. They lacked punctuation, and knew nothing of such devices as parentheses, footnotes, quotation marks, not to mention chapters and verses. All these are the work of subsequent editors. In discussing the disagreements (known as variants) between ancient manuscripts, attention will be paid chiefly to those which are noted in RSV. Some important MSS will be mentioned by their usual symbols, thus:

ℵ   Codex Sinaiticus (fourth century)
A   Codex Alexandrinus (fifth century)
B   Codex Vaticanus (fourth century)
D   Codex Claromontanus (sixth century)
G   Codex Boernerianus (ninth century)
$\mathfrak{P}^{46}$ Chester Beatty papyrus (about 200).

The MSS of the New Testament are often treated like members of families, because of their common characteristics (i.e. they resemble one another more than they resemble others). Chief among these families are the Alexandrian, represented by א, sometimes A, and B, and the Western, represented by D and G, and also by the Old Latin (symbol: it).

In discussing textual variations, several factors come into play. Obviously it makes sense to favour old and generally reliable MSS over later and generally less reliable ones, though this can never be a hard and fast rule. Obviously also, we look for a reading which makes sense in the context, though we have to be ready for an author to have written something not in line with his usual style and thought. The criterion usually regarded as crucial for choosing between variants is that the best reading is the one which most plausibly can account for the existence of the others. In practice this often means choosing the most awkward reading, on the grounds that copyists would tend to smooth over difficulties of grammar, sense, or theology, rather than to create new ones.

ANRW	*Aufstieg und Niedergang der Römischen Welt*, Berlin/New York
BCE	Before the Common Era (= BC)
Bib	*Biblica*, Rome
BJRL	*Bulletin of the John Rylands Library*, Manchester
CE	Common Era (= AD)
Diss.	Dissertation
ET	English translation
ExpT	*Expository Times*, Edinburgh
FS	Festschrift (i.e. a collection of essays in honour of someone)
ICC	*International Critical Commentary*, Edinburgh
JBL	*Journal of Biblical Literature*, Philadelphia
JSNT	*Journal for the Study of the New Testament*, Sheffield
JSNTMS	*Journal for the Study of the New Testament, Monograph Series*, Sheffield
JSOT	*Journal for the Study of the Old Testament*, Sheffield
KJV	King James Version (= Authorized Version)
LXX	Septuagint, the Greek version of the Old Testament, so called because it was believed to have been the work of seventy-two translators working independently. It often

differs from the Hebrew text on which our English versions are based.

MS	Manuscript
MSS	Manuscripts
NEB	New English Bible
NT	New Testament
NT	*Novum Testamentum*, Leiden
NTS	*New Testament Studies*, Cambridge
OT	Old Testament
RSV	Revised Standard Version
RV	Revised Version
SBL	Society for Biblical Literature
SNTSMS	*Society for New Testament Studies Monograph Series*
TDNT	*Theological Dictionary of the New Testament*, ET of G. Kittel and G. Friedrich, *Theologisches Wörterbuch zum NT*, 9 vols., Eerdmans, Grand Rapids, Mich.
TLZ	*Theologische Literaturzeitung*, Leipzig
TZ	*Theologische Zeitschrift*, Basel
ZNW	*Zeitschrift für die neutestamentliche Wissenschaft*, Berlin

Bibliography

In the first two sections, only those works regularly mentioned in the book are listed. In each case, they are cited in abbreviated form, and this is listed first, followed by fuller details.

A. Commentaries

Althaus: P. Althaus, *Der Brief an die Römer*, Göttingen: Vandenhoeck & Ruprecht 1978

Barrett: C. K. Barrett, *The Epistle to the Romans*, A. & C. Black 1957

Black: M. Black, *Romans* (*New Century Bible*), Marshall, Morgan and Scott 1973

Bruce: F. F. Bruce, *The Epistle of Paul to the Romans*, Tyndale Press 1963

Cranfield: C. E. B. Cranfield, *The Epistle to the Romans*, 2 vols., *ICC*, T. & T. Clark 1975, 1979

Dodd: C. H. Dodd, *The Epistle of Paul to the Romans*, Hodder & Stoughton 1932

Käsemann: E. Käsemann, *Commentary on Romans*, ET SCM Press 1980

Lagrange: M.-J. Lagrange, *Saint Paul: Épître aux Romains*, Paris: Gabalda 1950

Leenhardt: F. J. Leenhardt, *The Epistle to the Romans*, ET Lutterworth Press 1961

Metzger: B. M. Metzger, *A Textual Commentary on the Greek New Testament*, United Bible Societies 1971

Michel: O. Michel, *Der Brief an die Römer*, Göttingen: Vandenhoeck & Ruprecht [14]1978

Murray: J. Murray, *The Epistle to the Romans*, Eerdmans and Marshall, Morgan and Scott 1967

Nygren: A. Nygren, *Commentary on Romans*, ET SCM Press and Fortress Press 1952

O'Neill: J. C. O'Neill, *Paul's Letter to the Romans*, Penguin Books 1975

Robinson: J. A. T. Robinson, *Wrestling with Romans*, SCM Press 1979

Sanday & Headlam: W. Sanday and A. C. Headlam, *The Epistle to the Romans*, ICC, T. & T. Clark ⁵1902

Schlier: H. Schlier, *Der Römerbrief*, Freiburg, Basel and Vienna: Herder 1977

Schmidt: H. W. Schmidt, *Der Brief des Paulus an die Römer*, Berlin: Evangelischer Verlag 1963

Wilckens: U. Wilckens, *Der Brief an die Römer*, 3 vols., Benziger/ Neukirchenes Verlag 1978, 1980, 1982

B. Other Works

Badenas, *End:* R. Badenas, *Christ the End of the Law*, JSNTMS 10, JSOT Press 1985

Barrett, *Essays:* C. K. Barrett, *Essays on Paul*, SPCK 1982

Beker, *Apostle:* J. C. Beker, *Paul the Apostle*, Fortress Press and T. & T. Clark 1980

Bultmann, *Theology:* R. Bultmann, *Theology of the New Testament*, 2 vols., ET SCM Press 1952, 1955

Campbell, 'Freedom': W. S. Campbell, 'The Freedom and Faithfulness of God in Relation to Israel', *JSNT* 13, 1981, pp. 27–45

Campbell, 'Christ the End': W. S. Campbell, 'Christ the End of the Law: Romans 10:4', pp. 73–81 of E. A. Livingstone (ed.), *Studia Biblica 1978*, III. *Papers on Paul and Other New Testament Authors*, JSOT Press 1980

Dahl, *Studies:* N. A. Dahl, *Studies in Paul*, Augsburg Publishing House 1977

Davies, *JPS:* W. D. Davies, *Jewish and Pauline Studies*, Fortress Press and SPCK 1984

Davies, *PRJ:* W. D. Davies, *Paul and Rabbinic Judaism*, SPCK ²1955

Donfried, *Debate:* K. P. Donfried (ed.), *The Romans Debate*, Augsburg Publishing House 1977

Dunn, *Christology:* J. D. G. Dunn, *Christology in the Making*, SCM Press and Westminster Press 1980

Dunn, *Jesus and Spirit:* J. D. G. Dunn, *Jesus and the Spirit*, SCM Press and Westminster Press 1975

Dunn, 'Rom. 7, 14–25': J. D. G. Dunn, 'Rom. 7, 14–25 in the Theology of Paul', *TZ* 31, 1975, pp. 258–73

Feuillet, 'Loi de Dieu': A. Feuillet, 'Loi de Dieu, loi du Christ et loi de l'Ésprit d'après les épîtres pauliniennes', *NT* 22, 1980, pp. 29–65

Gamble, *Textual History*: Harry Gamble Jr, *The Textual History of the Letter to the Romans*, Eerdmans 1977

Hagner & Harris: D. A. Hagner and M. J. Harris (eds.), *Pauline Studies*, FS F. F. Bruce, Paternoster Press and Eerdmans 1980

Hanson, *Technique*: A. T. Hanson, *Studies in Paul's Technique and Theology*, SPCK 1974

Hooker & Wilson: M. D. Hooker and S. G. Wilson (eds.), *Paul and Paulinism*, FS C. K. Barrett, SPCK 1982

Hübner, *LPT*: H. Hübner, *Law in Paul's Thought*, ET T. & T. Clark 1984

Jewett, *Terms*: R. Jewett, *Paul's Anthropological Terms*, Leiden: Brill 1971

Kümmel, *Römer 7*: W. G. Kümmel, *Römer 7 und das Bild des Menschen im Neuen Testament*, Munich: Christian Kaiser Verlag 1974

Meeks, *Urban Christians*: W. A. Meeks, *The First Urban Christians*, Yale University Press 1983

Minear, *Obedience*: P. S. Minear, *The Obedience of Faith*, SCM Press 1971

Munck, *Israel*: J. Munck, *Christ and Israel*, Fortress Press 1967

Munck, *Salvation*: J. Munck, *Paul and the Salvation of Mankind*, ET SCM Press 1959

Newton, *Purity*: M. Newton, *The Concept of Purity at Qumran and in the Letters of Paul*, SNTSMS 53, CUP 1985

Räisänen, *PL*: H. Räisänen, *Paul and the Law*, Tübingen: J. C. B. Mohr 1983

Räisänen, *Torah*: H. Räisänen, *The Torah and Christ*, Helsinki: Finnish Exegetical Society 1986

Räisänen, 'Geistigen Ringens': H. Räisänen, 'Römer 9–11: Analyse eines geistigen Ringens', *ANRW*, 1987, Vol. 25.4, pp. 2891–2939

Reumann, *Righteousness*: J. Reumann (with J. A. Fitzmyer & J. D. Quinn), *Righteousness in the New Testament*, Paulist Press and Fortress Press 1982

Richardson, *Israel*: P. Richardson, *Israel in the Apostolic Church*, SNTSMS 10, CUP 1969

Sanders, *PLJP*: E. P. Sanders, *Paul, the Law, and the Jewish People*, Fortress Press 1983 and SCM Press 1985

Sanders, *PPJ*: E. P. Sanders, *Paul and Palestinian Judaism*, SCM Press 1977

Siegert, *Argumentation*: F. Siegert, *Argumentation bei Paulus: gezeigt an Röm 9–11*, Tübingen: J. C. B. Mohr 1985

Theissen, *Aspekte*: G. Theissen, *Psychologische Aspekte paulinischer Theologie*, Göttingen: Vandenhoeck & Ruprecht 1983. Now in English, *Psychological Aspects of Pauline Theology*, T. & T. Clark 1987

Watson, *PJG*: F. Watson, *Paul, Judaism and the Gentiles*, SNTSMS 56, CUP 1986

Whiteley, *Theology*: D. E. H. Whiteley, *The Theology of Saint Paul*, Blackwell 1964

Williams, 'Righteousness': S. K. Williams, 'The "Righteousness of God" in Romans', *JBL* 99, 1980, pp. 241–90

Ziesler, *Meaning*: J. A. Ziesler, *The Meaning of Righteousness in Paul*, SNTSMS 20, CUP 1972

Ziesler, *PC*: J. A. Ziesler, *Pauline Christianity*, OUP 1983

C. Other Important Commentaries

It would be impossible to list all the commentaries on Romans. The following are only some of those not cited:

P. J. Achtemeier, *Romans (Interpretation)*, John Knox Press 1985

J. D. G. Dunn, *Romans*, Waco, Texas: Word Books, forthcoming

K. Barth, *The Epistle to the Romans*, ET, OUP 1933

K. Barth, *A Shorter Commentary on Romans*, ET, SCM Press and John Knox Press 1959

E. Best, *The Letter of Paul to the Romans*, CUP 1967

C. E. B. Cranfield, *Romans: A Shorter Commentary*, T. & T. Clark 1985

J. Huby & S. Lyonnet, *Paul. Épître aux Romains*, Paris: Beauchesne 1957

J. Knox, 'The Epistle to the Romans', in *The Interpreter's Bible* IX, Abingdon Press 1954

BIBLIOGRAPHY

O. Kuss, *Der Römerbrief*, 3 vols., Regensburg: Pustet Verlag 1959, 1963, 1978

H. Lietzmann, *An die Römer*, Tübingen: J. C. B. Mohr ⁵1971

A. Maillot, *L'Épître aux Romains*, Paris and Geneva: Le Centurion and Labor et Fides 1984

D. Zeller, *Der Brief an die Römer*, Regensburg: Pustet Verlag 1985

Introduction

There can be few ancient letters ('epistle' and 'letter' are taken to be synonymous) which have been so influential and also so controversial as this one. Attempts to explain it and to interpret its message for one's own contemporaries go back at least to the second century, though it was at the time of the Reformation that it became most prominent, particularly with Luther. He found in Romans, together with Galatians, the chief support for his teaching that the Christian message was primarily about God's undeserved and unconditioned goodness towards men and women who were otherwise hopelessly sinful, and was in sharp contradiction to any notion that human beings could ever deserve God's favour. Indeed, such an idea was seen as leading to self-righteousness, which was the greatest of all barriers between God and humans.

A great deal of subsequent interpretation of Romans has been concerned with this 'Lutheran' interpretation, whether agreeing with it all the way, or wanting to modify it. This present book, in attempting to explain the letter, deliberately attempts to get underneath the centuries of interpretation, and to hear as far as possible what the original Romans heard when the letter was read to them (doubtless at more than one sitting!). Inevitably, because the attempt is being carried out by a twentieth-century Western European with his own cultural experiences and conditioning, the attempt can never be more than approximately successful. Yet, especially because of the immense weight of polemical and doctrinal interpretation that has accumulated, it is important to keep on trying to hear what they heard, *before* we start asking questions about the message the letter has for us today. Such matters will not be dealt with in this commentary, but will be left to the reader.

There is one particular respect in which this commentary differs from most of its predecessors. Until about 1977 it was usual to find commentators saying that Paul, especially in Galatians and Romans, was opposing the view allegedly held by most of his Jewish contemporaries, that good deeds, and in particular good deeds done in obedience to the *Torah*,[a] enabled one to acquire merit with God and so be acceptable to him. Paul, it was claimed, wrote to maintain that now, because of Jesus Christ, it must on the contrary be said that acceptance with God, and acquittal at the divine judgment, is entirely by grace on the divine side and by faith on the human side. In other words, Luther's problem was also Paul's problem, except that Luther's opponents were certain Roman Catholic theologians, and Paul's were Jewish ones. That granted, their targets were taken to be virtually the same.

In 1977 E. P. Sanders[b] in a massive study failed to find any such merit-dominated approach to God in Jewish sources of the relevant period. If he is right, then Romans must be construed differently. Even where its handling of some matters differs from that of Sanders, this commentary is heavily indebted to him. If Paul's target is not human and in particular Jewish self-righteousness, it must be something else, and in what follows an attempt is made to see what that something else is.

If we aim to hear as far as we can what Paul's first readers heard, we need to know who they were. They were without doubt Christians (cf. 1[1-8]), for the whole letter presupposes a Christian belief on the part of the readers. Were they Jewish Christians, Gentile Christians, or some of each? Internal evidence suggests that the readership was expected to consist of some of each. Often enough, what is said is applicable to both sorts of Christian, but sometimes Paul appears to be addressing Gentiles (e.g. 1[13]; 11[13-22]) and sometimes he seems be addressing Jews (e.g. 2[17-24]; 7[4]). It is sometimes pointed out that Romans is unique in the Pauline correspondence for the clarity of

a The Hebrew word for the Law, which held and holds a central place in Jewish piety. The definitive Torah is the Pentateuch, Genesis to Deuteronomy, though this was later interpreted and handed down in literature like the Talmuds. The books of the Law contain much more than laws: stories, and promises, for example, and we shall see that this wider meaning is important for understanding parts of Romans.

b PPJ, later developed in certain respects in *PLJP*.

the evidence that Jewish Christians are expected to be among the readers.[c]

It is natural that, in the case of a writing that has been so thoroughly studied as this one, there should be many issues thrown up over the years by the scholarly enterprise. What follows in the Introduction is a selection of the most critical of these issues. To many readers they may seem barriers to grappling with the text of the letter, rather than aids to its understanding. If so, there is a good deal to be said for moving straight to the commentary proper, and for returning to these introductory matters at the end of reading the commentary, or for referring to them from time to time.

I. WHY DID PAUL WRITE THIS LETTER?

Why did Paul write this very long letter, about precisely these matters, to precisely these people?

(a) Why a letter to Rome at all?

Apparently, the question is easily answered: both at the beginning and at the end (1^{10-15} and 15^{22-29}) he makes it obvious that he is preparing the ground for a visit to Rome, to a church which he does not know at first hand. Unfortunately, the two passages are not in entire agreement about Paul's reason for his visit, and this causes uncertainties about his reason for writing. In 1^{15} he says his visit is 'to preach the gospel to you also', in a church he has not visited but some of whose members he knows ($16^{3, 5, 7, 8}$; this is assuming Ch. 16 is part of the original letter). All the stress in Ch. 1 is thus on his visit to Rome for its own sake, and there is no mention of any other reason. In Ch. 15, on the other hand, his reason for coming is to 'see you in passing as I go to Spain, and to be sped on my journey there by you' (15^{24}). He needs their practical support for his mission farther west, and though he reiterates his eager anticipation of a visit, which he has wanted to make for a long time but from which he has been mysteriously hindered hitherto (15^{22-24}), the goal is not Rome but Spain.

[c] So Sanders, *PLJP*, pp. 182–4; Munck, *Salvation*, pp. 204–6, rather implausibly thinks that even the Roman church was an almost solely Gentile one.

It has been suggested[d] that this contradiction is one sign that our present letter is a stitching together of more than one epistle. There is something to be said for such a view. It would help to account for another discrepancy, between 15^{23-25} where Paul's plan to visit seems definite, and 1^{13} where 'thus far prevented' could mean that he is still unable to commit himself to a visit. It would also help, though only a little, to explain why in 1^{13} he seems to envisage making converts in Rome, yet in 15^{20} says it is his fixed policy not to preach where there are already Christian believers (it would help only a little, because we should still have a contradiction between two letters, though not within one letter). The aim of Schmithals is to explain how it is that in parts of the letter, as he sees it, Paul aims to persuade Gentile Christians who are still attached to the Jewish synagogue as godfearers[e] to loosen their ties to it, while in other parts he wants his readers to be tolerant of such unliberated people. There are, he suggests, different letters written for different but related reasons.

It is doubtful if thus dismembering the letter is very successful in removing difficulties. Incompatibilities within one letter become incompatibilities between letters written at different, but not vastly different, times. Certainly, the present difficulty about whether the projected visit was primarily for the Romans' own benefit, or to prepare the Romans to serve as a base camp for the Spanish mission, is not finally solved by the theory of Schmithals. Most scholars are reluctant to divide a letter into several originally separate entities unless there are powerful arguments for doing so, and unless alternative solutions are implausible. In this case it is not too difficult to think of a reason why it is not until the end of the letter that we discover that the Roman visit is not strictly for the Romans' sake: that reason is tact, or even good manners. At the beginning Paul courteously depicts his readers as the object of his visit, and only at the end lets them understand that they are a part of larger plans. By this time he

d See W. Schmithals, *Der Römerbrief als historisches Problem*, Gütersloh 1975; see also the useful discussion of the Schmithals thesis by A. J. M. Wedderburn, 'The Purpose and Occasion of Romans Again', *Exp T* XC.5, 1979, 137–41.

e Adherents who were not full proselytes, i.e. circumcised members committed to full Jewish practice.

has presumably gained their sympathy for his point of view and also their support for his whole enterprise.

(b) Why a letter of this length and on these topics?

Given that Paul needed to write to the Roman Christians at all, we still need to ask why it was precisely this letter that was written, one that has been regarded as his major theological achievement and even as his 'last will and testament', theologically speaking.[f] So far as we know, Paul's only letter of comparable length is I Corinthians, but there the length is caused largely by the series of questions raised, explicitly or implicitly, by the Corinthians themselves. There is no such reason for the length of Romans, at least on the surface.

It is commonly said that Paul wrote not as a systematic theologian but as a missionary pastor, and that his letters were responses to concrete problems and difficulties, whether theological, ethical, or disciplinary. Within these responses lies a great deal of theology, but they are not primarily theological disquisitions. In I Corinthians, for instance, when Paul has finished dealing with the series of issues that have been raised, he simply observes the normal conventions of ending letters, and then stops. He does not go on writing theology for its own sake. The same appears to be true of the other letters, except Romans, which for many readers bears the marks of a sustained theological argument.

It is indeed always the case that Paul responds to the issues in his own way, no doubt saying what he wants to say rather than necessarily what his readers wanted to hear, or even perhaps needed to hear. This is only to say that in his letters there is a mixture of material dealing with his own concerns and of material dealing with the recipients' concerns. Such is doubtless true of almost all except the most perfunctory of letters, whoever writes them. The peculiar problem of

---

[f] G. Bornkamm in Donfried, *Debate*, Ch. 2. This whole volume is of great importance for the matter here under consideration. See also, among many other contributions, J. W. Drane, 'Why did Paul Write Romans?', in Hagner & Harris, Ch. 13; W. S. Campbell, 'Why Did Paul Write Romans?' *Exp T* LXXXV.9, 1974, 264–9; Minear, *Obedience*; and not least Cranfield II, Essay I, pp. 814–23.

the letter to the Romans is that, while it is relatively easy to identify Paul's concerns, it is not immediately obvious how what he writes connects with the Romans' concerns, nor is it obvious what their concerns were.

(i) Romans as a presentation of Paul's theology

A considerable amount of the material in Romans is familiar to us, at least in its general orientation, from other letters. The question of how Jews and Gentiles relate to one another within one Christian community, the further questions of how that community relates to its Jewish roots, and of how men and women are to be accepted by God as his people, and of God's dealings throughout history with his special people, all have some sort of resonance with the letter to the Galatians, even though the treatment there differs at some points from that in Romans. Even the major ethical matter, the question of eating or not eating certain foods, has important similarities in its treatment with I Cor. 8, 10, whether or not the problem there is precisely the same. Is Paul, therefore, pulling together into one new structure materials which have emerged as crucial in his mission generally, without special regard for their relevance to the Roman church? It seems possible.

Moreover, there is remarkably little in Romans that is explicitly tied to any time, place, or set of people. Apart from Ch. 16, whose doubtful provenance will be discussed below, and apart from the travel plans in Chs. 1 and 15, the letter could have been addressed to almost any church, or so it seems. Again, therefore, it is hardly surprising that many have argued that alone of the letters of Paul, Romans arises out of Paul's own concerns, and hardly at all out of the needs of the recipient church. Indeed we find it hard at first blush to name one of those concerns, except the question of eating foods (Ch. 14), and even that could be a projection from Paul's experience in Corinth, which may or may not meet a similar Roman problem.

In addition, the body of the letter has, for Paul, a remarkably logical structure (see the analysis of the letter below). It forms the nearest to a systematic account of Christianity to be found in his writings, or indeed in the New Testament as a whole. This is consistent with its being an attempt by Paul to make a considered statement of his distinctive view of the Christian gospel.

So far as the manner of presentation is concerned, its nature is highly rhetorical, often in the style of a debate with a hypothetical partner, and does not appear to address real opponents as so often elsewhere in Paul. Whether this rhetorical question and answer technique can properly be called 'diatribe' is disputed, but the thing itself is certainly present.

'Diatribe' is usually defined as debate with an imaginary opponent, and has been widely supposed to have been a contemporary literary device. The most famous presentation of the case for its use by Paul is to be found in R. Bultmann, *Der Stil der paulinischen Predigt und die kynisch-stoische Diatribe*, Göttingen 1910, and the view is often taken as established. Yet Donfried in Ch. 8 of *Debate*, 'False Presuppositions in the Study of Romans', pp. 132–41, gives concise expression to two sets of doubts. First, was there ever such a *genre* as the Cynic-Stoic diatribe? Second, even if there was, can we really say that Paul used it, rather than less exactly defined rhetorical methods? Donfried thinks that uncertain answers must be given to both questions. In any case, there is no good reason why Paul should not both use rhetorical methods and at the same time address concrete situations and actual persons in Rome. Preachers do that sort of thing every week. A more recent discussion is in Stanley K. Sowers, *The Diatribe and Paul's Letter to the Romans*, SBL Dissertation Series 57, Chico Cal. 1981. He maintains that the diatribe did exist as a *genre*, but that it belonged not to propaganda but rather to philosophical discussion in a teacher–student setting. Paul does indeed use it, and appropriately enough for pedagogy, not for polemic.

So then, for reasons such as these, very many scholars, perhaps the majority, have found the reason for Romans to be some need on Paul's part to make a considered statement of his position on certain important issues. It is often observed that, where similar material is found in Romans and in another letter, the treatment in Romans is more careful, balanced, and within a larger theological framework.

Thus, it is said,[g] while the issues in Romans are similar to those in Galatians, they are not simply a matter of whether Gentiles need to become Jews in order to become Christians, and of how Gentiles and Jews can exist together in one Christian community, but are in a wider perspective. In Romans we see the issues within God's historical (*heilsgeschichtlich*)[h] treatment of his people, Israel, and face the questions as to how the Gentiles fit into both his ancient purposes and his ancient people, and as to how Jesus Christ is the solution to the problems of the whole human race, Jew and Gentile alike. In other words, it looks as if Paul is trying to make a thorough and even definitive statement of his viewpoint. Yet why should Paul feel the need to do such a thing, and why should he then decide to send the result to the Roman church?

(ii) Romans as a circular letter

As an answer to the last question, it has been proposed that originally what we call 'Romans' was a circular letter, the copy addressed to Rome being the one that has come down to us. There is some concrete evidence for this. A few manuscripts omit the words 'in Rome' in 1[7] and 1[15]: the chief one to do so is G, admittedly late (10th century?), but usually an important witness to the text of Romans. The evidence is hardly impressive, and it may be that at some stage the words were left out in order to make it plain that the letter was of universal application. Nevertheless, it is possible that 'in Rome' was originally found only in the Roman copy, and also possible (as is discussed below) that Ch. 16 was originally attached not to the Roman but to the Ephesian copy of the circular. We shall see that there is indeed a case to be made for seeing Rom. 16 as having originally been sent to Ephesus, though there is nothing impossible or even implausible about it as part of a letter to Rome.

g See J. W. Drane, 'Why Did Paul Write Romans?', Ch. 13 of Hagner & Harris, especially pp. 212, 223, as well as *Paul: Libertine or Legalist?*, SPCK 1975.

h A German adjective describing God's saving dealings with his people in the process of history, and also the history of those saving dealings. 'Salvation history' and 'History of salvation' are both acceptable translations of the German noun *Heilsgeschichte*, which is often used in theological and exegetical writing.

The circular letter theory would explain the general and almost systematic character of Romans, but it has its difficulties. First, the MS that lacks 'in Rome' in 1⁷, ¹⁵ does not have the name of another church instead, but simply nothing at all. Are we to suppose that there were some spare copies without the destination's having been inserted? This leads us to wonder if the whole notion of multiple copies is not a trifle anachronistic. Of course it is possible, even in Paul's time, but it fits more easily into an age like ours, where multiple copies can be made quickly, easily, and relatively cheaply. In the first century, we have to do rather with slow, laborious, and expensive copying by hand.

The second difficulty about the circular theory is that even without 'in Rome' in 1⁷, ¹⁵, there is still rather a lot that is tied to a particular time and place. Even if we discount Ch. 16 and its data as not originally sent to Rome, there is still the material about Paul's intention to visit in 1¹⁰ff. and 15²²ff.: to how many places could these precise intentions apply, and in particular of how many places could it be hoped that they would help him on his way to Spain? Moreover, did all these places also have a problem about eating or not eating certain foods? Did they all have a Jewish/Gentile problem? It cannot be said to be quite impossible, but it begins to look more and more improbable.

(iii) Romans as preparing the ground for Paul's Jerusalem visit

The more common answer to the question why Paul should wish to send a definitive statement of his thought on certain key issues to the Roman church is one that looks both before and after. It looks back to the controversy in Galatia (Gal. 2), where Paul had to face those who believed that Jews and Gentiles could not eat together in one fellowship unless Gentiles adopted certain key observances, notably food laws and circumcision. He saw this as requiring Gentiles to become Jews in order to be in the same Christian community as Jews, so that Christ and faith in him was no longer sufficient for entry into that community. The same controversy is presumably reflected also in Phil. 3 and II Cor. 3–6. It became a central issue in the Pauline mission, and was the reason for the so-called Apostolic Council in Jerusalem (Gal. 2 and Acts 15: whatever the precise relationship between the two passages and the events they describe, there certainly was at least one meeting on the issue). If it was so central, it is hardly surprising that it is strongly reflected in Romans.

However, the answer also looks forward, to Paul's impending visit to Jerusalem. He intends to return there, taking with him the monetary gifts of his churches (Rom. 15²⁵⁻²⁷) for the poor in that city. Evidently it is highly important to him that he should do this, not only for the sake of relieving hardship (Rom. 15²⁷; Gal. 2¹⁰; I Cor. 16¹⁻⁴; II Cor. 8–9) but also in order to express and to foster a genuine unity between Gentile and Jewish churches (Rom. 15²⁷). To this end, it is surely significant that he intends to be accompanied by some representatives of the churches that have contributed to the collection (I Cor. 16³⁻⁴). I Corinthians may suggest an even deeper purpose, namely to signal that the last days are very near now that the Gentiles are streaming to Zion,[i] though no hint of such a purpose emerges in Romans. At all events it is clear enough that the collection is of sufficient importance to Paul for him to be determined to appear with it in Jerusalem, despite the considerable personal danger that he runs. It is also clear that he is not by any means certain that the gift will be accepted (Rom. 15³¹), presumably because it may be held to have come from an unacceptable source.[j] Therefore, it is held, Paul in Romans looks forward to his Jerusalem visit, to the uncertainty of his reception there from Christian as well as non-Christian compatriots, and to the controversy he fears may take place. It has even been suggested that in the event the collection was declined on theological grounds, i.e. as implying endorsement of the non-observant Gentile churches, and that this is why Acts, with its ecumenical tendency, is virtually silent about it.[k]

i So Munck, *Salvation*, pp. 303f.; see Isa. 2²ᶠ·; 60⁵ᶠ·; Micah 4¹ᶠ··.

j Watson, *PJG*, pp. 174–6, suggests that by accepting the collection the Jerusalem church would implicitly accept the validity of Paul's Gentile, law-free churches, and so stop trying to influence them towards Jewish observances, such as circumcision, the sabbath, and the food laws. Paul rightly is not at all sure that his strategy will work.

k See for example J. D. G. Dunn, *Unity and Diversity in the New Testament*, SCM Press 1977, pp. 256–7. In Acts the only allusion to the collection comes at 24¹⁷, which suggests that the author knows about it, but chooses to pass over it in near-silence. If it mattered to Paul as much as his letters seem to indicate, an explanation is needed for its treatment, or lack of treatment, in Acts. That it was not accepted cannot be ruled out.

If his collection is to achieve its purposes, therefore, Paul is obliged to make a theological defence of his version of Christianity, arguing that he is not a renegade, that he has not turned his back on God's dealings with his ancient people nor on the covenant of God with Israel, if these are properly understood in the light of Christ. Romans looks ahead, then, to the coming controversy in Jerusalem, and constitutes a prior statement of his defence of himself and his churches. Yet we still need to know why it was sent to Rome, and not to Jerusalem. The answer often given is that there were rather close relations between the Jewish communities in Rome and in Jerusalem, and so also between the Jewish-Christian communities in the two centres. Paul was trying to enlist the support of the Romans, not only for his projected Spanish mission, but also for his case (and collection) to be presented before that in Jerusalem.[1]

That his visit to Jerusalem lies behind much that is said in Romans is by no means improbable, but that it controlled the content of the letter is impossible to demonstrate or to refute. Paul does not in fact ask the Romans for their support, except in their prayers (15^{30-32}). We may well be convinced that Romans fits well into what we know of Paul's concerns around the time of its writing; what is not so convincingly shown is why he should write at this length about these matters specifically to the Romans. Particularly in recent years, students of Romans have argued that the probable situation of the church in Rome at the time of Paul's writing does fit rather well with the matters discussed in the letter, and to this other side of the question we now turn.

(iv) Does Romans after all reflect the needs of the Roman church?

It is possible to argue that Romans is no different from Paul's other letters in reflecting the needs and problems of the church to which it is addressed. On this view, the concerns of the letter *are* reflections of

1 See J. Jervell, 'The Letter to Jerusalem', in Donfried, *Debate*, pp. 61–74; M. J. Suggs, 'The Word is Near You: Rom. X 6–10 within the Purpose of the Letter', in *Christian History and Interpretation: Studies Presented to John Knox*, ed. W. R. Farmer, C. F. D. Moule & R. R. Niebuhr, CUP 1967, pp. 289–98; A. J. M. Wedderburn, 'The Purpose and Occasion of Romans Again', 140f.; see also the summary of such views in Campbell, 'Why Did Paul Write Romans?', 266–7.

the concerns of the church in Rome, so far as they can be reconstructed. The relation of Jew to Gentile in one Christian community, the fulfilment in Christ and his church of God's historical dealings with his ancient people, the newness of salvation in Christ that is also part of the primal divine purpose as seen in the story of Abraham, and the need to accept one another without boasting over one another or judging one another, all these are matters that can be seen as directly relevant to the actual situation of the Christians in Rome. The tension between 'the weak' and 'the strong' in Rom. $14-15^6$ can also, at least on the usual reading of that passage, be taken as evidence of a Roman problem, though its precise nature is not easy to determine, as we shall see in the commentary proper.

There is a good case for thinking that the Roman church was exercised about Jewish-Gentile questions, and even that there was a problem about the relationship between Jewish-Christian and Gentile-Christian house churches. If the 'weak' in Ch. 14 are partly or wholly to be identified as Jewish Christians who feel obliged to maintain observance of Jewish food laws, and the 'strong' as Gentile Christians and doubtless some Jewish Christians also, who feel under no such obligation, then they might well have found it difficult to remain in communion with one another. Then it is possible that the different groups of Christians listed in Ch. 16 represent, at least in part, different attitudes to the matter of traditional Jewish observance, especially of food regulations. Even the fact that so many groups are mentioned may arise from a need to leave no section of the total Christian community in Rome out of account. All this is to a degree hypothetical: it is not certain that Rom. 14 does reflect a division along just these lines, nor that Ch. 16, if to Rome at all, does point to a divided church along these or any other lines. Nevertheless a reasonable case can be made for finding this sort of division and this sort of problem implied by the data.

However, there are more general grounds for suspecting that the Roman church was exercised about the relation of its Christian faith to its Jewish roots, in both theological and community terms. It has been argued[m] that the large Jewish community in Rome was considerably

m Notably by W. Wiefel, 'The Jewish Community in Ancient Rome and the Origins of Roman Christianity', Ch. 7 of Donfried, *Debate*.

varied in economic, social, and cultural status, and also in degree of strictness of adherence to the Torah (the Law). When Christianity first came to the capital, and we have no idea how or when that was, the Jewish population responded to it with great variety, roughly corresponding to its own internal variety. The result was a good deal of internal strife and even disorder. When the Emperor Claudius expelled the Jews from Rome, probably in or about the year 49, though an earlier date has been suggested, he did so, according to Suetonius, because of 'Jews who persisted in rioting at the instigation of Chrestus' (*Life of Claudius*, 25[4]). As it stands this is a puzzle: who on earth is Chrestus? The usual solution is to say that 'Chrestus' is the result of the Romans' misunderstanding of the title 'Christus' for a relatively common proper name. If this is correct, then the expulsion of Jews by Claudius was the outcome of their violent disagreements over the messiahship of Jesus: the emperor concluded that the only thing to do was to banish the lot of them. The event is mentioned in Acts 18[2]:

> And he found a Jew named Aquila, a native of Pontus, lately come from Italy with his wife Priscilla, because Claudius had commanded all the Jews to leave Rome.

This was not the first occasion on which all Jews had been expelled, and we do not have to assume either that every single Jew left, or that the expulsion lasted very long. There is no evidence that the order was rescinded, and it may simply have been allowed to lapse at the death of Claudius if not before.[n] If Rom. 16 was originally addressed to Rome, then by the mid-fifties Aquila and Priscilla were back in Rome (16[3-5]).

So far the picture can be tolerably well substantiated. What follows

---

n See E. M. Smallwood, *The Jews Under Roman Rule*, Leiden 1976, p. 216, and F. F. Bruce, 'Christianity under Claudius', *BJRL* 44, 1961–62 (309–26), 318. Dio Cassius, *Historia Romana* 60, 6, 6, makes no mention of the expulsion under Claudius, but does say that Jews had no right to assemble. Wiefel, art. cit., pp. 110f., takes this as indicating a first step in moderating the banning order: they were allowed back so long as they did not assemble. It is, however, more usually taken as an earlier attempt by Claudius to control Jewish turbulence: so Smallwood, pp. 211–14; Bruce, 314–15; Drane, 'Why Did Paul Write Romans?', pp. 216–17.

is more hypothetical. When the Jewish Christians returned to Rome, some time about the start of the reign of Nero, they found that Christianity in the city had gone on without them and was now a largely Gentile movement.[o] Exactly how, when, and under whose aegis this had happened are all unknown, but if it is correct it means that Roman Christianity had changed, during the expulsion period, from being a Jewish church to being a Gentile one, and after the return became a mixed one, with the Gentiles quite possibly now in the majority. It is even possible that if the first relaxation was to allow return but not assembly, Rom. 16 with its apparently rather small house groups reflects this early stage: it could have been a way of keeping within the letter of the law.

The importance of all this for understanding the purpose of Romans is that it provides a setting, constructed partly from known fact and partly from supposition, in which Jewish and Gentile Christians could have confronted one another on a number of issues. The most urgent of these issues might well have been the fundamental one of whether the Christian movement should be within the fold of Judaism and therefore ought to live Jewishly, or was a new and independent entity. It has been argued[p] that Paul saw and wanted to see his Gentile-Christian communities existing in sharp distinction from the Jewish synagogue. At least so far as Romans is concerned, this appears to draw the lines more sharply than the evidence warrants. What seems to fit the data more closely is M. D. Hooker's analogy of eighteenth- and nineteenth-century Methodists and Anglicans in Britain.[q] The communities overlapped, and many Jews found it possible to belong to both church and synagogue at the same time, if a little uneasily, just as many early Methodists also regarded themselves as Anglicans, again a little uneasily at times. Final separation may have been inevitable, but there was a period in both cases when the lines of differentiation were blurred. We cannot, needless to say, be sure about this, if only because Paul does not directly deal with the community question, yet on the whole Hooker's model is preferable.

We cannot be sure, but the content of Romans does encourage us

o So Drane, art. cit., p. 218; Wiefel, art. cit., p. 111.
p Watson, *PJG*, pp. 19–22 and passim.
q Continuity and Discontinuity, Epworth Press 1986.

to suppose that Paul took a middle position on the matter of the church and its Jewish roots, a position which he hoped to persuade both sides to accept, i.e. both those who still saw Christianity as a kind of Judaism, and those who saw it as an independent movement. This middle position, as set out theologically but not sociologically in Romans, was that the church cannot live independently of its Jewish roots, and that God's dealings with humanity from Abraham onwards are part of a consistent overall pattern, but that on the other hand Jewish Christians ought not to think that entering the church is the same as entering Israel *as it has come to be understood*. Rather, Gentiles who become Christians enter Israel as God always intended it to be, but in practice has not always been. On the one hand, both Jewish and Gentile Christians can trace their theological ancestry back to the faith of Abraham, and both alike inherit the promise God made to him. On the other hand, because faith is now seen as the crucial and only essential matter, the Torah in its entirety cannot be considered binding on all Christians, Jewish and Gentile alike. In particular, circumcision, the most notable outward sign of commitment to the Torah, has become a matter of indifference.

It is this mediating position, neither rejecting the Jewish ancestry of Christian faith, nor being bound by it in its present Judaistic expression, which may well account for what Schmithals notices, namely that part of the time Paul is urging liberation from the practices of the synagogue, and part of the time urging toleration of those who are not thus liberated. He was obliged to argue in both directions at once, if the unity and so the witness of the Roman house churches were not to be fragmented and debilitated.

(v) Does Romans reflect both Paul's and the Romans' concerns?

When such good cases can be made for opposite points of view, the view that Romans arises from Paul's concerns elsewhere in his mission, and the view that it arises from concrete problems in Rome itself, it is hard to resist the conclusion that both may well be correct. When he came to write Romans, in order to prepare for his visit and subsequent Spanish mission, the concerns that had been faced by Paul in his missionary work and that were likely to face him in Jerusalem, coincided to a considerable extent with a particular set of problems within the Roman church. The outcome is a letter whose topics do indeed reflect Roman interests and Roman problems, but whose length and careful structure reflect the apostle's mature consideration of such matters over a relatively long period.

2. SOCIAL FACTORS IN THE STUDY OF ROMANS

Some important work has been done in elucidating the social world of Paul's churches,[r] attempting to give an analysis of the sort of people in social and class and economic terms that made up those churches. If we grant that historical sociology of this sort is possible at all,[s] then some illumination may also be provided by looking at the behaviour of religious movements in general and using this as one key to the understanding of a Pauline letter. This is what Watson (*PJG*) has done with very interesting and often exciting results.

However, in the first case, mapping the social position of the Pauline churches, there is a considerable problem of obtaining adequate data for all the churches except Corinth[t] and in the case of the Roman church our concrete information is extremely slight. Except that the question of eating or not eating meat (Rom. 14) clearly has a social dimension, in that the poor could have it only on festival occasions, we are driven back to Ch. 16, but even there we shall see that the information is very scanty indeed. There is certainly not enough to provide substantial illumination for the interpretation of the letter.

In the second case, looking at Romans in the light of sociological theory, there is first of all the problem of having the right theory, and secondly the problem that it cannot be assumed without question that modern sectarian movements' behaviour is useful in mapping the development of Pauline or other churches away from Judaism. I have

r See especially G. Theissen, *The Social Setting of Pauline Christianity*, ET T. & T. Clark and Fortress Press 1982; W. A. Meeks, *Urban Christians*.

s See the somewhat reluctantly critical discussion by C. S. Rodd, 'On Applying a Sociological Theory to Biblical Studies', *JSOT* 19, 1981, pp. 95–106.

t See G. Schöllgen, 'Was wissen wir über die Sozialstruktur der paulinischer Gemeinden?', *NTS* 34.1, 1988, pp. 71–82, who thinks Meeks is too confident in *Urban Christians*, Ch. 2, 'The Social Level of Pauline Christians'. Schöllgen stresses the danger of extrapolating from one Pauline church to another.

already mentioned in 1 (*b*) (*iv*) above the work of Watson and Hooker: both are clearly right in placing Romans somewhere along the line of disengagement of the church from the synagogue. We certainly begin with Christianity within Judaism, and end with it as a separate religion; that is unquestionable. The difficulty is to know where we are in the case of any given writing. That can, finally, only be deduced from the writing itself, which in turn has to be illuminated by the deductions. In the case of church-synagogue (or Christianity-Judaism) there is a complication, in that we are not dealing simply with a new form of an old religion, but also with matters of national and racial identity of a sort unparalleled in degree in modern sectarianism. Caution is therefore essential.

In Romans, apart from the argument in the body of the letter which proceeds very much in the realm of ideas, what do we have that would help us to detect the way in which Paul saw his churches developing in relation to Judaism and the synagogue?

(i) Romans 16 contains a list of people, which includes at least several groupings indicating that the Roman church existed in a series of house churches, which *may* have corresponded more or less to degrees of Jewishness in their Christianity. This seems likely enough, though there is no hard evidence for it. If Rom. 16 was not originally addressed to Rome, this evidence disappears, but we shall see that there is a good case for retaining Ch. 16 as an original part of the letter.

(ii) If the issue in 14^1–15^6 centres on Jewish scruples about clean and unclean food, as many scholars think, then there was a division within the Roman church along Jewish-Gentile lines (or more precisely along observant and non-observant lines). This is far from certain, however, and in this commentary it will be argued that the non-eaters were not only Jewish Christians with 'kosher' scruples, but also Gentile Christians who, as in Corinth, feared to eat food that had been, or might have been, used in pagan sacrifices. If this is correct, then the passage does not give us unambiguous help in mapping the church-synagogue break.

(iii) If the historical setting suggested above in 1 (*b*) (*iv*) is anywhere near correct, then there would presumably have been a division within the Roman church along observant and non-observant lines, and this underlies a good deal of the theological argument in Paul's letter. Perhaps no more than this can be said: the matter is not provable, but is highly probable.

All this seems rather pessimistic, and to suggest that we should return to Romans as a presentation of purely theological ideas. On the contrary, whatever doubts we may have about the possibility of precise sociological work on this letter, the general point must be granted. The Romans as a church had some sort of relationship with the synagogue, so that in talking about the Jewish provenance of the Christian gospel Paul was talking at least partly about that relationship. Neither Judaism nor Christianity was disembodied. Both had concrete existences in persons and places. The same goes for disagreements within the church about the relationship between Gentiles and Jews: Paul is talking about people who occupy space and time, not only about ideas. Therefore, those who read this commentary with experience of some earlier ones may perceive that it consistently tries to see the issues in corporate and social terms at least as much as in individual or strictly theological terms. For example, justification is taken to involve not only 'being put right with God' but equally 'entering the people of God'. In this respect, Rom. 9–11 show us that for Paul the question of who constitutes the people of God, and where historical Israel now fits into the divine scheme, were absolutely crucial matters. That they are not such crucial matters for most modern readers can be a barrier against hearing the letter as its first hearers/readers perceived it.

3. PLACE AND DATE OF WRITING

These are comparatively uncontroversial matters that need be mentioned only briefly. Paul writes as he is about to go to Jerusalem bearing the collection of money taken up by the churches of Macedonia and Achaia (15^{25-26}). He is presumably, therefore, in Greece, and the place usually nominated is Corinth (cf. 16^1: Cenchreae was the port of Corinth). Other evidence that Corinth was the place of writing consists in the likelihood that Gaius, host to the church where Paul is (16^{23}), is the same Corinthian Gaius of I Cor. 1^{14}, and in that Erastus (16^{23} again) is associated with Corinth in Acts 19^{22} and II Tim. 4^{20}.

Certainty is impossible, and the evidence does come largely from Rom. 16, which may not have been addressed to Rome. Nevertheless Corinth remains the most likely place and has no serious rival.

The time of writing can be fixed without too much difficulty in relative terms, though absolute chronology is much more of a problem. Clearly Romans was written close to the end of Paul's active missionary work, before his final and almost fatal visit to Jerusalem, where he was arrested and eventually shipped to Rome as a prisoner. For our purposes the absolute dating matters very little. It depends on the date when Gallio was governor of Achaia (Acts 18[12ff.]: Paul appeared before Gallio), and when Felix was replaced as governor of Judaea by Festus (Acts 23[24]; 24[27]). It also, of course, depends on our estimate of the accuracy of Acts on these points, and on a reconstruction of Paul's activities around the rough datings provided by this external evidence. Several scholars have provided detailed (and differing) accounts of how a date may be fixed for the writing of Romans within reasonable limits, but here it must suffice to say that it must have been somewhere in the middle to late fifties of the first century.[u]

4. AUTHORSHIP AND INTEGRITY: THE PLACE OF ROMANS 16

That Paul wrote Romans is not disputed. What is disputed is whether he wrote all of it as it now stands (this will be discussed in (d) below) and whether he wrote all of it to Rome. Our present concern is with Ch. 16, which some believe was not originally part of the Roman letter.

u See Cranfield I, pp. 12–16 (the years 55–56, or less probably 54–55); A. J. M. Wedderburn, 'Some Recent Pauline Chronologies', Exp T XCII. 4, 1981, 103–8 (the years 52–58); R. Jewett, Dating Paul's Life, Fortress Press and SCM Press 1979 (the years 56–57); G. Lüdemann, Paul: Apostle to the Gentiles I: Studies in Chronology, ET SCM Press and Fortress Press, 1984 (the years 51–52, or 54–55, depending on the date assigned to the crucifixion); W. G. Kümmel, Introduction to the New Testament, ET Abingdon Press and SCM Press 1966, p. 220 (the years 55–56); J. Knox, Chapters in a Life of Paul, A. & C. Black 1954, pp. 85ff. (the years 53–54); J. A. T. Robinson, Redating the New Testament, SCM Press 1976, p. 55 (early 57). The list could go on, but the limits would not be significantly altered.

(a) The view that Romans originally had 15 chapters

The most famous name to support this view is that of T. W. Manson whose view it was that Rom. 16 was originally addressed to the church at Ephesus.[v] In fact the theory of an Ephesian destination comes in two varieties. The first is that Rom. 16 is part of a lost letter to the Ephesians. The second is that Romans was originally a circular letter, that Ch. 16 was appended to the copy addressed to Ephesus, and only later and wrongly became an apparently integral part of the whole letter. We have already discussed the circular letter theory and found it less than convincing (1.*b*, *ii* above), so shall now concentrate on the other form of the theory.

The matter is complex and is tightly bound up with the textual confusion of the last two chapters of our Romans.[w] Here we can do no more than point to some of the textual evidence and explain in outline the reasons why an Ephesian destination has been proposed.[x]

(i) Our oldest manuscript for Paul's letters, the papyrus 𝔓[46], which may date from as early as the beginning of the third century, places the closing doxology of 16^{25-27} instead at the end of Ch. 15. It is the only MS that does have it there, but its evidence cannot be lightly brushed aside, and seems to suggest that somewhere behind it lies an edition of Romans that ended with Ch. 15. This is one of the strongest weapons in the armoury of those who consider Ch. 16 an addition or an intrusion, at least in a letter addressed to Rome. Indeed the oldest surviving MS does not necessarily preserve the oldest text, and indeed we cannot simply accept without question the evidence of one MS, however valuable, and certainly as it stands 𝔓[46] does include the bulk of Ch. 16. We cannot, therefore, simply conclude that originally Romans was a 15-chapter letter. Nevertheless this MS does provide important grounds for suspecting the existence of such an earlier edition. It is possible that 𝔓[46] represents a Roman letter then adapted,

---

v 'St Paul's Letter to the Romans – and Others', now printed as Ch. 1 of Donfried, *Debate*.

w On the whole question see the excellent extended treatment in Gamble, *Textual History*.

x For a fuller discussion see Cranfield I, pp. 5–11; Kümmel, *Introduction*, pp. 222–6.

by the addition of Ch. 16, to be sent to another church. If so, we should expect the references to Rome in $17, 15$ to be lacking.[y] Did it omit them? Unfortunately we do not know, as the earliest chapters of the letter are missing from 𝔓[46].

To sum up, the presence of the doxology after 15^{33} does seem to point to the existence at one time of a 15-chapter form of Romans. Yet the only surviving MSS which omit Ch. 16 also omit Ch. 15. These are Latin MSS of the Vulgate. We can only conclude that this important evidence from a very ancient MS is not without its difficulties, and can scarcely in itself be regarded as decisive.

It may be added that 15^{33} does look rather like the ending of a letter. On the other hand it contains no reference to 'grace', and all Paul's other epistolary conclusions do have such a reference: cf. 16^{20}; I Cor. 16^{23}; II Cor. 13^{14}; Gal. 6^{18}; Eph. 6^{24}; Phil. 4^{23}; Col. 4^{18}; I Thess. 5^{28}; II Thess. 3^{18}; Philemon 25; even the Pastoral Epistles conform to this pattern. In Rom. 15 there has not been a reference to grace since v. 15, and even that is not invocatory, as is the case in all other Pauline letters.[z] Admittedly the grace is unusually far from the end in Ch. 16, but this is nothing compared with Ch. 15.

(ii) In Rom. 16 there is an unusual number of greetings to individuals and groups, and the question naturally arises as to how Paul could possibly have known so many people in a church he had never visited. In itself this objection does not point to Ephesus, but merely clears the ground for such a proposition. However, Paul does not claim to know all these people, but only some of them. If the suggested view is right, namely that the Roman church after its partial return from exile was in danger of fragmentation, the Jewish Christians in only uneasy alliance with the Gentile ones, and that in any case it existed in a number of distinct house-groups, then it may be plausibly supposed that in Ch. 16 Paul is simply trying to cover all such groups. Indeed he might well have been more comprehensive in sending greetings to a church he did not know than in greeting a

---

[y] G certainly lacks them, though it does include Ch. 16 but without vv. 25–27, the concluding doxology.

[z] Gamble, *Textual History*, pp. 182ff., shows that all Paul's letters end with the following sequence: hortatory remarks; peace-wish; greetings; grace; benediction, always in the same order.

community he knew well. The other undisputed letters (I and II Corinthians, Galatians, Philippians, I Thessalonians, and even Philemon) have relatively few personal greetings, and certainly nothing on the scale of Rom. 16. A letter to Ephesus, therefore, a church which he knew exceptionally well, might also be expected to have rather few personal greetings. So then, the heavy concentration of greetings in Rom. 16 may argue for a Roman destination and against an Ephesian one.

(iii) Nevertheless, it is often said that some of the people mentioned in Rom. 16 are more readily to be associated with Ephesus than with Rome. In particular, Prisca and Aquila were in Asia in I Cor. 16^{19} (probably in Ephesus, cf. Acts 16$^{18-19}$) having been expelled from Rome (Acts 16^2). Could they now have gone back to Rome? Indeed they could, if the expulsion order had lapsed as it must have done. The much later evidence of II Tim. 4^{19} that they were in Ephesus when Paul was in prison in Rome cannot be given much weight if, with most scholars, we hold II Timothy to be pseudonymous and post-Pauline. In any case, it is clear from Rom. 16$^{3-4}$ that the pair had travelled about a good deal: why else should 'all the churches of the Gentiles' give thanks for them? If the greeting to Prisca and Aquila fits an Ephesian destination, then it fits a Roman one almost equally well, and does not help to settle the question.

In 16^5 Epaenetus is called 'the first-fruits of Asia', which presumably means that he was the first Asian convert or at least one of the first. Does this mean that at the time of writing he was still in Asia? Of course it does not. There has been much discussion about whether such a description better fits one who is still living in Asia (i.e. in Ephesus) or one who comes from Asia but is now expatriate, living in Rome. The discussion has not been decisive, one way or the other. As with Prisca and Aquila, all we can say is that the reference would fit either Ephesus or Rome.

For the rest of the people named, it is frequently impossible to determine whether Paul's professions of esteem and affection imply personal acquaintance. The 'kinsmen' in 16$^{7, 11}$ are almost certainly just fellow-Jews. The most likely candidate for personal acquaintance is the mother of Rufus, 16^{13}, who has at some time, it appears, been active in Paul's welfare. This could have been in Ephesus, but it could equally have been somewhere else, and in any case it does not follow that she is still where she was then (this is assuming that calling her his 'mother' is not simply a verbal flourish). To sum up, while these personal references may fit Ephesus, Rome remains perfectly possible also, especially if we bear in mind the point made above under (ii) that Paul did not normally indulge in lengthy greetings to churches he knew well.

(iv) The warning against false teachers in 16^{17-20} comes decidedly oddly at the end of Romans. To what in the body of the letter can it possibly correspond? It seems to have nothing to do with the debate about Christ, the Law, and Israel which has dominated much of the letter, nor with the relationship between the church and the Jewish community. On the other hand, it can be argued, it does have similarities in tone with the attacks on false teachers which we find in Colossians. Colossae was not far from Ephesus, and this could be evidence for an Ephesian destination for the chapter. In the body of Romans he argues; in 16^{17-20} he denounces. There he tacitly allows for more than one view (e.g. in 14^1-15^6), even while strenuously proposing his own. Here he does not. The difficulty is evident to anyone who reads straight through the letter and suddenly lights on these verses. They seem out of key with the rest, and constitute a difficulty which is not easy to solve. For many scholars, consequently, this passage tips the balance in favour of a non-Roman destination for the whole chapter. It must be granted that it is the strongest piece of evidence for the Ephesian view.

There are, on the other hand, plausible ways of explaining the passage. Perhaps at the end of the letter Paul allows his irritation with those who want Christians to live Jewishly to burst out. More probably the passage 16^{17-20} has nothing to do with the questions hitherto discussed, but shows Paul's awareness that the Roman church has problems of a quite different character with which he has not hitherto been concerned to deal. False teachers known to be active elsewhere may now be threatening the Roman church too: they could well be teachers of the kind that were later known as Gnostic. General warnings against them would be appropriate, even if only perfunctory attention could be paid to them in this letter.[a]

a See Gamble, *Textual History*, pp. 52–3.

On the whole, then, while an Ephesian destination for Rom. 16 is by no means impossible, it seems preferable not to detach it from what precedes it.

(b) The view that Romans originally had 14 chapters

There is a slightly stronger case, at least so far as MS evidence goes, for separating both Chapters 15 and 16 from the rest of the letter, and proposing an originally 14-chapter edition. This leads us into the question of the ending of the letter as a whole. As Ch. 15 is plainly to Rome, if 15 and 16 belong together as they very probably do, the Ephesian hypothesis becomes impossible. Leaving that theory aside, however, there are still problems about the end of the letter. There are two interrelated sets of facts, some of which have already been mentioned, and a particular problem about one verse.

(i) The text of Romans issued by the second century 'heresiarch' Marcion had neither Ch. 15 nor Ch. 16. A few MSS of the Latin Vulgate also lack 15 and 16, though they have the doxology (16^{25-27}) after 14^{23}. On the other hand, the overwhelming majority of MSS, even including $\mathfrak{P}^{46}$, have 16 chapters.

(ii) The position of the doxology (16^{25-27}) varies in a peculiar fashion. In $\mathfrak{P}^{46}$ it comes after 15^{33}. Some MSS omit it altogether, e.g. G, though it does leave a space after 14^{23}. We have just mentioned the Vulgate MSS that have it after 14^{23}; there are also a few MSS (e.g. A, Codex Alexandrinus) which have it both after 14^{23} and at the end of Ch. 16. On the other hand it is at the end of Ch. 16 and only there in most MSS, including $\mathfrak{P}^{61}$, $\aleph$ (Codex Sinaiticus), B (Codex Vaticanus), D (Codex Claromontanus) and in many MSS in languages other than Greek. If we were treating the placing of the doxology in isolation, and if we were going strictly on the weight of the MSS, there is no doubt that we should place it at 16^{25-27}.

(iii) Rom. 16^{24} is a doubtful reading. It virtually repeats 16^{20b}, and is omitted by $\mathfrak{P}^{46}$, $\mathfrak{P}^{61}$ (apparently), and by most of the major MSS. However a number of Western MSS include it: D, G (Codex Boernerianus), which on the other hand omit it at 16^{20b}, and many of the Old Latin MSS. Some MSS have it after 16^{27}. It may be that, as the tendency was to expand liturgical formulations, not to delete them, this verse should be regarded as a later insertion or repetition. On the other side it has been argued that v. 20 is the end of a Pauline autograph which has run from 16^1, and that in 16^{24} the scribe adds his own grace-wish. [b]

Leaving aside the matter of 16^{24}, which does not affect the question of the existence of a 14-chapter edition, we can see that there is a case for seeing both 15 and 16 as having been added. The strange behaviour of the doxology points to editions of different lengths, and there is direct evidence for a 14-chapter edition. Nevertheless, if we rule out an Ephesian destination for Ch. 16, the evidence for either a 15- or a 14-chapter edition is nothing like as strong as for a 16-chapter one. We may therefore be content to accept as probably original the 16-chapter edition we now have. This is not just a matter of finding other cases unproven: Ch. 16 exhibits in sequence the usual elements of the conclusion of a Pauline letter, which would not be found in their completeness if the letter ended earlier. [c]

(c) Tentative reconstruction of the history of the end of Romans

Accepting a 16-chapter edition does not solve all the problems. We still have to explain how it came about that there is evidence for both 14- and 15-chapter editions. Something like the following is both plausible and widely proposed.

(i) Paul wrote to the Romans a 16-chapter letter, but without the concluding doxology, and perhaps also without the 'grace' in 16^{24}. We have already mentioned the strange 'repetition' (if it is that) of the grace. As for the doxology, the reasons for thinking it was not part of what Paul originally wrote are not only its floating position, but also its un-Pauline language. [d] We surmise, then, that Paul wrote Rom. 1.^{1}–16$^{23/24}$.

(ii) In the second century, Marcion chose to end his edition at 14^{23}, perhaps because of the OT quotations in Ch. 15: Marcion was implacably opposed to any notion that the OT or indeed the Just God of the

---

b For the first, and usual view, see Metzger, pp. 539–40; for the second view, Gamble, *Textual History*, pp. 94, 129–32.

c So Gamble, *Textual History*, Ch. III.

d On this, see Gamble, *Textual History*, pp. 107–10, 123f.

OT, had anything whatsoever to do with Christianity. It is possible, however, that both 14- and 15-chapter editions predated Marcion, and were relatively straightforward attempts to make the once specifically Roman letter applicable to a wider range of early Christians.[e] Then either Marcion or someone else before or after him, added 16[25-27] as an otherwise lacking suitable conclusion. If we hold that 16[25-27] is authentically Pauline, then Marcion or someone else transferred it to the end of Ch. 14. It may be worth repeating that it was not only Marcion who worked with a 14-chapter Romans: so it seems did the scribes responsible for some Vulgate MSS, and also probably (and ironically) Tertullian, a staunch anti-Marcionite, who never quotes from 15 or 16.

(iii) Eventually scribes engaged in copying 16-chapter versions of Romans discovered in existence other copies which ended with 14 or 15. What should they do with the doxology? In the end some played safe, and had it after 14 or 15, and also at the end of 16; others put it in one place and not another.

This commentary, then, works on the assumption that the 16-chapter edition is original and was directed by Paul to the Roman church. It also assumes that the doxology, if authentic, belongs at the end of Ch. 16 and there alone.

(d) The view that extraneous matter has intruded into Romans

It is sometimes argued that, as we now have it, Romans is the product of a process of expansion by other hands than Paul's.

(i) The theory of J. C. O'Neill

In *Paul's Letter to the Romans*[f] Professor O'Neill contends, mainly on the basis of incongruities of expression and thought in the letter as it now stands, that Romans evolved in three stages. First, there was

---

e This is Gamble's view. He also points out that the 14-chapter editions probably lacked 'in Rome' at 1[7], [15]: see pp. 29–33, 100–7, 115–26.

f Penguin Books 1975. For his procedure see especially pp. 14–21. The text of what he regards as the original and much shorter letter is printed on pp. 264–71.

Paul's original letter, which consisted of: 1^1, 5, 7–17; 3^{1-11}, 19–24, 26–31; 4^{1-2}, 5, 9–13 16, 18–21, 23–24; 5^{1-3}, 5–6, 8–11; 6^{1-4}, 8–17, 21–23; 7^4, 6–7, 12–13; 8^{2-4}, 11, 15–26, 28, 31–35, 37; 9^{1-3}, 6–10, 25–27, 30–33; 10^{1-6}; 15^{14-20}, 22–25, 27–33; 16^{1-3}, 5–16, 21–24. Clearly this is a relatively short letter, and indeed is really shorter than the list of passages shows, for sections within some verses are also excised by O'Neill.

The next stage was when scribes and editors put glosses (brief comments) in the wide margins that were not uncommon in ancient MSS. Eventually, in the process of copying, these crept into the text itself, when copyists who were unsure whether they were added commentary or accidentally omitted text, played safe by putting them in. In the nature of the case, these glosses seldom amounted to more than a line or two.

The third phase occurred at the same time as all this was going on, and consisted of longer pieces being inserted by an editor, a theologian who wanted to adapt the letter for a new time and a wider audience. In a few cases these added pieces (whether glosses or longer passages), which include most of 9–11, do represent some uncertainty in the MS tradition. In the main, however, O'Neill relies for his reconstruction not on MS evidence but on what he perceives as incongruities in expression, argument, or theology.

That there are these incongruities can hardly be denied by anyone who has wrestled with the letter. The usual way of dealing with them, and the way taken in the present commentary, is to accept that Paul was dealing with problems which he had not completely solved. Paradox, uncertainty, and sudden flashes of insight are thus just as characteristic of the apostle as are passages of clear and relatively systematic thought. To read Romans is to read theology in the making, rather than a piece of finished thinking. In the end, Romans is not a *summa*. The difficulties and awkward connections, both in thought and in language, are to be conceded, but are taken as the result of Paul's working out his argument as he goes along, probably as he dictates (see below, 5. Methods of authorship). They are also taken to be the result of his still being in the middle of formulating his precise views on some aspects of some matters, notably the relation between Israel and church.

Professor O'Neill, on the contrary, finds it more likely that Paul was an orderly and straightforward thinker, and that the difficulties and disagreements arise because other hands are at work. The tension that arises, for example, between what O'Neill sees as the predestinarian teaching of Rom. 9–11 and much of what Paul says elsewhere which assumes human freedom, is to be resolved by concluding that Paul did not write most of 9–11. If we ask why our MSS do not show clearer signs of this glossing and interpolating, the answer comes in two parts. First, there *is* some evidence of glossing and of additions, e.g. the variant readings noted at the foot of each page in RSV and discussed below in the commentary, and the uncertainty about Ch. 14 and Ch. 15. Secondly, it is argued, those signs that survive are but the tip of the iceberg, pointers to much more extensive variation that was covered up by the emergence in due course of official texts. Once the long text (glossed and supplemented) of Romans had become officially accepted, copies of the shorter original would be either ignored or deliberately suppressed. O'Neill notes that something like this is widely supposed to have occurred in the history of many OT books and wonders why it is found so controversial when he proposes it for a NT book.

It would be quite impossible to give his thesis a proper examination here, i.e. by working through his alleged glosses and additions one by one. A few general observations must suffice.

1. There are places where he clearly has a case, and where there is at least some MS evidence to back him. The most striking instance is the ending of the letter, already discussed at length.

2. We have seen that most scholars think the undoubted discontinuities and discrepancies are to be explained not by interpolation and addition, but from the existence of tensions within the thought of Paul as it develops.[g] Moreover, Paul was a first-century Jewish, not a twentieth-century Western, thinker, and in at least some Jewish thought there was a greater ability to encompass apparent contradictions than in ours. This was so in the matter of predestination: it was possible both to maintain human freedom and responsibility and to believe in divine providence, and leave it at that, without trying to provide a theoretical reconciliation of the two.[h]

g See, e.g. the work of Räisänen, *PL*.

h See M. Hengel, *Judaism and Hellenism*, 2 vols., ET SCM Press and Fortress Press 1974, I, pp. 219f., and II, p. 144.

3. It is not easy to see how O'Neill's extensive process of development could have taken place. It is not only that we might have expected more traces to survive in the MS tradition, it is also the shortness of the time-scale. If we take it that we have at least some evidence from the end of the second century (namely 𝔓⁴⁶), we have a rather short time not only for the expansions to occur, but also for the lapse of the memory that the original text was the short one. It is true that 𝔓⁴⁶ is very incomplete (it consists of a number of leaves of a codex) with large gaps, including the whole of the first four chapters. Yet the gaps in the papyrus do not at all coincide with O'Neill's excisions.

In the nature of things, it is unlikely that such interpolation and development theories can finally be proved or disproved. However, we have some evidence from the earlier part of the second century (II Peter 3[15-16]) which indicates that Paul's letters had already come to be regarded as Scripture. This would presumably make their text more likely to be treated as sacrosanct. The onus is therefore on the protagonists of interpolation to make their case, and O'Neill's, while argued with great skill, is not widely regarded as having been made.

(ii) *The theory of W. Munro*

Her theory, not dissimilar to O'Neill's though on a much narrower front,[i] is part of a general case about the interpolation into many NT writings of material about the ordering of society. This material is of an hierarchical character, i.e. it enjoins subjection of one group to another, of women to men, of slaves to masters, of citizens to the state, and so on. It is widely found in the NT, in Pauline, deutero-Pauline, Petrine and other letters, and it has usually been supposed that it was part of a stock of common catechetical matter drawn on independently by various ancient Christian writers. It has also often been suggested that it represents part of the baptismal preparation, not only in its general pattern and orientation, but also sometimes in its details.[j] Professor Munro, on the contrary, thinks the material is later,

i Winsome Munro, *Authority in Paul and Peter*, SNTSMS 45, CUP 1983. Romans is treated particularly on pp. 56–67.

j See, e.g. P. Carrington, *The Primitive Christian Catechism*, CUP 1940; E. G. Selwyn, *The First Epistle of St Peter*, Macmillan 1946, pp. 365–466.

not earlier than the written letters, and was introduced into them by a writer or school of writers. These had much in common with, and may even have been identical with, the circle responsible for the Pastoral Epistles, I and II Timothy and Titus, which certainly contain some significant submission material.

For Romans she proposes that Chs. 12 and 13 consist of two strata. The earlier and authentically Pauline is Rom. $12^{1-8, 11b-12b}$; 13^{11-14}. The rest interrupts a series of two-line parallels which not only have a common style, but also are coherent and consecutive in subject-matter. The intruded material does have its own coherence, is often in antithetically parallel form, and has a common orientation towards socially acceptable conduct. The most striking piece of this sort is Rom. 13^{1-7} with its apparent doctrine of total subservience to the state.

Munro's procedure is not dissimilar to O'Neill's in some ways, although her interpolations are by no means identical with his. What is distinctive about her thesis is that she finds the later stratum in 12 and 13 to be closely akin in manner and matter to a good deal of other NT material. It originated, she thinks, about the thirties of the second century, the time of the Second Jewish War when the Christian church was anxious to present itself as not subversive and as no threat to the Roman state. At about the same time it was also concerned, because of the threat of teachings it deemed heretical, to enjoin on Christian believers strict orthodoxy, and submission to the church authorities as the guardians of that orthodoxy. These two factors coincided to make it prudent to insert into Christian writings some matter that stressed the need for submission, both in the church itself and in relation to the political power.

Now Rom. 13^{1-7} has often been thought to fit awkwardly into its context.[k] Munro shows that removing it does not solve all the problems of continuity. The interpolated material is therefore seen as having been rather more extensive. About all this there are two fundamental questions to be asked. First, are the discontinuities in the passage(s) such as to require the solution that there has been interpolation? Secondly, does 13^{1-7}, and the material that coheres with it,

k See Michel, pp. 312–14. Like Munro he thinks the material an insertion; unlike her, he thinks it is a Pauline insertion. See also Cranfield II, pp. 651–3.

really reflect the later emphasis on submission that she thinks they do? The only satisfactory answers to both questions must be those that arise from working through the passage, and the readers must therefore be referred to the commentary to judge for themselves. However, a few words may be in place here.

1. In answer to the first question, there obviously must come a point where interpolation is the only plausible solution. Yet it does not seem to be so in Rom. 12–13. There are awkward transitions and disjunctions, but not noticeably more so than often in Paul's writings. We need to remember that Paul's first draft was almost certainly his final one, and that he may even have dictated it at a sitting. Literary polishing was therefore impossible, and tiredness must have often been acute. There must have been breaks from the work, even if only short ones, and awkward connections could arise at the resumption of dictation. In short, Paul was not working under modern conditions.

2. In considering the second question, we must agree that submission is a major theme in the passage. Yet submission did not become an important theme only in the second century. As is noted in the commentary, it was an element in Hellenistic Jewish tradition, and in any case was taken for granted in the ancient world as a whole. It may have received fresh impetus in Christian circles at the time Munro proposes, and certainly it is a leading theme in the Pastorals, but it need not have begun then, even in Christian circles. It is true that there are other elements in Paul's thought (cf. Gal. 3[28]) which run counter to such an hierarchical approach to social life, but the usual explanation of this conflict of attitudes is that Paul is grappling with the contradiction between life in the new age introduced by Jesus Christ, and life in the present age which is the concrete setting of Christian obedience. The conditions of discipleship are given, not chosen.

Finally, it must be agreed that the discontinuities of thought and expression within writings, and the similarities of wording and content between the submission material in different writings, are explicable on Munro's theory. They are also, however, explicable on the other theory, that common catechetical material is being independently used by different authors. As with O'Neill's theory, in the end the reader must judge how far interpolation must be posited in order to explain the disjunctions.

5. METHODS OF AUTHORSHIP

At 16²² we read 'I Tertius, the writer of this letter, greet you in the Lord.' What does this mean? First, it must mean that the actual putting of pen to papyrus was done not by Paul but by Tertius. It could further mean that Tertius did this at Paul's dictation, word for word, though over an extended piece of writing like this one wonders if that could be sustained exactly. It could, perhaps, rather mean that Paul told Tertius what to write in general terms, that Tertius wrote it up a piece at a time, and that he then showed it to Paul for his approval, before going on to the next section. Finally, it could mean that Tertius took it down in ancient shorthand, and then wrote it out in longhand for Paul's approval. There is a long discussion in Cranfield (I, pp. 2–5); here we can treat the issues only in summary.

It has long since been argued that because taking dictation in longhand would be intolerably slow and tedious, and because the use of shorthand for correspondence began after Paul's time, we must assume that Paul gave Tertius the gist of what he wanted to say and that Tertius then wrote it out.[1] Yet the mind quails at the task given Tertius, even if he had to tackle only one piece at a time. The subtlety and complexity of the argument, not only occasionally but almost throughout the long letter, would demand in Tertius a theological grasp virtually identical with Paul's own. There do, in fact[m] seem to be instances of dictation into longhand, cumbersome though it must have been. If this was the method, then it is no wonder that there are theological and syntactical disjunctions. How many times must Paul have said, 'Now where was I?'

However, it is not as certain as Roller thought that the use of shorthand is to be excluded.[n] Conventional abbreviations were in use two

[1] See O. Roller, *Das Formular der paulinischen Briefe: ein Beitrag zur Lehre vom antiken Briefen*, Stuttgart 1933.

[m] See Cranfield I, pp. 3–4.

[n] Cf. Sanday and Headlam, p. lx, writing well before Roller, of course. See also Cranfield I, pp. 4–5.

and a half centuries before Paul, and a full system was in use about a century later; what is difficult is to know whether there was anything like a complete system in Paul's time. On the whole we may suspect it did exist: there was a Latin system, apparently invented by Cicero's freedman Tiro, which is referred to by a Greek name (Cicero *Att.* 13³²). This may imply that the system, or a system, was used in Greek first. At all events, we cannot rule out the possibility of a reasonably well-developed system of shorthand's being in existence at the time of Paul and Tertius.

Even if this possibility be granted, however, it must have taken a long time to complete the letter. Therefore, whatever the method of composition, it must have been slow and cumbersome, so that occasional awkwardness of expression and argument would be inevitable. This is why I am being so cautious in inferring interpolations or glosses, especially in cases where there is no MS support.

6. THE STRUCTURE OF THE LETTER

We have noted (1 *b* above) that of all Paul's writings, Romans is the closest to an organized and carefully constructed treatise. Nonetheless it is a genuine letter, if an unusually long one, and it follows the epistolary conventions of the time. We now have large numbers of papyrus Greek letters, enough to enable us to see that there was a quite stereotyped pattern in letter-writing. Most of these ancient letters are very brief, and consist of the following formal elements:

Name of sender
Name of recipient
Greetings
Thanksgiving, often ending with a transition to the letter-body
Letter-body
Final greetings and blessing.

Although Paul's letters generally conform to this pattern, some of the elements that are usually very brief can become extended to a considerable degree. The letter-body may be relatively enormous, as it is in Romans. So much have some of the elements been extended that it has been asked whether Paul's letters (except Philemon) really fit into the ordinary letter structure at all. Among the large number of works on ancient letter-writing, especially in relation to early Christianity,[o] have been some that suggest that Paul's letters belong to a more specialized epistolary *genre*, e.g. the apologetic letter[p] or the letter-essay.[q] Like Paul's other letters, Romans is a real letter and not a discourse artificially cast in epistolary form. Nevertheless its very length forces it to take on something of the character of a treatise, and this is why Donfried argues for the letter-essay as the model: it is a real letter, but of essay dimensions. The very simple form proposed for this letter-essay is:

Heading (sender and recipient)
Epistolary introduction
Transition to the letter-body
Letter-body
Closing.

Paul's letter corresponds quite well to these formal structures, but it has some formal features of its own, in common with many of his other letters.[r] Thus the body of the letter is often followed by, or includes, ethical instructions (often given the technical name 'parenesis'). Further, the closing frequently includes the expression of an intention to make a visit, what has been called the 'apostolic *parousia*',[s] the importance of which is enhanced if we take it that Paul's letters were regarded by him and by his readers as surrogates for his personal presence. The letter-closing is also sometimes greatly expanded, as it is in Romans, by a prayer for peace, personal greetings, and a doxology or benediction.

o See, for example W. G. Doty, *Letters in Primitive Christianity*, Fortress Press 1973; John L. White, *The Form and Function of the Body of the Greek Letter*, Scholars' Press 1972. There is an excellent summary in Calvin J. Roetzel, *The Letters of Paul*, John Knox Press and SCM Press 1983, Ch. 2.

p H. D. Betz, *Galatians*, Hermeneia, Fortress Press 1979, pp. 14ff.

q Donfried, *Debate*, esp. pp. 143–8, building on the work of Martin Luther Stirewalt Jr, 'The Greek Letter-Essay', Appendix to *Debate*, pp. 175–206.

r Set out most conveniently by Roetzel, *Letters of Paul*, p. 40.

s See R. W. Funk, 'The Apostolic *Parousia*: Form and Significance', in W. R. Farmer, C. F. D. Moule, and R. R. Niebuhr (eds), *Christian History and Interpretation*, CUP 1967, Ch. 12.

This concern with structure may seem irrelevant to gaining an understanding of what the letter says. In fact, however, it does at times clarify particular matters or give reinforcement to points that are already evident. For example, the absence of any opening thanksgiving from Galatians becomes even more striking when we learn that this violates not only usual Pauline practice, but also normal etiquette of the time. In the case of Romans, it has often been noticed that 1^{16-17} is a pregnant summary of at least a large part of the letter. If we now further observe that it comes precisely at the body-opening, at the end of the thanksgiving, and is thus the transition to the letter-body, then its pregnant character is exactly what we should expect.

The bones of Romans may be set out thus:

Sender 1^{1-6}
Addressees 1^{7a}
Greeting 1^{7b}
Thanksgiving 1^{8-15}
Transition to body and body-opening 1^{16-17}
Letter-body $1^{18}-11^{36}$
Parenesis 12^1-15^{13}
Body closing (travel plans, intention to visit) 15^{14-32}
Closing of letter: peace wish 15^{33}
              greetings $16^{1-15, \; 21-23}$
              blessing/doxology 16^{25-27} (?).

Into this scheme 16^{17-20} does not fit naturally, any more than into the general theme and mood of the letter. Was it, perhaps, the ancient equivalent of a postscript?

As for the structure of the argument of the letter-body, including the parenesis, perhaps too much should not be said at this stage. After all, it is part of the purpose of the commentary to elucidate Paul's sequence of thought, and that means we should not start with too many preconceptions.[t] Nevertheless it may be helpful to give a very broad outline of how the argument will be understood to develop, especially in $1^{18}-11^{36}$, so long as it is borne in mind that this is only

---

t Beker, *Apostle*, Ch. 5, thinks that working too hard at a coherent argumentative structure for Romans plays havoc with interpretation.

one exegete's view of it and that he does not make great claims for it.[u]

1^{18}–3^{20} God condemns human sinfulness among the pagans, but equally among the Jews. All peoples suffer from the power as well as the guilt of sin.

3^{21-31} In Jesus Christ, dying and rising, God has provided the solution to the problem of human sinfulness for Jews and Gentiles equally. Both may now be within his people.

This solution has four main aspects:

(a) 4^1–5^{21} There is no longer divine condemnation, for those who have faith in Christ, whether Jew or Gentile. They now belong to the people of God by the Abraham-Christ line of descent (the line of faith), and no longer belong to Adamic humanity.

(b) 6^{1-23} There is no longer bondage to sin.

(c) 7^{1-25} There is no longer the divided self, which even the Law cannot heal, but only diagnose.

(d) 8^{1-25} Life for Christ's people is no longer 'in the flesh', i.e. life centred on something other than God, but is life in the Spirit, in the power of God.

It is noteworthy that each of (a) to (d) ends with a similar formula, 'in/through Jesus Christ our Lord', 5^{20}; 6^{23}; 7^{25}; 8^{39}. Everything that is said in these chapters is addressed to those who are now a new humanity under the sovereignty and protection of Christ as Lord.

9^1–11^{36} The existence of this community composed of Gentiles as well as Jews and based on faith does not nullify God's ancient promises to Israel. His election was always of a restricted group within the total community of Israel. In any case, if most of national Israel is not now within God's people, it is their own fault. Finally, the aim of the divine strategy is that in the end national Israel also, as a whole, will be restored to that community.

12^1–15^{13} Ethical instructions about various matters, including civil obedience and the eating of certain foods.

---

u A recent and very valuable analysis of Romans by J. D. G. Dunn is to be found in *ANRW*, 25[4], pp. 2842–90.

7. THE PLACE OF CHAPTERS 9–11

In the summary immediately above, these chapters are given a crucial place. This needs stressing because it has sometimes been thought that they are an intrusion; even if written by Paul himself, they are self-standing, and have been placed here rather intrusively and awkwardly. This was the view of C. H. Dodd (pp. xxxf., 148–50), and is still occasionally to be met. To some, these chapters are an embarrassment because of the support they give, or appear to give, to a doctrine of predestination.[v]

Most recent commentators have rejected the idea of an intrusion, whether of genuinely Pauline material or not, largely because these three chapters are not seen as an appendix to the main argument of the letter, but as its climax, theologically speaking. It used to be thought that by the end of Ch. 8 Paul had finished his main theological work about justification and its consequences, and then from Ch. 12 outlined the practical outworkings of the theology. On this view 9–11 constituted a digression. We could quite well go from 8^{39} to 12^1 immediately.

On the contrary, according to a great deal of modern reading of the letter, 9–11 constitute a climax (even *the* climax) to the total argument, which is less about the individual and God than about the definition of the people of God, and the relationship between Jew and Gentile within that one people. If justification is by faith, i.e. if we are acceptable to God (and therefore within his people) by faith, and if the life of his people consists above all in faith, and further if faith is equally accessible to Gentile and Jew, then what becomes of God's special promises to Israel? Behind this lies the crucial question of the faithfulness, or in more everyday terms the reliability, of God. The implicit question is thus: 'Can we rely on God's grace in Christ if his earlier grace to historical Israel is now to be put in question?'

The business of 9–11 is to find an answer, or even a series of answers, to that central and critical question, for which see the commentary.[w]

[v] O'Neill, pp. 13, 148–51, 154–5, excises them. He finds the predestinarian teaching incompatible with Paul's known ideas.

[w] See also H. Räisänen, 'Geistigen Ringens' for an extended treatment of the chapters.

Some specific points about the chapters may now be noted briefly.

(i) There is a more diffuse manner of arguing in these chapters than in 1–8. This may well be true (though these things are notoriously difficult to determine). However, they come in the latter part of the letter-body, which does sometimes become more diffuse in Paul's letters. ˣ

(ii) There is a remarkably high incidence of OT quotation in these chapters in comparison with the rest of the letter, where allusion is common enough, but where there is not much direct quotation except in the latter part of Ch. 3 and Ch. 4. The answer to this is that it is particularly in Chs. 4 and 9–11 that the nature of the argument gives rise to the copious use of OT quotations: Paul is discussing God's dealings with Israel as recorded in Scripture. The OT material is the basic datum of the problem.

(iii) Perhaps 9–11 could stand as a self-contained unit, even (as Dodd suggested) as a sermon which Paul for some reason decided to ·
insert at this point in his letter. Could they have stood as an ancient sermon? It is impossible to be certain, but they are nothing like the examples of ancient sermons provided by the Acts of the Apostles. In any case, even if the chapters do contain material Paul has used before, whether or not in a sermon, it is worth observing that if he includes them here it is because he chooses to do so, and that their place in the argument of the letter has been deliberately made.

(iv) There are important connections in detail, as well as in overall theme, between material in 9–11 and material in the rest of the letter. Chapter 4 is a case in point, with its stress on the continuity between God's dealings with Abraham and with Gentiles who are now in Christ. The best example, however, is 3^{1-8} which virtually requires 9–11 to expand and expound it. Further, Ch. 8 ends with hope, and hope by its nature depends on the faithfulness or reliability of God; this is the fundamental concern of 9–11. To go from 8^{39} to 12^{1} without the intervening discussion would be to leave a major question-mark against hope. Such a question-mark may not be inevitable for modern readers for whom the problem of historical Israel is often hardly acute. It would surely have been inevitable for Paul's readers,

x So White, *Body of the Greek Letter*, pp. 47, 54.

especially his fellow-Jews in the church, but also those Gentiles who had a history of attachment to the synagogue.

(v) The fact that Ch. 11 ends with a doxology does not necessarily mean that it concludes a self-contained unit. Doxologies can occur not only at the end of something, but also in the middle of pieces at appropriate points: Rom. 9⁵ is an instance.

In the commentary, therefore, these chapters have been taken as integral to the letter and even as essential to the proper understanding of the whole. Indeed they have been deemed to show that a strictly individualist interpretation of 1–8 is inadequate (though of course they have an individualist aspect). Paul's fundamental concern is with the people of God who are in Christ, the new Adam, and who are the true children of Abraham as well as the new humanity. Thus the questions 'How do I become acceptable to God?' and 'What is the nature of my life in Christ?' come within the setting of the prior question: 'Who, and under what conditions, are the people of God, those who are the God-intended humanity?'ʸ

8. THE PLACE OF THE LAW IN THE THOUGHT OF ROMANS

This matter is so controversial that it seems justifiable to break the rule of letting the exegesis speak for itself, and to erect a few signposts in advance. This is especially so in that the view taken in this commentary would not, by any means, be universally shared.

At root the problem is that in the one letter Paul says some things which suggest that the Law (the Torah) has no relevance at all for believers in Christ, and other things which suggest it is still valid and binding on them. Moreover, it is not universally agreed why he says the negative things, nor what precisely is meant by the positive things. We begin by putting what he says about the Law in the context of the purport of the letter as a whole.

If Romans is about who are God's people and on what conditions, it is at the same time about being saved. We are not given a definition of salvation, but the term occurs significantly in the transition to the

---

y On the whole question of these chapters, see further Campbell, 'Freedom and Faithfulness', especially 38–41, as well as Räisänen, 'Geistigen Ringens'.

letter-body, 1^{16}: the gospel is 'the power of God for salvation to every one who has faith, to the Jew first and also to the Greek'. If we say that the letter is about who are God's people, we must also say that this cannot be understood solely in an ecclesiastical or sociological fashion. It must also be understood in terms of acceptability with God, now, at the Judgment, and for ever (cf. Rom. 4). Those who are God's people are those who are in a right relationship with him, and it is impossible to work through the letter asking whether, in any given passage, the focus is on the community question or on the relationship-with-God question. In the end, the two questions are the same.

As the brief outline of the letter indicates (above 6), the first two and a half chapters are devoted to showing that Jews, like Gentiles, are sinful. If Jews should object that, unlike Gentiles, they have God's Torah (Law) to guard them against sin, Paul's reply is that indeed they do, but they fail to live by it. In practice, their having the Law does not preserve them from sin. What is needed is what Christ and the Spirit bring: justification (i.e. acceptance by God as his people) by grace through faith, and new life in righteousness. The first is the major concern of 3^{20}–5^5 or thereabouts, and the second dominates the rest of Ch. 5 and 6–8, though there is a case for putting the shift at the end of Ch. 5. Moreover, the latter part of Ch. 5 has Paul talking about Christians as a new sort of human race, a new start, in their belonging and submission to Christ as the last Adam. This raises, as we have seen, the issue of historical Israel, which is treated at length in 9–11, as well as the issue of the sort of life required of this new humanity.

The Law is not dealt with at length in any one section of the letter, but appears in many of them. We must, then, return to Paul's apparent ambivalence about it. Is it good or bad, valid or invalid for Christians? In the first instance we must resist the temptation to answer these questions by looking at material from other letters, until we have examined *this* letter on its own terms. Reference to other Pauline writings will therefore be parenthetical, not determinative; it can scarcely be avoided altogether, but it must be after we have done our best to make sense of Romans as it stands. The first readers could not cross-check with other letters, and we must presume that Romans was intended to be comprehensible on its own. The letters are separated from one another by time, audience, and circumstances, and we cannot say what preconceptions the first readers may have had about Pauline teaching. In short, we cannot too readily interpret one letter from another.

When, in 1^{18}–3^{20}, Paul argues that the Jew as well as the Greek needs both forgiveness and deliverance from sin, he does not appear to be entirely consistent in doing so. If the aim of the whole argument is to prove that all human beings, without exception, are helplessly under the control of sin (3^{9-18}), then unexpected things are said in Ch. 2. In arguing that the Jews cannot boast over the Gentiles, he says that while Jews who have the Law fail to observe it, Gentiles who do not have it nonetheless contrive to observe it, as it were 'by nature' ($2^{14-15,\ 26-27}$). If there are some Gentiles who do keep it, what happens to the end of the argument that none is righteous, not even one (3^{10})? Paul apparently did not notice the incongruity, though it has been emphasized by some modern study.[z] Perhaps, in his determination to show that Jews are no better than Gentiles, he fails to notice that one small part of his argument (viz. that Gentiles do better than Jews, or at least in some cases), defeats the aim of the whole (viz. that all are sinful). In concentrating on some trees, he forgets about the wood, in other words. Perhaps, as Sanders suggests, he was incorporating a synagogue sermon which helped to make the point in general, but ran against it in particular. It may also be, however, that we have got 3^{9-18} wrong, and that the point is not to prove that every single human individual is irretrievably sinful, but that all *races*, Jews as well as Gentiles, are sinful and under the divine judgment.[a]

Another oddity about Rom. 2 is that in v. 13 (cf. vv. 6ff.) Paul says that it is those who do the Law who will be justified. We may well ask what has happened to justification by faith! Some suggest that justification by faith does not exclude judgment by works, that faith has to work itself out in love, and that life and behaviour are the tests

---

z Cf. Sanders, *PLJP*, pp. 123–35; Räisänen, *PL*, pp. 101–9.

a Thus Wendy Dabourne, *The Faithfulness of God and the Doctrine of Justification in Romans 1:16–4:25*, unpublished dissertation, Cambridge 1988, who mounts a powerful argument for seeing God's faithfulness as the 'governing strand', and the doctrine of justification as a secondary one.

of true faith, cf. Gal. 5[6]; 6[7]; II Cor. 5[10].[b] While this must be granted, in Rom. 2 there is no suggestion that justification is by anything else but doing the Law: there is no place given to faith at all. It therefore seems more likely that we are to see the argument here as still within a Jewish frame of reference. Paul is trying to show that Jew and Gentile, apart from Christ, are on the same footing before God. Within that Jewish frame of reference, it is not *having* the Law but *doing* it that characterizes those who are agreeable to God and who are within his people, cf. *Aboth* 1[17].

Despite the difficulties of Rom. 2, it is generally clear that the drift of the argument up to 3[20] is to show that both Jews and Gentiles are sinful and in need of a gospel of release. This placing of Jews and Gentiles on the same footing is a dominant theme throughout the letter: thus 2[10], and by implication 2[12–16, 25–27]; 3[9, 22, 29]; 4[9, 11–12, 16, 18]; 9–11 as a whole, but especially 9[30–31]; 10[12]. Up to 3[20] the Law has been given no role, except that having it is not much use unless it is kept, and that since those who have it seem to keep it no better than some who do not have it, it constitutes no solution to the power of sin.

What the solution is emerges in 3[21ff.]: faith, God's grace in Jesus Christ and his cross, behind which lies the saving righteousness of God (cf. 1[17]). Now the Law comes into the foreground for the first time since 2[12–29]. Boasting is excluded because justification is by faith and not by keeping the Law. But who wanted to boast to whom about what? The usual answer has been that the Jews, representing all who think they can win God's favour by their piety and good deeds, believed that keeping the Law was the way to salvation. By obeying the Law and by good deeds they won merit before God, and this merit would be recognized at the Judgment. On this view, boasting was about one's own achievement, and was, overtly or implicitly, before God. This is seen as a fundamentally wrong attitude for two reasons. First, no one can in practice ever be good enough to warrant such boasting before God. Secondly, it would in any case be a thoroughly sinful thing to do, as it would infringe the majesty and

b Cf. Cranfield I, pp. 150–3; Black, p. 55; Klyne R. Snodgrass, 'The Place of Romans 2 in the Theology of Paul', *NTS* 32, 1986, 72–93.

'Godness' of God. In the end, we are dealing with the sin of pride.[c]

As we have already noted above (p. 2), it is now widely agreed that this is a serious misreading both of Paul and of the Judaism contemporary with him. After 70 the idea of achieving merit before God at the Judgment is to be found, notably in 2(IV) Esdras, but earlier than that it is not found. The notion of merit certainly occurs, but its reward is strictly in this life, in terms of prosperity, health and success, and especially in terms of national success and peace. In the Jewish literature contemporary with or earlier than the NT, salvation is clearly by God's grace in election and covenant. Obedience to the Law is the proper response on the part of Israel as the beneficiary of election and covenant, but it is not the prerequisite for receiving them. Moreover, when examined carefully, Paul's writings do not mount an attack on Law-obedience on the grounds that it leads to self-righteousness. Rather, Paul's attack is either on the grounds that if salvation is through Christ, then it cannot be by any other means, or on the grounds that in some matters at least (the food laws, sabbath-observance, and circumcision) it creates a division between Jews and non-Jews. Such a division is at radical odds with Paul's belief that God accepts Gentiles and Jews equally and on the same terms.

If, in the light of all this, we now return to the question of boasting in 3[27ff.], it appears much more likely that the boasting Paul opposes is that of Jews over Gentiles ('we have the Torah, but you are lesser breeds without the Law' so to speak), than that it consists of saying to God 'See what good people we are!' The whole direction of the argument up to this point has been to show that Jews and Gentiles are in the same predicament 'under sin', and 3[27-30] does readily lend itself to the interpretation of the impossibility and inappropriateness of the Jews' boasting over the Gentiles. *All* are justified by faith, Jew and Gentile alike, just as both sorts of people have been under sin's power. No doubt Paul thought very poorly of any suggestion of boasting before God, and some hint of this may appear in 4[2] and even perhaps in 9[11], but this is not what he is talking about here, and

c This 'self-righteousness' interpretation is so often to be found in commentaries and other books about Paul that it scarcely requires documentation. Perhaps its most eloquent expression is in Bultmann, *Theology* I, pp. 259ff., 281f., 340ff. For a more recent and sophisticated approach, see Hübner, *LPT*.

it is unlikely that it was a primary target in any of his writings.[d]

So, then, the Law plays no part in justification, in becoming acceptable to God as part of his people. It is hardly surprising, in the light of this, that Paul in diatribe fashion asks the question (3[31]), 'Do we then overthrow the law by this faith?' Most readers coming fresh to the passage would probably expect the answer, 'Yes, we do.' The expectation would be the greater among those who had read Galatians, as the first readers obviously had not. 'On the contrary,' he says astonishingly, 'we uphold the law.' In the light of all that has gone before, how can he claim this? Three main answers have been proposed.

(i) Paul is saying that he upholds the Law when it is correctly understood as carried out in faith, and *not* to establish our own righteousness. If we do the Law without supposing that we are thereby saved, but letting our obedience proceed from our consciousness of having been justified by faith, then that is good. If we do it in order to be saved, that is bad. The Law has been overthrown in the latter sense, but in the former sense it has been established.[e]

We may recall two points made earlier, in casting doubt on this answer. First, it is not evident that Paul's Jewish predecessors or his contemporaries thought they were saved by keeping the Law. Secondly, if we read the present passage free from preconceptions, especially Reformation preconceptions, it is not easy to find any such notion in it. It is not a natural reading of this passage that Paul is condemning Law-obedience if it is done for the wrong reasons, but applauding it if it is done for the right reasons.

(ii) Another answer is that Paul points forward to passages like 8[4] and 13[8-10] in which he does appear to confirm the Law as an obligation laid on Christians.[f] In this case, 3[31] is a cryptic clue given in advance that there is more to be said on the subject, and that readers ought not to take it that Paul is simply rejecting the Law. This possibility cannot be ruled out, but in a communication that is presumably meant to be *heard*, it is extremely bad strategy to make the meaning of what has been said depend on something that will not be said for a considerable time.

---

d Sanders, *PLJP*, pp. 32–6; Räisänen, *PL*, pp. 170f. and passim.

e See e.g. Hübner, *LPT*, pp. 140–4; also probably Cranfield I, pp. 223f.

f So, it appears, Sanders, *PLJP*, p. 103.

(iii) If we look at 3³¹ in its context, and go on to Ch. 4 without a break,ᵍ then it is natural to think that 3³¹ is explained by Paul's use of Gen. 15⁶ and the story of Abraham, taken from the Torah itself. We recall that the Torah, the Law, is not only regulation, but is also story and *promise*. The last is important, not only in the sort of detail represented by the story of Abraham, where the promise that he would be the father of many nations is taken as being fulfilled in Jesus Christ, but also in a more general sense that it points beyond itself to something further that God would do. Certainly early Christians saw the Law in this way. So, Paul could be claiming here that his teaching about justification *is* in line with the Law in its character of promise.ʰ If this is right, then Paul is claiming that the story of Abraham and the promise given to him, in the Torah itself, gives crucial support to what he has been saying, and he goes on to spell this out.

A difficulty with this view is that 4¹ does sound like a change of tack and the introduction of a new subject. Rather than 'What shall we then say . . .?' we should have expected something like '*For* what shall we say . . .?' On the other hand, the discussion proper does begin at 4¹, with 3³¹ as a transitional verse to the new topic, so that the connection is not as awkward for this answer to the problem as at first appears. In any case, it is not a sufficient difficulty to prevent our taking 3³¹ in the most straightforwardly sequential way: it is in Ch. 4 that Paul demonstrates how he can claim to be establishing the Law, even though so far he has given no positive place to its legislation, so far as Christians are concerned.

Still, therefore, the Law has been given no positive role except for the promise-character of one of its narrative parts (Gen. 15⁶). In Ch. 4, the story of Abraham is used to show that it always was by faith that people found favour with God. Not circumcision but faith is what

---

g We cannot be too often reminded that Paul did not know he was finishing one chapter and beginning another. Both chapters and verses are devices introduced many centuries after Paul.

h So Käsemann, p. 105; Wilckens I, pp. 249f.; on the general point about the Torah as promise, see W. D. Davies, 'Paul and the Law. Reflections on Pitfalls in Interpretation', in Hooker and Wilson, Ch. 1 and esp. pp. 4–6. See also Rhyne, *Faith*, Ch. 2, who shows that a rhetorical question, followed by *me genoito* ('by no means!'), always introduces a topic for immediate treatment and never concludes one. Romans 4 is thus the clarification of 3³¹.

God wants, and the important thing about faith is that it is open to Gentiles and Jews equally. The Jews are right when they claim Abraham as their father, so long as they recognize that it is sharing his faith that makes them his children, not sharing in his subsequent circumcision (Paul simply passes over the fact, 4[11], that circumcision was a sign and seal of faith, and ignores completely the fact that in the story it was God himself who commanded Abraham to be circumcised). Abraham, he argues, is as much the father of Gentiles who believe as of Jews who believe, and much more the father of believing Gentiles than of unbelieving Jews. In the argument he more or less fuses Christian faith and the faith of Abraham. Quite clearly the point is once more to put Jews and Gentiles on the same footing before God and as members of his people.

While all this is the main thrust of the passage, it ought to be conceded that in the background is a theme or an implication that it is not by anything we do or are that we enter and remain within God's favour and his people. This is clearest in 4[2]: 'if Abraham was justified by works, he has something to boast about, but not before God.' Boasting before God *is* excluded explicitly by Paul, even if it is only parenthetically. Certainly Paul's main point is that even Abraham became the father of Israel by faith, and not by what he did, so that even he cannot boast over Gentiles. The emphasis is on the equality of Jews and Gentiles in God's people. Nevertheless there is the implication in the chapter that if justification is by faith, it cannot be by anything else, and that includes human achievement, cf. vv. 4–8, as well as v. 2. This implication or even sub-theme has been of tremendous importance in Christian history, yet it must be repeated that it is not what the passage focusses on.

It is only in Ch. 5 that we at last come to a positive role for the Law, understood not as story or promise but as legislation. This is to make sin recognizable, concrete, computable (5[13]). It is not that the Law creates sin; sin was there already, but somewhat in the fashion of a disease that is active but cannot be identified and treated because symptoms have not yet appeared. The Law enables the symptoms to be recognized and thus the disease to be treated, and this is surely good. In 5[20] he does seem to go beyond this and to say that the Law exacerbates sin: 'Law came in to increase the trespass.' It is probable, however, that we should take 'trespass' not as a synonym for sin, but as a concrete and therefore perceptible infringement of the divine will. In other words, by giving rise to trespass, the Law exposes symptoms, and indeed creates them: God gives a specific command, a law, and if we disobey it, that reveals our disease, our sinfulness. If this is correct, then 5^{20} also says that the Law makes potential sin actual, like 5^{13}.

Now in some circles Paul was suspected of saying, or of opening the door to saying, that if all is by God's grace then it does not matter what we do, indeed that sinning is good because it gives God greater scope for his grace (cf. 3^8; $6^{1, 15}$). On the contrary, he argues (6^{14}), being under grace deals with sin more successfully than the Law ever could. In fact the Law does not deal with sin at all: it simply exposes it. At least in the short term it seems to make it worse by making it perceptible and concrete. In 7^{1-6} he depicts Christians as dead to the Law in so far as it is a régime under which people live. This picture must be given its full value. His statement is unqualified: he does not say that people are dead to the Law only as a means to salvation. He simply says they have died to it. How then, a few verses later (7^{12}), can he turn to saying quite positive things about the Law? If, until now, the only positive role for it has been that it brings out the symptoms of sin, how can it now become holy, just, good, and spiritual? Now, apparently, with the best part of me, I want to do what the Law prescribes (especially $7^{12, 13f., 16}$). Most important of all, being in the Spirit means that I can now at last do what the Law commands (8^4). Have we died to it, only in the end to be obliged to obey it as never before? If so, why is the language of dying to it early in Ch. 7 so strong and unqualified?

Despite what has just been said, it must be noted that many have held that Paul rejects the Law only in so far as it is treated as a means to salvation. As a rule of life it is not rejected at all, but rather reinforced. This is held to explain the seeming internal contradictions in Rom. 7.[i] It is also now suggested that what is rejected is the Law only in so far as it separates Jews from Gentiles.[j] Yet neither of these

i See most notably Cranfield, passim, but especially II, Essay II, pp. 845–62, and I, e.g. pp. 349f.

j See especially Sanders, *PLJP*, Ch. 3.

explanations quite accounts for the strong and categorical statements about dying to the Law. It may therefore be suggested that Paul is talking about dying to the Law as a régime, as that which governs people's lives, but does not thereby propose that everything in the Law is to be rejected. It is clear that he does not, for instance, propose to jettison the law against coveting (and in the commentary it is suggested that throughout 7^{7-25} and on to 8^4 it is this particular law that is the subject). This law certainly still stands for Christians, as do others, cf. 13^{8-10}, most notably the law to love one another. On the other hand, 14^5 and 14^{14}, whether or not primarily concerned with Jewish observances of the sabbath and the food laws, show that Paul does not regard some aspects of the Law as binding on all Christians. This means that he is prepared to discriminate within the Law, holding to some parts and not to others. This is to deny it a ruling function; it is no longer the sole and sufficient arbiter of life that is pleasing to God.[k] It must be repeated that this does not mean that he rejects everything or even most things that are in the Law, and it equally does not mean that he denies that men and women ought to obey God's will. It is simply that the Law is no longer the decisive criterion. In that sense Christians have died to the Law, as well as in any sense that it is a means to salvation (if it ever was). Only in I Corinthians does he explicitly cite the Law in order to settle an issue of behaviour; he does so twice, and in both cases (the financial support of the apostle, 9^9, and female silence at worship, 14^{34}) the issues are scarcely central to his theology, while in the second case there is serious doubt about the authenticity of the text. This almost total ignoring of the Law when he deals with practical, ethical matters, makes us doubt whether we can plausibly hold that for Paul the Law still stood, apart from things that divide Jews from Gentiles (particularly the sabbath, circumcision, and the food laws). There are remarkably few signs that the Law functioned for him as a criterion of behaviour, with the exception of the command to love. This (love) is not only the first of the fruit of the Spirit in Gal. 5^{22} (cf. I Cor. 13), but also emerges as the first strictly ethical element in the parenesis of Rom. 12 (v. 9); it is seen as the fulfilment of the Law in 13^{8-10}.

k Cf. Räisänen, *PL*, pp. 23–41.

In the last passage (13^{8-10}), the commands against adultery, killing, stealing and coveting are specified as fulfilled in the love-commandment. So, somewhat surprisingly, is 'any other commandment'. This can hardly mean any other commandment whatsoever, for we know from the next chapter that Paul proposes sitting loose to the food laws, at least in principle, if not (for pastoral reasons) in practice. Presumably love, and not the Law itself, is now the criterion of behaviour, and therefore only those things that can be subsumed under the heading of love are matters of obligation: thus refraining from adultery is, but circumcision is not. Thus when Paul says 'any other commandment', this is not to be taken without qualification unless he is guilty of incoherence on a large scale. Something more restricted must be at stake, which is why I have suggested that he refers to things that can be subsumed under the heading of love.

This view of Paul's implicit attitude to the continuing validity of the Law for all Christians will be supported by the line taken in the commentary on 9^{30-33}. This is that it was true righteousness at which Israel failed to arrive, not the Law, and that they failed to arrive at it because righteousness (i.e. life as God's people) basically consists not in doing the Law but in having faith in Christ. As Sanders has argued, this doubtless gives the game away: the real thing wrong with the Law is that it can hardly lead to true life with God if that can be found only through faith in Christ.[1] Only Christ gives life (7^{10}), and this is true not only of entry into the people of God, but also of continuing existence as that people.

So then, whatever may be true of the letter to the Galatians,[m] in Romans there are two reasons given for negative statements about the Law. The first comes at the end of Ch. 3 and the beginning of Ch. 4, namely that if acceptance into God's people is equally open to Jews and Gentiles on the basis of faith, then circumcision can hardly remain as the basis. Since circumcision is the sign of life under the Torah, it follows that Torah-obedience can no longer be seen as *the* distinguishing mark of the people of God. The second reason emerges in 9^{30-33},

[1] See, e.g. *PPJ*, pp. 474–84.
[m] See Hübner, *LPT*, Ch. 1; J. D. G. Dunn, 'The New Perspective on Paul', *BJRL* 65. 2, 1983, 95–102; Sanders, *PLJP*, pp. 17–29; Drane, *Paul: Libertine or Legalist?*, Ch. 2. The precise shape of the attitude in Galatians is much disputed.

where we learn that faith in Jesus Christ is the criterion of righteousness, from which it follows that nothing else can be, including Torah-obedience. These two reasons merge into one: faith in Jesus Christ, for Jews and Gentiles equally, is the crux of what God wants. The Law, on the other hand, applies in its fullness only to Jews, and is moreover a competitor to faith in Christ.

That this is the heart of the divine requirement is elaborated in 9–11 as a whole: Israel was indeed called to be the people of God, yet this was always primarily a matter of call and promise rather than one of keeping the Law or indeed of doing anything ($9^{11, 16, 30-32}$; $10^{3, 4}$; 11^6). It was also never intended to be a racial matter, 10^{11-12}.

Of course it is clear enough that Paul believed that Christians have an obligation to live as God's people should,[n] but this is set out in terms that overlap with, but are not identical with, the OT Law. To borrow an idea from I Cor. 9^{20}, although the written Torah as such and as a whole is not binding on Christians, the fundamental will of God certainly is, and this includes such things as the law against coveting and the command to love. In Rom. 10^4 when we read that 'Christ is the end of the law for righteousness for everyone who believes'[o] we may debate whether 'end' is to be taken in the sense of 'fulfilment' or that of 'termination'. Either way, it is likely that we should see Christ as now in some way taking the place of the Law at the centre of piety and life.

In sum, Paul's statements about the Law are problematic and difficult to reconcile with one another. It would be rash to claim that the interpretation offered here does away with all the difficulties; perhaps no interpretation is likely to do that, and we may be forgiven for suspecting that Paul had not managed to sort the whole matter out for himself. Nevertheless the contention now being made is that in · Romans Paul does reject the Torah both as a means to salvation, and also as the definitive guide to life under God, more radically and more consistently than is sometimes allowed.

As a footnote, mention may be made of the view of Wilckens[p]

n See M. Hooker, 'Paul and "Covenantal Nomism" ', Ch. 5 of Hooker and Wilson; also Sanders, *PLJP*, pp. 93–105.
o This is a literal rendering of the Greek.
p II, pp. 84, 86, 121–3.

that there is in Romans a stress on the Law as curse (from which Christ on the cross gives redemption). The view taken in this commentary is that though there may be echoes of such an idea, it is not central as it is in Gal. 3. In Rom. 1^{31} Paul speaks of the divine decree that 'those who do such things deserve to die', and in 4^{15} we learn that the Law brings wrath. In 8^1 the condemnation that does not apply to Christian believers may well refer back to $7^{11, 13}$. Yet there does not seem to be sufficient basis for a specific link between Law and curse in Romans, let alone for supposing that it is a critical element in Paul's thought in the letter.

9. POWER-LANGUAGE IN ROMANS

In this letter, Paul does not discuss only the conditions under which people may be justified, and enter the people of God. He also speaks often, and especially in Chs. 5, 6, and 8, of the powers under which men and women live. That the NT is permeated by the language of the powers, forces that are supernatural but operate through social and political institutions, is widely agreed. q Though this idea does occur in Romans (see $8^{38f.}$), a more fundamental idea is more prominent, which is equally hard for most moderns to grasp. This is the notion that human life is lived within one sphere of power or another: either the sphere of God and his Spirit, or the sphere of sin (or something associated with it). This idea is expressed in various ways, and it starts as early in the letter as $1^{21ff.}$ (and cf. 1^{24}, 'God gave them up . . .'), and is particularly prominent in 3^9; 5^{12-21}; 6^{5-22}; 8^{1-4}.

Salvation consists, at least in part, in being transferred from one dominion (sin) to the other (Spirit). This basic idea is clearly related to the notion of supernatural powers already mentioned, and also to the eschatological scheme of two ages, the present evil age ruled over by wickedness, and a future age in which God will rule absolutely. Yet it surely has more general roots in the ancient world's experience of subjection. Human life was carried on in the knowledge that choice was severely limited: not only were there the 'angelic' forces,

q It has been denied by W. Carr, *Angels and Principalities*, SNTSMS 42, CUP 1981, but reaffirmed and expounded by W. Wink, *Naming the Powers*, Fortress Press 1984.

demons and astral forces,[r] there were also their human counterparts or agents. Even where democracy existed, its franchise was extremely limited, while imperial power was dominating and pervasive. It is hardly surprising, then, that in Paul's letter we hear the recurring note of impotence under unfriendly power, particularly the power of sin, and the offer of release not into absolute freedom, but into a benign dominion, that of God himself. Although the connection with the notion of the people of God is largely left to the reader to make, it is surely plain that to be in that people is also to be within the dominion of God. Therefore, being within God's people is freedom from other powers, notably the power of sin.

Perhaps all this is not as remote from our contemporary experience as at first sight it seems. The element of free choice may be not as secure for us as we like to think: not only are we too subject to political power which may or may not rule with our consent, but we are also subject to fashion, habit, public opinion, the past, and so on. The alcoholic and the drug addict without doubt know what being under an alien and unfriendly power is like. That their addiction began from a choice, is not to the point: now they are not free to choose. At all events, this notion of living within and under some power or other is taken for granted in Romans.

[r] It is clear that by the time of Paul, astrology was widespread and popular, embraced by, among others, the Stoics, who had a natural receptivity towards its determinism. See S. J. Tester, *A History of Western Astrology*, Woodbridge and Wolfeboro: The Boydell Press 1987, esp. Chs. 2 and 3.

Romans 1-16

Commentary

I ¹*Paul, a servant of Jesus Christ, called to be an apostle, set apart for the gospel of God ²which he promised beforehand through his prophets in the holy scriptures, ³the gospel concerning his Son, who was descended from David according to the flesh ⁴and designated Son of God in power according to the Spirit of holiness by his resurrection from the dead, Jesus Christ our Lord, ⁵through whom we have received grace and apostleship to bring about the obedience of faith for the sake of his name among all the nations, ⁶including yourselves who are called to belong to Jesus Christ:*

⁷To all God's beloved in Rome, who are called to be saints:

Grace to you and peace from God our Father and the Lord Jesus Christ.

Letters of the period usually began with the name of the writer, the name of the recipient, and the simple word 'Greeting'. There could be a little elaboration, especially of the greeting and of the recipient's name, for example, 'Serapion to his brothers Ptolemaus and Apollonius greeting'[a] or 'Irenaeus to Apollinarius his dearest brother many greetings'.[b] It is very unusual for there to be as much elaboration as there is in the letters of Paul, who seems to want to include some matters of central Christian belief even in the formal opening. There are three main themes:

(*a*) an account of himself that is theological rather than biographical;

(*b*) the place of Jesus Christ in the divine plan for humanity;

(*c*) the universal scope of the Christian mission.

a 154 BCE. Cited from Doty, *Letters in Primitive Christianity*, p. 13.

b Second or third century CE. Cited from C. K. Barrett, *The New Testament Background: Selected Documents*, SPCK 1956 and New York: Macmillan 1957, p. 29.

Everything Paul writes has its ultimate centre in Jesus Christ, and here he identifies himself as Christ's servant or slave, who is therefore committed to obeying him, and who is his apostle by virtue of a divine call. He thus places himself within the prophetic tradition as someone set apart by God not so much for special honour as for a special task. We know that this special task was not simply to spread the gospel (explained in 1¹⁶), but specifically to be the apostle to the Gentiles, i.e. to all those who were not Jews (v. 5; 11¹³; and Gal. 1¹⁶) and so had hitherto been outside historical Israel, the people of God. This alerts us to the fact that throughout the letter Paul's concern is not just with individuals and their salvation, but with communities and people.

The coming of Jesus is no abrupt or isolated incursion of God's activity into the stream of history. Rather is it the culmination and fulfilment of a long process of divine dealings with Israel, especially through the prophets (v. 2), but now seen to embrace people of all traditions, histories, and races (vv. 5–6). Jesus is the Messiah, the deliverer expected by many Jews (v. 1), and in accordance with the usual form of the expectation, he is of Davidic descent, indeed a new and greater David (v. 3). From another angle, however, seen in the light of the world-changing event of the resurrection, he is much more than the son of David: he is the powerful Son of God. Although this term is never really explained by Paul, it probably means that as God's agent, he is as totally obedient to him as any good son was expected to be to his father. Moreover, he bears not only God's endorsement and authority, but also his power, the power signally demonstrated in the resurrection. In short, Jesus is seen as *Lord*. This is a term difficult to define in relation to God, but so far as human beings are concerned it means that Jesus is the one to whom they are servants or slaves (cf. v. 1). From this passage, therefore, we may not be able to deduce much about Paul's view of the relation of Jesus to God except in terms of function: God acts authoritatively through him. Nevertheless we can certainly learn that the relation of men and women to Christ the Lord is to be one of service and obedience.

It is through this Lord that 'we' (Paul himself, and also presumably those associated with him in his task) have been given the commission of spreading the gospel not just to Israel but all nations. This commission, or apostleship, arises from God's great saving kindness ('grace') and is intended to lead to Christian discipleship ('the obedience of faith') everywhere, not least among the Romans.

At last in v. 7 Paul gets to the point of naming the recipients, who are all the people in Rome who belong to Christ and who are already aware of being loved by the God who spoke through the Jewish prophets. They are 'saints', i.e. those whom God has called to be his people. Then, instead of the usual word 'greeting' (Greek *chairein*), he invokes upon them 'grace' (Greek *charis*), perhaps making a mild theological pun. He also invokes upon them 'peace', a translation of the common Hebrew greeting *Shalom*, but he does this in no conventional way. If grace is God's undeserved saving kindness, peace in the biblical tradition is more than mere absence of conflict. It is total well-being, and especially that well-being which includes a proper relationship with God.

א

1

Paul: a Roman name. In Acts he is called Saul up to 13⁹, and Paul thereafter. Contrary to what is often supposed, the change of name does not coincide with his becoming a Christian. It is true that names were regarded as highly significant, and a change of name often accompanied an important change of life (compare Abram-Abraham and Jacob-Israel in the OT, and Simon-Peter in the NT). Nevertheless, if there was once some such significance to Saul-Paul, it is now irretrievable. It is on the other hand quite possible that Saul was his Jewish name and Paul his Roman name from the beginning. In his letters he never refers to himself as Saul.

servant: servants were normally slaves, and 'slave' undoubtedly provides the better translation (Greek *doulos*), implying as it does total obedience and belonging. To Gentiles (non-Jews), it must have sounded unpleasantly demeaning. Jewish readers, however, would probably not have been startled by the word, as it is often used in the Septuagint (LXX) for those who serve God, e.g. Ps. 89³ (David) and II Kings 17²³ (the prophets). Paul uses it for Christian missionaries, e.g. Gal. 1¹⁰; Phil. 1¹.

Jesus Christ: Jesus is the Greek form of 'Joshua' and is straightforwardly his personal name, a not uncommon one. 'Christ' (Greek *Christos*) literally means 'anointed', and in itself would convey little to an ordinary Greek reader. For Jews and instructed Gentiles it would have been a different matter, for *Christos* translates the Hebrew *Meshiach*, Messiah; in Israel anointing was an important matter and a solemn one, usually signifying divine endorsement and authorization for an important task. Kings were anointed (e.g. II Sam. 2⁴) as were priests (Num. 3³), a prophet (Isa. 61⁶) and even Cyrus king of Persia (Isa. 45¹). By NT times, however, many Jews expected one particular anointed one, divinely sent and commissioned, who would restore and purify the national life under God. This expectation was neither universal in Judaism nor always of the same sort of figure, but probably most Jews hoped for another king like David who would release the nation from bondage to foreign powers, which in our period meant the power of Rome. As was usual in early Christianity, Paul believed that Jesus was this expected figure. Nevertheless he often seems to use the title 'Christ' in a way that is almost devoid of content, as little more than a name. Perhaps this was because it would have been unintelligible to most non-Jews, or perhaps because those who did understand it would take it in narrowly nationalist and political, even military terms. There is no question of Paul's rejecting the messiahship of Jesus (see v. 3 and 9⁵), but there is no sign that he accepted its usual connotations. Apart from perfunctory occurrences, he tends to use it especially in contexts where he is concentrating on the sufferings of Jesus, as in Rom. 6. It stands above all for the idea of fulfilment, for the culmination of all God's dealings with his people; as Paul believed that Jesus was that fulfilment, it was natural for him to retain the title Messiah/Christ for Jesus. Yet it may be that he was trying to redefine it in terms of suffering and rejection rather than in terms of straightforward triumph, and that this is why he uses it in the particular way he does.ᶜ

called to be an apostle: it is a divine call, like that to a prophet (cf. Gal. 1¹⁵; Jer. 1⁴ᶠᶠ.; Isa. 6; 49¹; Ezek. 2¹–3¹⁵), which gives Paul his authority. In several of his letters he writes of his apostleship in a fashion that is not only emphatic but also defensive (see I Cor. 9¹⁻²; 15⁸⁻¹⁰; II Cor. 10–13; Gal. 1–2). An apostle (*apostolos*) is literally 'one who is sent', cf. the verb

---

ᶜ See M. Hengel, ' "Christos" in Paul', Ch. 4 of *Between Jesus and Paul*, ET SCM Press and Fortress Press 1983; see also G. Vermes, *Jesus the Jew*, Collins 1973, reissued Fortress Press and SCM Press 1983, Ch. 6.

'to send', *apostellō*. Behind the NT use of the term may lie the Jewish idea of the *shaliach*, the plenipotentiary representative,[d] and it seems to be used in the NT in more than one way. In Acts 14[4, 14] Paul and Barnabas are both referred to as apostles, yet in the rest of Acts the term is reserved for the Twelve, and Paul is nowhere else so described, even though he is the hero of much of the book. There are thus at least two different fields of reference for 'apostle': one which can include a figure like Barnabas (cf. II Cor. 8[23]), and one which is limited to the Twelve as in all of Acts except 14[4, 14]. The matter may well be much more complicated than this,[e] but what is important for understanding Paul is that he claims to be an apostle in the *narrower* sense, i.e. in the same sense as Peter. He claims that his experience of Christ on the road to Damascus counts as a resurrection experience which qualifies him for apostleship (I Cor. 9[1]; 15[8]), yet for him the crucial qualification is not this, but his call and commission by God.

set apart: the Greek word (*aphōrismenos*) is rich in LXX associations. There it is used for special appointment to the cultic service of God, but also for God's choice of Israel to be his special people (compare Num. 8[11] with Lev. 20[24-26]).

gospel of God: the word here rendered 'gospel' (*euangelion*) is literally good news. It and its verbal cognate *euangelizō* (to tell good news, or even to preach) are used in LXX for any sort of good news, but in some passages like Ps. 40[9] and Isa. 41[27] the particular good news is that of God's saving action, and it is doubtless these passages that have influenced the early church's use. In the pagan world, on the other hand, they were associated with good news about the emperor, such as his accession to the throne, so that Gentile as well as Jewish readers would find the terms familiar. For Paul and other Christians, the good news was from and about *God*. What this news is will emerge more exactly at I[16].

2

promised beforehand: the early Christians believed that, as Christ was the fulfilment of God's ancient purposes, the OT (roughly speaking: it was not yet precisely defined) contained promises that pointed forward to him. In order to maintain this view, arguments that often seem im-

d Cf. K. H. Rengstorff, in *TDNT* I, pp. 407ff.
e See C. K. Barrett, *The Signs of an Apostle*, Epworth Press 1970, esp. pp. 71–3.

plausible to modern readers were constructed from OT passages. Here, Paul does not say which, if any, particular passages he has in mind, but we may suspect he would have included Hab. 2⁴ (cf. Rom. 1¹⁷; Gal. 3¹¹) and Gen. 15⁶ (cf. Rom. 4³ff·; Gal. 3⁶).

3–4

In these verses Paul is widely believed to be quoting an already traditional confession of faith. This is for two main reasons.

(*a*) There are two statements about Jesus which, in the Greek, fall into a neatly rounded couplet, much more neatly than RSV indicates with its 'descended from David according to the flesh and designated Son of God in power according to the Spirit of holiness . . .' Barrett (p. 18) brings out the parallelism thus:

> 'in the sphere of the flesh, born of the family of David;
> in the sphere of the Holy Spirit, appointed Son of God.'

This parallelism has led to the suspicion that we have something that has been honed by repetition, and made memorable, and that this has taken place in worship. If this suspicion is justified, then the couplet may be a very early confession of faith about Jesus, perhaps 'in power' being Paul's own addition to the formula.

(*b*) There is a rather high incidence of expressions which are not characteristically Pauline. These include the reference to Jesus as son of David; 'according to (or 'in the sphere of') the flesh' used without negative connotations; 'the Spirit of holiness' instead of the usual 'Holy Spirit'; and the possible implication that Jesus became Son of God at the resurrection (see below under *designated*).

Even if he is quoting, it ought to be added, he means what he says. He accepts Jesus as the Messiah, but sees him as much more than that.

3

descended from David: this is no mere genealogical comment. It is a way of saying that Jesus is the Davidic Messiah, cf. Isa. 11; II Sam. 7¹¹⁻¹⁴.

according to the flesh: the phrase *kata sarka*, unusually for Paul, must here mean 'humanly speaking'. Elsewhere it means often something like 'apart from God', 'worldly' in the sense of being centred on something other than God (cf. Rom. 8⁴, ⁵, ¹², ¹³; II Cor. 1¹⁷; 10²,³; 11¹⁸; perhaps Gal. 3¹⁹). This, however, is not the only place where the phrase simply refers to human descent: see Rom. 4¹; 9³,⁵; I Cor. 10¹⁸; even perhaps

Gal. 4²³ and II Cor. 5¹⁶. Paul's use of the word 'flesh' (*sarx*) is complicated. Sometimes he can use it for the physical stuff of which we are
made, as in I Cor. 15³⁹ and II Cor. 7¹ (in the latter translated 'body' by
RSV). Sometimes he can use it, as here, for natural kinship and common humanity. His more negative use, sometimes called 'ethical',
is strongly represented in Rom. 8 and Gal. 5, and requires some
explanation.

(*a*) In its negative sense 'flesh' (*sarx*) is not particularly and certainly
not exclusively physical. 'The works of the flesh' in Gal. 5¹⁹⁻²¹ include
physical sins, but also religious and above all social sins. In Rom 8⁹ Paul
says that his hearers are not in the flesh but in the Spirit, yet they plainly
were still in physical embodiment.

(*b*) In crucial passages, especially Rom. 8 and Gal. 5, being in the
flesh, or living according to the flesh, is bad and hostile to God, while
being in the Spirit, or living according to the Spirit, is good and means
commitment and obedience to God. The opposition is not between
physical and non-physical, but between life centred in something other
than God, and life centred in God.

(*c*) The terminology is not consistent. In II Cor. 10³ Paul makes a
useful distinction (obscured by the RSV translation) between living *in*
the flesh (*sarx*) which is the proper and universal human lot, and carrying on the struggle *according to* the flesh, which is acting in the wrong
way and accepting the world's standards, goals, resources, and con-
straints. Unfortunately, in Rom. 8 this distinction is not maintained,
and 'in the flesh' and 'according to the flesh' come to be used synonym-
ously for the wrong way of living.

(*d*) How such a straightforward word like *sarx* came to have this
astonishing range of meaning is not clear. It is often held to have taken
its negative/ethical meaning from the OT use of *bāsār*, translated *sarx* in
LXX, which can mean human nature in a neutral sense, but can also
mean human frailty as opposed to divine strength: see Isa. 31³, 'The
Egyptians are men, and not God; and their horses are flesh, and not
spirit'; see also Isa. 40⁶, 'All flesh is grass'. In Qumran, moreover, 'flesh'
and 'Spirit' can be used as expressions of the opposition between the
two ages, the Age of Belial and of wickedness on the one hand, and the
Age of God, the New Age, on the other, cf. IQS 4, 11. There was thus
in Paul's background the notion of 'flesh' as a mark of the evil realm,
and not just of natural humanness.

It is also possible that it was in the Galatian dispute that Paul began to
use *sarx* in so strongly negative a fashion, and that it was there prompted
by his polemic against any attempt to impose circumcision upon

Gentile Christians. If he knew that circumcision was sometimes called 'the covenant in the flesh' (Ecclus. 44²⁰), then he could have developed his use of *sarx* to cover anything that replaced God-in-Christ as the centre of life.

4

designated Son of God: it is convenient to take the expressions in reverse order.

(*a*) Son of God: to read into this term the later trinitarian teaching about God the Son is anachronistic. To call someone a son of God was neither difficult nor unusual in Judaism or in the Hellenistic world generally. Israel as a nation was called God's son (Hos. 11¹), angelic beings were sons of God (Gen. 6², ⁴), and so were kings of Israel (II Sam. 7¹⁴; Ps. 2⁷). Later the term was applied especially to the righteous man (Wisdom 2¹⁷⁻¹⁸), and to charismatic figures.ᶠ Further, although evidence outside the NT is not plentiful, it appears that the Messiah, the Davidic king of the future, was also thought of as God's son, and this is certainly borne out in the Gospels, cf. Mark 14⁶¹; Matt. 26⁶³. In the non-Jewish Hellenistic world, 'son of God' appears to have been a regular way of referring to a very powerful or charismatic person, a ruler, an ancient hero, or even a great thinker.ᵍ In at least some Hellenistic circles, divinity was much more easily shared by human beings than it was in Judaism, where being a son of God certainly did not mean that one was divine. In a Jewish context, use of the term did not imply that the person in question was eternal, nor even that he existed before his birth. What it did imply was God's endorsement and commissioning, and on the human side, obedience to God. There is no doubt, however, that Christians very early began to think of Jesus as Son of God in a special way, though it was some centuries before this special way was given definition. How far Paul believed Jesus to have existed before he was born of Mary is a matter of dispute: the most favourable texts for the view that he did are Gal. 4⁴ and Rom. 8³.

(*b*) designated: the problem here is the precise force of the verb.

(i) The Greek *horisthentos* normally means 'appointed, established', which would suggest that Jesus became Son of God only at the resurrection. This would lead to what later became called 'adoptionist christology', in effect that at some point Jesus was elevated to divine sonship. This meaning of the verb with its implication is used, as we

ᶠ See the evidence in Vermes, *Jesus the Jew*, pp. 206–10.
ᵍ See the succinct treatment in Dunn, *Christology*, Ch. 2.

noted above, as evidence for Paul's quoting earlier material in these two verses. When Paul is writing freely, it is argued, he does not say that Jesus *became* Son of God at the resurrection. To judge from the quotation of Ps. 2^7 in Acts 13^{33}, there was such a view in the early church, but it is usually held that Gal. 4^4 and Rom. 8^3 show that Paul did not share that view.[h]

(ii) *Horisthentos* could just possibly mean not 'appointed' but 'manifested', with the implication than an already existing but hidden sonship was revealed at the resurrection. This would avoid finding Paul guilty of the 'heresy' of adoptionism, but it also seems to avoid taking the Greek word in its obvious sense.

(iii) It is possible that we ought to take seriously, as the key to the phrase, the connection between sonship, *power*, and resurrection. In that case, Paul (and the formula before him) may be saying that it was at the resurrection that Jesus became, not Son of God, but Son of God *in power*. This would not contradict the apparent meaning of Rom. 8^3, where God *sends* his Son, nor would it avoid the obvious meaning of *horisthentos*, 'appointed'. It would also lend support to those who think that this is an enthronement formula.

The most striking aspect of these verses, however, especially in the light of the references to the resurrection and to the Holy Spirit, is that they point to the inauguration of the New Age of God and of his power, with the clear implication that the Old Age is therefore at an end. This belief, which is of great importance for the understanding of Paul, will be considerably developed later in the letter.

Spirit of holiness: the adjectival genitive, 'of holiness', rather than the simple adjective 'holy', is an indication that we have an Hebraic idiom here. It is unlikely that the meaning is any different from 'Holy Spirit'.

5

the obedience of faith: there are several ways this could be taken, but there are two of special importance.

(*a*) It could be the faith that consists in obedience, or indeed the obedience that consists in faith.

(*b*) It could be the faith that leads to, or requires, obedience.[i]

h See, however, Dunn, *Christology*, pp. 33–46 for doubts as to whether the passages do show this. Dunn thinks it possible that Paul did believe that Jesus became Son of God at the resurrection.

i For a full list of the possibilities see Cranfield I, p. 66.

The most likely meaning is that faith, the positive response to the Christian message, is in itself an act of obedience to God.[j] Nevertheless, while we may prefer such a meaning, something of (*b*) cannot be ruled out. The act of response to the gospel is the primary obedience, but Paul certainly expects that to lead to further obedience, obedience in life (cf. Rom. 6$^{15-19}$). It is possible that this is the primary meaning, but the context is about *becoming* Christian, and this gives (*a*) a slight edge, as concerned with the initial act of faith.

for the sake of his name: in effect, 'for his sake'. 'Name' is commonly used in the Bible as a surrogate for the person, and this is particularly so in the case of God and the name of God.

among all the nations: almost at the very beginning of the letter, still within the formal opening, we have a signal that we are to be concerned with the Christian gospel as for Gentiles and Jews equally. The word 'nations' here (*tois ethnesin*) is that normally used for Gentile nations, i.e. non-Jews.

7

in Rome: one important MS omits these words both here and from v. 15 (see the Introduction, 1.*b*, *ii*), and this has been used to support the view that Romans was originally a circular letter. It is more likely, however, that the words are original; the vast majority of MSS include them.

called to be saints: the biblical usage of 'saint' (*hagios*) is markedly different from the modern. Today, a saint is a hero of the Christian faith, or a particularly notable and godly person, like St Peter or St Theresa, or else in common speech someone who has special qualities of goodness. In the NT, on the other hand, it is the regular term for ordinary Christians. *Hagios* can also be translated 'holy': saints are holy ones, and the essential biblical meaning of 'holy' is 'belonging to God'. At root, therefore, saints are simply the people of God. Indeed they are expected to live in a way that is appropriate to being God's people, but this moral and behavioural meaning is consequent and not primary. It is thus quite possible for Paul to refer to a group of Christians as saints, and yet proceed to castigate them for their behaviour, as he does in I Corinthians (cf. 1^2 with Ch. 5).

Here, he reminds the Roman Christians that they are the people of

j So Wilckens I, p. 67.

God by *call*. It is not by birth, and this marks a difference from Judaism, where the normal thing was to be a member of Israel by being born into it (together with subsequent circumcision and commitment to keeping the Torah).

I$^{8-15}$ THANKSGIVING

⁸*First, I thank my God through Jesus Christ for all of you, because your faith is proclaimed in all the world.* ⁹*For God is my witness, whom I serve with my spirit in the gospel of his Son, that without ceasing I mention you always in my prayers,* ¹⁰*asking that somehow by God's will I may now at last succeed in coming to you.* ¹¹*For I long to see you, that I may impart to you some spiritual gift to strengthen you,* ¹²*that is, that we may be mutually encouraged by each other's faith, both yours and mine.* ¹³*I want you to know, brethren, that I have often intended to come to you (but thus far have been prevented), in order that I may reap some harvest among you as well as among the rest of the Gentiles.* ¹⁴*I am under obligation both to Greeks and to barbarians, both to the wise and to the foolish:* ¹⁵*so I am eager to preach the gospel to you also who are in Rome.*

As we saw in the Introduction (6), in all his letters except Galatians Paul follows the formal opening with a thanksgiving. This is here intimately connected with his own role in the Christian mission. The whole thing is delicately worded, probably reflecting the fact that the Roman church was not his foundation; we know that he had a policy not to conduct a mission in a place that had already been evangelized by another apostle (cf. Rom. 15²⁰; II Cor. 10¹⁵⁻¹⁶). In the case of Rome there is no evidence that at the time of Paul's writing any other apostle had been active there, but he is still taking pains not to seem to be patronizing the church. Thus he writes of *mutual* enrichment and of *sharing* ministry with them. It is in this passage that we get our first firm indication that the Roman church was predominantly Gentile, though this does not preclude there being a substantial Jewish element as well (see Introduction, 1.*b*, *iv*). The whole section is clearly preparing the ground for a personal visit.

ನಞ

9

with my spirit: Paul can sometimes speak of the spirit (*pneuma*) as a distinct human entity, that part of a person which has relationship with God (I Thess. 5^{23} is a probable instance). More commonly in his writings, however, *Pneuma* refers to the divine in-breathing, or else the human self as quickened by God (cf. Rom. 8$^{1-11}$). It thus has the sort of meaning we should indicate by giving the word a capital letter: Spirit/Pneuma. It is possible, therefore, that here Paul is saying that he serves God by means of God's own empowering.

13

prevented: by whom or what has he thus far been prevented from visiting them? It has been suggested that Satan has been the obstacle (cf. I Thess. 2^{18}), but there is nothing in the context here to argue for that. It is more likely that this is a 'divine passive', common in the Bible. Where the agent of a passive verb is left unstated, as here, it is usually to be inferred that God is the agent. The device may well have been used to avoid speaking of God too humanly, having him do this and that just as if he were one more actor on the human stage, and also to avoid using the name of God unnecessarily and so 'in vain' (Ex. 20^7). So, if God is implicitly the one who has prevented Paul's visiting the Romans, we should understand that it is the demands of the divinely given mission elsewhere that have hitherto made it impossible for him to come to Rome.

14

under obligation: literally, 'I am a debtor to'. This is not to say that the Romans have given Paul something which he must repay. The sense is rather something like 'I have a responsibility towards'. If there were a specific debt, Paul would no doubt regard it as due to God.

to Greeks and to barbarians: this presumably includes all who are not Jews, the cultured and the uncultured from the point of view of Hellenistic-Roman civilization. 'Barbarian' is a quite usual term for people outside that civilization (cf. Cranfield I, pp. 84f., and Wilckens I, p. 81).

to the wise and to the foolish: this may be another way of saying the same thing, or it may refer to the educated and the uneducated in both groups. The former is more likely, as it is doubtful whether the ordinary person in the Graeco-Roman world would have considered that barbarians could be educated!

15

in Rome: as in v. 7, one important MS (G) omits these words.

> ¹⁶*For I am not ashamed of the gospel: it is the power of God for salvation to every one who has faith, to the Jew first and also to the Greek.* ¹⁷*For in it the righteousness of God is revealed through faith for faith; as it is written, 'He who through faith is righteous shall live.'*

These two verses form a bridge between the thanksgiving and the beginning of the body of the letter, and put in a nutshell the message of the letter as a whole. This means that the letter itself is their true exegesis: almost every word of them is pregnant. The good news (gospel) serves to bring liberation (salvation) to all believers, i.e. to all who respond to it, whatever their racial or religious background (to the Jew first and also to the Greek), though historically and in the divine economy it came first to the Jew. It can provide this liberation because God's consistent faithfulness to his people now embraces the rescue of all races, and can be openly seen doing so. To benefit from this divine rescue, men and women are required only to be willing to do so (from faith to faith), as the words from Habakkuk show: it is those whose righteousness is based on faith who will find true life. So then, what God has been to his ancient covenant people, he now will be to all people, the only condition being readiness to receive.

ॐ

16

I am not ashamed: this strikes the ear oddly. Why should Paul be ashamed of his Christianity?

(*a*) It could be that he was abashed by the cultural and religious sophistication of the ancient world in general and Rome in particular, and here is in effect whistling to keep his courage up. There is no evidence that he felt like that, but quite a lot to show that he was highly critical of much contemporary culture (see vv. 18–32, and I Cor. 1–4).

(b) It could be that he is facing the charge that his version of Christianity is destructive of both true Judaism and true morality. The whole letter can then be seen as his answer to these twin charges.[k] This would fit in with the argument that *euangelion* (gospel) is always Paul's *own* preaching of Christianity, so that he is maintaining here that, whatever others may say, he is not ashamed of his version of the Christian message.

(c) Perhaps, on the other hand, Paul is saying that the gospel does not let him down; it will stand the test of experience.[l] This meaning is supported by somewhat similar expressions in Phil. 1^{20}; II Cor. 10^8; Rom. 9^{33}; 10^{11}.

Both (b) and (c) make good sense in the context, (b) picking up 'to the Jew first and also to the Greek', and (c) picking up the stress on the power of the gospel. To decide between them is not easy, but the parallels adduced for (c) perhaps tilt the balance in its favour. The gospel does not and will not fail those who receive it.

of the gospel: we have now been brought to the point of learning what the gospel is. It is the power of liberation, but from what and to what is still to be made plain.

the power of God: it is crucial that this should be mentioned in the transitional summary, for a major part of the human problem, as Paul sees it, is that men and women are not free. It is not just that they need forgiveness, though they do, but even more that they are under alien power, especially that of sin (see Introduction, 9). To release them, they need a superior power, and a large part of the argument will be that they *can* be transferred from the power-sphere of sin and death to that of the divine Spirit, which brings true life as the people of God. See 1$^{18-39}$; 6$^{1-23}$; 8$^{1-11}$.

for salvation: the desire for salvation in the Hellenistic world took various forms. People wanted deliverance from the bondage of the material world, or from the meaninglessness of a life controlled by astrological or other forces, or from ultimate descent into annihilation (or at best a shadowy attenuated existence that could hardly be called

k See K. Grayston, ' "Not Ashamed of the Gospel". Romans 1.16a and the Structure of the Epistle', *Studia Evangelica* II, ed. F. L. Cross, Berlin: Akademie Verlag 1964, pp. 569–73.

l See C. K. Barrett. *New Testament Essays*, SPCK 1972, Ch. 8, esp. pp. 117f.

life). They also, like people in every age, wanted deliverance from sickness, poverty, and a host of other ills. Various cults aimed to provide the solution to one or another of these problems. Among the Jews, on the other hand, 'salvation' (*sōtēria*) was a regular way of referring to God's deliverance of Israel at the Exodus (see for example Ex. 14^{13}; 15^2; Isa. 45^{17}; 52^{10}). It also came to refer to the hoped-for liberation when God would act in the future through his appointed agent (e.g. *Ps. Sol.* 10^8; 12^7; Wisdom 5^2; Isa. 25^9). Although LXX uses *sōtēria* for almost any kind of deliverance, it is this last usage that is characteristic of Paul, see Rom. 10^1; 13^{11}; II Cor. 6$^{2,\ 12}$; Phil. 1^{28}; I Thess. 5$^{8,\ 9}$; II Thess. 2^{12}. Thus for him it is particularly an eschatological term (i.e. to do with the End of the present evil age and the beginning of the New Age of God). It is something to which believers must still look forward, even though in a sense it has already dawned with Jesus Christ (see especially Rom. 11^{11}; II Cor. 7^{10}).

At this point Paul does not say from what it is that the gospel gives salvation/deliverance; for that see Chs. 5–8. To anticipate, we can say that it gives liberation from all powers that are hostile to God, and into a life with him and under him, a life as his people.

to every one who has faith: an understanding of faith (*pistis*) is crucial in reading Romans.

(*a*) Here, as so often in Paul's writings, faith is the human response to God. *Pistis* can also be translated 'belief' or 'faithfulness', for which there are no separate Greek words, and Paul can use it in a variety of ways. In Rom. 3^3 he uses it for 'faithfulness'; in Rom. 4^{20} it is confidence in the divine promise; in II Cor. 5^7 it is assurance of the unseen, and in places · it may even mean 'the faith', i.e. Christianity, in something like the modern sense (so perhaps Gal. 1^{23} and even 6^{10}). Usually, however, especially where Paul is talking about salvation or justification, it is simply the human response to God's initiative. In his kindness (grace), God offers men and women a new life: all they need to do is to accept it. That is faith. This initial response must lead on to other things, to faithfulness in life, and probably implies some sort of belief, but the starting point is the faith that is simple response. It is almost a non-thing, as Rom. 4 makes clear. It is not something one must strive after, and it is not *doing* anything, or having any qualification of any sort. It is the acceptance of the divine overtures.

(*b*) If salvation comes to those who have faith, it therefore means that belonging to a particular religious tradition, or to a particular race, and that being especially virtuous, cannot be requirements. On the contrary, if faith is lacking, none of these things is of use as a substitute. Moreover, though Paul does not say so in this verse, it is clear from the rest of the letter (see especially 3$^{21-31}$) that faith is to be understood specifically as faith in Jesus Christ.

(c) The gospel is for *every one* who has faith (cf. v. 5), Jew and Gentile alike. The only advantage the Jew has over the non-Jew when it comes to salvation is a chronological one, though in other ways Israel has had considerable advantages (cf. 3$^{1f.}$; 9$^{3-5}$), in effect advantages of preparation. Now that the only condition for salvation on the human side is faith, which is equally open to everyone, Jew and Greek, there can be no advantages. This theme is at the heart of Romans.

17

the righteousness of God: this is not simply the strict justice of God, which would hardly be good news! In the OT and much later Jewish writing, the righteousness (*dikaiosunē*) of God is his acting to sustain his people, his loyalty to his own promises, and his total reliability. This may mean that he judges those who are oppressing Israel, or those within Israel who are being unfaithful. At the same time it may mean that he acts to vindicate the oppressed, and so to save or liberate. In later times, when Israel was almost permanently under foreign and oppressive powers, his righteousness was increasingly seen as synonymous with his salvation. Yet it is too much to say that the two simply become identical in Jewish writing, for it is rather that salvation is the *form* that God's righteousness increasingly takes. Other meanings are not lost, but become less common.[m] In the light of the context here, while a suggestion of the even-handedness of God, to Jew and Gentile alike, is not to be dismissed, the dominant note is a saving one. In Judaism, God's righteousness was essentially for his people Israel, with whom he had established a covenant that he would be their God and protect them, while on their side they would worship him alone, and live as a people under his direction. In practice this last meant obeying his Torah, his Law. Now, however, in Paul's view, this saving righteousness of God is opened out to *all* who respond to him (have faith), with no restrictions of race or history. This leaves a problem of how to relate this development to Israel as God's ancient people: Paul deals with it briefly in Ch. 4, but at length in 9–11.

There may be something more in the term here. God's righteousness is a power (v. 16) *for* those who have faith, and the second half of the present verse seems to concern those who may themselves become

m Cf. Ziesler, *Meaning*, Chs. 1–5.

righteous (by their faith). This latter part of the verse looks rather like an explanation of the first half. Moreover in both v. 16 and v. 17 there is a stress on the human response, on faith: God does not just act however humans may react. As in the somewhat similarly worded 3^{22}, it is possible that here God's righteousness is something into which believers are drawn, so that in their own selves and their own lives, that righteousness which is essentially God's becomes a reality. In other words, they begin to live in his power, and his righteousness is effective in their lives. Some have thought[n] that God's righteousness becomes ours in the sense that a right standing/status is freely granted by God. No doubt this is so, but it is not just that. God's righteousness is how he acts, and when human beings are drawn into its power, they begin to act as they should, as his covenant people.

is revealed: the reference to power shows that this is not mere depiction, as of something static, but is effective. The present tense indicates that it is now in progress.

from faith to faith: it is not certain what this means precisely, though the general point is plain enough. On the human side, faith is the essential requirement.

(*a*) The phrase may be a rhetorical way of saying that what counts is faith, faith alone, faith all the way (Luther's *sola fide*).

(*b*) It may be saying that God's righteousness arises from *his* faith(fulness), and is to be met by *our* faith.

(*c*) It could be saying that it begins with the faith of some but spreads to all who have such faith.

(*d*) Perhaps the phrase is shorthand for 'the obedience of faith' (cf. 1^5, and Wilckens I, p. 88).

None of these ways of taking the phrase is impossible, but (*a*), the rhetorical view, is on the whole preferable. Paul is simply underlining the necessity and the sufficiency of faith. If any of the other options is correct, then Paul has not in the least made himself clear.

'*he who through faith is righteous shall live*': a quotation from Hab. 2^4, taken from LXX but omitting 'my' after 'faith'. The same quotation is used in Gal. 3^{11}. The LXX probably means 'the righteous will live by my (i.e. God's) faithfulness', or else possibly 'the righteous will live by faith in me'. The Hebrew means that the righteous will live by faithful-

---

n E.g. Bultmann, *Theology* I, pp. 270–80.

ness (to God). For Paul, this quotation from one of the prophets is important because it supports his contention (cf. Ch. 4) that the Scriptures themselves show that faith always was the one thing necessary for acceptance by God into his people. He maintained that the heart of his gospel was in accordance with the Scriptures, and that God's way of dealing with humankind was consistent.

What then does this quotation mean? KJV reads 'The just shall live by faith', but many think its place in the argument requires that we should read 'the righteous-by-faith shall live', which is the effect of the RSV translation. It is argued that Paul is not saying that those who are already righteous will live by faith, but that faith is the way to righteousness. In fact both statements are true and can be supported from within the letter: faith is the way to righteousness, *and* it is how the righteous live (cf. 3^{22}; 9^{30-32}; 10^4). [o]

We are still left with the question of what Paul here means by 'righteous'. In biblical Greek, especially in LXX, 'righteous' and 'righteousness' tend to mean those who live as God's people (righteous), and in the abstract, life as that people (righteousness). Particularly in the case of the adjective, it is often difficult to determine how far the word is about being in a right relationship, and how far it refers to actual life and behaviour. Ideally the two would go hand in hand. In this verse, then, Paul could be saying that it is those who are in a right relationship with God who will live, and this is how the quotation is usually taken. Yet it is possible that more is meant: a whole renewal of life and being, life as the people of God in all its aspects, comes about by faith on the human side. [p] In the chapters that follow, Paul is indeed concerned with the restoration of men and women to right relationship with God, but he is equally concerned that they should live day by day in a manner befitting their role as the people of God. Both their standing before God and a totally renewed life are important. This reinforces the suspicion that in quoting Hab. 2^4 he uses 'righteous' in the wider and not the purely relational sense.

shall live: this could be taken as the verdict in a legal process, if 'righteous' is understood as a right standing before God at the Judgment.

[o] The Greek *dikaios* can be translated either 'righteous' or 'just'. Since 'just' and 'justice' tend nowadays to have narrowly judicial connotations, I shall use 'righteous' and 'righteousness', even though they are not commonly used words.

[p] See Ziesler, *Meaning*, pp. 175-7, 188.

However, without denying a relational aspect, we may also see it as referring to the whole life of the redeemed, free from oppressing powers.

¹⁸For the wrath of God is revealed from heaven against all ungodliness and wickedness of men who by their wickedness suppress the truth. ¹⁹For what can be known about God is plain to them, because God has shown it to them. ²⁰Ever since the creation of the world his invisible nature, namely, his eternal power and deity, has been clearly perceived in the things that have been made. So they are without excuse; ²¹for although they knew God they did not honour him as God or give thanks to him, but they became futile in their thinking and their senseless minds were darkened. ²²Claiming to be wise, they became fools, ²³and exchanged the glory of the immortal God for images resembling mortal man or birds or animals or reptiles.

²⁴Therefore God gave them up in the lusts of their hearts to impurity, to the dishonouring of their bodies among themselves, ²⁵because they exchanged the truth about God for a lie and worshipped and served the creature rather than the Creator, who is blessed for ever! Amen.

²⁶For this reason God gave them up to dishonourable passions. Their women exchanged natural relations for unnatural, ²⁷and the men likewise gave up natural relations with women and were consumed with passion for one another, men committing shameless acts with men and receiving in their own persons the due penalty for their error.

²⁸And since they did not see fit to acknowledge God, God gave them up to a base mind and to improper conduct. ²⁹They were filled with all manner of wickedness, evil, covetousness, malice. Full of envy, murder, strife, deceit, malignity, they are gossips, ³⁰slanderers, haters of God, insolent, haughty, boastful, inventors of evil, disobedient to parents, ³¹foolish, faithless, heartless. ³²Though they know God's decree that those who do such things deserve to die, they not only do them but approve those who practise them.

From now until 3²⁰ the letter focusses on the plight of a human race (or rather, human races) which is neither free from sin nor free for God. Through the gospel which has just been stated in summary, we

come to an understanding not only of the way of deliverance that
God has provided, but also of the situation that makes it necessary,
not only for Gentiles but also for Jews. This situation is a dire one, which
evokes the wrath of God. The wrath of God is not a matter of God's
emotions, as if he were in a state of chronic ill-temper with humanity,
but is rather something like his constant pressure against evil of every
kind. This pressure is perceived as wrath by those who resist it, but
it is nonetheless part of the beneficent provision of God. It works in
various ways, and for Paul as for much of the biblical tradition it is
to be operative particularly at the Judgment, at the End. In this passage, however, it is especially seen in the decadence and degradation
of the pagan world. Although they were capable of knowing better,
men and women turned away from God to what is not God, especially to idols of their own devising. The result was to become incapable of proper discernment in ethical matters. Paul takes for granted
the common Jewish idea that idolatry leads to immorality and to
sexual immorality in particular, cf. for example Wisdom 13–14. q
This idea may go back to an awareness of the practice of sacred
prostitution in some pagan cults; it may also arise from observing
pagan idolatry and pagan immorality, and inferring a causal connection between them. At all events, it appears to have been a deeply-
rooted idea. Although in this passage Paul endorses it without
hesitation, in 2$^{14-16, \ 26-27}$ he equally does not hesitate to tell the Jews
that many Gentiles are much more moral than they are.

The main drift of vv. 19–32 is that the wrath works by God's *not*
interfering to stop a downward spiral. People begin by choosing
wrongly (the creature rather than the Creator) and end by being
unable to distinguish between right and wrong. What they at first
choose to do, they are finally unable to avoid, for God does not protect them from the consequences of their own actions. This is the
wrath of God (v. 16). God gives them their collective head, and the
result is degradation (vv. 24, 26, 28). It is a sort of moral hardening
or blindness, that is self-inflicted. In other words, radically wrong
choices produce radically wrong people who are in the end pro-

q It is widely suspected that in this passage Paul is drawing directly on Jewish
materials, not least from the Wisdom of Solomon. See Wilckens I, pp. 96f.

foundly unfree. It may be that behind all this is an allusion to the story of the fall of Adam in Genesis.^{r}

֍

18

the wrath of God: this passage is the chief piece of evidence for the view propounded by C. H. Dodd (see pp. 20–4) that 'the wrath' (*orgē*) was used 'to describe an inevitable process of cause and effect in a moral universe'. He pointed out that only here in the undisputed letters of Paul is it the wrath *of God*. Elsewhere it is simply 'wrath' or 'the wrath', the full phrase being found, apart from here, only in the doubtfully Pauline Eph. 5^6 and Col. 3^6. Moreover, nowhere is the verb 'to be angry' used by Paul with God as the subject. Dodd argued that Paul was not ascribing to God the irrational passion of anger, in anthropomorphic fashion, but chose his words carefully to indicate that he saw the wrath as the effect of wrongdoing in a divinely created moral world. We may take the analogy of fire: if I put my hand in the flames I suffer acute pain, not because God is angry with me, but because that is the way the world is. Further, the world is that way in order to dissuade me from putting my hand in the fire and so be harmed. So *orgē* (wrath) is God's wise provision in order to dissuade us from evil. It is the sign that evil is not intended to be congruous with a good life.

Even those who think that the wrath is straightforwardly God's punishment of sin may agree that for Paul its ultimate purpose is beneficent, aiming at human goodness (cf. Rom. 11^{32}). Yet Dodd allowed too little weight to the connection, both in Jewish tradition and in Paul, between the wrath and the Day of Judgment. It was at the End that *orgē*/wrath was to be revealed, especially against those who oppressed God's people (e.g. Isa. 2$^{10-22}$; Zeph. 1^{18}; Dan. 8^{19}), and Paul too saw the End as the Day of Wrath (I Thess. 1^{10}; Rom. 2^5; 5^9). As God is indubitably the Judge, it is unlikely that Paul saw the wrath, even in its present operation as in this passage, entirely in impersonal terms. The wrath that belongs to the End is nonetheless already evident in the ordinary life of people who turn against God, and operates not by God's intervention but precisely by his *not* intervening, by letting men and women go their way (vv. 24, 26, 28) into that downward spiral in which sin becomes its own punishment. In short, the more we sin, the more we sin, and what that makes of us is the verdict of God's wrath.

r So M. D. Hooker, 'Adam in Romans I', *NTS* 6, 1959–60, pp. 297–306.

We shall see that Paul also connects the operation of the wrath with the civil power, with 'law and order' in Rom. 13⁴, and less directly with the working of human conscience in 13⁵.[s]

is revealed from heaven: the revelation of wrath in this verse parallels the revelation of righteousness in the previous verse. Some commentators (e.g. Cranfield I, pp. 106ff.) think that this implies that *the gospel* reveals the wrath of God as well as the righteousness of God. In effect, it is argued, it is only when we understand God's liberation that we can understand fully that from which we are being liberated. This is a possible reading of the verse, yet there are difficulties.

(a) While Paul says clearly enough that God's righteousness is revealed in the gospel, he does not say at all clearly that his wrath is. The use of the connecting particle 'for' (*gar*) at the beginning of v. 18 is the nearest he comes to that.

(b) In what follows, he argues that everyone ought to know what sin is and what it does. No special revelation of the wrath appears to be needed.

(c) There is something decidedly odd about saying that the revelation of the wrath is good news. Perhaps if the wrath was seen as an aspect of the End-time, then its manifestation could be regarded as a sign that the time of release was very close; in this sense it could be good news.

We must therefore be cautious in connecting the wrath too exactly to the gospel, though the possibility cannot be ruled out. There is plausibility in the notion that diagnosis and cure go hand in hand, and that it is only those who come to experience real health who properly grasp the extent of their former sickness. Nevertheless this remains only a possible interpretation of the passage, and cannot be seen as altogether secure.

of men: Paul does not restrict what he says explicitly to pagans, but in view of what follows it is likely that he is speaking of them in particular. This likelihood is strengthened by the parallels with Wisdom 13–14, which are certainly aimed at the Gentiles.[t]

who suppress the truth: this is not just any truth, but 'the truth about God as Creator, Judge, and Redeemer' (Barrett, p. 34; cf. II(4) Esd. 7²¹⁻²⁴).

s On all this see the excursus in Wilckens I, p. 128, and A. T. Hanson, *The Wrath of the Lamb*, SPCK 1957.

t For further evidence see Wilckens I, p. 104 and n. 166.

19

what can be known about God: this is so reminiscent of the Wisdom of Solomon that it seems highly probable that Paul is dependent on that book, which also argues that pagans are capable of knowing God.ᵘ Paul is talking not about knowledge of God gained through the coming of Jesus Christ, but about a basic perception of God that is possible for all human beings (cf. v. 20). Nonetheless this verse makes it plain that this basic perception is not reached unaided, but comes from God's own disclosure of himself.

20

his invisible nature, namely, his eternal power and deity, has been clearly perceived in the things that have been made: it has been much debated whether this implies a natural theology, i.e. a view that men and women can come to know God without his deliberate revealing of himself. At times this debate verges on the anachronistic, yet it is clear enough that Paul does think that something of God, namely that he exists and has power over the world, can be known by all people. The creation implies the Creator, and as v. 19 shows, Paul believes that God has so arranged things that men and women are able to draw this inference. *All* people are so able, so that those who fail to make a proper distinction between God and what he has made, especially those who indulge in idolatry, are culpable. If this is natural theology, then Paul is a natural theologian. In fact he simply takes the existence of God as a given fact, and argues no more than that his invisible nature and power as God can be discerned in (not from) the created world (cf. Wisd. 13$^{1-9}$). The culpability of those who fail to grasp this possibility of discernment is the only conclusion he draws, cf. v. 21.

21

they did not honour him as God: they did not let God be God. This was their dire and fundamental error, which led to a deadening of perception, especially moral perception. The idea that idolatry as the confusion of creation with Creator leads to immorality is common in Jewish tradition, see for example Jer. 2$^{5ff.}$; Wisdom 13–14; *Sib. Or.* III 8–26, 763f.

23

glory: the precise meaning of this word (*doxa*) is difficult to pin down.

u See C. Romaniuk, 'Le Livre de la Sagesse dans le NT', *NTS* 14 1968, pp. 498–514.

In secular Greek it can mean praise, or opinion, reputation, or belief. In LXX it is used to translate the Hebrew *kābhōdh*, 'splendour' or 'honour'. There is usually about its use in biblical Greek some connotation of brightness, and by NT times it regularly denoted the brightness which surrounded God and which both revealed his presence and also prevented his being seen directly. Paul believes that believers will ultimately share God's glory (Rom. 8^{30}; II Cor. 3^{18}; 4^{17}). In this verse there may be an allusion to Adam's fall, as well as a very probable one to Ps. 106^{20} ('They exchanged the glory of God for the image of an ox that eats grass'); there is a close connection between 'glory' and 'image' (*eikōn*), cf. I Cor. 11^7; Rom. 8$^{29f.}$, and Adam was regarded as made in the image of God.[v] Moreover there was an old Jewish tradition that at the fall Adam lost the glory of God which he had hitherto shared (see *Apoc. Mos.* 20–21). It is possible, therefore, that here *doxa* denotes something of God's splendour that was intended to be shared by the human race, but was lost.[w]

24

God gave them up: he let them go their own way and take the consequences, cf. vv. 26, 28. The result is sexual degradation. They go 'from guilt to fate' (Käsemann, p. 44), from wrong choice to bondage. See Wisdom 11^{16}, 'one is punished by the very things by which he sins.'

26

natural relations: both here and in v. 27 Paul is clearly talking about homosexuality, sometimes regarded as acceptable in the Gentile world, but not in Judaism (see for example Lev. 18^{22}; 20^{13}; I Kings 14^{24}; *Sib. Or.* III, 396ff.). The reference to it supports the supposition that throughout this passage Paul is talking about the moral characteristics of paganism, as he sees them (though cf. 2$^{14-15}$).

27

the due penalty for their error: it is impossible to be sure what this means. It may refer to sexually transmitted disease, or to an increase of effeminacy in men and masculinity in women, or (most likely) it may be saying that the perversion is its own punishment. There is more here than an instinctive Jewish recoil from homosexuality: Paul sees sexual abnormal-

v See Gen. 1^{27}, though of course the name Adam is not used in the first creation story in Gen. 1.

w See Hooker, 'Adam in Romans I', pp. 304–6.

ity as the outcome of that fundamental abnormality, the confusing of
Creator with creation, which is idolatry.

28

a base mind: it is not just morality that becomes corrupt, but reason
itself.

29–31

The range of sins mentioned is now widened, and sexual matters are not
discussed again. The list is conventional: [x] it is not that these things and
these alone are the result of the basic wrongness, but rather that these
are the *kinds* of thing that result. Omission of something, e.g. dishonesty,
means nothing.

32

God's decree: there is probably no particular OT decree being alluded to
here, unless it be Gen. 3^{19}, which would fit the view that the story of
Adam lies behind the whole passage. A more general explanation is that
Paul sees the human race as in bondage to death, as in Rom. 5$^{12-21}$. The
latter is also, of course, Adamic, so that the two explanations are not
mutually exclusive. We are not told how pagans can be expected to
know of this decree, whatever it is. Perhaps Paul is thinking as a Jew
and simply generalizes from his own world of ideas, assuming that
'everyone knows' that such conduct deserves death. If we reply that
everyone does *not* know that, perhaps Paul's rejoinder would be that
this is a sign of the base mind of v. 28.

they not only do them but approve those who practise them: it seems strange
to say that consenting to something wrong is worse than doing it oneself. There is some textual confusion in this verse, which may arise from
ancient scribes' finding it strange in their day. There is little doubt that
RSV is correct, and that Paul did write just this. Moreover there are
parallels for the idea (see *T. Ash.* 6^2), and it is not unreasonable to
maintain that while it is bad enough to do wrong things (with a bad
conscience), it is even worse to give the wrongdoing one's approval,
for this shows that one has lost the ability to distinguish between right
and wrong. Thus the passage reaches its climax in demonstrating the
depths of moral impotence and blindness into which people fall when
they turn away from God to something that is not God.

x See Cranfield I, pp. 129–33, and Wilckens I, pp. 112–13.

THOSE WHO CONDEMN OTHERS ARE
THEMSELVES TO BE CONDEMNED

2 *Therefore you have no excuse, O man, whoever you are, when you judge another; for in passing judgment upon him you condemn yourself, because you, the judge, are doing the very same things.* ²*We know that the judgment of God rightly falls upon those who do such things.* ³*Do you suppose, O man, that when you judge those who do such things and yet do them yourself, you will escape the judgment of God?* ⁴*Or do you presume upon the riches of his kindness and forbearance and patience? Do you not know that God's kindness is meant to lead you to repentance?* ⁵*But by your hard and impenitent heart you are storing up wrath for yourself on the day of wrath when God's righteous judgment will be revealed.* ⁶*For he will render to every man according to his works:* ⁷*to those who by patience in well-doing seek for glory and honour and immortality, he will give eternal life;* ⁸*but for those who are factious and do not obey the truth, but obey wickedness, there will be wrath and fury.* ⁹*There will be tribulation and distress for every human being who does evil, the Jew first and also the Greek,* ¹⁰*but glory and honour and peace for every one who does good, the Jew first and also the Greek.*

It is not until v. 17 that Paul explicitly says he is talking to Jews. In this section it is possible that he includes all who pride themselves on their high morality and therefore despise those who do the sorts of things listed in the previous passage. Throughout the whole of this chapter, however, Paul seems to use a good deal of Jewish material, and it has even been proposed that he has taken over a Jewish synagogue sermon.ʸ Certainly even in this passage there are links with Jewish material (cf. Wisdom 15¹⁻³) which could be taken as engendering complacency, at least on a superficial reading. In any case Paul·attacks those who lightly condemn others, saying that they themselves are in no better case, and that simply to vote for righteousness is not enough.ᶻ God requires the practice of righteousness, and not

y So Sanders, *PLJP*, pp. 123–35.
z Cf. Watson, *PJG*, pp. 110–22: the argument is against those Jews who rely on their covenant status and on God's grace, supposing that performance is unimportant.

just assent to it. His rewards and punishments are on that basis, whether one is a Jew (and so knows of God's requirements as set out in the Law) or a Greek (and so is ignorant of them). As things have stood, it is only by right action and right character that God's approval is to be obtained. At this stage in the letter Paul is still dealing with the human situation apart from God's gracious action in Jesus Christ, which he will not reach until 3^{21}. Meanwhile, if we are thinking in terms of deserving, then what matters is strictly what we do; those who condemn others do not, in fact, do very well. Paul is building up a picture in which sin grips Jews as well as Gentiles, cf. $3^{9ff.}$.

יהוה

1
Therefore: the transition is rather abrupt. It is probable that 'therefore' refers back not to 1^{32} in particular, but to the whole of 1^{18-32}.

whoever you are: we have noted that we cannot rule out the possibility that Paul is attacking all who pride themselves on their moral superiority, Gentiles as well as Jews. Yet there is a strong case for suspecting that this is directed especially to Jewish despisers of Gentile (im)morality.

(a) This would be a neat sequel to the characteristically Jewish indictment of Gentile immorality in 1^{18-32}.

(b) Whether or not we can say that this was originally a synagogue sermon, there is much in it that would have been at home in such a setting, and virtually nothing that would not. Therefore it is highly likely that throughout Rom. 2 it is Jews who are being addressed.[a] The parallels with Wisdom 11^{15} are striking: God's wrath rests on the Gentiles for their immorality and idolatry. Israel, however, is saved by her knowledge of God and of his will; even as he condemns the heathen, God is always giving them opportunity to repent. When the Jews judge the heathen, they must always remember that they too are subject to judgment and are in need of God's goodness and mercy (see especially Wisdom 12^{19-22}).

(c) Those who 'presume upon the riches of his kindness and forbearance and patience' are much more likely to be Jews than Gentiles (v. 4), who are not expected to have experience of such a God at all.

[a] As well as Sanders, already cited, cf. Wilckens I, pp. 124f.; Cranfield I, pp. 105f.

you ... are doing the very same things: cf. vv. 21–23. This is not to be taken with absolute literalness, so that point for point Jewish immorality is identical with pagan. It means rather that Jews too are guilty of immorality of various kinds.

3

Do you suppose ... you will escape the judgment of God: if we ask why anyone should think it possible thus to escape, while others are condemned for the same or similar things, the only immediately plausible answer is that some Jews might be tempted so to think. Knowing the Law, and being descended from Abraham, in short being the people of God, *could* be held to lead to God's treating them as special cases (cf. Amos 3^2). It would be possible to take Wisdom 15^2 ('Even if we sin we are thine') in such a way, though this would involve ignoring the rest of the sentence: 'but we will not sin, because we know that we are accounted thine'.

4

repentance: a rare word in Paul's writings, whether as noun or verb. The only other instances are in II Cor. $7^{9, 10}$; 12^{21}. Its use here is some modest support for the view that Paul is relying on Jewish material, of the sort found in Wisdom 11^{23-24}. [b]

5

the day of wrath: in 1^{18-32} we observed that the wrath can be seen already at work in human moral decadence. Here we see its definitive expression at the End, in the Judgment. It *is* being revealed (1^{18}) and it *will be* revealed (2^5). This tension between already and not yet is characteristic of Paul, and reflects his belief that with Jesus Christ the world has come to the close of the Old Age, the old scheme of things, and to the beginning of the New Age, the new day of God. Yet this is still in the process of happening. We are at the point of transition, so that the future is still the future even though in important respects it is being experienced already. No doubt this means, in the case of the wrath, that what is already perceptible in human degeneration will emerge with full force, and without being able to be ignored, at the End.

6

according to his works: cf. Ps. 62^{12}; Prov. 24^{12}. This is a notoriously difficult statement, because of the problem of reconciling it with Paul's later

b See again Romaniuk, 'Le livre de la Sagesse', pp. 506–7.

statements (3^{20}; 4^5; 5^1) that if we are to be judged according to our works there is no hope for any of us, and that we are justified solely by faith. There are many solutions offered to this problem,[c] but there are two which demand special consideration (if we exclude the possibility that Paul was simply confused and did not notice that he was contradicting himself in a matter right at the heart of his message).

(*a*) The first possibility is that he is still talking strictly and solely about the human condition apart from Christ, and is going along with normal human – and in this case also Jewish – assumptions. If he is using Jewish sources, then he is going along with those sources. Thus, here in 2$^{6-11}$, he is still setting out how things are without the Christian good news: those who do right are accepted by God, and those who do wrong are condemned. This is not how things are now, in a Christian frame of reference; it is how they would still be apart from Christ, and apart from justification by faith. Put in community terms, those who are God's people are those who live and behave as God's people.

(*b*) The second main possibility is that Paul *is* talking within a Christian frame of reference, and that justification by faith is compatible with judgment by works. Although men and women are accepted as God's people solely on the basis of faith in Jesus Christ, nevertheless the proof of the pudding is in the eating. That is to say that if faith is genuine it will issue in a character and a life pleasing to God. Faith works itself out in love (Gal. 5^6), and judgment is in effect a testing of the reality of faith, a testing by results (see also Gal. 6^7; II Cor. 5^{10}).[d]

Both explanations are possible, and both have their difficulties. The second is difficult because in the end we seem to have returned to performance rather than faith as the crucial criterion, though we have seen that elsewhere Paul does talk about judgment by performance. The first is difficult because Paul does not make it clear that he is still talking within a pre-Christian context. On the other hand it has the advantage that it does not create confusion about how one is justified. In the end, it is the structure of the letter that tips the balance in favour of (*a*): after stating the gospel in 1$^{16-17}$ Paul does not return to it until 3^{21}. The intervening material depicts in stark terms the condition in which all

---

[c] Ten are listed by Cranfield I, pp. 151f.; see also the excursus in Wilckens I, pp. 142–6.

[d] Cf. Watson, *PJG*, pp. 119–21, who also thinks that 3$^{20ff.}$, 2$^{7f.}$, and 4$^{2-8}$ are about *Jewish* Law-works, not good deeds in general. Yet 2^{13} seems to say clearly enough that it is precisely by Jewish Law-works that people will be justified.

peoples, Jew as well as Greek, exist (3$^{9ff.}$). This condition is that of being dominated by sin and unable to escape. This passage is thus part of the statement of the problem, not part of the solution. It is about how things are without the grace of God in Christ. The precise point is then that there are no privileges, no special cases. Without that grace in Christ, both Jew and Gentile have to produce good and obedient living in order to satisfy God. Doubtless Paul knew well enough that in Judaism being God's people was not brought about by human achievement, and also that obedient living was not taken to mean *perfect* obedience. These matters are not at issue here. What is at issue is simply the fact that in living according to the divine requirement, no less is expected of Jews than of anyone else. Any Jew who expects to get special treatment at the Judgment is mistaken.

7

eternal life: this expression is common in the Fourth Gospel, where it is regularly used for Christian life here and now, though as an anticipation of the life to come hereafter (e.g. John 5^{24}; 6$^{40, 47}$; 17^3). It is comparatively rare in Paul (cf. Rom. 5^{21}; 6$^{22, 23}$; Gal. 6^8) and has a primarily future reference, for life in the world to come.

9

the Jew first and also the Greek: see also v. 10. Both judgment and reward fall evenly, and the Jew has no advantage in this matter, whatever other advantages there may be (cf. 3$^{1-2}$; 9$^{4-5}$).

2$^{11-16}$ WHAT MATTERS IS DOING THE LAW,
NOT HAVING IT

^{11}*For God shows no partiality.* ^{12}*All who have sinned without the law will also perish without the law, and all who have sinned under the law will be judged by the law.* ^{13}*For it is not the hearers of the law who are righteous before God, but the doers of the law who will be justified.* ^{14}*When Gentiles who have not the law do by nature what the law requires, they are a law to themselves, even though they do not have the law.* ^{15}*They show that what the law requires is written on their hearts, while their conscience also bears witness and their conflicting thoughts accuse or perhaps excuse them* ^{16}*on that day when, according to my gospel, God judges the secrets of men by Christ Jesus.*

Paul now proceeds to disabuse his fellow-Jews of any notion that belonging to the people who have and know the Law/Torah constitutes a passport to special treatment. On the contrary, good deeds are good deeds, good character is good character, whether they spring from knowledge of God's Law or from some other cause. The world cannot be divided into virtuous Jews and wicked pagans: a good many people who do not know the Law nonetheless obey the will of God more devotedly than many people who do know it, and God goes strictly by performance. There is no indulgent favouritism towards the Jews who, as the Elect (see especially 9–11), have the Law. In arguing that Gentiles are doers of the Law 'by nature', Paul appears to go against both what he has said in 1^{18-32} and the point of $1^{18}-3^{20}$ as it is usually understood, namely that all people, without exception, are helplessly under the dominion of sin. The morality of the pagan world is certainly viewed very favourably here.

This oddity is not easily explained.[e] If Paul is using traditional Jewish material, perhaps he has not noticed that it contradicts his main theme of proving the sinfulness of everybody, while making his immediate point that Jews are no better than Gentiles. On the other hand, there seems to be an increasing suspicion that we have misunderstood the purpose of $1^{18}-3^{20}$, and that it is not to prove the irretrievable sinfulness of absolutely everybody, but only that Jews are just as much sinners as Gentiles. In this case, 'all men' in 3^9 (cf. v. 23) does not mean literally all, but something like all races, all sorts.[f]

שמא

12
the law: this must be the Mosaic Law, the divine guidance (Torah) classically expressed in the Pentateuch, the first five books of the OT.

[e] O'Neill solves the problem by treating none of Ch. 2 as part of Paul's original letter, and moreover by taking vv. 14–15 as marginal glosses on non-Pauline material, p. 51.

[f] See Dabourne, *The Faithfulness of God*, pp. 119–21: the Jews are simply being put on the same footing as the Gentiles before the righteous, i.e. impartial, judgment of God.

13

the doers of the law who will be justified: cf. the comments on v. 6. This is the first appearance in Romans of the Greek verb *dikaioō* ('justify') which is of such great importance in Paul's presentation of the Christian gospel. In biblical and other ancient Jewish literature this verb (or its usual Hebrew equivalent *tsādaq*) is used in a broadly forensic way to mean either 'vindicate' or 'declare right/innocent'. A formal court of law is by no means always implied; often enough in a more general way we have to do with restoration to proper relationship within the community or with God. For Paul, the verb may mean 'acquit' in the divine court, but it is often used where the forensic note is at best muffled and where the main thing is restoration to relationship with God. The simple verb 'accept' is frequently an adequate translation. [g] Paul does not always use 'justify' in the same tense: as past it can be transfer terminology, i.e. it denotes the move from unacceptability into acceptance with God, or from being outside his people, into it, e.g. Rom. 5^1; as future it can refer to the Last Judgment and the verdict of God as in the present verse; as present it is often taken to denote the continuing acceptance by God of those who have entered his people, as in the view of many at Gal. $2^{16, 17}$.

Here it is plain that it is God's acquittal at the Judgment that is in view. That verdict will be heard not by those who have merely listened to the reading of the Law in the synagogue, but by those who have carried it out. This passage is polemic against those who think that possession of the Law is enough (see similar polemic from the Jewish side in *Aboth* 1^{17}, and from the Christian in James $1^{22f., 25}$). This hearing *versus* doing theme is found only here in Paul. As in v. 6, there is a substantial problem in reconciling what is said with justification by faith alone (see the comments on that verse).

14

Gentiles: if we are right to think that in this part of the letter Paul is still with the problem, and has not yet reached the Christian solution, then the Gentiles in this verse are those who are not Christians. They are not[h] Gentile *Christians*. The point then is that even though they do not

---

g See Ziesler, *Meaning*, Chs. 8, 10, 11. For a similar view, but one which also makes 'righteousness' (*dikaiosunē*) often a virtual equivalent for 'justification', see Reumann, *Righteousness*.

h *Contra* Cranfield I, p. 156.

know the Jewish Law as the revealed will of God, the Gentiles are nonetheless moral agents (cf. vv. 26–27).

by nature: this is not philosophically 'loaded', but simply means 'naturally'.

do . . . what the law requires: cf. II(4) Esd. 3^{36}, 'Thou mayest indeed find individual men who have kept thy commandments, but nations thou wilt not find', where the writer is talking about the world at large. So here, Paul cannot be saying that all Gentiles keep all the Law. For one thing, all the ritual provisions must be excluded. For another, the wording is far from implying a universal obedience. All we can infer is that some Gentiles observe some of the Law without knowing it. It is hard to resist the conclusion that for practical purposes the Law is being reduced to something like what we may call its moral aspects. This[i] remains the case even if there is an oblique reference to the so-called 'Noachian commandments', which according to Jewish tradition were laid on the whole human race, as against the Torah, which was laid on Israel alone.[j]

We have already noted the difference between this picture of Gentile morality and that presented in 1^{18-32}, and also the difficulty of harmonizing it with $3^{9ff.}$, especially v. 12: 'no one does good, not even one'. See the introduction to this section.

they are a law to themselves: this certainly cannot mean that they can do what they like, as it does in common English parlance. Greek writers used this expression to describe virtuous people whose goodness came from within, and who did not need external sanctions (cf. Cranfield I, p. 157). This statement runs counter to the idea of the total depravity of all men and women. Nevertheless the aim is not so much to praise the Gentiles, or some of them, as to point up the inappropriateness of Jewish claims to special privilege on account of their knowing and possessing the Law. Such special privilege will not be allowed at the Judgment; God goes strictly by performance.

i So Räisänen, *PL*, pp. 26, 28, 64.
j See Davies, *PRJ*, pp. 114ff. He lists seven Noachian commandments as those most widely agreed: (i) not to worship idols; (ii) not to blaspheme the divine name; (iii) to set up courts of law; (iv) not to kill; (v) not to commit adultery; (vi) not to steal; (vii) not to eat meat cut from a living animal p. 115 n. 1).

15

what the law requires: as in the previous verse, this can hardly be the
Law in its entirety.

conscience: this is not a characteristically Jewish idea, for the Jews tended
to find their moral arbiter in the Torah, and in the will of God as disclosed through the prophets, rather than in any human faculty. Conscience (*suneidēsis*) was a Greek and Roman notion, especially in popular
morality. It tended to be retrospective and individual, and to manifest
itself in the pain felt by someone who is aware of having done wrong.
It was very often negative: to have a conscience about something was
the same as what we call having a bad conscience. The NT uses the
word very much in the Greek tradition, so that here Paul is saying that
although the Gentiles lack the Torah, they do have a moral sense, and
that is conscience. [k] It often involves inward debate, hence *their conflicting
thoughts accuse or perhaps excuse them.* Either conscience is to be seen as
the arbiter of the debate, or (as Wilckens thinks, I, pp. 136f.) it is one of
the participants in the discussion. The beginning of v. 16 appears to
imply that conscience operates at the Day of Judgment, but this would
be a strange and almost inexplicable thing for Paul to say. The essence
of conscience is that it operates as moral director or moral sanction now,
just as the Law operates for Jews. On the Day of Judgment it is hard to
see what role it could have. Then God will be the only arbiter and
director.

At this point we need to be reminded that Paul lacked simple literary
devices that we take for granted, such as footnotes and parentheses. A
parenthesis is exactly what vv. 14–15 appear to be, for the beginning of
v. 16 connects admirably with the end of v. 13.

16

on that day: despite the parenthetical character of vv. 14–15, we need
not rule out all connection between conscience and the day (of Judgment), for what conscience has provisionally grasped may be seen as
being brought into the open by God at the End.

according to my gospel: why is the Judgment part of Paul's good news
(gospel)? Perhaps the point is that unveiling the cure also involves unveiling the nature of the disease, cf. the comments on the wrath and the
gospel at 1^{18} above. It is also, however, possible that what is 'according ·

[k] See Davies, *JPS*, Ch. 13.

to my gospel' is not the fact of judgment in itself, but the even-handedness of God in treating Jews and Gentiles exactly alike.

God judges the secrets of men by Christ Jesus: God does not act upon superficialities, but upon the springs of character and action. Paul is still talking about the situation apart from its solution in Christ, and still demonstrating the general need of God's free and gracious acceptance (justification). It is notable that judgment is here by Christ, the one who justifies the sinner (cf. 8^{32-34}), though later in the letter judgment is in the hands of God himself (14^{12}).

2^{17-24} CONDEMNATION OF THOSE WHO DO NOT
            PRACTISE WHAT THEY PREACH

[17]*But if you call yourself a Jew and rely upon the law and boast of your relation to God* [18]*and know his will and approve what is excellent, because you are instructed in the law,* [19]*and if you are sure that you are a guide to the blind, a light to those who are in darkness,* [20]*a corrector of the foolish, a teacher of children, having in the law the embodiment of knowledge and truth –* [21]*you then who teach others, will you not teach yourself? While you preach against stealing, do you steal?* [22]*You who say that one must not commit adultery, do you commit adultery? You who abhor idols, do you rob temples?* [23]*You who boast in the law, do you dishonour God by breaking the law?* [24]*For, as it is written, 'The name of God is blasphemed among the Gentiles because of you.'*

The argument does not proceed in logical steps,[1] and to some extent this section repeats and expands vv. 1–3 from a somewhat different angle. We are back with the problem of Jews who have the Law and who purport to be moral teachers of the human race, but who are in fact no better than those they condemn. They thus incur widespread obloquy both on themselves and on the God whom they claim to represent. This very negative view of Jewish practice is at odds with Rom. 10^2 (and cf. Gal. 2^{15}), and presumably the charges here are much exaggerated in order to make the point that the Jews are not,

---

1 On the rhetorical structure of the passage see Wilckens I, p. 147.

any more than the Gentiles, free from the power of sin (cf. 3$^{9ff.}$). It is not easy to determine what is meant by the charges in vv. 21–23: they could be taken non-literally, so that Paul is not accusing the Jewish community of ordinary theft, adultery, or temple-robbery, but rather of depriving God of his due (v. 21, cf. Mal. 3$^{8f.}$), of consorting with other gods (v. 22, cf. Jer. 3^8), and of committing sacrilege by putting themselves as judges in the place of God.^{m} It is usually thought, however, that the charges are to be taken literally, and that Jews are accused of the same sins which they condemn in Gentiles. The whole passage is directed to showing that there is no point in having the Law if it is not kept; it is indeed a privilege to have it and know it (cf. 9^4), but that privilege does not result in automatic protection. The Law is to be *done*.

ဢၕ

17

boast of your relation to God: what is at stake is not self-righteousness, but over-confidence in being the people of God. It is failing to recognize that Israel's undoubted privileges (3$^{1-2}$; 9$^{4-5}$) put her under deeper obligation to carry out God's will (cf. Wisdom 15$^{1-3}$; II *Bar.* 48$^{22-24}$). Her failures in obedience are more serious, not less, than those of people who have not shared her privileges.

19

a guide to the blind, a light to those who are in darkness: this is a not un-common theme in Jewish, and indeed in Christian sources. Among many examples see Isa. 42$^{6-7}$; 49^6; Wisdom 18^4; Matt. 5$^{14-16}$; see also Isa. 42$^{19-20}$ and Matt. 15^{14}; 23$^{16, 24}$ on the blindness of some who are supposed to be guides.

21

you then who teach others: at the end of v. 20 the syntax has become out of control, and Paul makes a new start at the beginning of this verse. In vv. 21–22 we may have a series of statements, but it is more likely to be a series of rhetorical questions. This is how RSV takes it. We must again remember that the punctuation is the work of modern editors, not of Paul himself.

m This figurative explanation is suggested by Barrett, pp. 56–7.

The idea of Israel as a teacher of other nations is not uncommon, cf. *Sib. Or.* III, 195; Josephus, *Ap.* ii. 293; Philo, *De Abr.* 98, especially in Judaism outside Palestine (and cf. Käsemann, p. 70).

22

do you rob temples?: it is at this point that a figurative interpretation of the charges against the Jews is more plausible. Surely Jews did not go in for literal temple-robbing? They certainly would not rob their own temple in Jerusalem, and it seems far-fetched to suppose they took valuables from heathen temples. Perhaps, therefore, Barrett (pp. 56f.) is right, and all the charges in vv. 21–22 are to be taken non-literally. Jews generally did not make a habit of stealing or adultery any more than of theft from temples. Nevertheless it must be remembered that the argument is that Jews are no better than others, not that they are universally prone to these things. If we take the charges literally, then the one of temple-robbing may allude to a case noted by the Jewish historian Josephus (*Antiquities* XVIII, iii, 5), in which there had been embezzlement of funds given as contributions for the temple in Jerusalem. If so, then it was the *Jewish* temple that had been robbed. On the other hand there is some evidence in contemporary or near-contemporary sources that on occasion some Jews were not above stealing or receiving valuable items from pagan temples, despite the ban on such actions in Deut. 7$^{25f.}$ [n] It may be relevant that in Acts 19^{37} Paul and his companions are exonerated of being 'sacrilegious' (RSV), where the Greek word is virtually the same as that here rendered 'temple-robbers' (*hierosuleis*). Apparently the charge was a plausible one, if mistaken, and so it is possible that there were Jews whose hands were not altogether clean in this matter. It is therefore quite possible that all these charges are to be taken literally.

23

do you dishonour God . . . : as Paul used no punctuation, it is a matter of interpretation whether this should be taken as a question, as in RSV, or as a statement. It could well be the latter, in which case it is a summary of the accusations.

24

as it is written: the quotation is quite close to the LXX text of Isa. 52^5. In

n Cf. Josephus, *Antt.* IV, viii, 10, and the references in Wilckens I, p. 150 and n. 388.

Isaiah, God's name is blasphemed (i.e. by impugning his honour, or arrogating his glory) by those who oppress Israel; here it is by Israel's own inconsistency.

'*The name of God* . . .': cf. the note on 1⁵. In good biblical fashion, 'name' here stands for God himself in his essential nature, power, and authority. It is thus God himself who is slandered, treated slightingly or insultingly.

2²⁵⁻²⁹   IS THERE ANY VALUE IN CIRCUMCISION?

²⁵*Circumcision indeed is of value if you obey the law; but if you break the law, your circumcision becomes uncircumcision.* ²⁶*So, if a man who is uncircumcised keeps the precepts of the law, will not his uncircumcision be regarded as circumcision?* ²⁷*Then those who are physically uncircumcised but keep the law will condemn you who have the written code and circumcision but break the law.* ²⁸*For he is not a real Jew who is one outwardly, nor is true circumcision something external and physical.* ²⁹*He is a Jew who is one inwardly, and real circumcision is a matter of the heart, spiritual and not literal. His praise is not from men but from God.*

Circumcision is the outward mark of belonging to the covenant people, that people chosen by God as his special possession. In the previous sections, Paul has been cutting the Jews down to the Gentiles' size, and so the question inevitably arises whether circumcision and what it represents are of any value at all. Surely it ought to make some difference to the way God treats people, and in particular surely it ought to make some difference at the Judgment, that one is circumcised and a member of the people of God? Paul's answer is that it does, but only if circumcision is truly reflected in an inward belonging. If that inward belonging and a true devotion to the God of Israel are lacking, then circumcision becomes devoid of meaning. It works the other way as well: someone who is not physically circumcised, but who does exhibit inward belonging and devotion by keeping the Law in general, must be regarded as in effect circumcised. It is this person who is the true member of the people of God.

ﬡﬡ

25

circumcision indeed is of value if you obey the law: it is not just one part of the Law, but represents the whole of it, cf. the inextricable connection between circumcision and covenant in Gen. 17^{10-14}. The present passage is directed against any who think these can be separated, and suppose that by itself circumcision has some kind of apotropaic power. On the contrary, it has meaning only when it genuinely represents the will to obey the Law as a whole.

26

will not his uncircumcision be regarded as circumcision: this was not a point of view at home in Palestinian Judaism, though it was possible outside Palestine.[o] Once again we meet the assumption (contrary, it appears, to $3^{9ff.}$) that Gentiles may keep the Law rather well. Such Gentiles will be regarded by God at the Judgment as having been circumcised, and so as belonging to his people. 'Be regarded' is a divine passive, i.e. the un-stated agent of the verb is assumed to be God, in this case God acting as Judge.

29

real circumcision is a matter of the heart: this is not a new idea, cf. Deut. 10^{16}; 30^6; Jer. 4^4; $9^{25f.}$; Ezek. 44^7; *Jub.* 1^{23}. The heart in biblical usage is not specifically the seat of the emotions, as it is in our popular speech, but covers many aspects of the inner self, including the emotions and the will, and most frequently refers to the mind. Circumcision of the heart is thus synonymous with being a Jew inwardly, with having an inner commitment to God and to his will. It is possible that Jer. 31^{33}; Ezek. $11^{19f.}$; 36^{26} are in the background (so Wilckens I, p. 156).

spiritual and not literal: perhaps all that is meant is a recapitulation of the contrast between inward and outward circumcision, figurative and literal. It is possible, however, that 'spiritual' refers to the Holy Spirit, and that it is *that* Spirit which effects inward circumcision.[p] Certainly in the OT passages cited in the previous note, it is usually God himself who effects circumcision of the heart. If this is right, then 'spiritual' here means 'in the sphere of God's power', and 'literal' means 'following the written Torah'.

o Cf. Philo, *Migr.* 92 and *Quaest. Ex.* II 2; see also Sanders, *PLJP*, pp. 131, 135.

p Cf. Käsemann, pp. 75–7; Wilckens I, p. 157; Robinson, p. 31.

It has sometimes been asked[q] whether this contrast, or even contradiction, between inward and outward circumcision is not destructive of Judaism. It would be common enough to insist that the inward must accompany the outward, cf. the passages in the previous note again, but to suggest that the outward should lapse in favour of the inward seems to go beyond Jewish bounds. The expression may be rhetorical, designed to drive the point home by exaggerating it. On the other hand, like v. 16, this may be where Paul goes beyond the Jewish material he has been using.

3$^{1-8}$ WHAT HAS HAPPENED TO JEWISH PRIVILEGE?

3 Then what advantage has the Jew? Or what is the value of circumcision? ^{2}Much in every way. To begin with, the Jews are entrusted with the oracles of God. ^{3}What if some were unfaithful? Does their faithlessness nullify the faithfulness of God? ^{4}By no means! Let God be true though every man be false, as it is written,
  'That thou mayest be justified in thy words,
   and prevail when thou art judged.'
^{5}But if our wickedness serves to show the justice of God, what shall we say? That God is unjust to inflict wrath on us? (I speak in a human way.) ^{6}By no means! For then how could God judge the world? ^{7}But if through my falsehood God's truthfulness abounds to his glory, why am I still being condemned as a sinner? ^{8}And why not do evil that good may come? – as some people slanderously charge us with saying. Their condemnation is just.

We now come back to a matter briefly raised in 2^4, ^{17}, and only just below the surface in much of the latter part of Ch. 2. What is the point of being God's special people Israel, if at the Judgment God treats Jew and Gentile even-handedly? Even more seriously, if more stringent demands are made of Jews because of their better opportunity to know God and his will, are they not in the end at a *disadvantage*? Paul develops his argument by debate with an imaginary or typical interlocutor[r] and with the problems to be dealt with in

q Cf. Hübner, *LPT*, p. 90 and n. 24.
r On the literary device of the diatribe, see the Introduction, 1 (*b*) (*i*). See also Robinson, p. 33, for a schematization of the questions and answers.

9-11 already in view. The imaginary opponent suggests that Paul has ignored God's covenant with Israel. Paul argues that the opponent is looking for the wrong kind of special treatment, for special indulgence at the Judgment. There will be none of that. Israel's advantage is real, but it consists in the privilege of knowing God and his will and receiving his call. In fact Israel has been disloyal to God[s] but this in no way impugns his loyalty to her.

Israel certainly cannot claim that her unfaithfulness is excusable because it sets in bolder relief the faithfulness and reliability of God. That is to say that it is permissible to do something wrong in order to point up the contrast with God; in that case, it would scarcely be wrong at all. Yet it is. At this point Paul notes that he himself has been accused of teaching (presumably when he speaks of justification by faith) that human sin leads in the end to the greater exercise of the divine grace, and therefore has laid upon it a gloss of acceptability. He indignantly repudiates this charge and condemns those who make it, but makes no rebuttal until 6$^{1ff.}$.

כ‍ל

1

what is the value of circumcision? Is he talking about inward or outward circumcision? After 2$^{28-29}$ we might expect him to mean inward, because he has been arguing that this is what matters. Yet it is more likely that we are back with literal, physical circumcision, for two reasons:

(a) that inward circumcision is of value is not in question and does not need defending;

(b) outward circumcision (cf. 2^{25}) has stood and does stand as the sign of commitment to God and to his covenant. In what follows, as in 9-11, it is the place of historic Israel in God's dealings with humankind that concerns him, and it is above all physical circumcision that marks historic Israel out from other peoples.

2

much in every way: in fact not quite every way! It does not give any advantage at the Judgment, as Ch. 2 has shown. The precise advantages

s Räisänen, *Torah*, Ch. 8, suggests that this refers specifically to most Jews' rejection of the Christian gospel, cf. 9-11.

are left unstated here, but will be enumerated in 9^{4-5}. All he says here is that Israel was –

entrusted with the oracles of God: it is not immediately obvious what these are. The Greek *logia* could mean oracles, or promises, or sayings.

(*a*) If the *logia* are God's promises, especially in the OT, then Paul is saying that, when rightly understood, the OT points forward to Jesus Christ and to the way of faith (e.g. Hab. 2^4 quoted in Rom. 1^{17}; Gen. 15^6 quoted in Rom. $4^{3ff.}$; Deut. 30^{12-14} quoted in Rom. $10^{6, 8}$). There could be a specific reference to the promise to Abraham and his descendants 'that they should inherit the world', Rom. 4^{13} and cf. Gen. 17^{4-6}; 22^{17-18}.^{t}

(*b*) Perhaps the *logia* are not particular passages in the OT, but the OT as a whole viewed as some kind of implicit promise for the future (cf. Acts 7^{39}; Deut. 33^9; Ps. 19^{8-14}, and Wilckens I, p. 164).

(*c*) The *logia* could be the divine sayings in the Torah not only in their promise-character, but also as guidance for Israel, i.e. in the widest sense (so Cranfield I, p. 179).

As the section deals quite largely with the divine demands, the last suggestion is preferable. In effect, then, we should understand the statement to mean: 'they have been entrusted with knowledge of the will of God'.

3
some were unfaithful: the Greek *ēpistēsan* could mean either 'unfaithful' or 'unbelieving'. Some (e.g. Käsemann) think it means 'unfaithful' here, while others (e.g. Cranfield) think it means 'unbelieving'. As elsewhere, the distinction between the two is far from absolute: a greater emphasis on unfaithfulness suits the contrast with God, but a stress on unbelieving fits well with the discussion of the Jews' unbelief in Christ in Ch. 11.^{u}

the faithfulness of God: his reliability and loyalty to his own covenant. This was an absolutely fundamental conviction for Israel, cf. Deut. 7^9; Isa. 49^7; Ps. 36^5; 40^{10}; $89^{1f.}$; 92^2; 119^{90}. Paul, however, does not limit that faithfulness to historical Israel, but believes it is extended to all who respond to God in faith, whether Jew or Gentile. However unfaithful men and women may be, God's reliability remains unimpaired.

t See Williams, 'Righteousness', pp. 266–8, and Käsemann, pp. 78f.
u So Räisänen, *Torah*, Ch. 8, esp. p. 189.

4

By no means: this is the first occurrence of an expression that is found six times in the letter. It is a particularly strong denial (*mē genoito*, literally 'may it not be'), for which it is difficult to find an adequate English translation. 'Not on your life' or 'Not in a thousand years' gives something of the flavour. 'By no means' is really far too prim to convey the considerable *force* of the denial. Human faithlessness can *never* (repeat, *never*) undermine the divine faithfulness.

true: God's truth is often synonymous with his faithfulness or reliability. It is truth in action as much as truth in utterance.

though every man be false: perhaps an echo of Ps. 116^{11}. Paul may be out-bidding the interlocutor's question in v. 3 about *some* who were unfaithful, by saying that even if everyone is unfaithful, God is still true. It is possible that he is widening the scope of unfaithfulness from that of Israel alone to that of the whole human race, just as he widens the scope of God's covenant dealings from Israel to all who have faith (cf. Ch. 4).

as it is written: the quotation is from Ps. 51^4 in the LXX version, where the numbering is 50^6.

justified: see above on 2^{13}. The meaning here is 'vindicated'/'be shown to be in the right', in a lawsuit.

when thou art judged: the Greek *en tō(i) krinesthai se* is ambiguous. It is possible that we should translate 'prevail when you take issue with (humanity)'. The difference in effect is not great: the RSV rendering has men and women taking God to task, and the alternative has God taking men and women to task. Either way, God is shown to be in the right.

5

the justice of God: despite the RSV rendering, this is the same phrase translated 'the righteousness of God' in 1^{17} (see the discussion *ad loc.*), cf. also 3$^{21, 22, 25, 26}$; 10^3. It was suggested for 1^{17} that the righteousness of God was primarily his saving activity, while not excluding the notion of his even-handedness towards Jew and Gentile. Here it appears to mean his own quality of rightness in judgment, as opposed to human wickedness, which does not soften that judgment because it puts the divine righteousness in a sharper light. Yet it can be argued that even here it is still God's covenant faithfulness that is in view, which is not nullified by human unfaithfulness.^v

wrath: used here for the Last Judgment, cf. 2⁵. On wrath (*orgē*) generally see above on 1¹⁸.

I speak in a human way: this somewhat apologetic aside (cf. also 6¹⁹; Gal. 3¹⁵; I Cor. 9⁸) may indicate Paul's awareness of the anthropomorphism involved in speaking of God's wrath. More plausibly, it may indicate that he knows it is impertinent to discuss the rightness or unrightness of God's actions.

6

By no means: cf. 3⁴, for this emphatic denial.

For then how could God judge the world? this looks like a *reductio ad absurdum*. God does judge the world, and could not do so if he were unjust. He therefore cannot be unjust. It is axiomatic that he is fitted to judge, cf. Gen. 18²⁵, 'Shall not the Judge of all the earth do right?' and Deut. 32⁴; Job 8³; 34¹⁰ᶠᶠ.

There is, however, another possible meaning. Paul may still be concentrating on the wrath (v. 5) and asking if that is not in itself unjust. In that case his answer is that the wrath is part of the judgment, and since that is inevitable, so also is the wrath. On the wrath as not the divine spleen but the divine condemnation and defeat of evil see on 1¹⁸.

7

God's truthfulness: the effect of this verse is the same as that of v. 5, except that here the language is that of being true, whereas there it was that of being righteous. We are still with God's covenant faithfulness.

why am I still being condemned: in the context 'I' is almost certainly to be taken as 'I, as a Jew'.

his glory: see on 1²³. Here glory (*doxa*) is probably his splendour, or even his Godness, his own distinctive character. The drift is thus that God's being true makes his divine nature even more evident.

v So Williams, 'Righteousness', pp. 265, 268–9, and Watson, *PJG*, p. 126. See the discussion in Räisänen, *Torah*, p. 197.

8

why not do evil . . . ?: this is parenthetical, as Paul appears to be looking ahead to the point where he faces the charge that his teaching on justification by faith cuts at the root of morality, see especially $6^{1, 15}$. Here he does not answer the charge, but merely denounces it.

some people slanderously charge us with saying: even in his lifetime Paul had to face the accusation that his teaching was immoral or at least opened the door to immorality.

3^{9-20} NO ONE IS RIGHTEOUS

⁹*What then? Are we Jews any better off? No, not at all; for I have already charged that all men, both Jews and Greeks, are under the power of sin,* ¹⁰*as it is written:*
    '*None is righteous, no, not one;*
    ¹¹*no one understands, no one seeks for God.*
    ¹²*All have turned aside, together they have gone wrong;*
        no one does good, not even one.'
    ¹³'*Their throat is an open grave,*
        they use their tongues to deceive.'
    '*The venom of asps is under their lips.*'
    ¹⁴'*Their mouth is full of curses and bitterness.*'
    ¹⁵'*Their feet are swift to shed blood,*
    ¹⁶*in their paths are ruin and misery,*
    ¹⁷*and the way of peace they do not know.*'
    ¹⁸'*There is no fear of God before their eyes.*'
¹⁹*Now we know that whatever the law says it speaks to those who are under the law, so that every mouth may be stopped, and the whole world may be held accountable to God.* ²⁰*For no human being will be justified in his sight by works of the law, since through the law comes knowledge of sin.*

Paul has now reached the climax of his statement of the human problem, having argued that it affects Jews as much as Gentiles. If the aim was to show that every single human being was utterly under the control of sin, he has failed, for he has argued that some Gentiles obey God's will remarkably well, without even being aware that it is God's will. In any case, the most that could be proved is that a great many people are very sinful. It has usually been assumed that the demonstration of universal human bondage under sin is the aim, and that on the way to achieving that aim Paul has inadvertently used arguments, or borrowed material, which goes against it.[w] This is certainly possible, the more so if Paul is using Jewish synagogue material for Christian ends.[x] However, it is also possible that Paul is not concerned with every single human individual, but with peoples, and that the aim is to show that as a people the Jews are under the power of sin, just as the Gentiles as peoples are. That some individuals nonetheless do rather well (like Paul himself according to Phil. 3^6, and like some Gentiles according to Rom. 2$^{14, 27}$) may not be in dispute. The suspicion that Paul is not trying to prove universal human depravity is increased when we notice that the OT passages quoted here in vv. 10–18, when read in their original contexts, do not concern *universal* human wickedness, but rather the wickedness of the wicked in contrast to the righteousness of the righteous. Paul's aim up to this point, therefore, may be more modest than has sometimes been thought: it is to show that both Jews and Gentiles are sinful, and under the power of sin, and need the rescue that Jesus Christ provides. Into the question of whether in some way every single human being must be regarded as helplessly sinful, Paul simply does not go. That was a later debate, not Paul's. This means that finding individual instances of righteousness, whether in a Jew or in a Gentile, does not affect Paul's general point, nor does the fact that most people are a mixture of goodness and wickedness.

Despite these caveats, it remains true that we have been brought to the point where humanity as a whole, Jew and Greek, is in need of liberation. In achieving this the Law is not effective: it holds everyone accountable to God, but while it excellently exposes the need for salvation, it cannot itself provide that salvation. Something else is needed.

෩

---

[w] See the discussion above, at the introduction to 2$^{11-16}$.

[x] Sanders, *PLJP*, pp. 123–35.

9

Are we Jews any better off? No, *not at all:* as it stands in RSV, this means that in the matters of doing what God wants and of being the sort of people God wants, Jews have no edge over pagans. However, both text and translation have been viewed in widely different ways, and the solution to the difficulties is far from clear. These difficulties are chiefly the following:

(i) the ambiguity of the Greek *proechometha* rendered in RSV 'Are we Jews any better off?' ('Jews' is not in the text, but is the translators' clarification);

(ii) the ambiguity of the Greek *ou pantōs*, rendered in RSV 'No, not at all';

(iii) the confusion of the textual tradition, which includes some witnesses which replace *ou pantōs* and have *prokatechomen* instead of *proechometha* so that the whole runs 'What extra do we (Jews?) possess?'[y]

There are four main ways to take the apparent question and answer, bearing in mind the difficulties just listed.

(a) There is the way of RSV, which is that preferred by the majority.

(b) The question could be, 'Do we Jews excuse ourselves?' The answer would then be as in RSV, 'No, not at all.'

(c) As a variant on (b), Dahl proposes 'What, then, do we plead as a defence?' He then omits *ou pantōs* following one Greek MS, and mounts a spirited defence of this very weakly supported reading, i.e. the omission of *ou pantōs*. The argument then runs straight on: 'What, then, do we plead as a defence? I have already charged . . .' The question is a strictly rhetorical one.

(d) The question could be 'Are we (Jews) excelled?', i.e. are we in fact *worse* off, and the answer is again 'No, not at all.'

To make matters more complicated, in (a), (b), and (d) the answer each time could be 'Not altogether', rather than in effect 'Altogether not.' If we look at the same expression in I Cor. 5^{10}, it seems that 'No, not at all' is more likely, and in I Cor. 16^{12} the similar *pantōs ouk* also suggests 'Altogether not.' Both ways of taking the expression make sense. I Cor. 5^{10} and 16^{12} argue for 'No, not at all', while 'Not altogether' fits better with 3^{1-2}, where in important respects the Jews *are*

---

[y] The textual confusion is in fact much greater than this, too great to be discussed here. For a full account, though from a very individual standpoint, see N. A. Dahl, 'Romans 3.9: Text and Meaning', Ch. 16 of Hooker and Wilson.

better off, though not in terms of living according to God's will nor in their freedom from sin.

The difficulty with Dahl's suggestion (c) is that he implausibly argues for omitting *ou pantōs*. Of the other possibilities, (a) is on the whole to be preferred, i.e. the text and translation behind and in RSV. If (b) were right, the verb ought to have a direct object, something like 'ourselves', which it does not. If (d) were right, then we should have a not impossible but certainly very rare use of this form of the verb. Any solution can be only tentative, but (a) is the least unlikely.

As for the textual confusion already noted, this suggests that the difficulties were noticed very early, and that various copyists have tried to improve and clarify the Greek in different ways. The insertion of the word 'Jews' is clearly required if any of (a), (b) or (d) is to be chosen, on the grounds that it is there by implication.

I have already charged: for some reason RSV translates a Greek 'we' by an English 'I'. As at the beginning of Romans Paul does not associate, himself and his writing with anyone else, 'we' here is presumably epistolary, akin to the editorial 'we'. If this is the explanation, then RSV brings out accurately what is meant.

all men, both Jews and Greeks: when has he charged them? Evidently in the whole argument from 1^{18} onwards. This expression reinforces the view noted in the introduction to the passage that Paul is aiming less at all human beings as individuals than at all races, all sorts of people, Jews as much as other races.

under the power of sin: it is very important to Paul's total presentation of the Christian gospel that sin is not just something wrong that people do, nor just a wrong disposition, but a power under which they are confined (cf. the Introduction, 9 and Rom. 5^{21}; $6^{12, 14, 16}$). This understanding of sin as more than guilt-inducing, and as a constraining power, is introduced here apparently out of the blue. Most of the argument has been to establish all races' guilt, in a forensic rather than a psychological sense, or so it seems. Yet we saw in 1^{18-32} that Paul did argue that wrong choice led to inability to make right choices, and so to a kind of moral atrophy and even a bondage to evil. Thus 3^9 does not really come without advance warning, though it is only at the climax of the argument that this aspect of sin comes to the fore. It is in fact a crucial element in his view of sin, an element in which he differed markedly from most of his contemporaries. To repeat, sin for Paul is not just a wrong act, or a series of wrong acts, or even a wrong disposition, though it includes or is manifested in all these. The point, which will recur and with force, is that sin is a power which so grasps men and women that they are profoundly unfree. Both repentance and forgiveness are important, but they are not enough. What is required is liberation, release from slavery. The twin notes of justification (acceptance despite guilt), and release from the hostile power of sin, are seldom if ever given equal emphasis at any given point, but where one is stressed the other is usually found as well, as here. Thus this verse gives us the knowledge that for Paul the dilemma of sin is double-headed: all are guilty, and all are enslaved. If we ask how people can be both responsible and powerless, then Paul never gives an answer. The nearest he comes to doing so is in 1^{18-32}, where, as we have seen, a culpable going-wrong at the heart of things results in a total and inescapable bondage. We begin by being free to choose; we choose wrongly; and then we become incapable of choosing rightly.

10

as it is written: Paul invokes Scripture to support his charge that all peoples have failed. He may have put this catena of quotations together himself, or he may (cf. Wilckens I, p. 171) have found it already formed in Christian tradition. The first part comes from Ps. 14, and at some stage the rest of the catena was inserted into that psalm in LXX, and thence into the Book of Common Prayer.

Too much need not be made of detail; the thrust is rhetorical, making a vivid picture of human wickedness. The sources of the quotations are:

vv. 10–12 from Ps. 14^{1-2} or 53^{1-3};
v. 13 in its first part from Ps. 5^9 and in its second from Ps. 140^3;
v. 14 from Ps. 10^7;
vv. 15–17 from Isa. 59^{7-8} (but cf. Prov. 1^{16});
v. 18 from Ps. 36^1.

We have already noted that in their original contexts these passages concern the wickedness of the wicked in contrast to the righteousness of the righteous.^{z}

z This is emphasized by G. N. Davies, *Faith and Obedience in Romans*, unpublished dissertation, University of Sheffield 1987, who argues strongly that 3^{9-18} is not saying that all human beings are totally sinful, but that sinfulness is spread indiscriminately among Jews and Gentiles.

'*None is righteous, no not one*': the word 'righteous' does not occur either in the Greek or in the Hebrew of Ps. 14 or 53. Here it means the opposite of being under the power of sin (v. 9) and not just 'innocent, free of guilt'. It is this verse as much as any other that gives rise to the view that Paul has been building up to a declaration of total and universal human sinfulness. Taken by itself, it does suggest just that, yet we have seen that we may be right to take it to mean 'No *people* is righteous, no not one.' If the obvious meaning is pressed, then we have to admit that the argument hitherto has not led at all convincingly up to it.

19

whatever the law says: this must refer to the passages just quoted, even though none of them comes from the Torah, the Pentateuch, but all come from Psalms or Isaiah. A similar phenomenon occurs in I Cor. 14²¹; John 10³⁴; 15²⁵, and it is not unknown for 'the Law' to be used in this loose way in Rabbinic writings. The reference is to Scripture in general, which is interesting in that it shows that Paul classes the Psalms among the Scriptures, something that had not been officially decided at this date.

under the law: Law is like sin in the respect that, like sin, it is a régime, a power, under or in which one may live (the Greek preposition is *en*, 'in').

the whole world may be held accountable: this seems decidedly odd. If the Law speaks to those who are under it, which presumably means to Israel, then how can the whole world be held accountable? Most of the world was not 'under it'. It would seem more logical to say that as only Israel is under the Law, only Israel will be called to account. Perhaps the argument is *a fortiori*: if Jews are accountable, how much more will everyone else be (no Jew doubted that at the Judgment the Gentiles would be called to account). The point would then be that the whole human race is to be included in accountability.

20

no human being will be justified in his sight by works of the law: Paul quotes Ps. 143², but adds 'by works of the law', cf. Gal. 2¹⁶, and thus defines the scope of the Psalmist's statement. This is the third time in the letter that he has used the verb 'justify' (*dikaioō*), discussed above at 2¹³; cf. also 3⁴. Here for the first time he uses it in explicit connection with his teaching on justification by faith. In this verse it is used negatively, denoting how justification does *not* happen. If we take the verb to mean the bringing of men and women into right relationship with God, whether or not in terms of a forensic acquittal, then this verse says that such a relationship is not achieved by keeping the Law.

It has been common to say that Paul is here attacking the notion that men and women can earn God's favour by Law-obedience, or indeed by good works of any kind. It has further been common to suppose that Jews generally believed that this was the way to God's favour. We have seen (Introduction, 8) that it is very unlikely that contemporary Judaism taught any such thing,[a] even if after CE 70 there was a strand within Judaism that did teach it. At the time of Paul, the emphasis remained that entry into God's people was entirely by his grace especially in election, and that obedience to the Law was the task and mark of those who *were* his covenant people. If all this is correct, then Paul is not here attacking a merit-centred view of the way to enter into relationship with God, let alone a self-righteous kind of piety. There is, moreover, no hint at all that Law-obedience is in itself sinful because it leads to self-righteousness.

In that case what is it that Paul is opposing? There are two main possibilities.

(*a*) He may be opposing a perversion of Judaism, arising out of official Judaism but in spite of it, a popular perversion which *did* think of earning God's favour. One may think of a parallel in some popular Protestantism where, despite official teaching that justification is by faith and faith alone, people can still think of good living as that which earns God's favour. A variant on this possibility is that some Gentile Christians, on discovering their adopted Jewish roots, misunderstood them, and took it that doing the Law was what made them acceptable, or more acceptable, to God, instead of seeing it as a consequence of their acceptance.[b]

(*b*) The other main proposal is that Paul is opposing any notion that salvation comes only or especially to Jews and is stressing that it comes only by faith, which is open to Jew and Gentile on equal terms. 'Works of the Law' would be open only to Jews and proselytes (full converts to Judaism). In other words he is refusing the Jews a privileged position in this matter.[c]

The strength of the second possibility lies largely in the context,

---

a See the whole argument of Sanders, *PPJ*.
b See Räisänen, *PL*, pp. 260–2.
c See Sanders, *PPJ*, p. 489.

which is concerned with the even-handedness of God's treatment of Jews and Gentiles. The strength of the first possibility lies in the verse 3²⁰ itself: it would be reasonable to read it as saying: 'the Law cannot justify; its role is only to reveal sin'.

Whatever the precise position against which Paul is arguing, what he says is clear enough and will be made even more clear in what follows. Acceptance with God is by faith in Jesus Christ, and not by obedience to the Law.

through the law comes knowledge of sin: the function of the Law is diagnostic (there will be more about this in Rom. 7), giving people a divine standard against which to measure themselves. They thus discover how far they fall short, and so come to an awareness of their own sin, or even of the power of sin over them.

3²¹⁻³¹   THE SOLUTION TO THE HUMAN SITUATION

²¹*But now the righteousness of God has been manifested apart from law, although the law and the prophets bear witness to it, ²²the righteousness of God through faith in Jesus Christ for all who believe. For there is no distinction; ²³since all have sinned and fall short of the glory of God, ²⁴they are justified by his grace as a gift, through the redemption which is in Christ Jesus, ²⁵whom God put forward as an expiation by his blood, to be received by faith. This was to show God's righteousness, because in his divine forbearance he had passed over former sins; ²⁶it was to prove at the present time that he himself is righteous and that he justifies him who has faith in Jesus.*

²⁷*Then what becomes of our boasting? It is excluded. On what principle? On the principle of works? No, but on the principle of faith. ²⁸For we hold that a man is justified by faith apart from works of law. ²⁹Or is God the God of Jews only? Is he not the God of Gentiles also? Yes, of Gentiles also, ³⁰since God is one; and he will justify the circumcised on the ground of their faith and the uncircumcised through their faith. ³¹Do we then overthrow the law by this faith? By no means! On the contrary, we uphold the law.*

We are now at a major turning point in the letter, where we move from problem to answer, an answer which will be elaborated in the ensuing chapters (e.g. vv. 22b–23 in Ch. 4; vv. 24–25a in 5¹⁻¹¹; vv. 25b–26 in 5¹²⁻²¹, though the divisions are only approximate). The double-headed problem of human sin, which affects Jews and Gentiles alike, is solved by the divine righteousness which, as in 1¹⁷, is primarily saving, and comes to the rescue of human beings in their collective predicament. This saving righteousness is promised in the Scriptures, the Law and the Prophets, but is not conditional upon human fulfilment of the Law's requirements. God's righteousness is the opposite of human sin in two ways: on the one hand, where men and women have been unfaithful (have sinned), God has been consistently faithful (righteous); on the other hand, where human beings have been imprisoned under the power of sin, God's righteousness provides a power for deliverance. This saving power is available to all who respond to Jesus Christ (have faith). Just as Jew and Gentile, those who have the Law and those who do not have it, have been shown to be in the same situation of guilt and powerlessness, so both now have access to the same deliverance by the same means: free generosity (grace) on God's side, and faith on the human side. All this comes about through the cross, which enables sin to be obliterated and guilt removed. Exactly how it does these things is not immediately apparent.

God's free acceptance must not be taken to indicate that sin does not matter. On the contrary, far from showing his lack of concern about righteousness, it shows the depth of his concern for it. It is in his grace centred on the cross that we encounter the only thing that can deal effectively with sin. Human sin and by the same token human goodness matter so much to God that he does the only thing that will solve the problem: he freely puts men and women into a new and fruitful relationship with himself, as his people. In that new relationship they can at last begin to live and be free. Moreover, as there is only one God, so there can be only one way to life with him as his people. That way cannot be Law-obedience, but is rather faith, the willingness to be accepted freely through Jesus Christ.

If this seems to leave no place for the Law, that is because the proper place of the Law as preparation and promise has not been understood.

Now in all this, the guilt aspect of the problem of sin has been in the foreground, and will remain so until the end of Ch. 5. The other aspect, that of the powerless of the sinner, will be taken up in Ch. 6. Nevertheless the stress on the centrality of the cross shows that while concentrating on the first, Paul is not altogether ignoring the second, for at the heart of his distinctive understanding of the death of Christ is the belief that men and women participate in it by dying to sin and the old life and by enjoying the resurrection-promise of new life and freedom.

ᔓᔓ

21

But now: the Greek *Nuni de* is emphatic, suggesting that what follows is the answer not only to the immediately preceding statement, but to the whole analysis of the human situation since 1¹⁸. Further, 'Now' is not just a logical contrast, as if to say 'You have heard the problem, now here is the solution.' It is also chronological or even eschatological: *now* is the dawning of the New Age, *now* in the time of Jesus Christ (cf. 3²⁶; 5⁹⁻¹¹; 6²¹; 7⁶; 8¹; 11³⁰⁻³¹; 13¹¹).

the righteousness of God: this phrase dominates the whole passage up to v. 26. On it see the discussion at 1¹⁷. Here, it could denote God's own integrity, but the drift of the passage and the meaning of the term elsewhere suggests that it is likely to be more than this. It has sometimes been thought here to denote God's activity of justifying and, taken together with the same phrase in v. 22, to mean that through Christ the righteousness of God becomes ours, so that we stand before God bearing *his* righteousness and on the basis of that will be acquitted. It is hard to find any hint of such an exchange (often called 'imputed righteousness') in this passage. More likely, as in 1¹⁷, God's righteousness is his saving activity, especially evident here in his justifying (accepting) those who do not deserve it. Whereas in Isa. 46¹³ and 51⁵ it was directed towards Israel, now it is directed even-handedly towards the whole human race, both Jews and Gentiles. God still comes to the rescue of his oppressed people, but his people are now not just historical Israel, and the oppressor is now sin.

has been manifested apart from law: it is not the manifestation that is apart from Law, for in fact Law and Prophets witness to the saving righteousness. It is righteousness that is apart from Law, which must mean that God saves without requiring adherence to or obedience to the Law, but there may be a further connotation. As in 1¹⁷, Paul may be saying that men and women are drawn into God's righteousness as a power in which and under which they may live, so that he not only accepts them as his people but also empowers them to live as that people. The true way of righteousness is living in this power, and not Law-obedience. To say this is to say that to be part of historical Israel is not necessary.

the law and the prophets bear witness: for the Law see Gen. 15⁶ and Rom. 4³ff., where the point will be developed, and for the prophets see Hab. 2⁴ and Rom. 1¹⁷. The Law here has the character of promise, pointing to something beyond itself, namely to Christ and the way of grace and faith, rather than the character of regulation. It is possible that the mention of both Law and prophets is a reflection of the Jewish view that in order to establish important matters two witnesses are required (cf. Deut. 19¹⁵).

22

through faith in Jesus Christ: the Greek is ambiguous, and it is possible that we should translate 'through the faith(fulness) of Jesus Christ'. The verse would then provide a neat contrast between Christ's faithfulness in obeying God even as far as the cross, and human faith as response to that action. The matter is not susceptible to a dogmatic answer, but on the whole it is more likely that we should follow RSV. It fits well with the whole passage that we should see the righteousness of God as his saving action, and 'faith in Jesus Christ' as the human response to that action.

there is no distinction: the God-given solution to the human dilemma is available to *all* who believe, Jew and Gentile, just as the whole preceding argument has been attempting to show that Jews as well as Gentiles are in need of rescue.

23

since all have sinned: cf. the whole passage 1¹⁸–3²⁰, and the discussion in the introduction to 3⁹⁻³⁰ about whether 'all' means literally every single individual. It was suggested there that the argument has not been to prove that every single human individual is irretrievably wicked, but rather that in the matter of sinfulness the Jews as a nation are in the same dire situation as the Gentile nations. In the course of that argument he incidentally suggested that some Gentiles obey God rather well, just as in Phil. 3^6 he claimed that as a Jew he kept the Law rather well. Nevertheless, although he cannot be said to have proved it in 1^{18}–3^{20}, he doubtless did want to maintain that all human beings were sinful to some degree, even if some were less so than others. There is no contradiction here to what he said in $2^{14-15, \ 26-27}$.

fall short of the glory of God: this gives one explanation of what sin is. It is to miss the true vocation of human beings as reflecters of the divine glory (*doxa*, see above on 1^{23}). There may be an allusion to Gen. 1^{26} where the human being is made in the image of God, for 'image' (*eikōn*) and 'glory' (*doxa*) are sometimes used interchangeably in Jewish writing in Greek. There was also a Rabbinic idea that human beings before the fall shared the glory of God, cf. *Apoc. Mos.* 21^6; Gen. R. 12^5; III *Apoc. Bar.* 4^{16}. However, Paul's focus is not on the story of creation and fall in Genesis, but on the present plight of the human race. We were intended to reflect the splendour of God himself, and we fail to do so.

24–25a

It is often, and with reason, argued that at this point Paul quotes a formula already in use in the church and quite possibly familiar to his readers.[d]

(*a*) The RSV translation hides an awkward connection between the end of v. 23 and the beginning of v. 24. Literally, v. 24 begins 'being justified . . .' where one would expect something like 'they are now justified'. This rough connection may be an indication that a quotation is being inserted into a context which it does not fit smoothly.

(*b*) The passage is so condensed and pregnant that it looks remarkably like a well-honed formula.

(*c*) There are some expressions in the verses which, while they are hardly impossible for Paul, are sufficiently uncharacteristic of him to increase the suspicion that he is quoting. The most striking example is the word 'expiation' (*hilastērion*), a word not found elsewhere in Paul's letters, and taken from the Temple cult which is not Paul's most usual field of reference. Some think that 'God's righteousness' in v. 25 is used in a different way from v. 21, to mean God's strict justice. Other unusual items of vocabulary include 'the blood of Christ' (v. 25), which occurs elsewhere only in 5^9, almost certainly a reference back to this passage,

---

d See, e.g. Käsemann, pp. 92ff.; Wilckens I, pp. 183f., and the discussion in Ziesler, *Meaning*, pp. 209f.

and I Cor. 10¹⁶ and 11²⁵, both of which come in traditional eucharistic material.

It remains the case that even if Paul is quoting, he means what he quotes. The importance of the theory that we have a quotation here, probably annotated by Paul himself, is twofold. First, it may help to interpret some of the difficulties of the verse. Secondly, it may show that justification by faith was not Paul's invention, but in at least some measure was already known and accepted in the primitive church.ᵉ

24

justified: see on 2¹³; 3²⁰. God's saving righteousness gives people a new status as his own people.

as a gift: this clarifies *by his grace*, and may be a Pauline gloss on the traditional formula.ᶠ

through the redemption: redemption is deliverance (*apolutrōsis*). The word had connections with the slave market and with buying a slave's freedom, and could also be used for any deliverance from bondage. In LXX it was associated with Israel's deliverance from bondage in Egypt (especially in a cognate verbal form), e.g. Ex. 6⁶; 15¹³, ¹⁶; Deut. 7⁸; 9²⁶; 13⁵; 15¹⁵; 21⁸; 24¹⁸. Here, the deliverance is from bondage to sin as in v. 9, an idea that is already found in the OT (Isa. 43²²⁻²⁸; 44²¹⁻²²) and actually in connection with *apolutrōsis* in Dan. LXX 4³⁴. In the NT compare Col. 1¹⁴; Eph. 1⁷.

The use of this image reminds us that though the focus of the passage is on acceptance/justification, and so on the removal of guilt, the idea of release from slavery to sin is also present. There is no reason to suppose that in the use of this word there is any suggestion of a price paid to the Devil or to anyone else, any more than there was in the case of Israel's redemption from Egypt. Yet this is not to deny that the redemption was costly, for it involved the death of Christ on the cross.

which is in Christ Jesus: why not 'through Christ Jesus' or 'by means of Christ Jesus'? No doubt something like that is included in the meaning,

---

e See the case built up by Reumann in *Righteousness*, pp. 27–40.

f So K. Kertelge, '*Rechtfertigung*' *bei Paulus*, Münster: Aschendorff 1966, pp. 52f., though he thinks 'by his grace' is also a Pauline addition. *Contra*, Käsemann, p. 96. Reumann, *Righteousness*, pp. 36f., on the other hand, thinks 'as a gift' was in the formula and 'by his grace' was the Pauline addition.

but there is probably more. When Paul uses the preposition 'in' (*en*) it is sometimes with the connotation 'under or in the power of', and this is especially so when he speaks of being *in* Christ or *in* the Spirit.^g Christ is regarded as a sphere of power which can overthrow other and malign powers, especially the power of sin. Here, 'redemption in Christ Jesus' is the transfer from one power/dominion to another, from that of sin to that of Christ, and this is nothing less than a liberation. Absolute freedom is not envisaged: true freedom is the ability to live under God and in the power of God in Christ.

25

whom God put forward: the verb *proetheto*, in RSV rendered 'put forward', could be taken in a quite general way to mean 'purpose' (so Cranfield I, p. 209), but it may be used as a technical term for the bringing of a sacrifice (so cautiously Barrett, p. 77). In view of what immediately follows, a sacrificial meaning is quite likely.

as an expiation: the Greek word, *hilastērion*, is rare, and its meaning here is highly controversial.

(*a*) In non-biblical Greek it normally means something done, like bringing a votive offering, to influence the gods. The usual translation to convey this meaning is 'propitiation', which in the biblical context is taken to mean something done to avert the wrath of God (cf. 1¹⁸; 2⁵; 3⁵). What is done in this case is the offering of Christ on the cross, which thus averts God's wrath and enables the sinner to be justified. It must be added that on this view it is God himself who provides the means of propitiation, and there is no suggestion that God is placated by anything men and women do or offer. This view has at least the merit of being straightforward.^h

(*b*) The meaning favoured by many commentators and represented by RSV is 'expiation', which differs from propitiation in that it is directed towards sinners, not towards God. Expiation is removing sin and guilt, not placating God, and it was argued by C. H. Dodd that in the Bible and the Jewish tradition in general, it was expiation and not propitiation that was the central concern and also the usual meaning of

g See Ziesler, *PC*, pp. 47–63. Compare 2¹² and 3¹⁹, where 'under the law' is literally 'in the law'.

h For its modern proponents see Murray, pp. 117f., and most notably L. Morris, *The Apostolic Preaching of the Cross*, Tyndale Press 1955, pp. 125–85.

hilastērion and its cognates.[i] In detail, Dodd's argument is vulnerable, as there are places where we do seem to find propitiation in the sense of that which averts the divine wrath. In general, however, he is right that in Jewish literature the tendency in this connection is towards dealing with sin rather than dealing with God. We cannot rule out all notion of propitiation here in any dogmatic fashion, and there is something of a parallel to such a meaning of *hilastērion* in IV Macc. 17^{22}, where the propitiatory death of the martyrs had a cleansing effect on Israel.[j] Nevertheless it is not easy to extract from Rom. 3^{25} in its context any notion that God is being placated by the death of Jesus, even if God himself is taken to be the prime mover. Moreover, any reference to the wrath is either too far back to be plausibly at stake here (1^{18}; 2^{5}) or only mentioned parenthetically and not brought into connection with *hilastērion* (3^{5}). The whole section is concerned with how God deals with sin, and that is where the emphasis should lie in interpreting *hilastērion*. In short, RSV is probably right to translate it as 'expiation'.[k]

(c) A variation on the 'expiation' view arises from taking *hilastērion* in its invariable LXX sense: the mercy-seat, i.e. the lid of the Ark of the Covenant in the Holy of Holies within the Jerusalem Temple.[l] It was here that on the Day of Atonement, Lev. 16, the High Priest performed on behalf of the whole nation the ritual which obtained forgiveness of sins, and which repaired the damage done to the covenant by those sins. *Hilastērion* would thus mean the place where, or the means by which, sins are dealt with. For Paul, this is now the cross of Christ.

The difference between this explanation and the second, 'expiation', is mainly one of vividness and concreteness. Both (b) and (c) differ from the propitiation explanation (a), not only in having human sin rather than God as the object of the action, but also very often in failing to make clear exactly how the action works.

i Dodd, *The Bible and the Greeks*, Hodder & Stoughton 1935, pp. 82–95. Dodd's case has been subjected to searching criticism by David Hill, *Greek Words and Hebrew Meanings*, SNTSMS 5, CUP 1967, Ch. 2.

j The passage contains the genitive of the adjective.

k For the view that the death of Jesus is here seen as atoning in line with Jewish martyr theology (cf. IV Macc. 17.22) see J. S. Pobee, *Persecution and Martyrdom in the Theology of Paul*, JSNT Supp. 6, JSOT Press 1985, pp. 61–4.

l On the word-usage see K. Grayston, '*Hilaskesthai* and Related Words in LXX', NTS 27.5, 1981, pp. 640–56. On 'mercy-seat' as the meaning here see Nygren pp. 156–60, and the discussion in Wilckens I, pp. 192–3; also Newton, *Purity*, pp. 76–7, who sees it as serving as a guarantee of the divine presence in the community.

It must be admitted that in this passage Paul does not explain how the cross functions in God's plan of salvation, that is unless we adopt the propitiation explanation. Elsewhere (e.g. I Cor. 15³) he can say in common with much early Christianity that Christ died 'for our sins', and that he died to reconcile us to God, Rom. 5⁶⁻¹⁰, though these are statements and not explanations. One possible way to clarity is to argue from a parallel with the Jewish sacrificial system: Israel did not try to rationalize how the Temple sacrifices worked, but simply took it that they were the divinely ordained way of removing sin and its effects, with not the worshippers but God himself as the effective agent.ᵐ Similarly Paul may have seen the death of Christ as the divinely provided way, in the new Christian scheme of salvation, to deal with sin and its effects, without trying to rationalize how it worked beyond seeing God himself as the effective agent.

This is possible. However, when he does talk at any length about the cross, notably in Rom. 6, Paul uses what we may call participatory terms. The cross is not something over against human beings, apart from them, or even in some way operating instead of them. Rather is it something in which they are involved. They die *with* Christ to sin (in their case, but not his, in that he was held to have been sinless). It is as if Christ's death on the cross represents the end of the old world, the Old Age, and so our dying with him represents our leaving that Old Age and entering, or being prepared for entering, the New Age. Put slightly differently, it is escaping from the old powers and dominions, and entering or being prepared for entering the new. If we then ask how in Rom. 3²⁵ the cross expiates our sins or acts as the mercy-seat, the answer is clear enough. It enables us to die to sin, to the power which hitherto has held us prisoners. Thus justification, the cross, and dying to sin are inextricable.

by his blood, to be received by faith: the sprinkling of blood had a central role in the ritual of the Day of Atonement (cf. Lev. 16¹⁴). The sacrifice Paul is talking about is that of the death of Christ, and so the blood here is Christ's. Yet in sacrificial contexts blood tends to represent not only death: it is also life released and offered up through death (cf. Lev. 17¹¹). In Jewish anthropology the blood was the life (e.g. Deut. 12²³). Here, then, we probably have more than a reference to the death of Christ; also included is the idea of new life through death, available to all who have died with Christ.

m On this see Wilckens I, pp. 233–43.

RSV rightly connects 'by his blood' with 'expiation' and not with 'faith', against some older versions which read 'by faith in his blood'.[n] The human response of faith is an entering into the whole action of Christ's dying.

This was to show God's righteousness: if one takes the propitiatory meaning of *hilastērion*, then this clause could mean that the divine justice was satisfied by the death of Jesus. In effect, due reparation has been paid, not by sinners themselves, but by Jesus Christ in their stead. We have argued that a propitiatory meaning is unlikely, however, and that in all probability *hilastērion* has some sort of expiatory meaning. It is also likely that God's righteousness has here its usual Pauline saving connotations, and so does not mean his strict justice of the 'eye for an eye' sort, but his action to restore and maintain the divine-human relationship. Indeed here as elsewhere his righteousness is his concern for the right, but it is shown by his releasing those who are labouring under the guilt and power of sin. Justification is a first step which puts people into that relationship with God in which they can exist as his people within his freedom-giving power.

It is thus not at all certain that 'God's righteousness' is used here differently from Paul's normal usage, and therefore this phrase cannot be taken as evidence that he is quoting a formula. That evidence must be looked for elsewhere. At all events, if a formula does underlie what he is saying, Paul uses 'the righteousness of God' in his usual way so far as we can see.

because in his divine forbearance he had passed over former sins: on a propitiatory interpretation, the point would be that by not punishing the sinners themselves God might have given the erroneous impression that he did not care about right and wrong. Then the sacrificial death of Jesus would be the proof that such an impression was indeed erroneous: the due punishment was visited upon him, in the place of sinners. If, on the other hand, we take an expiatory explanation, we may read this clause not 'righteousness *despite* his passing over former sins in his forbearance' but rather 'righteousness *observed in* his passing over former sins in his forbearance'. That is to say that the passing over sins is not a problem to be solved, but the way to the solution itself, the first step taken in putting wrong people right.

But what does 'passing over' mean? The word (*paresis*) is found only

n For a discussion, see Wilckens I, pp. 193–4.

here in the whole NT, and its force depends to some extent on whose sins were passed over: the sins of people in former times, or the sins formerly committed by people who are now receiving the gospel? The latter is on balance more likely, i.e. the former sins of those to whom salvation is now offered, because 1¹⁸⁻³² shows that God has not passed over the sins of people hitherto. On the contrary, they have been (1¹⁸) and will be (2⁵) the objects of the wrath. If all this is correct, then *paresis* does not mean ignoring sins, but forgiving them, as part of God's total strategy of dealing with and overcoming sin.° It is now, in the light of Jesus Christ, and because of God's freely granted acceptance, that their former sins are not held against those who have faith, cf. 'at the present time' in v. 26.

26

it was to prove: this is a translation of words closely similar to those rendered 'This was to show' in v. 25. Perhaps in v. 25 Paul was talking of showing God's righteousness in the light of sins passed over in former times, but here he is talking of showing God's righteousness now. In that case we do not have a repetition of the statement in v. 25. It is more likely, however, in the light of what was said about the end of v. 25, that v. 26 does function as a summary and does contain a degree of repetition. 'It was to prove' thus takes the argument to its conclusion. The whole event of the death of Christ in its bearing on the problem of human sin and guilt goes to show that God's righteousness and the justification of sinners are entirely compatible. Indeed the justification is an expression of the righteousness, not its contradiction; this is because God's righteous purpose is carried out and human righteousness becomes a possibility *through* God's freely given justification.

that he himself is righteous and that he justifies: we need to recall that in Greek the words 'righteous' (*dikaion*) and 'justifies' (*dikaiounta*) are similar, so that we have a kind of solemn pun. God's being righteous, and his being a justifier (of the undeserving) are two sides of one coin. It is because he is a faithful, reliable, consistent God, forever working for goodness, that he accepts those who respond to his offer: nothing else, in Paul's view, can succeed.

27

our boasting: who has been boasting, or has been tempted to boast, over

---

o See further Ziesler, *Meaning,* pp. 210f.

whom and about what? It has been common to say that the Jews have boasted about their good works and their Law-obedience, and have felt confident in their own righteousness before God. In short, it is the boasting of self-righteousness.[p] It is thinking that one has some claim on God, or has some rights and dues from him, because one has earned them. On this view, Paul is saying that on the contrary no one can boast before God, God can never be put in our debt, and to think he can is a reprehensible and sinful way of thinking. Moreover in fact no one can boast, for all must rely on God's grace and on that alone.

Despite the support it has received, the above interpretation is difficult to sustain from the text and the context themselves. The argument so far has not been about Jews who think they can boast about their own righteousness before *God*, but rather about Jews who think they can boast over *Gentiles* to whom they are morally superior and also superior in the purposes of God. The boasting is of those who think they have a special status because they are Jews. 'Our boasting' therefore probably means 'our Jewish boasting'.[q] What follows in vv. 29f. bears out the contention that what is excluded here is the boasting of Jews over Gentiles, as does the whole argument up to 3^{20} (cf. especially $2^{17, 23}$ and the comments on these verses).

All this being said, it can still be argued that the Bultmannian position is implied by what Paul says. He was not accusing the Jews of being self-righteous before God, but rather of seeing themselves as better than the Gentiles. Yet *any* sort of boasting before God is ruled out implicitly.

principle: the Greek is *nomos*, normally translated 'law', and very often referring to the Torah, the Jewish Law. How it ought to be rendered (three times) in this verse is much disputed.

(*a*) It could, as usual, mean the Torah. In that case we have a Torah of works set in opposition to a Torah of faith. If we paraphrase the verse giving this value to *nomos*, we can get something like: 'What Torah excludes boasting? Not the Torah used as a basis for proving our own righteousness before God, but the Torah regarded as showing God's will for those who approach it in faith.' What this boils down to is that

p A view vividly represented by Bultmann, *Theology* I, pp. 259ff., 281f., 340ff. 'Jews' are taken as representative of people of any time and any race who try to establish themselves before God by their own merit.

q For this way of reading the verse see Sanders, *PLJP*, pp. 32–6; Räisänen, *PL*, pp. 170f.; also Wilckens I, p. 248.

the Torah is good if we know that obeying it does not win/earn our acceptance/justification, but bad if we think it does.[r]

(b) *Nomos* could mean something like the RSV 'principle'; perhaps 'régime' or even 'system' would be better. Then Paul is saying that boasting is excluded by the régime of faith, under which all are on an equal footing, Jew and Gentile alike. It is not excluded under the régime of works, under which Jews must do better because they are circumcised, observe the sabbath and the food laws, and so on.[s]

The second view is to be preferred. Although it is a relatively unusual meaning for *nomos*, 'principle' is not impossible[t] and it avoids the problematic expression 'Torah of faith' which has to be taken in the sense 'Torah as requiring faith' or 'Torah as pointing forward to faith' or even 'Torah as approached in (Christian) faith'. If Paul was saying any of these it is a pity he did not make himself clearer. The first view takes for granted that there were some people (Jews) who approached the Torah thinking that by observing it they earned God's favour, whereas Christians approached it knowing that they could never so earn that favour. We have seen that this whole contrast is now under serious doubt, and in any case it does not fit well with the course of the argument up to this point.

28

justified by faith apart from works of the law: cf. 3^{21f}. Faith (in Christ) is the criterion, not doing the Law. The next verse explains why.

29

is God the God of the Jews only?: If he were, then acceptance by God as his people could indeed require the observance of the Law, which would automatically exclude the mass of the Gentiles. Paul cannot, however, allow any infringement of his basic principle that God's salvation is for Jews and Gentiles equally; this is why the Law can play no part in making men and women acceptable to God. He cannot envisage the possibility that the Torah should be kept in its entirety by all nations

r See Hübner, *LPT*, p. 115; Cranfield I, pp. 219f. There is a good discussion of such views in Räisänen, *PL*, pp. 50–2. Cranfield thinks that the 'law of faith' is the law as summoning men and women to faith.

s See Sanders, *PLJP*, pp. 15, 92f.; Räisänen, *PL*, p. 52, and especially his article 'Das "Gesetz" des Glaubens und des Geistes', in *Torah*, pp. 95–118, as well as pp. 143f.

t Despite Wilckens II, p. 122; see Räisänen, *PL*, pp. 50f.

(see the sustained argument in Galatians). He argues from God's concern for Jew and Gentile alike, with an unexpressed minor premise that Gentiles cannot be asked to keep the whole Torah, and concludes that acceptance with God as his people cannot be by keeping the Law.

30

he will justify the circumcised on the ground of their faith and the uncircumcised through their faith: there are several points to notice here.

(*a*) The circumcised and the uncircumcised are the two communities, Jewish and non-Jewish.

(*b*) The unity of God is the reason why the two communities are treated in the same way. The one God (Deut. 6⁴) cannot have two different ways of working.

(*c*) Thus there is only one way to God's acceptance. Justification by faith is not a second-best way for those who cannot rise to the best, viz. obedience to the Torah. It is the way for Jews just as for Gentiles.

(*d*) The RSV 'on the ground of (their faith)' and 'through (their faith)' attempts to indicate that different Greek prepositions have been used with reference to the faith of the Jews and of the Gentiles. Some (cf. Robinson, p. 50) have therefore supposed that some sort of difference is implied in the way to God for the two groups. Yet the whole drift of the argument is against this supposition, and the difference in prepositions is probably no more than a stylistic variation (so Cranfield I, p. 222, and Wilckens I, p. 248).

31

we uphold the law: a very surprising answer. We might well have expected, 'Yes, we do indeed overthrow the law'. There are two main ways of taking these words.

(*a*) Paul is not saying that Christians can now regard themselves as absolved from obedience to any of the Law, just because they are absolved from obedience to some parts of it, or because obedience to it is not what makes them God's people. Passages like Rom. 8⁴; 13⁸⁻¹⁰ can be cited as supporting evidence.[u] In this case Paul is saying that if one really wants to do God's will in general, then where one must start is with justification by faith. In the long run, far from militating against the doing of God's will, it on the contrary enables it to be done. There is no doubt that this is a Pauline position, though the precise relation between God's will and the Torah in Paul's thought is not easy to

[u] See Sanders, *PLJP*, pp. 93–105, 149; Robinson, p. 51.

determine. The question, however, is whether this is what he is saying at this point, and there is little in the context to suggest that it is.

(b) Paul is not talking about the Law in its regulative aspect but its predictive (cf. 3[21b]), and in particular about Gen. 15[6] and the story of Abraham to which he is about to turn. In short, Ch. 4 is the explanation of 3[31], which is a transition. In effect he is saying that if you read the Law carefully, you will see from Gen. 15[6] that it too teaches justification by faith.[v]

The likelihood that (b) is correct has been increased by the observation that *mē genoito* (*By no means!*) after a rhetorical question, as here, regularly introduces a topic for immediate discussion, and never concludes a matter. Thus Rom. 4 is the clarification of 3[31].[w]

4[1-8]   FAITH RECKONED AS RIGHTEOUSNESS

4 *What then shall we say about Abraham, our forefather according to the flesh?* [2]*For if Abraham was justified by works, he has something to boast about, but not before God.* [3]*For what does the scripture say? 'Abraham believed God, and it was reckoned to him as righteousness.'* [4]*Now to one who works, his wages are not reckoned as a gift but as his due.* [5]*And to one who does not work but trusts him who justifies the ungodly, his faith is reckoned as righteousness.* [6]*So also David pronounces a blessing upon the man to whom God reckons righteousness apart from works:*

[7]*'Blessed are those whose iniquities are forgiven, and whose sins are covered;*
[8]*blessed is the man against whom the Lord will not reckon his sin.'*

Abraham was revered as the father of the Jewish people, but Paul does not take him as the example of how to be God's people by observing the Torah (he was sometimes regarded as having kept the Torah before it was given, by anticipation, cf. Ecclus. 44[20]; II Apoc. Bar. 57[2]). Paul rather takes him as the example of the way to God through justification by faith, and so for the whole human race with-

---

[v] So Käsemann, p. 105; cf. Hübner, *LPT*, pp. 53, 118, 141–3; Williams, 'Righteousness', p. 280.

[w] See C. Thomas Rhyne, *Faith Establishes the Law*, SBL Diss. 35, Scholars Press 1981, exp. Ch. 2.

out distinction, Gentiles as well as Jews. Of course this carries the implication that acceptance with God cannot be obtained by human achievement, as v. 2 may indicate, but the target of the argument from 3^{27} to 4^{25} is clearly to show that God deals with Jews and Gentiles in the same way and on the same conditions.^{x} Paul quotes and re-quotes Gen. 15^{6}, arguing that as Abraham was accepted by God before he had any Law to obey, on the ground of his faith alone, even before circumcision had been instituted, justification by faith is no latter-day innovation. It always has been the divinely ordained way. It certainly comes to new expression and new clarity with Jesus Christ, but it is as old as Abraham and David. Therefore the Law itself shows that this is and always was the way to enter right relationship with God as his people.

꩜

1

What shall we then say about Abraham: many MSS, including most of those usually reckoned to be the best, have in addition the word 'found'. Despite its absence from RSV, it almost certainly ought to be included. The question then runs, 'What shall we say that Abraham – our forefather according to the flesh – found?' The answer presumably comes in v. 5, and there may be an allusion to Gen. 18^{3} LXX where Abraham 'found grace'.

There is, however, disagreement in the MSS about the placing of 'found' (*heurēkenai*). Some have it in the order implied by the translation just given, i.e. immediately before 'Abraham' (*heurēkenai Abraam ton propatora hēmōn kata sarka*). Others have it immediately before 'according to the flesh' (*Abraam ton propatora hēmōn heurēkenai kata sarka*), which would require the translation 'What then shall we say that Abraham our forefather found according to the flesh?' In order to determine which reading is more original, we need first to consider the meaning of 'according to the flesh' (on *sarx* see 1^{3} above). If the first text and rendering are correct, 'according to the flesh' means 'in terms of human relationship, kinship, or race', so that the whole question runs 'What shall we say that Abraham – our forefather racially speaking – found?' If the second text and rendering are correct, 'according to the flesh' means something like 'in purely human terms', so that the whole question runs 'What shall we say that Abraham our forefather found,

x See Sanders, *PLJP*, p. 34; Wilckens I, pp. 281f.; Räisänen, *Torah*, p. 82.

humanly speaking?' On balance the arguments tilt in favour of the first text and rendering.

(a) The MS evidence is stronger for 'our forefather racially speaking'.

(b) It is hard to make much sense of 'found humanly speaking', for of what other kind of finding was Abraham capable?

(c) It fits with the whole argument if Paul begins with Abraham as the Jewish progenitor, and shows that even he supports the way of faith for Jew and Gentile without distinction.

(d) Against all these points, one may bring forward a textual principle of prime importance, that we should prefer that reading which best explains the rise of the others. In practice this usually means choosing the more awkward one, because later copyists are more likely to have smoothed over existing difficulties than to have created new ones.

Despite the force of this last point, we may cautiously take it that 'What then shall we say that Abraham (our forefather racially speaking) found?' is as close as we are likely to get to the original text. Unfortunately there is still further textual disagreement in this verse: some Western MSS have not 'forefather' but 'father'. The latter is by far the more usual Jewish way of referring to Abraham, but it might not be so familiar to a non-Jewish audience. Therefore, although the MS support for it is relatively slight, there is a chance that 'father' is the better reading, having been altered to the more comprehensible 'forefather' by a copyist.

our forefather: the question immediately arises, whose forefather (or father)? Is Abraham the forefather of 'us who are Jews', or is he the forefather of all the Roman Christians, Gentile as well as Jewish? If the first, does this imply that the Roman church was predominantly Jewish? If the second, how can Paul say that Abraham was the forefather of Gentiles? On balance it is more likely that Abraham is seen as the forefather of *all* Christians.

(a) Paul is about to argue that all who share Abraham's faith – which is taken as a type or anticipatory parallel to Christian faith – are his children and heirs.

(b) He does appear prone to universalize Jewish experience when talking to Christians. This is seen, for example, in I Cor. 10$^{\text{1}}$ where he talks of 'our fathers' as having been under the cloud, although he is writing to a very largely Gentile church.[y]

[y] For further evidence and discussion of this Pauline habit, see Sanders, *PLJP*, pp. 82, 183, 209.

(c) It is unlikely that the bulk of the Roman church was Jewish Christian, because part of the argument of this letter is dedicated to persuading Gentiles that they must not brush aside the Jewish Christians and their problems. Indeed he has to tell them that it is the tree of historical Israel into which they are being grafted (see Rom. 11), as if to curb their pretensions. There certainly is no way of working out the relative strengths of Jews and Gentiles in the church in Rome; all we can confidently say is that both seem to have been substantially represented.

2

if Abraham was justified by works: it is clear that 'works' (*ergōn*) here are specifically works of the Law, not just good deeds in general.[z] We have already noted in the introduction to this passage that in some circles Abraham was believed to have kept the Law even before it was given (see *Jub.* 23^{10}), and was the model of the perfectly righteous. The faith referred to in Gen. 15^6 was thus taken to be faithfulness. For Paul, however, almost the opposite is the case: Abraham was reckoned righteous and accepted as the father of Israel solely on the basis of his faith, understood not as his faithfulness but as his response to God. Paul does not, for instance, link Gen. 15^6 with Abraham's later willingness to be obedient even to the point of offering Isaac as a sacrifice, a linkage made by I Macc. 2$^{51-52}$.

he has something to boast about but not before God: this is a key text for the view of Bultmann and others that Paul opposes, and uses Abraham as a case-study for his opposition, the idea that human beings can pile up merit before God and so have something to boast about before him. In short, this verse is held to betray the fact that Paul's target is self-righteousness. On the contrary, if that element is present at all, it is at best only parenthetically,[a] for the true target is the notion that the Jews have some inbuilt advantage, the notion that they alone can be the people of God because they alone have and observe the Torah. Paul's riposte is that even the great Abraham, the father of Israel, was justified by faith, a faith which is accessible to Jews and Gentiles equally.[b] Abraham is thus the paradigm for Gentiles as well as for Jews, and a

z Cf. Watson, *PJG*, p. 140.
a Cf. Räisänen, *Torah*, p. 82.
b See Bultmann, *Theology* I, pp. 259–67; on the other side, Sanders, *PLJP*, p. 57, and Räisänen, *PL*, p. 69.

paradigm in terms of his faith, God's chosen way then as now, cf. vv. 9–13.

'Not before God' does indeed indicate that even if Abraham could have been conceded some right to boast over others, he could have no such right before God. To this extent we do have evidence of Paul's opposition to self-righteousness. Yet it is a parenthesis in the argument, not the main argument itself, and must not be read into other passages where it is not even mentioned.[c] The main argument remains that even if Abraham, the archetypal Israelite, was accepted by God not on the basis of his works, his Law-obedience, but on the basis of his faith, how much more will this apply to anyone else. It was not that he was not good enough to be accepted on the basis of his works; it was that this was not the divinely chosen way. There was a tradition that Abraham was a quite exceptionally good person who, as we have seen, was considered to have kept the Law (the whole Law) before it was given. He was seen as perfectly righteous, as one who therefore had no need to repent of anything.[d] If it was not appropriate for him to be justified by works, how much less so for the rest of the human race!

3
believed: this is to be taken, despite the obvious anachronism, in a specifically Christian sense. In this argument, there is no doubt that Abraham's faith is a paradigm of Christian faith. Abraham relied for acceptance on God, and God alone, and so should Christians.

it was reckoned to him as righteousness: this probably does not mean that his faith (or his faithfulness) was to be regarded as equivalent to or as constituting righteousness, but rather that it was to be counted in lieu of righteousness, instead of it.[e] This runs counter to the usual Jewish interpretation, which does take Abraham's faith(fulness) to constitute righteousness. Nevertheless there may be a sense in which faith, as a crucial aspect of the life of the people of God, is seen by Paul as part of righteousness, and not just in lieu of it.

However difficult it may be to unpack it in detail, this expression stresses the fact that God accepted Abraham as his child, and as the pro-

c Its importance is exaggerated by Hübner, *LPT*, pp. 118–20; see the criticisms of Sanders, *PLJP*, pp. 33–4, 44.
d See *Jub.* 23^{10}; *m. Kidd.* 4^{14}; *Or. Man.* 8.
e See the discussion in Ziesler, *Meaning*, pp. 180–5.

spective father of many more children, simply because of his faith. Paul does not say that by some process righteousness was transferred from someone else's account to Abraham's, as a parallel to some transference from Christ's account to the Christian's. The whole notion of 'imputed righteousness' rests only on this passage and on Gal. 3⁶, and on the use of 'reckoned to him as' (*logizesthai auto(i) eis*) in both passages. It is a weight that the passages do not readily bear.[f] It is only when discussing Gen. 15⁶ that Paul uses the 'reckoning to him as' terminology; it is not elsewhere a part of his justification vocabulary. Its importance ought not, therefore, to be exaggerated, and certainly the idea of transferring righteousness from one account to another ought not to be added to it, at least in the exegesis of Paul, whatever may be the case in the history of theology.

To sum up, 'faith reckoned as righteousness' means that for acceptance by God into his people only faith is needed. That no transaction is involved is made clearer by what now follows.

4

to one who works his wages are not reckoned as a gift but as his due: this statement, together with v. 5, forms a major piece of support claimed by those like Bultmann who think that Paul is arguing against self-righteousness and the earning of status before God. Taken by themselves, these words could tend in that direction, and doubtless Paul would have been strongly opposed to any notion of earning status with God, as would his Jewish contemporaries. Yet once again we must recall the context, which is about the non-advantage of the Jew over the Gentile, because both are accepted on the basis of their faith and that alone. The target, to repeat, is not Jewish self-righteousness, but Jewish claims to privilege.

5

one who does not work but trusts: this makes it crystal clear that for Paul, faith is not anything one does, and is not equivalent to faithfulness. It is almost a non-thing, the simple willingness to receive and to be received. We might call it openness to God.

him who justifies the ungodly: it is possible that, if there is still a reference to Abraham, he is being seen as ungodly, i.e. a Gentile.[g] However, it is

_f_ Cf. Sanders, *PPJ*, p. 491 n. 57.
_g_ So, e.g. H. Moxnes, *Theology in Conflict*, Leiden: Brill 1980, pp. 43f.

possible that attention has switched rather to contemporary ungodly. These are not the totally godless, who would scarcely be interested in being justified and brought into the people of God. They are rather those who, like the Gentiles, cannot claim that they are particularly righteous and deserving people, and above all those who cannot claim to be within the people of God. Bultmann and the Reformation tradition are indeed right to maintain that Paul's teaching on justification means that God accepts the undeserving, freely and graciously, if they only have faith. This statement here is in contradiction to some OT texts like Ex. 23⁷: 'I will not justify the wicked' (LXX has 'the ungodly', cf. also Prov. 17¹⁵; Isa. 5²³). In the OT tradition, God can be relied upon *not* to acquit those who are guilty. For Paul, the gospel is that he can be relied upon to do precisely that, so long as there is faith on the human side.

6

David pronounces a blessing: the quotation is from Ps. 32¹⁻², LXX.

to whom God reckons righteousness apart from works: there is a difference in formulation from vv. 3 and 5, where we read of 'faith reckoned as righteousness'. It is this variant that has given most impetus to the imputation theory of justification, the theory according to which God imputes Christ's righteousness to sinners. Yet there is nothing here that suggests the righteousness reckoned is transferred from one account to another. Indeed, if righteousness is life within the covenant, and so life that is pleasing to God, it is hard to see what it would mean to transfer it from Christ's account to any other.

It is possible that this variant formulation means nothing different from 'faith reckoned as (in lieu of) righteousness'. It could, however, be that faith is now understood as that which pleases God, so that those who have faith are to be reckoned righteous. If so, it may be important that it is only now in v. 6 that this particular formulation is used, because it is only after vv. 4 and 5 have made it clear that faith is not the same as faithfulness (and thus works under another name), but is tantamount to receptivity.

7

whose iniquities are forgiven, and whose sins are covered: it is now apparent that

      faith reckoned as righteousness = justification by faith
                               = forgiveness of sins.

To be more precise, forgiveness of sins is included in justification by faith; while forgiveness may be taken to mean a restoration to right relationship, it need not. This is one of the very few places where Paul talks about forgiveness, and even here he does so only by way of a quotation that is presumably used because of its latter part. No one thinks that Paul rejects the idea of forgiveness; in itself, however, it does not go as far as justification.

4$^{9-25}$ THE PROGENY OF ABRAHAM:
PROMISE AND FAITH

⁹*Is this blessing pronounced only upon the circumcised, or also upon the uncircumcised? We say that faith was reckoned to Abraham as righteousness.* ¹⁰*How then was it reckoned to him? Was it before or after he had been circumcised? It was not after, but before he was circumcised.* ¹¹*He received circumcision as a sign or seal of the righteousness which he had by faith while he was still uncircumcised. The purpose was to make him the father of all who believe without being circumcised and who thus have righteousness reckoned to them,* ¹²*and likewise the father of the circumcised who are not merely circumcised but also follow the example of the faith which our father Abraham had before he was circumcised.*

¹³*The promise to Abraham and his descendants, that they should inherit the world, did not come through the law but through the righteousness of faith.* ¹⁴*If it is the adherents of the law who are to be the heirs, faith is null and the promise is void.* ¹⁵*For the law brings wrath, but where there is no law there is no transgression.*

¹⁶*That is why it depends on faith, in order that the promise may rest on grace and be guaranteed to all his descendants – not only to the adherents of the law but also to those who share the faith of Abraham, for he is the father of us all,* ¹⁷*as it is written, 'I have made you the father of many nations' – in the presence of the God in whom he believed, who gives life to the dead and calls into existence the things that do not exist.* ¹⁸*In hope he believed against hope, that he should become the father of many nations; as he had · been told, 'So shall your descendants be.'* ¹⁹*He did not weaken in faith when he considered his own body, which was as good as dead because he was about a hundred years old, or when he considered the barrenness of Sarah's womb.* ²⁰*No distrust made him waver concerning the promise of God, but he grew*

strong in his faith as he gave glory to God, ^{21}*fully convinced that God was able to do what he had promised.* ^{22}*That is why his faith was 'reckoned to him as righteousness.'* ^{23}*But the words, 'it was reckoned to him,' were written not for his sake alone,* ^{24}*but for ours also. It will be reckoned to us who believe in him that raised from the dead Jesus our Lord,* ^{25}*who was put to death for our trespasses and raised for our justification.*

Since the pronouncement of blessing on Abraham occurs in Gen. 15^6, and the institution of circumcision is not until Gen. 17$^{10ff.}$, it follows that circumcision is the seal of justification and not its cause. Therefore, runs the argument, if Abraham could be accepted without having been circumcised, so can Gentiles now. There is thus no case for requiring the circumcision of Gentiles before they can be regarded as full Christians (cf. Galatians, where this is a major theme; here it is comparatively incidental). What was good enough for Abraham as the archetypal Israelite is good enough for Gentile Christians.

Abraham's faith was met by God's promise that his descendants would be numerous enough to dominate the world. This connection between human faith and divine promise has nothing to do with the giving of the Law, and is certainly not conditional upon obedience to that Law. Everything rather rests on God's ability to create life out of death or nothingness. This is what God did for Abraham and Sarah who, naturally speaking, had no chance of becoming parents. This is also what he did in the case of Jesus Christ, whose crucifixion was turned into the triumph of the resurrection. Therefore, those who believe in Jesus Christ, and so echo the faith of Abraham, will inherit the promise of life, and find acceptance as the people of God.

‿◦‿

11
the father of all who believe without being circumcised: from a Jewish point of view Paul's argument is a radical one. Abraham was the father of Israel, 'the circumcision', yet Paul maintains that if the Genesis stories are taken in sequence he is at least as much the father of those who are uncircumcised but have faith. This is because Gen. 15^6 shows that it is his faith that is the crucial thing about him, so that his true children are those who share that faith. The time between Abraham and Christ is collapsed, and the faith Paul is talking about is faith in Jesus Christ.

12

not merely circumcised but also follow the example of the faith: to be a child of Abraham it is necessary to have faith, whether or not one is also circumcised. Those who are circumcised but do not believe (in Jesus Christ) are therefore not true children of Abraham. True Israel consists of those who have a faith like that of Abraham. In Paul's eyes justification by faith is not a newly contrived arrangement, but a very old one now brought to fulfilment and clarity in Christ.

our father Abraham: it is now evident that 'our' embraces not merely Jews, or even especially Jews, but all who have faith in Christ, whatever their race and lineage. In one sense this was not altogether new. In Israel Abraham was universally regarded as the national father, but in some circles he was also regarded as the father of proselytes (i.e. converts, see *Mekhilta* 101a on Ex. 22²¹; *b. Sukk.* 49b). For Paul, on the other hand, the order is almost reversed: he is the father of Gentiles who have faith more than of Israelites who do not. Yet the apostle never denies that Abraham was the father of unbelieving Jews, though such a denial cannot be far away when such a heavy stress is laid on faith as the sole criterion.

13

The promise to Abraham and his descendants: Gen. 15⁵; 22¹⁷ᶠ. In Gen. 17²²⁻²⁷ we have the story of the circumcision of Abraham and his extended family, and just before that the promise that he would be the father of a vast number is repeated (17¹⁶ᶠᶠ·). Paul concentrates exclusively on the connection of the promise with Abraham's faith (Gen. 5⁵, ⁶). To give attention to the connection between promise and circumcision in Gen. 17 would destroy his argument. We need to remember that for Paul Abraham's true descendants are those who have faith, whether circumcised or uncircumcised. On Abraham's promised descendants see also Gen. 12²; 13¹⁶; 18¹⁸.

inherit the world: in Genesis Abraham is promised not only innumerable descendants but also a *land* in which to live, the land of Canaan (Gen. 12¹, ⁵, ⁷; 13¹⁴⁻¹⁷; 17⁸). In some later writings the promised land becomes the world itself (e.g. Ecclus. 44²¹), and there may be an allusion here to that idea. Alternatively, 'the world' may be the world to come.

the righteousness of faith: it is not immediately obvious what this means. (a) It could be the righteousness that depends on faith, taking righteousness (*dikaiosunē*) to be equivalent to justification/acceptance (*dikaiōsis*). This is unlikely because it is not righteousness itself that is equivalent to justification, but the whole expression 'faith reckoned as righteousness', cf. v. 5. Moreover the meaning of *dikaiosunē* in both biblical and secular Greek tells against such an equivalence.

(*b*) It could be a somewhat cryptic reference to the fact that in Paul's view faith is the sufficient condition for life as God's people, cf. I Cor. 1^3; II Cor. 5^{21}; Phil. 3^9, and see below on Rom. 9^{30-32}.

(*c*) As a variant of (*b*), it could be a summary reference to 'faith reckoned as righteousness', cf. vv. 3, 5, 9.

The issue is far from clear, and both (*b*) and (*c*) are feasible. In any case, the place of this verse in the whole argument consists in its picking up the point of 3^{29}, and in its stressing that to be God's people and to inherit his promise to Abraham, what is needed is neither possession nor observance of the Law, but faith and faith alone. Once again, this means that Jews and Gentiles are on an equal footing.

14

faith is null and the promise void: if being God's people were based on possession and observance of the Law, then faith and promise would have no role to play. It would be a simple matter of fulfilling the condition of keeping the Law. In fact, however, faith is crucial, and the promise cannot be void, because it is *God's* promise. Therefore it follows that being the people of God does not depend on having and keeping the Law.

15

the law brings wrath: for 'wrath' (*orgē*) as the divine opposition to and judgment on sin, see above on 1^{18}; $2^{5, 8}$; 3^5. It is hardly likely that the Law is seen as the cause of wrath; rather, given the Law and given human sin, *orgē* is the inevitable divine reaction. Law is the condition (*conditio*, not *causa*) which makes it appropriate for sin to be met by the divine wrath.[h] There is here an allusion to a matter which will be expanded in $7^{7ff.}$, and referred to briefly in 5^{13}: the Law does not solve the problem of human sin, but exposes it in all its sharpness. It is only when there is a concrete command against which I sin that my sinful nature becomes evident to myself and to others. The Law thus brings potential sin into actuality, and reveals what is already there, but lying dormant for lack of opportunity. It thus 'brings wrath', because it identifies and makes concrete the sinfulness against which God reacts. This is

h See Hübner, *LPT*, pp. 79–80.

an important function for the Law, but it has nothing to do with making people heirs of God's future. That future is left undefined, but as the whole argument is about bringing life out of death, we may infer that eternal life with God is at issue (and cf. v. 13).

where there is no law there is no transgression: see the comments immediately above. Paul does not say that where there is no law there is no *sin*, but that there are no recognizable, definable *acts of sin*: transgressions are infringements of a norm, a law. This is therefore no more than a statement of plain fact.[i] Unfortunately it is a statement at partial odds with what Paul says elsewhere: see 5¹³, where there were sins 'from Adam to Moses'.[j]

16

That is why it depends on faith: it is possible that from here to the end of the chapter the meaning of 'faith' (*pistis*) shifts slightly, so that it no longer is simply response to God, but means something like 'confidence that God will do as he has promised'.[k]

As it stands, this statement seems to look back to v. 15: everything depends on faith because Law brings only wrath, through the actualization of transgressions. Yet it looks forward also to the second part of the verse, to the fact that the true children of Abraham are those who have faith, both Jews and Gentiles. It depends on faith not only, and perhaps not primarily, because Law does not work, but because faith is the only way by which *all* can have Abraham as their father.

17

'I have made you the father of many nations': LXX Gen. 17⁵ (and cf. 15⁵) is used to show from the Book of the Law itself, as Rom. 3³¹ promised, that God has made Abraham the father of the Gentiles as well as of Israel. This can be so only on the basis of faith, as Paul takes it for granted that Gentiles cannot be asked to keep the whole Torah. God's promise, the human response of faith, and the inclusion of the Gentiles within the people of God, all belong together as one whole. How this can be so is explained in the next part of the verse.

i Wilckens I, p. 271, thinks Paul may be saying that Gentiles are in the same situation, without the Law, that Abraham was in Gen. 15⁶, and like Abraham in Rom. 4⁶⁻⁸ they receive forgiveness so that they are free from transgressions. This seems unnecessarily complicated.
j On the Pauline logic see Räisänen, *PL*, p. 146 n. 91, and pp. 147f.
k Cf. Sanders, *PPJ*, p. 490.

who gives life to the dead and calls into existence the things that do not exist:
this is the centre of the 'promise-faith-Gentile-inclusion' entity, and
indeed of the whole section. 'Life from the dead' echoes the Genesis
story (Gen. 15-18) in which Abraham and Sarah are promised a child.
Humanly speaking this was ridiculous because of their age, and indeed
Abraham and Sarah themselves find it ridiculous, despite Gen. 15⁶
where Abraham believed God. Such a conception and birth really
would be 'life from the dead'. The phrase also echoes the second of the
Eighteen Benedictions, an ancient part of the synagogue service: 'Thou
quickenest the dead.'

In 'calls into existence the things that do not exist' we have the idea
of *creatio ex nihilo*, creation out of nothing. This idea is familiar to
Jewish tradition, for even in Gen. 1 God creates simply by his word,
and cf. II Macc. 7²⁸; Isa. 48¹³.[l] The idea of *new* creation is found in Paul
most notably in II Cor. 5¹⁷, cf. Eph. 2¹⁰. In the present verse the point
is that God has created life where there was no life, in giving a son to
Abraham and Sarah, in calling the Gentiles into his people, and we look
forward to v. 25 where he creates life in the resurrection of Jesus Christ.

18

In hope he believed against hope: in the Bible 'hope' (*elpis*) has two characteristics that are foreign not only to modern English usage but also, it
appears, to secular Greek usage of the time. For us, and for the Greeks,
there is an element of risk in hope. If I say 'I hope to come', I mean that
I wish to come, and probably think there is a good chance that I shall
come, but cannot be certain of coming. In the Bible, on the contrary,
hope has an element of security and even certainty. The ground of this
characteristic of biblical hope is the reliability of God and his promises:
that is its second notable characteristic.[m] People in the Bible may hope,
not because of a calculation of what is probable, nor as a form of wishful
thinking, but because God is who he is, and therefore provides confidence in facing the future. So Abraham's believing in hope means that
his confidence in God had a strongly forward thrust, because he could
rely on God's continuing to be the faithful God he had already been.
There was no need for doubt about the outcome (though of course this
is a somewhat idealized picture of Abraham, who in the Genesis story
did not exhibit such consistent confidence in God).

l See Cranfield I, pp. 244f., for further examples and discussion.
m On hope in the Bible see Turner, *Words*, pp. 213-15, and the references
there given.

'Hope against hope' thus means that while in human terms there was no ground for hope, there was ample ground in the promise of God.

19

He did not weaken in faith when he considered his own body . . .: even when he took a candid look at his own and Sarah's inability at their age to have a child, he maintained his confidence in God's promise that he would become the father of many descendants. He faced the facts, but still believed in the power of God to create life where there was no life.

However, some MSS of importance, especially from the Western family (including D and G), have 'he did *not* consider his own body . . .' so the whole verse runs, 'He did not weaken in faith because he did not consider his own body as good as dead, although he was about a hundred years old, or the barrenness of Sarah's womb.' This would mean that he refused to contemplate his own lack of potency, or Sarah's inability to conceive, but simply went on believing in God's promise. Perhaps the difference between including and omitting 'not' is not great, for either way he trusted in God rather than in human probabilities (cf. Murray, pp. 149f.).

Most scholars prefer to omit 'not', i.e. take the text implied in RSV, partly because that has the better MS support, partly because 'not' could have been inserted by a scribe in the mistaken belief that it made the point better, but also because the text without 'not' fits the context better. Abraham did not blind himself to the facts but still trusted in the promise of God, just as he 'hoped against hope' according to v. 18. We may accept the text as represented in RSV.

23

not for his sake alone: this long excursion into the story of Abraham has not been a digression, but a focussing of important matters about the people of God in Paul's own day. Abraham is not only the father of Israel, he is also the model for Christian faith, applicable equally to Jews and Gentiles. The faith that made him acceptable to God and the father of God's people, humanly speaking, is the same faith that will justify Jews and Gentiles alike.

24

It will be reckoned to us who believe . . .: Paul has now completed his elaborate parallel between Christians and Abraham, a parallel that is also a fulfilment. Promise, faith not works, and life from the dead, all apply equally to Christians and to Abraham, though for Christians life from the dead centres on the resurrection of Christ, and for Abraham on the conception of Isaac. The purpose of this parallel is to show that justification by faith for both Jews and Gentiles is no innovation. On the contrary it is as old as Abraham and has always been the way by which men and women were accepted as God's people. The true children of Abraham are those who live out this fulfilment-parallel by responding in faith to Jesus Christ. The statement of 3³¹, that justification teaching does not nullify but rather establishes the Law, has now been worked out in detail.

25

put to death for our trespasses and raised for our justification: it is possible that the first half of the statement looks back to the crucifixion of Christ to deal with human sin,[n] while the second half looks forward to the life that lies ahead of Christians, in parallel with the unexpected life promised to Abraham when 'he believed God'. This would explain the unusually strong link between justification and resurrection in this chapter, though cf. I Cor. 15¹⁷.

An alternative, and perhaps more likely, possibility is that the double statement is a formula which Paul is quoting.[o] It would then be a mistake to take the two halves of the statement as distinct: cross and resurrection together procure forgiveness and justification together. Thus, it is not that the cross deals with sins, and then the resurrection procures justification (and compare 3²⁴ᶠ·; 5⁹, ¹⁸, where justification is connected not with the resurrection but with the cross). In short the formulation is more rhetorical than providing precise distinctions.

    ★   ★   ★

Up to this point Paul has argued that as all peoples, Jewish and Gentile, are under the power of sin, so the way for all to escape is through faith in Jesus Christ, dying and rising. They become the people of God by that same faith, for escaping from sin's power and becoming God's people are not two different things, but one. Ch. 4 does not change the subject, but explores a particular angle of it.

n Echoing the common early Christian belief that the cross was a sacrifice for sin, cf. 5⁶⁻¹⁰, and M. Hengel, *The Atonement*, SCM Press and Fortress Press 1981, esp. Ch. 2.

o See Reumann, *Righteousness*, pp. 38f.; E. Käsemann, *Perspectives on Paul*, ET SCM Press and Fortress Press 1971, pp. 39f.; contrast the scepticism of Wilckens I, pp. 279f.

The next four chapters form a centre-piece, and though Paul did not write in chapters and verses, it is plausible that here he did pen (or dictate) four deliberately more or less distinct sections, each of which explores the change of life and circumstances consequent upon accepting the free grace of God and becoming his people. Until now the stress has been on the means of acceptance, faith not works. Now the other side of the solution to the problem of universal human sinfulness comes into the foreground. The righteousness of God is a power (1^{17}), which provides *a new dominion under which men and women may live.* Each of the four chapters, 5–8, closes with a similar formula, 'through Jesus Christ our Lord', see 5^{21}; 6^{23}; 7^{25}; 8^{39}. Each deals with a different aspect of the new life offered by God, though these aspects overlap and the division of subject-matter is only approximate. Chapter 5 is about freedom from wrath and condemnation; Chapter 6 deals with freedom from sin; Chapter 7 deals with freedom from Law; and Chapter 8 with freedom from flesh. All deal at some point with deliverance from death.

Commentators disagree about the place of 5^{1-11}. Some think it belongs to the explication of 3^{21-26}, so that the new section begins only at 5^{12}.[p] Others think that 5^{1-11} belongs with what follows and introduces it.[q] The disagreement is not sharp, and perhaps 5^{1-11} ought to be seen as the transition to the next part of the letter.

5^{1-11} FREEDOM FROM CONDEMNATION
AND WRATH

5 *Therefore, since we are justified by faith, we have peace with God through our Lord Jesus Christ.* [2]*Through him we have obtained access to this grace in which we stand, and we rejoice in our hope of sharing the glory of God.* [3]*More than that, we rejoice in our sufferings, knowing that suffering produces endurance,* [4]*and endurance produces character, and character produces hope,* [5]*and hope does not disappoint us, because God's love has been poured into our hearts through the Holy Spirit which has been given to us.*

[6]*While we were yet helpless, at the right time Christ died for the ungodly.* [7]*Why, one will hardly die for a righteous man – though perhaps for a good man one will dare even to die.* [8]*But God shows his love for us in that while we were yet sinners Christ died for us.* [9]*Since, therefore, we are now justified*

p See Wilckens I, pp. 181f.; Black, p. 81.
q See Robinson, p. 57; Cranfield I, pp. 252–4.

by his blood, much more shall we be saved by him from the wrath of God. ¹⁰*For if while we were enemies we were reconciled to God by the death of his Son, much more, now that we are reconciled, shall we be saved by his life.* ¹¹*Not only so, but we also rejoice in God through our Lord Jesus Christ, through whom we have now received our reconciliation.*

Those who already know freedom from God's condemnation of their sin because they have been justified by faith will at the Judgment enjoy freedom from God's wrath against sin. Past (and present) and future are closely linked. We have been justified, we have been re-conciled to God, and we do have peace with him, for Christ has died for us. On these bases we have the guarantee that at the End we shall be saved and shall share the glory of God. In other words we have hope. In the meantime there may well be suffering, but when rightly endured this suffering can lead to even greater confidence in God, because through it all we can be sure of God's love for us. This love has been demonstrated in his gift of the Holy Spirit (mentioned here for the first time in the letter as available to Christians). Whatever may befall them, therefore, Christians can have joy as well as peace, knowing that their destiny is secure. While the general drift of this passage is tolerably clear, many of its details are contentious.

ಐ

1

since we are justified by faith: this may refer back to the whole of 1^{18}–4^{25}, and certainly refers at least to the discussion from 3^{21} onwards.

we have peace with God: in biblical usage 'peace' (Greek *eirēnē*; Hebrew *shālôm*) tends to mean much more than the absence of conflict. It carries connotations of well-being, and can include health and prosperity as well as good order. Here it points forward to the idea of reconciliation in vv. 10–11. Peace may well include a subjective feeling of peace with God, but the focus is on the objective reality which would give grounds for the feeling.

The MSS differ about 'have' (*echomen*). The balance of the evidence is strongly in favour of *echōmen*, 'let us have', so that the sentence runs 'Since we are justified by faith, let us have peace with God.' Where the text behind RSV makes it a statement, this text makes it an exhortation, an exhortation to enter into the life obtained by justification. Despite the very strong MS evidence for *echōmen*, 'let us have',^{r} most texts and translations, like RSV, prefer the less well-attested *echomen*, 'we have', mainly for theological reasons. It is considered more likely that, given the argument that has been mounted since 3^{21}, Paul is proclaiming peace with God as an established fact, than exhorting people to have it.

The usual procedure of preferring the more difficult reading does not work well in this case, because the difference in sound was probably minimal between *echomen* and *echōmen*. If Paul dictated the letter, or if dictation was involved at a subsequent stage in the transmission of the letter, confusion would be understandable and even inevitable. In these circumstances it is impossible to reconstruct how one reading was changed into the other, and scholars tend to choose that reading which better fits the theological argument. So, despite the weight of the MSS, and despite the usual rule of choosing the reading which better explains the rise of the other, *echomen* ('we *have* peace') is usually adopted. It is worth noting that some of our most ancient MSS have marginal notes correcting 'let us have' to 'we have', which shows that the confusion is a very old one indeed.

2

access: as with entry to a monarch's audience chamber, where someone with influence is needed to introduce a suppliant, or as with entry to the sanctuary of God's presence, so believers are enabled to enter a state of grace through Christ, cf. Eph. 3^{12}. Some MSS add 'by faith': the textual evidence is quite evenly divided, though perhaps it is slightly stronger for omitting the words, as RSV does. It make very little difference to the sense whether they are included or not, for v. 1 has shown that in any case Paul sees faith as indispensable.

this grace in which we stand: for 'grace' (*charis*) see above on 1$^{1-7}$. It is primarily God's undeserved kindness, especially in saving his people. Here, however, the focus is slightly different. It is almost the condition in which those who have received God's kindness now exist, and is thus close in meaning to peace.

we rejoice: the Greek *kauchōmetha* is ambiguous, and could also mean 'let us rejoice'. If in v. 1 we read 'let us have peace', then presumably here

---

r Evidence which includes the MSS A, C, D, and the original hand in both B and ℵ.

we shall read 'let us rejoice'. If we have agreed with RSV in reading 'we have peace' in v. 1, then we shall probably read 'we rejoice' here. The verb is a strong one, so that something like 'exult', expressing a firm confidence, would be an appropriate translation.

in our hope of sharing the glory of God: on 'hope' see 4^{18}, and on 'glory' see 3^7. Because of the acceptance they already enjoy, believers have total confidence that in the world to come they will be in the presence of God himself, and will share in his blessedness and splendour. There may be an allusion to the belief that the glory of God, which human beings now lack (Rom. 3^{23}) but which was intended at the creation to be theirs, will be restored and more than restored to them at the End. See IQS 4^{23}, 'all the glory of Adam shall be theirs', i.e. theirs as the people of the covenant.[s]

3

we rejoice in our sufferings: 'rejoice' is again *kauchōmetha*, and could again be rendered 'let us rejoice'. As in v. 2, if we have read 'we have peace' in v. 1, we shall probably read 'we rejoice'. 'Sufferings' (*thlipsesin*) in the NT are very often specifically the sufferings as a result of persecution, and it is likely that here too they are the unpleasant experiences that Christians have to face simply because they are Christians (cf. Matt. 13^{21}/Mark 4^{17}; Matt. $24^{9, 21, 29}$; John 16^{33}; Acts 11^{19}; 20^{23}; Rom. 8^{35}; II Cor. 6^4). Such sufferings are to be recognized as precursors of the joys of heaven and the new world, cf. v. 2 and sharing the glory of God.

suffering produces endurance: Cranfield (I, p. 261) is doubtless right to say that this should not be taken as an unqualified statement. Suffering does not automatically produce endurance: sometimes it may instead produce bitterness, or even collapse. It is those who have the faith referred to in v. 1, and the hope referred to in v. 2, who will not collapse under suffering but will meet it with active fortitude.

4

endurance produces character: this is doubtless true, sometimes at least, but is it what Paul is saying? The word here translated 'character' is *dokimēn*, literally 'proved, tested'. The question is, what is tested? RSV implies that it is the believer's own character, but it seems more likely that it is

s Cf. CD 3.20; IQH 17.15, and R. Scroggs, *The Last Adam*, Blackwell 1966, pp. 23–31.

God's constant support that is tested and found adequate. We should then translate: 'endurance proves God's sustaining power'.

character produces hope: perhaps we should rather translate, bearing in mind the previous note, 'Finding in experience that God is an unfailing source of support, we are led to have confidence in the future.' On 'hope', *elpis*, see 4^{18}. It is not very plausible that Paul should say that our own character produces hope, since hope in the NT is confidence *in God* for the future. On the suggested interpretation of the verse, there is good reason to rejoice in sufferings, for they lead to this assurance for the future, based on God's character, not ours.

5
hope does not disappoint us: or rather, 'Hope does not let us down; we are not living in a fools' paradise' (cf. Ps. 22^5; 25$^{3,\ 20}$; 119^{116}, and see Wilckens I, p. 292). When the End comes, we shall not be left looking foolish, but shall be fully vindicated for our trust in God. See the comments on 'ashamed' in 1^{16}: the Greek verb is the same.

God's love: in the end, our assurance for the future expressed in vv. 2–5a rests on God's love, active through the Holy Spirit. This must surely be God's love for us, not ours for him, because of the spelling out of this love in vv. 6–8. Most recent commentators agree, despite the Western view, common since Augustine, that it is our love for God, at least partly because it seems to fit with 'poured out in our hearts'.^{t} Not only the context as a whole, but more particularly v. 8 with its stress on the demonstration of God's love for us, makes it difficult to suppose that in this verse Paul is talking about human love for God.

has been poured into our hearts: the language of pouring recalls Joel 2^{28}; Isa. 44^3. This need not mean a love which, as a result of the pouring, is now ours towards God or one another. It can just as well mean our experience of God's love to us. It is this love which forms the basis of our confidence for the future.

through the Holy Spirit: it is surprising to note that this is the first clear reference in the letter to the Holy Spirit, apart from 1^4. Nothing more is said at this stage: the Spirit is simply the means of the pouring out of

t On the history of interpretation see Wilckens I, pp. 300ff., who thinks, however, that it must be God's love for us.

God's love. Later, especially in Ch. 8, it will become clear that the Holy Spirit is the power in and under which the Christian community lives.

6

helpless: incapable of saving ourselves, of extricating ourselves from the situation so graphically described in $1^{18}-3^{20}$. Cf. also 8^3, and 6^{15-23} where men and women are seen as slaves of sin.

at the right time: although this may mean at the same time as when we were weak (see Wilckens I, p. 295), it is more likely to mean 'at he time of God's choosing', the time when he resolved to provide the solution to the human problem of sin.

Christ died for the ungodly: this illuminates the character of the divine love (v. 5). It is love for the unlovely, and is motivated only by the generous nature of God himself. In what precise sense Christ died *for* (*huper*) the ungodly is not self-evident in this passage (see the comments above on 3^{25} and 4^{25}). Clearly it was common early Christian teaching that in some sense Christ had died for men and women. More will be said on this when we discuss 5^{12-21} and Ch. 6. It is probable that the notion of vicarious suffering is present (cf. vv. 7–8), but its *modus operandi* is not explained. We may see a parallel in the way Judaism carried out the Temple sacrifices because they were divinely ordained, without trying to rationalize how they worked.

Elsewhere in Paul (notably in Rom. 6) Christ's death is *for* us in that it enables us to die *with* him, but there is no hint of that in this passage.

7

one will hardly die for a righteous man: it is not certain whether 'a righteous man' is the same as, or different from, 'a good man' in the second half of the verse. If they are not the same, then the difference is probably that a righteous person is upright but not necessarily attractive or lovable, while a good person is both upright and attractive. [u] At all events, Paul's point is that Christ dies for those who are neither righteous (*dikaios*) nor good (*agathos*).

though perhaps for a good man one will dare even to die: the translation is uncertain for two main reasons.

[u] The distinction is maintained by, among others, Sanday and Headlam, pp. 127f., and opposed by, among others, Murray, pp. 167f. Cranfield I, pp. 264f., thinks that a good man here is a benefactor.

(a) 'A good man' is literally 'for the good one' or even 'for the good cause' (*huper tou agathou*). It is therefore possible that 'a good man' is being contrasted not with a righteous man, nor being identified with one, but that a good cause is being contrasted with a righteous man. This is because we cannot be sure whether *tou agathou* is masculine or neuter.

(b) The word rendered 'even' (*tacha*) may alternatively be translated 'gladly/willingly', so that we could read 'for a good cause, or for a benefactor, one would readily dare to die'.

However these matters are decided, sinners fall into none of these categories, so that the love of Christ remains astonishing.

8

God shows his love: there are four things to note here.

(a) The character of the divine love is sharply accented. It arises purely from God himself, and not from the attractiveness or lovableness of its objects.

(b) Christ's dying is *God's* love in action. His love is God's love, and his action is God's action.

(c) Thus in vv. 5–8 the love of God that provides the basis of future hope of believers is precisely the love that goes to the lengths of dying.

(d) Once more Paul does not explain in what sense Christ dies *for* sinners.

9

justified by his blood: in effect this is a recapitulation of what was said in 3$^{\text{24f.}}$ about the link between cross and justification. See the comments on 4^{25}, where Paul appears to link justification with the resurrection rather than the cross. They can scarcely be alternative methods of justification; more probably death and resurrection, as a total event, bring about justification. This strengthens the suspicion that, even while using traditional statements about Christ's dying for our sins (as here, and e.g. in I Cor. 15^3), Paul is talking about believers' participation in the death and resurrection.[v]

The preposition translated 'by' is literally 'in' (*en*), which means it is possible that even here a participatory view of the cross is explicit. However, in the Greek of the period the use of *en* had become so flexible that such an argument is precarious.

v Cf. Rom. 6, and Whiteley, *Theology*, pp. 130–51, who argues that Paul saw the effect of the cross primarily in participatory terms.

saved by him from the wrath of God: see on 1^{16} for 'saved'. The readers' eyes are being firmly directed towards the End, the Judgment, when those who have already received justification will find that acceptance confirmed and that verdict endorsed. In the Greek 'the wrath' (*hē orgē*) stands without qualification; 'of God' has been added by the translators as clarification. In a way they are right, for it is *God's* wrath (cf. 1^{18}) that Paul is talking about, but the result of the insertion is to obscure the fact that the wrath is not an outburst of divine anger, but is the fact of judgment which is now seen within this life (1^{18-32}) and will be seen fully at the End (2^5).

10

while we were enemies we were reconciled to God: this verse is closely parallel to v. 9, but instead of the language of justification we have that of reconciliation. It can be debated whether or not justification and reconciliation are precisely the same in effect. [w] It is clear that the metaphorical field of the latter is that of human relationships. The enmity was on the human side, not the divine, and is now over. We are reconciled to God, not he to us, cf. II Cor. 5^{18-20}: 'God was in Christ reconciling the world to himself.' In this reconciliation the initiative is solely with God.

As in v. 9, there is a contrast between the future and the past/present, though here there is rather more emphasis on the present than in the previous verse. We were reconciled; we are now in a state of having been reconciled; we shall be saved.

saved by his life: the future reference is again important. Salvation is the consummation to which believers may look forward with confidence (though in 8^{24} we shall see that there is an anticipatory sense in which Christians are saved already). 'By his life' may refer to the resurrection, so that while the cross brings about reconciliation, the resurrection enables the reconciled to share in Christ's life, to be 'in Christ'. On the other hand the formulation may be rhetorical, as in 4^{25}: just as cross and resurrection are a unity, so are reconciliation and salvation. In view of the usual assignment of salvation to the End, it is more likely that the first view is right, and that we have a stress on the once-for-all nature of

---

w See for example Cranfield I, pp. 258, 267, who tends to want to distinguish them; contrast Sanders, *PPJ*, pp. 469–71, who does not. On reconciliation see R. P. Martin, *Reconciliation*, John Knox Press and Marshall, Morgan & Scott, 1981.

the cross on the one hand, and on the permanent nature of the resulting life on the other hand.

11

we rejoice in God: we come back to the present time, which is one of joy because reconciliation with God is an established fact. As in 3^{27}, the reason for joy (or exultation, or even boasting – it is the same Greek verb) lies strictly in God.

5^{12-21} CHRIST AND ADAM

^{12}*Therefore as sin came into the world through one man and death through sin, and so death spread to all men because all men sinned –* ^{13}*sin indeed was in the world before the law was given, but sin is not counted where there is no law.* ^{14}*Yet death reigned from Adam to Moses, even over those whose sins were not like the transgression of Adam, who was a type of the one who was to come.*

^{15}*But the free gift is not like the trespass. For if many died through one man's trespass, much more have the grace of God and the free gift in the grace of that one man Jesus Christ abounded for many.* ^{16}*And the free gift is not like the effect of that one man's sin. For the judgment following one trespass brought condemnation, but the free gift following many trespasses brings justification.* ^{17}*If, because of one man's trespass, death reigned through that one man, much more will those who receive the abundance of grace and the free gift of righteousness reign in life through the one man Jesus Christ.*

^{18}*Then as one man's trespass led to condemnation for all men, so one man's act of righteousness leads to acquittal and life for all men.* ^{19}*For as by one man's disobedience many were made sinners, so by one man's obedience many will be made righteous.* ^{20}*Law came in, to increase the trespass; but where sin increased, grace abounded all the more,* ^{21}*so that, as sin reigned in death, grace also might reign through righteousness to eternal life through Jesus Christ our Lord.*

This passage demands of the reader something of a change of mental gear. We move from the first person plural to the third person, and into a didactic mode from a more declamatory. Such changes in the epistles are not unusual. Another change is that the notion of two realms of power, already hinted at, now comes to the fore (see the Introduction, 9). Paul's apocalyptic framework betrays itself more clearly than hitherto, and we see that he envisages Christ as the bearer of the power of God in the New Age, one which replaces the era of Adam.[x] Much research has been done into the use of the figure of Adam in Judaism about this time, and into the use of similar 'Man' figures in the Hellenistic world. Although much remains uncertain, it is likely that Jewish speculations about Adam as Everyman, as the representative Man, at least facilitated Paul's use of Adam as a foil to Christ here.[y] In this passage Paul concentrates on the Adam of the Fall (Gen. 3), whereas in I Cor. 15 he focusses rather on the Adam of Gen. 1 and 2. The Christ on whom he concentrates is the obedient, earthly figure, whereas in I Cor. 15 he focusses on the exalted Lord. Adam and his story are taken seriously not just as what once happened, but even more as the picture of every human being. Similarly, the story of Christ is taken seriously as what happened, but even more as a picture of what can be the case for those who move from Adam's dominion to Christ's. The Adam story is the story of disobedience and death; the Christ story is the story of obedience and life. Both Adam and Christ represent realms in which one may live, and not just models to follow, for now and in the next three chapters Paul is dealing with life in alternative spheres of power. There is the sphere of sin, Adam, *sarx*/flesh, and disobedience. There is also the sphere of God, Christ, the Spirit, and obedience. Moreover, throughout this passage there is concern with life and death: the Adam-way leads to death as it always has, but the Christ-way leads to eternal life.

Paul's vision of Christ is not just of someone who can release men and women from guilt and give them a new and fruitful relationship to God. More than that, he sees Christ as inaugurating a new way of being human (his being the new Adam must mean at least that), a way that is free from oppressive powers like sin. This is no merely individual matter, but concerns the human race in its solidarity,

---

x See Käsemann, pp. 141f.; Beker, *Apostle*, pp. 83ff., 100 and *passim*.

y See Scroggs, *The Last Adam*, but also Ch. 3 of Davies, *PRJ*; Ch. 1 of C. K. Barrett, *From First Adam to Last*, A. & C. Black, 1962; Dunn, *Christology*, Ch. 4; A. J. M. Wedderburn, 'Adam in Paul's Letter to the Romans', pp. 413-30 of E. A. Livingstone (ed.), *Studia Biblica 1978 III*, JSOT Press 1980.

indeed its alternative solidarities, that of Adam/sin/death, and that of Christ/righteousness/life. Adam is the head and representative of the kingdom of Death, and Christ of the kingdom of Life.

All this is not something independent of the movement of history. On the contrary, the contrast includes an element of time, for the Christ-humanity has only become possible with the death and resurrection of Jesus. It is not surprising that within this historical movement in the passage the question of the Law recurs (vv. 13f., 20). Paul is hardly crystal clear, but it is likely that the main use he grants the Law is its role in exposing sin for what it is, but without doing anything to deal with it.

ငာ

12

sin came into the world through one man: we note at the outset (with Wilckens I, p. 314) that Adam is not the agent of sin, but the host of the active agent, which is sin itself. Paul assumes that his readers will know that 'one man' is Adam: certainly in contemporary Judaism there was the view that sin began through Adam and Eve, but there were other views, e.g. that it sprang from the lustful intercourse of angelic powers with human women recounted in Gen. 6, or that it was connected with the incident of the golden calf.[z] For his part, Paul assumes an Adamic explanation of some sort. So far, he is saying no more than that Adam gave sin its foothold within the human race, yet in saying this he once more implies (cf. 1[24, 26, 28]; 3[9]) that sin is more than something people do that is wrong. It is a power that can act, and once let loose, cannot easily be stopped.

death through sin: it is probably ordinary physical death that comes through sin.[a] Although the theme is not stressed in the Genesis story itself (though see Gen. 2[17]; 3[19]), it was common in Judaism to think of death as the consequence of sin, and Paul may even be alluding to

---

[z] See Wedderburn, 'Adam in Paul's Letter to the Romans', pp. 414f.; Cranfield I, p. 280.

[a] Cf. A. J. M. Wedderburn, 'The Theological Structure of Romans V.12', *NTS* 19, 3, 1973, pp. 339–54, at pp. 347f.; on 'death' in this chapter and later see C. Clifton Black II, 'Pauline Perspectives on Death in Romans 5–8', *JBL* 103. 3, 1984, pp. 413–33.

Wisdom 2^{24}, 'through the devil's envy death entered the world.'[b]

It is tempting to ask if Paul is talking about more than physical death, for in $8^{6, 10}$ he does speak of godless life as tantamount to death, since death could be thought of as being without God. It is just possible that in this passage we should hear overtones of that sort of death.

death spread to all men: Paul does not say that sin spread to all men, let alone that it was inherited by all men, with the result that all die. He begins at the other end, and works from the observable universality of death, back to the universality of sin.

because all men sinned: a notorious difficulty of translation lies behind these apparently straightforward words.[c] It is partly a question of whether two small Greek words *eph ho(i)* should be rendered 'because', and partly a question of the underlying thought in the passage. These two parts of the problem cannot easily be kept apart, but at the risk of distortion we shall take them in turn.

(*a*) The words *eph ho(i)* could mean not 'because' but 'in whom' or 'in which', so that possibly Paul is saying, as Augustine thought,[d] that all men and women sinned 'in Adam'. It is not easy to see what this would mean, but it is usually taken that in some sense all future human beings were already seminally in Adam, and therefore (*sic*) guilty of the sin of disobedience together with him. Even if it be held that this idea is coherent, there are formidable difficulties about it as an interpretation of this verse.

(i) The antecedent for 'whom', if it is Adam, is uncomfortably far back in the passage.

(ii) By analogy with 'in Adam' and 'in Christ' elsewhere, we should expect not *eph ho(i)* but *en ho(i)*.

(iii) In Paul *eph ho(i)* usually seems to mean 'in that' or simply 'because' (II Cor. 4^5; Phil. 3^{12}; 4^{10}), and the natural presumption is that it has that meaning here.

[b] See J. Cambier, 'Péchés des hommes et péché d'Adam en Rom. V.12', *NTS* 11, 1964–65, pp. 230f., and Romaniuk, 'Le livre de la Sagesse', pp. 504f. Further instances of the sin-death connection include Deut. $30^{17f.}$; Ecclus. 25^{24}; II (4) Esd. $7^{11f.}$; II *Apoc. Bar.* 17^3.

[c] For a fuller account of the possibilities see Cranfield I, pp. 274–9.

[d] However, Augustine considered more than one possible interpretation; the one he seems to have favoured, and the one usually associated with him, is set out in *Contra duas epistolas Pelagianorum* 4.4.7; *De civitate Dei* 13.14.

(b) Even if Paul is saying that all people sinned in Adam, it does not follow that they were seminally in him or sinned when he did. In the light of contemporary and near-contemporary Jewish thought, it is more likely that Adam is Everyman (and Everywoman), so that to say that Adam sinned is a way of saying that everybody sins. Everyone is his or her own Adam (cf. *II Apoc. Bar.* 54¹⁹) and cannot put the blame on the historical Adam. The suggestion has often been made in Christian history that sin and guilt can be inherited, much as blue eyes can be inherited, but this is implausible. It does not seem to have been a Jewish belief up to Paul's time,ᵉ and if he is now propounding it for the first time, he fails to make his point clearly. What is hereditary in this passage is *death*, and while death is the consequence of sin, each person after Adam (or even in Adam) deserves that consequence. Death comes not because of Adam's sin, seeing Adam as an individual only, but because of their own. Moreover, Paul is drawing a parallel between Adam and Christ and their respective effects, and he certainly does not say that righteousness passes automatically or genetically from Christ to his people. It is therefore unlikely that he is saying that sin passes from Adam, seen as an individual, to all people automatically, or genetically, or by sexual transmission. Finally, we saw in (a) that the meaning of *eph ho(i)* tells against the idea of transmission.

In this verse, then, Paul is saying that death did indeed spread to all people, in so far as they, like Adam (or even in Adam, if Adam is Everyman), sinned. In fact they do all sin, and naturally therefore they all die. Adam started the infection in the human race, and with it the penalty of death; to that extent there is an element of transmission and even determinism. On the other hand men and women are not absolved of responsibility, for they too have voluntarily embraced sinfulness. In short we have here a mixture of fate and guilt.ᶠ

13

sin is not counted where there is no law: counted by whom? This is another instance of the divine passive, where the unstated agent of a verb in the passive is normally to be understood as God. It is *God* who does not count sin where there is no Law. The reference to Moses in the next verse makes it obvious that 'Law' here means, as usual, the Torah, the Mosaic Law, which was not given until long after Adam. There was

---

e See Wedderburn, 'Theological Structure of Romans V.12', pp. 341f.

f See Hübner, *LPT*, p. 132, and the carefully nuanced treatment of Wedderburn, 'Theological Structure of Romans V.12'.

sin in the world in the interim, but it could not be identified until there was a norm, a law, against which human behaviour could be measured. Law is given this role in 7^8, and probably also in 5^{20}. Even in the Adam story, Adam may have been potentially rebellious, but he could not actually rebel until there was a concrete command to disobey. It is not that sin does not matter where there is no law, but simply that it cannot be identified and made concrete.

14

death reigned from Adam to Moses: as death is the consequence of sin, its presence between Adam and the giving of the Law (for which 'Moses' is shorthand) shows that sin must also have been present even if it could not be explicitly identified.

those whose sins were not like the transgression of Adam: i.e. those whose sins were not in response to a definite command or prohibition.

a type of the one to come: a good deal is here condensed.

(*a*) It is possible (Robinson, p. 65) that we should translate 'a type of what was to come', i.e. Adam was a type or prototype of the sinning of the future.

(*b*) It is more usual, in the light of the Adam–Christ contrast in the passage, to see 'the one to come' as Christ. It may have been a messianic designation (cf. Matt. 11^3; Luke 7^{20}), or simply a reference to Jesus as the coming Man, the Last Adam (I Cor. 15^{45}).

(*c*) Whether as Messiah or Last Adam, Christ would bring in the new Age. Correspondingly, Adam stands as the head of the old Age, representing sin and death in what now follows. Throughout the passage Paul's primary focus is on Christ, with Adam brought in as a foil to him. It is not primarily on Adam, with Christ brought in as fulfilment and antithesis.[g] This becomes especially evident in vv. 17, 21. Of the two ages, it is the new that is the main object of attention.

(*d*) 'Type' (*tupos*) usually refers to a correspondence in characteristics or historical pattern between two realities, with one as the enhancement or fulfilment of the other. The interpretation of both is thereby enriched. To take a twentieth-century parallel, during the Battle of Britain reference was sometimes made to 'singeing Hitler's beard', an allusion to the saying about singeing the king of Spain's beard at the time of the Armada. In this passage the correspondence is not simple

g See Wilckens I, p. 322; Ziesler, *PC*, pp. 50–4.

but antithetical, between the primal and the end times, between the
first man and the new or last Man, between the old and the new regimes
and spheres of power. It is as much reversal as fulfilment.

15

the free gift is not like the trespass: the free gift must be justification (see
the whole argument since 3²¹). The trespass is Adam's disobedience.
These two are not in equilibrium, for grace far outweighs sin, and in
any case they lead in opposite directions, one to life and the other to
death.

many: in this passage, 'many' is in contrast to 'one' (Adam or Christ),
not in opposition to 'all', as if only some were affected by Adam's sin
and Christ's grace. In the case of Adam's trespass, the many are in fact
all, but we cannot say the same about the grace of Christ, though we
cannot deny it either. Paul is not discussing the question whether all men
and women will ultimately receive grace.

16

the judgment following one trespass brought condemnation: but how did it
do so? This is where it becomes important not to see Adam as simply
an individual, unless we are to suppose that all men and women are
condemned for what Adam did, in something like the Augustinian
sense (see above on v. 12). The morality of that is worse than doubtful,
and we saw that in any case it does not appear to have been an idea
current at the time. On the contrary, Adam is a representative figure,
Everyman and Everywoman, whose story is the story of all who remain in his sort of humanity, the sphere of sin and death (see again the
Introduction, 9). For such people, condemnation is the only possible
verdict.

the free gift following many trespasses brings justification: the free gift is that
grace of God which entered the world in the person of Jesus Christ.
What Paul finds so remarkable is that while one sin brings condemna-
tion, the great mass of sin which he has delineated in 1¹⁸–3²⁰ is met by
God's mercy. So we have justification: the word here is *dikaiōma*, which
can have more than one meaning (cf. v. 18), but is here in parallel with
katakrima, condemnation, and so means God's justification, his free
acceptance or acquittal.

17

death reigned through that one man: Adam's infringement of the known will of God incurred the sentence of death (Gen. 3^{19}), and as Adam is Humanity, it naturally follows that death is universal, cf. v. 12. However, it is not just that Adam as an individual started the whole nexus between sin and death, though Paul does appear to assume that death is universal because of Adam's sin. It is further that every man and every woman experiences afresh the nexus of sin with death. Such a strict connection is strange in modern ears, and we may wonder how far Paul himself would push it. After all, even Christ was not immortal, but had to die, even if not of natural causes.

death reigned: we again see that we are dealing with powers, cf. Introduction, 9.[h]

the free gift of righteousness: in the first instance *dikaiosunē* ('righteousness') may well be God's saving righteousness which leads to justification (*dikaiōma*, v. 16, and cf. 3^{21-26}; 5^{6-9}). Yet because of the consequent 'reigning in life' (see below) it is possible that there is the further connotation that those who have faith share in God's righteousness, and thus begin to live in a manner befitting people who reign. Such reigning would obviously include being victorious over sin.

will . . . reign in life: those who allow themselves to be placed under the sovereignty of Christ, and who accept what he graciously offers, will enjoy a life that is tantamount to reigning. They reign because he reigns; it is not an independent sovereignty but a sharing of his. Yet by speaking not of being reigned over by Christ but of active reigning, Paul points to freedom from the powers of sin and death that cripple human existence.

'Life' is not defined, but it presumably includes life here and hereafter. It is not just a matter of the past's having been wiped clean and sins' having been forgiven. The future tense indicates that such life properly belongs to the future, though the present reception of justification points to a future already partly realized.

[h] Räisänen, *PL*, pp. 99–100, thinks that the power-language is merely metaphorical. Yet it is power-language that Paul finds appropriate for his metaphorical field, conveying the idea of helplessness. Death, for example, is inescapable.

18

one man's trespass led to condemnation for all men: this recapitulates v. 17a, and the Everyman figure is again implicit. If I remain within his realm, Adam's story is my story, but there is an alternative, as the other half of the verse shows.

one man's act of righteousness leads to acquittal and life for all men: if I enter his realm, Christ's story is my story. This recapitulates v. 17b. Paul does not specify Christ's act of righteousness,[i] but in the light of vv. 6, 8 it must be least primarily his death on the cross (cf. his 'obedience' in v. 19, and Phil. 2⁸).

'Acquittal and life' is literally 'justification of life' (*dikaiōsin zōēs*). This either means justification that leads to life, or justification that is the judicial sentence which consists in 'life', as opposed to death. The first is to be preferred on balance, as part of the thrust of the passage is the overcoming of death. Justification then inaugurates the situation in which life, here and hereafter (v. 17), becomes possible.

Ought we to take 'for all men' strictly? Is Paul saying that all people, without exception, will be justified and find life? In view of other passages where he speaks of those who are perishing (e.g. Rom. 2¹²; I Cor. 10⁶⁻¹²), we should probably take him to be talking not about all men and women without qualification, but about all people in Christ.[j] However, this is not to deny that acquittal and life are intended to be available to all.

19

many were made sinners: for 'many' see on v. 15. If we ask how the many/all were made sinners, we must look back to v. 12: Adam is the starting-point of the infection, yet the infection has been voluntarily accepted by all his successors. Once again we see that Adam is both an individual and a representative figure, Everyman.

many will be made righteous: it may be repeated that the question of how many human beings will be saved in the long run (i.e. whether here 'many' is to be equated with 'all') is not the present topic. We may

---

i The word is *dikaiōma*, rendered 'justification' in v. 16. It can hardly mean that here, cf. Cranfield I, p. 289, especially because of the parallel with 'trespass' (*paraptōma*) in v. 18a. See also Ziesler, *Meaning*, pp. 199, 209.

j See, however, Sanders, *PPJ*, p. 473, who thinks that Paul has been carried away by his own analogy.

suspect that, if pressed, Paul would have found 'many' more accurate than 'all', but this is no more than a suspicion.

Some think we should take 'righteous' (*dikaioi*) in a strictly forensic or relational sense, to mean 'justified' accepted, acquitted',[k] not least because throughout the passage there is a stress on justification and the absence of condemnation. Yet 'righteous' is in parallel with 'sinners', and the latter really are sinners who do wrong things, not just those who have the status of sinners. It seems likely, therefore, that in this verse we have a complete reversal: the many will find a whole new life, not just a new status, a new life that reverses the spread of sin, cf. v. 12.[l]

20

Law came in: it was not always there, though the divine will had been there from the beginning, and was rejected by Adam (v. 14). In this verse and the following one, it is clear that God is seen as having a strategy of salvation.

to increase the trespass: this dogmatic statement is not explained.[m] Paul does not say that the Law increases sin, but rather trespass, suggesting that we should take it that the Law turns potential or implicit sinfulness into concrete acts of sin, i.e. into trespasses (cf. v. 13). He does not say that Law caused sin to increase, just that where it did increase, grace increased more. Thus while it is possible that in this verse he says that Law increases sin (and not just concrete transgression), we cannot be sure that he does. The main thing, however, is that the Law does not contribute to salvation; it rather shows up the need for it. Only through God's grace can the human problem be solved (see also v. 21).

21

grace also might reign: this climactic and summary verse adds little that is new, but underlines that we are dealing with lordships, that of sin/death and that of grace/righteousness (and see again Introduction, 9). The latter leads to life which is eternal, going beyond the present Age and

---

k Cf. Murray, pp. 205f.; Barrett, p. 117.

l See Ziesler, *Meaning*, p. 199.

m See Robinson, pp. 37, 66; Sanders, *PLJP*, p. 71. Wilckens I, p. 329, thinks that Law gives its definitive form to the connection between sin and death, so that only when Law comes does sin achieve its final annihilating power. For a succinct treatment of the relation of Law to sin in Paul see Räisänen, *PL*, pp. 141–9.

the present existence. It is this reign of grace to which the whole passage leads.

through Jesus Christ our Lord: this is not just a neat semi-liturgical way of ending an important section of the letter. It is the key to what is at stake: a choice between lordships. All that has been said in the section about grace depends on allowing Jesus Christ to be Lord, upon abandoning the old realm of Adam/sin/death, and entering the sphere of God's rule and power in Christ. How one is abandoned and the other entered is the subject of the next section.

6 *What shall we say then? Are we to continue in sin that grace may abound?* ²*By no means! How can we who died to sin still live in it?* ³*Do you not know that all of us who have been baptized into Christ Jesus were baptized into his death?* ⁴*We were buried therefore with him by baptism into death, so that as Christ was raised from the dead by the glory of the Father, we too might walk in newness of life.*

⁵*For if we have been united with him in a death like this, we shall certainly be united with him in a resurrection like his.* ⁶*We know that our old self was crucified with him so that the sinful body might be destroyed, and we might no longer be enslaved to sin.* ⁷*For he who has died is freed from sin.* ⁸*But if we have died with Christ, we believe that we shall also live with him.* ⁹*For we know that Christ being raised from the dead will never die again; death no longer has dominion over him.* ¹⁰*The death he died he died to sin, once for all, but the life he lives he lives to God.* ¹¹*So you must consider yourselves dead to sin and alive to God in Christ Jesus.*

¹²*Let not sin therefore reign in your mortal bodies, to make you obey their passions.* ¹³*Do not yield your members to sin as instruments of wickedness, but yield yourselves to God as men who have been brought from death to life, and your members to God as instruments of righteousness.* ¹⁴*For sin will have no dominion over you, since your are not under law but under grace.*

The transition from the rule of Adam/sin to the rule of Christ is not a smooth one. It requires a death, especially to sin. Since the crucifixion of Christ, cf. 5^{6-8}, death has taken on a new nuance.[n] It no longer stands simply for the result of condemnation, but now constitutes the gateway to life. When shared in by the believer, Christ's death is liberating. Justification by faith is more far-reaching than may at first have appeared, and any who have thought that it undercut morality have misunderstood it completely. The faith-response required in justification is in fact a dying, dramatically conveyed in baptism when the person being baptized goes under the water as an act of sharing in the death of Christ. It is also an entry into new life which the person being baptized shares with Christ, who rose not from the water but the from the grave. Yet while Christ lives already, the believer's life lies essentially in the future. On the other hand Christians are to be aware of themselves as people who already live, and belong to that future.

There has been a vast amount of discussion about the background to and the meaning of Paul's language of dying and rising with Christ. It has been maintained that it is a Christianized version of a mystery religions idea, in which the initiate, perhaps by ceremonial washings and/or sharing in a sacred meal, participates in the death and rebirth of the cult hero or heroine. This participation secures freedom from controlling powers, such as astrological forces, and promises a life after death that is no mere shadowy survival but an enrichment. It is difficult to believe that such parellels never occurred to Paul's readers, but it is unwise to make too much of them, for they are not as close as some have thought.[o] Paul's dying-and-rising teaching centres not on a mythical figure, but on an historical one of the very recent past. Moreover his piety in general is not one of mystical absorption, and in any case we know too little of how widespread and

[n] On the varying meaning of death in this passage, see again Black, 'Pauline Perspectives on Death in Romans 5–8', esp. pp. 421–4.

[o] The literature on the subject is enormous. Mention may here be made only of a little of it, including G. Wagner, *Pauline Baptism and the Pagan Mysteries*, Oliver & Boyd 1967, who finds little connection, perhaps too little; see U. Schnelle, *Gerechtigkeit und Christusgegenwart*, Göttingen: Vandenhoeck & Ruprecht 1983, pp. 77f., 208f. n. 418. See also R. C. Tannehill, *Dying and Rising with Christ*, Berlin: Töpelmann Verlag 1967, pp. 7–43; R. Schackenburg, *Baptism in the Thought of Saint Paul*, Blackwell 1964, Ch. 2; Wilckens II, pp. 57–9.

well-known the mysteries were in his day. More importantly, he talks not of death and rebirth, but of death and *resurrection*, and this puts the material in this chapter into the category of eschatology: resurrection was seen as a sign of the New Age. We are therefore not in the Hellenistic realm of sharing in the fate of a cult hero, but in a Jewish realm where the shift of the ages is taking place and where the New Adam is displacing the old.[p] To die and rise with Christ is thus to move from the Old to the New Age, to come to live in the power of that New Age, so that one is no longer under the power of sin and no longer 'in Adam'.

If one is no longer under sin's power, it is anomalous to go on sinning. The question with which the chapter begins, 'Are we to continue in sin . . .?' is thus seen to be a foolish one. It is nonsense to suppose that justification by faith enables people to sit loose to morality; on the contrary, justification entails a transfer from one age to another, from death to life, from sin to righteousness.

ɞɔ

I

What shall we say then?: Paul continues to use the device of debate with an imaginary opponent, used spasmodically since 2^1.

Are we to continue in sin that grace may abound?: cf. 3^8, which shows that this is a real charge made against Paul's teaching. It may have been a proposal seriously made by some Christians with amoral and libertine tendencies, or it may be an attempt by opponents to show the consequences of Paul's view. In the light of 3^8, the latter seems more likely, and the objection runs something like this: if acceptance with God as his people, and remaining that people, depend solely on faith in Christ, then manner of life becomes unimportant and sin even becomes good, in that it gives ever more scope to the divine grace.

p In addition to the references in the preceding note, see the seminal work of A. Schweitzer, *The Mysticism of Paul the Apostle*, ET A. & C. Black 1931, Ch. 6, and note Schnelle, *Gerechtigkeit und Christusgegenwart*, pp. 206f. n. 397, for evidence that Paul's 'with Christ' language tends to refer to sharing in his resurrection, e.g. I Thess. 4^{14}; II Cor. 4^{14}; see also Käsemann, pp. 161f.

2

By no means!: on the strength of the expression (*mē genoito*) see on 3^4. The idea is indignantly repudiated.

How can we who died to sin still live in it?: Paul is not suggesting that Christians are sinless, as the exhortatory material in the chapter demonstrates. Sinless people do not need to be encouraged to be good. Rather, people live either under the power of sin or under that of God, and those who have died to sin cannot any longer be dominated by it.

'Died' (*apethanomen*) is an aorist verb, which means that it refers to a definite event. This is reinforced almost at once by the talk about baptism, also a definite event. Those who have become Christians and have been baptized have died to sin. '*To* sin' may indicate possession, so that 'died to sin' means release from possession by sin. In any case there is complete separation. q

3

Do you not know: similar expressions sometimes introduce traditional material, and this is what we may have in vv. 3–4. r At any rate Paul expects his readers to know the significance of their baptism.

baptized into Christ Jesus: this is commonly taken to be equivalent to baptism 'into the name of Christ', thus referring to belonging to Christ as Lord, and being marked with his name as his property. It is possible, however, that the more direct expression here indicates entry into the new Adam, the people of the New Age. There is a good case for seeing the two-Adams contrast of 5^{12-21} as still operating in the first part of this chapter. s

baptized into his death: the only Christ to whom one can belong is the Christ who died. To belong to him must therefore mean to share his

q See Wilckens II. pp. 10f.; Schnelle, *Gerechtigkeit und Christusgegenwart*, p. 75. One should note, however, the careful treatment by C. F. D. Moule, 'A Note on Certain Datives', in A. Descamps and A. de Halleux, *Mélanges Bibliques (en hommage au R. P. Béda Rigaux)*, Gembloux: Duculot 1970, pp. 367–75.

r For the debate see Schnelle, *Gerechtigkeit und Christusgegenwart*, pp. 75f., 204f.

s See J. D. G. Dunn, *Baptism in the Holy Spirit*, SCM Press 1970, pp. 140f. On the equivalence of baptism into Christ and baptism into the name of Christ, see Cranfield I, p. 301; Wilckens II, pp. 11, 48–50.

death (and his resurrection too, but that is not at issue at the moment). Of course there has been only one relevant literal, physical death, that of Christ himself. The physical deaths of Christians are not of interest at this point. So what does baptism into Christ's death mean? 'Into his death' cannot have the same connotations of possession that 'into Christ Jesus' has. There may be a reference to the material in the Gospels which speaks of suffering with and for the sake of Jesus, like 'being baptized with the baptism with which I am baptized' (Mark 10[38]), which clearly looks forward to his death (cf. Luke 12[50]). There may also be a reference to the practice of immersion in baptism (cf. v. 4), which conveys the idea of total death to the old life and the old belonging.[t] At all events belonging to Christ involves dying, not in the meantime a physical dying, but a dying to all that has controlled the old self and in particular to sin.

4

buried therefore with him by baptism into death: it is virtually certain that RSV is correct, and that 'into death' goes with 'baptism' and not with 'buried'. The picture is that of going down into the water in baptism and of being covered by it, thus representing and conveying death and burial. The old is left behind as finally as the world is left behind by someone who has been buried, cf. Col. 2[11-12] and especially I Cor. 15[3-4]. In the latter the stress is on the past event of Christ's death and burial, while here it is at least as much on the believer's participation in that event.

as Christ was raised from the dead by the glory of the Father, we too might walk in newness of life: if one world is lost, another immediately replaces it. We have noted that the stress in this passage on resurrection points to the shift of the Ages, to eschatology. Christ's death consequently not only represents but brings about the end of the Old Age, the old world, and his resurrection not only represents but brings about the beginning of the New Age, the new world. Those who die and rise with him are those who have joined him in leaving the Old Age and embracing the New. So Christ's death leads to life, not only for himself but also for those who belong to him, those who respond to him in faith (cf. 7[6]).

'Walk' is a common biblical term for the ordinary conduct of life. The ordinary life of those who belong to Christ is altogether new, and

t See Wilckens II, pp. 10f., 50, 60–2; G. R. Beasley-Murray, *Baptism in the New Testament*, Macmillan 1962, pp. 129–31. See also below on v. 5.

therefore hardly ordinary at all. We note that Paul does not say that Christ rose, but that he was raised (implicitly, by God); as usual it is not something he did, but something achieved through him by God. God did it by his 'glory': the presence, power, and greatness of God are to be discerned in the event.[u] Paul does not say whether this new life is here and now, or in the future (but see below on vv. 5, 8, 11). Here he says only that the purpose of dying with Christ in baptism is that Christians should enjoy risen life with him.

5

united with him in a death like his: 'united' is literally 'grafted', 'become vitally joined' (*sumphutoi*), but it would be unwise to press the etymology. 'United' is adequate as a translation. It is not easy to be precise about the meaning of 'a death like his'. In one sense, the believer's death with Christ is not at all like his, for unlike him the believer does not yet literally die. Moreover, while the believer dies to his or her own sin, there is no suggestion that Christ did that. If there are such clear points of dissimilarity between Christ's death and believers' death with him, in what does the similarity lie? Any answer must be tentative, but two things may be said.

(*a*) The believer's death in baptism is an end to the old life, just as the cross represents the end of the old world. This is reinforced by the fact that sometimes in the primitive church the cross was seen as a baptism (Luke 12^{50}).

(*b*) The baptism of the believer represents a working out in individual terms of that shift of the ages which took place with the cross and resurrection of Christ.

If we thus put together the baptismal imagery and the eschatological assumptions about the cross, it does make sense to talk about believers' undergoing a 'death like his', despite the patent differences.

we shall certainly be united with him in a resurrection like his: Christ has already been raised from the dead, but the resurrection of believers is still in the future. Paul does *not* say that they have already been raised, nor that they already enjoy the life of heaven. See I Cor. 15^{20} for the temporal priority of Christ's resurrection, 'the first fruits'. Christians may indeed be assured of the life of heaven, and belong to it and the New Age in principle, but until the consummation this can only be a

u For 'glory' (*doxa*) see above on 1^{23}, and for the biblical association of it with power see Cranfield I, pp. 304f.

matter of anticipation. They belong to the future but they still live in the present. This is why they still need to be exhorted (vv. 12–14), but it is also why they can be expected to respond to the exhortation. They still need to be reminded to resist sin's control, yet it is not impossible now for them to elude that control. Contrast 3^9, where without Christ escaping sin is not possible.

6

our old self was crucified with him: literally, 'our old man' (*anthrōpos*), so that a reference back to the Adam figure of 5^{12-21} is quite possible. The old Adam is no more. Characteristically, Paul does not see the effect of the cross on men and women as from outside, and certainly not by some transaction which averts punishment. Rather is it something into which they enter and share,[v] though there are echoes in the letters of the common early view of the death of Christ as a sacrifice (cf. I Cor. 15^3 for example, and see above on 5^6). The tense of 'crucified' is aorist, indicating a definite past event; doubtless the act of baptism is what is meant.

that the sinful body might be destroyed: does this mean the physical as the gateway of evil, so that it is in our physicality that sin is especially active? If 'body' (*sōma*) always denotes the physical, then that is the meaning to be presumed here.[w] It is more usual to take *sōma* in this verse to mean the whole person, neither excluding nor concentrating solely on the physical.[x] It is unlikely that Paul is saying that the physical body is the special location and gateway of sin; it is probable therefore that 'the sinful body' is the sinful person as a whole.

(*a*) 'The works of the flesh' in Gal. 5^{19-21} include physical sins, but also include religious sins like idolatry, and concentrate on social sins, such as envy. In that passage it is the whole person, within a network of social, physical and religious relationships, that is wrong, and there is at least a presumption that the same is true here.

(*b*) Here, it is the whole person, the old man/*anthropos*, v. 6a, that has

v See Sanders, *PPJ*, pp. 463–8 for a useful discussion of the Pauline emphasis.

w See R. H. Gundry, *Sōma in Biblical Theology*, SNTSMS 29, CUP 1976, pp. 39, 57–8, who thinks that here Paul refers to the future death of the physical body.

x So, e.g. Cranfield I, p. 309; Wilckens II, pp. 16–17. Bruce, p. 139, rightly stresses that it is no merely individual matter, and that 'sinful body' refers to human solidarity in sin, cf. also and notably Käsemann, pp. 169, 326–8.

been under the control of sin; it is natural to suppose that in this second part of the same verse Paul is also talking about the whole person.

(c) In LXX *sōma* does indeed usually mean the physical body, but it can refer to the whole person without any special emphasis on the physical, though the latter is never excluded.[y] Other Pauline passages where this more general meaning of *sōma* is likely include Rom. 12^1.

(d) The subject of this passage is not the dissolution of the physical body, but the change in lordship and direction of the whole person. What must die is not just the person's physical side, but the whole self that has hitherto existed. The RSV translation of *anthrōpos* by 'self' in v. 6a brings this out well. It could even be argued that since Paul is looking forward to continuing life in this world (see the last clause of v. 6, and vv. 7–8), the physical aspect must be decidedly muted.

It seems, therefore, that we ought to deny any special emphasis on the physical as the seat of evil in this verse. We should think rather of the person as embroiled in the relationships and dominations of this world and this age.

no longer be enslaved to sin: this is the outcome of dying with Christ, a life freed from sin's reign. We recall that sin is not just something wrong which we do, nor just a wrong disposition of the person, but enslavement. Paul now sees the Christian as enjoying life rather in the power of Christ, within the humanity of Christ, and no longer within the humanity of Adam (cf. 5$^{12-21}$).

7

he who has died is freed from sin: literally, 'he who has died has been justified from sin'. The RSV translation does not quite bring out the nuance provided by the use of 'justify' (*dikaioō*, cf. on 2^{13} and 3^{20}). In the context we might have expected deliverance language, but instead there is the language of acquittal/acceptance. We must therefore allow for the possibility that more is being said than that when we are dead we are free from sin's power. The Rabbinic near-parallels in *Shab.* 30a, 151b that when a man is dead he is freed from the Law and the commandments have more bearing on Rom. 7$^{1-6}$ than on this passage.[z] The idea that death brings atonement for sin (*Sifre* Num. 112 on 15^{31}) is more relevant, but does not take account of the fact that it is sin as a power with which we are chiefly concerned at this point.

[y] So Ziesler, 'SOMA in the Septuagint', *NT* 25. 2, 1983, pp. 133–45.
[z] See Wilckens II, p. 17, for further Rabbinic material.

The choice of verb is unexpected, but the explanation may be that justification-language is regularly transfer-language, transfer from not being God's people to being his people, and also that Paul sees the human problem as double-edged, involving both guilt and powerlessness. Here Paul says that those who die with Christ are justified: nothing further is required of them. At the same time, to be justified and to die with Christ is to be released from one dominion and to enter another. It is to be released from sin and to enter the power of God in Christ. Justification language is thus not inappropriate here, for it is a reminder that we are dealing with one process, not two separate ones. The expression is so condensed as almost to be a mixing of metaphors, but the point is simple enough. Justification involves a transfer of powers, just as dying with Christ involves acceptance/acquittal, for at root the two are one.[a]

If Paul is consciously echoing some Rabbinic statements (and that is by no means certain), there is nonetheless a major difference in that the death he talks about is the death with Christ now, not the death that comes at the end of natural life. This is made plain by v. 8a.

8

we shall also live with him: Paul appears to draw back from saying that Christians have not only died with Christ but have also risen with him. Logic may seems to demand the latter, yet while Christ has died and *has* risen (vv. 9–10), Christians have died and *will* rise. Their present life is not yet risen life, though v. 11 shows that in their self-understanding they are to keep their risen destiny firmly in mind. The character of their present life is for the moment left undefined, but the rest of the chapter shows that it is to consist in a struggle to live out in practice the freedom for God and for righteousness that is rightly theirs. Although their resurrection is still future, its effect is to be evident in the present time.

9

Christ being raised from the dead will never die again: this is unlike the case with believers, who have died with Christ but must still face natural death. It is the definitiveness of Christ's resurrection that is the ground of hope for Christians who die with him (v. 8). This resurrection lasts for ever, unlike the resuscitation of someone, like Lazarus in John 11, who must still die at some future time.

a Cf. Sanders, *PLJP*, p. 10; Cranfield I, p. 311.

10

he died to sin: the force of this expression is not easy to determine. The fundamental problem is the dative, *'to sin'.* As in v. 2, this is probably a dative of possession, so that the clause as a whole is saying that in his death Christ ended the grip of sin on human beings generally.

once for all: this gives some indication of how Christ's death ended sin's grip, without also saying that Jesus himself was sinful. The point is that the death was not only a personal but also an eschatological event. That is, it ended not only the earthly life of Jesus of Nazareth, but also the Old Age of the human race. It was literally the end of an era, the end of the powers and goals of that era. Most notably, it ended sin's possession and domination of men and women. On this eschatological-power language, see the introduction to this section, and Introduction, 9.

the life he lives he lives to God: the risen life is life under the power and in the possession of God. We again take the dative as one of possession, and again the point is eschatological: we are not talking about the personal biography of Jesus of Nazareth, after death any more than before it, but about the fundamental change in the human condition brought about by his death and resurrection.

11

you must also consider yourselves dead to sin and alive to God: cf. above on v. 8. The resurrection remains future, yet it dominates the lives of Christians who are expected to live in the present as those whose destiny is life with Christ. They are to think of themselves always in the light of that destiny, and therefore not as still bound to sin to which they have died. This ought to be their basic 'self-understanding'.

in Christ Jesus: this strange expression occurs here for the first time in the letter (cf. also 'in the Lord' and 'in him', neither of which has appeared up to this point). Its background and meaning have puzzled interpreters of Paul since critical study of the letters began, and it must be confessed that agreed results from the consequent scholarly industry are hard to find.[b] Something along the following lines may be a

---

b One can do no more than indicate a few of the more influential studies: F. Neugebauer, *In Christus: eine Untersuchung zum paulinischen Glaubensverständnis,* Göttingen: Vandenhoeck & Ruprecht 1961; M. Bouttier, *En Christ: étude d'exégèse et de théologie pauliniennes,* Paris: Univ. de France 1962; C. F. D.

reasonable explanation of 'in Christ' language.

Although clues to the meaning have been proposed in Hebrew corporate thinking and in incipient Gnosticism, none has proved convincing. It is doubtful if Hebrew thought ever conceived of an individual who could incorporate others in himself, though representation of the many by the one is a different matter. It is therefore not plausible that Paul should be following some supposed ancient Jewish models (such as Jacob/Israel) and be seeing Christ as an historical or even exalted individual who somehow includes believers within himself. On the other hand, in Gnosticism it did become possible to think of the spiritual parts of some human beings as destined to be literally within the redeemer figure, whom they thus, in effect, complete. Quite apart from the difficulty, in the present state of knowledge, of being sure that this idea existed at the time of Paul, there is the more important objection that for Paul the destiny of the believer was not to be absorbed into Christ, but to be *with* him. It is now, on earth, that the believer is *in* Christ; in heaven the Christian will be with him (cf. Phil. 1^{23}). More probably the clue to the meaning lies in the apparent interchangeability of being in Christ and being in the Spirit. Being in the Spirit is to be within the sphere of the divine power, but for Paul the Spirit is now the Spirit of Christ, so that being in the Spirit is in effect being in Christ, and *vice versa*. Thus we have to do not with the inclusion of Christians as individuals within Jesus Christ as an individual, but with the existence of Christians within the sphere of power of Christ the Lord.

Therefore, to be in Christ Jesus here means to live in the present time before the resurrection under the lordship and in the effective power of Christ, see again Introduction, 9. It is sometimes pointed out that talk of being *in* Christ is a different language-game from that of dying and rising *with* him, and so it is. Yet in this passage Paul shows himself capable of playing both games at once: dying and rising with Christ in vv. 1–10, and being in him in v. 11. We have died and shall rise with him, and meanwhile we are in him. Perhaps we can rationalize the matter by saying that with him we die to sin, thus endorsing the end of sin's dominion. The result is that we are in him, in his new dominion

---

Moule, *The Origin of Christology*, CUP 1977, Ch. 2. For a recent discussion which builds a great deal on the parallel with Abraham, see A. J. M. Wedderburn, 'Some Observations on Paul's Use of the Phrases "In Christ" and "With Christ" ', *JSNT* 25, 1985, pp. 83–97. The position taken in the present commentary is set out at somewhat greater length in Ziesler, *PC*, pp. 47–63.

which is also that of the Spirit, cf. Ch. 8. The final outcome, however, is that we shall be with him in the presence of the Father. Dying with him is thus the means of entry into being in him, while being risen with him is the ultimate destiny. It must be said that Paul himself never spells things out like this, and to do so may be to deserve the charge of over-systematizing his thought.

12

Let not sin therefore reign: we now come up against the anomaly that those who have died to sin still need to be told not to let it continue reigning over them. We may have expected them to need no such advice, because they are already sinless. If so our expectation is wrong. The Christian may have died with Christ to sin, and so no longer be under sin's dominion, but Paul obviously does not expect immediate sinlessness. What is crucial, however, is that there is now the possibility of defeating sin. It is no longer futile to encourage people not to be governed by sin; it is not futile, but it is necessary. This is a measure of the degree to which a victory won in principle still has to be worked out and made specific in practice. 'Become what you now can become' (Käsemann, p. 173).

in your mortal bodies to make you obey their passions: as with the 'sinful body' of v. 6, we are obliged to ask if this is strictly the physical body with its appetites for sex, food, drink, and comfort, or if it is the whole person in all its connections with the present world. In the latter case, the physical would certainly be included, but would not exhaust the reference. Since Paul has the whole of life in his purview in this passage, the more general meaning seems more likely. The word for 'passions' (*epithumiais*) may seem to tilt the balance of probability in favour of a physical reference, but in fact it cannot decide the question, since it can be used for sexual desires, for coveting in general, or even for the wish to be in heaven with Christ (see Rom. 1^{24}; $7^{f.}$; Phil. 1^{23}; I Thess. 2^{17}). 'Mortal' (*thnēton*) is more inclined to give the clause a specifically physical reference, for elsewhere it does tend to stand for the natural, physical body (I Cor. $15^{53, 54}$; II Cor. 4^{11}; 5^4; perhaps also Rom. 8^{11}). It is therefore not impossible that in this verse Paul is turning from a more wide-ranging freedom from sin to freedom from physical sins in particular. Yet if this is so, the move is not clearly made, and it remains preferable to suppose that Paul is still talking about freedom from all kinds of sin. In effect, 'Let not sin therefore reign in your mortal selves.'

13

Do not yield your members to sin: 'members' (*melē*) are human faculties or parts, cf. I Cor. 12$^{12ff.}$, where 'members' include the foot, the hand, the ear, the eye, and the head. The verbs 'Do not yield' and 'but yield' are in different tenses. 'Do not yield' could well be translated 'Stop yielding' or 'Do not go on yielding'; this is a regular possibility of meaning of a prohibition using the present imperative. 'But yield yourselves to God', on the other hand, is an aorist imperative, which usually has the nuance 'make a definite act'. In other words, Paul's readers are being urged to stop being subject to sin, and in a decisive step to make themselves available to God for righteousness.

If we adopt a strictly physical interpretation of 'mortal bodies' in v. 12, then this verse may be seen as endorsing it. On the other hand the apparent equivalence of 'yield your members' and 'yield yourselves' may support an understanding that whole persons are at stake throughout.

from death to life: have they already moved from death to life, or is life still in the future as in vv. 1-10? Even if the resurrection is future, Christians are to live now as people who have found life out of death. More than this we cannot say.

14

sin will have no dominion over you: not only common sense, but also the fact that Paul offers his readers ethical warning and encouragement, show that this clause cannot mean that Christians are incapable of sinning. It means just what it says: they are not under sin's power. Escape is now possible, though not a foregone conclusion.[c]

because we are not under law but under grace: Paul now pre-empts any suggestion that being the recipients of God's grace conveys freedom to sin. If the ruling principle is not adherence to the Law, but the boundless and undeserved grace of God, this does not imply (cf. v. 1) that we can do as we like. On the contrary, we are free not *to* sin but *from* sin. The whole argument of the chapter up to this point has shown why: being under grace is having died to sin with Christ, and its effect is freedom from sin. Grace has effected the transfer from one dominion, that of sin, to another, that of Christ and righteousness. This is a transfer that the Law could not make (NB 5^{20}: Law increases concrete acts of sinning and does nothing to rescue those who are caught in sin's toils).

c See the excellent more extended treatment in Cranfield I, pp. 318f.

¹⁵*What then? Are we to sin because we are not under law but under grace? By no means!* ¹⁶*Do you not know that if you yield yourselves to any one as obedient slaves, you are slaves of the one whom you obey, either of sin, which leads to death, or of obedience, which leads to righteousness?* ¹⁷*But thanks be to God, that you who were once slaves of sin have become obedient from the heart to the standard of teaching to which you were committed,* ¹⁸*and, having been set free from sin, have become slaves of righteousness.* ¹⁹*I am speaking in human terms, because of your natural limitations. For just as you once yielded your members to impurity and to greater and greater iniquity, so now yield your members to righteousness for sanctification.*

²⁰*When you were slaves of sin, you were free in regard to righteousness.* ²¹*But then what return did you get from the things of which you are now ashamed? The end of those things is death.* ²²*But now that you have been set free from sin and have become slaves of God, the return you get is sanctification and its end, eternal life.* ²³*For the wages of sin is death, but the free gift of God is eternal life in Christ Jesus our Lord.*

Paul does not envisage a life of absolute freedom, but two sorts of life under alternative masters. He now sets out these alternatives: sin, and righteousness. Those who have died with Christ have escaped the domination of sin, and entered the domain of righteousness, which means that they have abandoned a destiny of death for one of eternal life. This is why it is nonsense to suggest that being 'under grace' is a licence to sin. Paul does not spell out all the steps of the argument, but behind what he says is the treatment of justification by faith in Chapters 3 and 4. Our being so justified, accepted as God's people, is an act of pure grace on God's part, but on our part it involves dying with Christ. In that dying we leave the realm of sin and enter the realm of righteousness and life. It thus cannot be held that grace makes sin unimportant. On the contrary, it is *the* way to conquer sin.

∽

15

Are we to sin . . .: Paul returns to the question of v. 1. Cf. also 3^8.

By no means: as in v. 2, Paul responds with the strongest negative in his vocabulary, *mē genoito.*

16

if you yield yourselves to any one as obedient slaves: behind this clause probably lies the practice of voluntary slavery. People in dire poverty could offer themselves as slaves to someone simply in order to be fed and housed (so Barrett, p. 131). 'Slaves' is an apt translation of the Greek *douloi;* 'servants' would not bring out the idea of total belonging and complete obedience that is needed.

you are slaves to the one whom you obey: this is not mere tautology, for it conveys the idea of exclusiveness that is inherent in slavery. No one can serve two masters (cf. Matt. 6^{24}). In the present context, no one can serve both sin and righteousness, righteousness here being shorthand for Christ and his régime. People must therefore choose, and thanks to God's grace that is a freedom they do have. They are not irrevocably committed to the régime of sin, but can 'die' to that and enter the service of God's righteousness in Christ. See again Introduction, 9.

either of sin, which leads to death: it is clear enough by now that Paul sees sin as a dominion under which, left to themselves, men and women have to live. Then what does it mean to say that sin leads to death? Certainty is impossible, but this is probably a reference back to $5^{12ff.}$ where death is the consequence of sin, and behind that to the Adam story in Gen. 2^{17}; 3^{19}. The natural outcome of a life under sin is death. Paul does not tackle the questions we may wish to ask: for example, does he mean that life under sin leads to total annihilation, or to that separation from God which is tantamount to death? The considerable amount of vagueness may well be because the main concern is to stress the alternative, namely life in and with Christ (v. 23).

or of obedience, which leads to righteousness: the expression is unexpected. The reader is ready for something like 'or of Christ, which leads to righteousness' or 'of righteousness which leads to life'. How can one be obedient to obedience? We are probably to recall that in 5^{19} Paul has identified Christ with obedience to God, so that 'obedience' here is shorthand for submission to Christ, who is characterized by his obedience to God. In 5^{19} Christ's obedience leads to righteousness for many, and this is echoed here in obedience that leads to righteousness. In the structure of the verse 'righteousness' in the second half corresponds to 'death' in the first half, so that righteousness (*dikaiosunē*, see on 1^{17}; $3^{5, 21}$ above) includes 'life' among its connotations here.[d] It is certainly not 'acceptance', but since it is the opposite of sin (v. 18) neither is it simply 'life' without further qualification. Probably the nearest we can get to the meaning is to see righteousness as the life of the people of God, life under him as Lord. The life that is with God for ever (v. 23) lies beyond righteousness and sanctification (v. 19).

17

the standard of teaching to which you were committed: it is not obvious what the standard of teaching is.[e] 'Standard' is *tupos*, which can be translated 'type' or 'pattern', cf. I Thess. 1^7; II Thess. 3^9; Phil. 3^{17}. The 'pattern of teaching' here could be either credal or ethical, and it could be either the form or the content.[f] It almost certainly cannot mean one type of teaching, viz. the Pauline, as against other types. In view of the context, this undoubtedly opaque expression most probably refers to baptismal teaching about Christ and his lordship. Whether we are to think of this in primarily ethical or primarily credal terms is not a matter for dogmatism.[g] The whole of life may well be in view, especially since Paul's readers were handed over ('committed') to it when they were baptized. Indeed it is possible that the *tupos* is the pattern of dying and rising into which they have entered.

18

have become slaves of righteousness: more than any other in the passage, this verse sets out the alternatives starkly. There is sin (and all that goes with it) on the one hand, or righteousness (and the one from whom it springs) on the other. Righteousness is the appropriate antonym to sin, and like sin is treated as if it were a power. Yet it is clear from v. 23 that the true Lord is Christ himself. In vv. 18, 19, and 20 therefore, righteousness is virtually a surrogate for Christ and his lordship. At the same time, its character as the opposite of sin is to be taken seriously: it is that

d See Sanders, *PPJ*, p. 494.

e For the view held, e.g. by Bultmann, that this is a rather inept insertion, see the discussion in Wilckens II, p. 35.

f For a full discussion of the various possibilities see Wilckens II, pp. 35–7.

g For the credal view, see Käsemann, p. 181; for the ethical, Robinson, p. 75.

quality of life which is the antithesis to sin, life entered by those who
escape the power of sin.[h]

19

I am speaking in human terms: Paul's apology for his terminology is not
surprising. His use of the language of slavery is only partly appropriate,
and has the disadvantage that it is not naturally appealing (it would be
no more attractive to Paul's contemporaries than it is to people today).
In the minds of many of his readers, the language might well have had
deeply unpleasant associations. Moreover, it is only partly apt: for most
slaves their situation was involuntary. Indeed in Paul's view, slavery to
sin was equally involuntary, but slavery to Christ/righteousness was
chosen, involving response and consent. The rest of the verse certainly
speaks of deliberate and voluntary submission. A further reason for
Paul's uneasiness with the slavery terminology may be that it expresses
only one side of being Christian: in 8^{15} he rejects the language of slavery
and turns instead to that of children and parent, so that Christians are
sons.

because of your natural limitations: literally, 'because of the weakness of
your flesh (*sarx*)'. It is unlikely that *sarx* here has those connotations of
living without God that it often has (cf. above on 1^3) and does have in
8^{4-9}. It is evident from the whole sentence that Paul is aware of using
terms that are inadequate for their subject, but are unavoidable given
the natural limitations of human thought and expression. In other
words it is natural human inadequacy, not human sinfulness, that is
meant here, and the RSV rendering is appropriate.

you once yielded your members: as in v. 13, 'members' (*melē*) are human
parts or faculties. The physical side is certainly included, but as in v. 13
it is not clear that only this is meant.

to impurity and to greater and greater iniquity: the latter phrase does not
quite bring out the force of the Greek, which is that iniquity leads to
more iniquity, *tē(i) anomia(i) eis tēn anomian*, an idea reminiscent of
1^{18-32}.

so now yield your members to righteousness for sanctification: see the comments on v. 18 for righteousness as not only an antonym to sin, but also

[h] See Käsemann, p. 180; Ziesler, *Meaning*, pp. 201f.

as a surrogate term for Christ as Lord. In effect, righteousness here is the power of God in Christ, under which believers live. Sanctification (*hagiasmon*) is its outworking in concrete terms. In the Bible holiness/ sanctification has moral connotations very often, but behind these is the notion of belonging to God and being fit for him, sharing in his holiness.[i]

20

you were free with regard to righteousness: this is not as difficult as it looks. Paul is simply adverting to the basic point made in v. 16, that servitude to one power or master excludes obligations to all others. If one is serving sin, then one is not at the same time serving righteousness.

21

But then what return did you get: as punctuation is a later addition to the text, there are places like this where it is in dispute. It is possible that the correct way to punctuate and read the first half of the verse is 'But then what return did you get (from your servitude to sin)? Things of which you are now ashamed.[j] If this does produce a slightly smoother reading, it does not make a great difference to the overall sense, which is that service to sin leads to things of which the readers are now ashamed, and which issue in death. No doubt the things of which they are ashamed are the practical outworkings of sin, in other words *sins*.

The end of those things is death: cf. vv. 16, 23. There may here be an echo of the choice between obedience to God's commandments and life in the land on the one hand, and disobedience and not living long in the land, of Deut. 30^{15–20}. Once again Paul fails to make it plain in what sense we should understand death, though vv. 22–23 show that it is the opposite of eternal life.

22

slaves of God: the power-sphere that is the alternative to that of sin can be described in more than one way. It is the sphere of God (as here); the sphere of obedience (v. 16); and the sphere of righteousness (vv. 18ff.). It is the same reality throughout.

the return you get is sanctification: on sanctification, *hagiasmon*, see v. 19.

i See on 1⁷, also Wilckens II, p. 39; Käsemann, p. 183; Cranfield I, p. 327.
j This reading is strongly argued for by Cranfield I, p. 328.

Literally, 'you have as fruit what leads/tends towards sanctification'. They are not at once sanctified, but are set on the road to becoming God's true and holy people (Cranfield I, pp. 328f.).

its end, eternal life: cf. v. 23. In comparison with John's Gospel, Paul seldom uses the expression *zōē aionios*, 'eternal life', and when he does it is usually with a strictly future reference, for life with God in the world to come (Rom. 2⁷; 5²¹; 6²², ²³; Gal. 6⁸).

23

the wages of sin is death: 'wages' (*opsōnia*) in contemporary usage often meant the pay given to soldiers, but could also mean the pocket money allowed to slaves. In view of the emphasis on slavery in this passage, the latter seems the more likely image here. The point is the same as in vv. 16, 21 (and cf. 5¹²).ᵏ

the free gift of God: not wages, not earned, but freely granted by God's grace. The Greek word is *charisma*, grace-gift.

eternal life: see on v. 22. It is not unimportant that eternal life is treated as a gift of God's special kindness, and not as a natural possibility, let alone an inevitable destiny.

in Christ Jesus our Lord: for 'in Christ' see on 6¹¹. Most unusually for Paul, the phrase here refers to the future life, and not to Christian existence here and now.

This is no mere rounding-off phrase, though each of Chapters 5–8 ends with some such formula. It has a crucial function in the passage in that it underlines that everything good happens under the lordship of Christ. Paul has been describing life that is the outcome of dying with Christ, life that is in him (cf. v. 11), in the sphere of his power and lordship. The power aspect will be brought to the fore in Ch. 8, but the lordship of Christ that has been implicit all along is at this point made explicit.

7¹⁻⁶ DEATH FREES FROM SUBJECTION TO THE LAW

7 *Do you not know, brethren – for I am speaking to those who know the law – that the law is binding on a person only during his life?* ²*Thus a*

ᵏ On the metaphor, see further Cranfield I, p. 329 and nn. 2, 3.

married woman is bound by law to her husband as long as he lives; but if her husband dies she is discharged from the law concerning the husband. ³Accordingly, she will be called an adulteress if she lives with another man while her husband is alive. But if her husband dies she is free from that law, and if she marries another man she is not an adulteress.

⁴Likewise, my brethren, you have died to the law through the body of Christ, so that you may belong to another, to him who has been raised from the dead in order that we may bear fruit for God. ⁵While we were living in the flesh, our sinful passions, aroused by the law, were at work in our members to bear fruit for death. ⁶But now we are discharged from the law, dead to that which held us captive, so that we serve not under the old written code but in the new life of the Spirit.

Although the point being made is relatively straightforward, the passage is complicated by the fact that the analogy Paul uses only partly fits the case. Whereas Ch. 6 was concerned mainly with Christians' freedom from the reign of sin, Ch. 7 deals with their freedom from the reign of Law. As Christ enables the first, so he also enables the second. In both cases the freedom comes about by dying and rising with Christ. Here, however, the apostle uses the analogy of a woman who is subject to the rule and authority (literally 'the law') of her husband during his lifetime. Once he dies, she is no longer subject to that authority or law. The trouble with the analogy is that it is not the Law (parallel to the husband) that dies, but the Christian (parallel to the wife) who dies with Christ, and is therefore free from the Law's rule. Probably we should accept that the analogy is inexact without trying to find a more obscure level on which it does operate well.

What is more important is deciding what Paul means by dying to the Law. If we take this passage on its own, it looks as if he is saying that, so far as Christians are concerned, the Law is over and done with. Yet it cannot be quite as simple as this, because of passages like 8⁴ and 13⁸⁻¹⁰ which seem to retain a positive role for the Law. Nevertheless no qualifications are introduced at this point. As Christians die to sin (Ch. 6), so now with Christ they die to the Law ('through the body of Christ'). Indeed for people who live 'in the flesh', the effect of the Law is not to combat sin, but actively to foster it, though there is no explanation how this can be so until vv. 7ff. Those who now live in the Spirit have found freedom from the captivity of the Law. This freedom, however, is not a licence to sin, but on the contrary it is freedom 'to serve', whereas the Law arouses sin. This is all highly paradoxical: far from arguing that the Law fosters morality and obedience to God, Paul is saying the reverse. The way to true service of God is not through the Law ('the letter') but through the Spirit, about which he will have a good deal more to say in Ch. 8. Nevertheless, to anticipate a little and also to look back to Ch. 6, we may say that the fundamental point is that the only way to counter evil life under the old dominion of sin is to enter into the new and beneficent reign of God and his Spirit.

ဢ

1

I am speaking to those who know the law: the argument of vv. 1–3 does not require identifying the law as the Law of Moses, and could fit any system of marriage law. Yet it is clear from the verses that follow that it is the Mosaic Law, the Torah, that Paul is talking about. Does this mean that we can assume that Paul's Roman readers were themselves Jews, or at least former adherents of the synagogue? The question continues to be debated, but probably all we can properly deduce is that *some* of his readers were expected to be versed in the Mosaic Law (cf. also the discussion on v. 4).

the law is binding on a person only during his life: Paul's argument here is that the rule of a law, any law, is over when a person dies. This is as true of the Torah as of any other system of law.[1]

2

if her husband dies: we have noted that here the analogy fails to run on parallel lines. It ought to be the wife who dies, as the believer dies with Christ (v. 4). Paul's illustrations usually resist being pressed too far, and we probably ought to think here more in terms of parable than strict analogy, let alone allegory. As often, one reasonably straightforward point is being made, and any attempt to work out the illustration in

---

l For Rabbinic references to this effect, see Wilckens II, p. 64 n. 241, and see above on 6⁷.

detail runs into confusion.^m The reasonably straightforward point here
is that legal obligations are removed by death, and that therefore any
obligation believers may have had to the (Mosaic) Law is cancelled
when they die with Christ. The inexact analogy with marriage law is
solely to make the point about cancelling obligations. The verse that
follows is no more than the flesh on the bones of the illustration; nothing subtle is to be deduced from it about the relation of the believer to
the Law.

4

you have died to the law: cf. v. 6, where the same point is made with different imagery, that of escape from imprisonment. Both verses show
that the Law is seen as a rule or régime, one under which Christians no
longer live. As noted on v. 1, Paul by now is talking specifically about
the Law of Moses: v. 7 makes this clear, as there was no law against
coveting in secular codes. Yet how can Paul assume that the Roman
Christians as a whole had died to the Law? Many of them had never
been under it, surely. Perhaps Paul is still speaking, as in v. 1, particularly to those with experience of the synagogue, who had, whether
Jews or not, tried to be Law-observant at least in most matters. They
had died to the Law. On the other hand this may be an instance where
Paul generalizes from his own experience, and writes of former pagans
as if they too had been under the Law. It is as if he forgets that not all
Christians had shared his experience or his people's history, but may
have had quite different experiences and histories of their own.ⁿ

What is 'dying to the law'? If it is parallel to dying to sin, it must be
escaping from the rule/régime of the Law. It is important that this discussion of freedom from the Law comes *after* Ch. 6, in which such heavy
stress was laid on the ethical renewal that ensues from dying with
Christ, disarming the criticism that justification could mean sitting
loose to morality. There can thus be no suggestion that dying to the
Law is a licence to be immoral; indeed perhaps it is only now that it is
safe to argue against the reign of the Law, when another basis for good
living has been established in Ch. 6. Dying to the Law therefore does
not mean being free from all authority, nor does it mean never doing

m A very thorough exploration of this matter is found in H. M. Gale, *The
Use of Analogy in the Letters of Paul*, Westminster Press 1964. For the present
passage see pp. 192–201.

n Cf. for example Rom. 4¹; I Cor. 10¹. The point is made and the passages
discussed in Sanders, *PLJP*, pp. 81–3.

anything that the Law prescribes (cf. 8^4; 13$^{8-10}$). It does mean that the Law is no longer the régime under which the Christian lives.^{o}

It is sometimes argued (e.g. Cranfield I, pp. 331f.) that it is a death to the Law only in so far as the Law condemns sinners and so only as a means to justification. Yet Paul has argued in Rom. 4 that doing the Law never was the way to justification, so there is nothing new about that. Moreover the unqualified language and its strong terms suggest that Paul means just what he says. The régime of the Law is over, so far as Christians are concerned. Ch. 6 shows that the will of God, and a high morality, still stand, but not because they are in the Law. Rather, they stand because they are demanded by life in Christ, in the Spirit, life that follows dying with Christ.

'You have died' is strictly 'you have been put to death' (*ethanatōthēte*), God being the implicit agent. Wilckens (II, p. 64) is probably right to suggest that this refers back to 6$^{3ff.}$ and dying with Christ in baptism, which can be seen as the divine action, or at least the divine enabling.

through the body of Christ: there may be a double reference.

(*a*) In view of the dying-with-Christ theme in the preceding chapter, a reference to the dying body of Christ on the cross is likely here. This then becomes another way of saying 'through dying with him'.

(*b*) However, as Paul is known to use the figure of the body of Christ to denote the church (see I Cor. 12$^{12ff.}$ and, less directly, Rom. 12$^{4-5}$), here too there may be a reference to the church. Through baptism, believers are in Christ's body, the church, and therefore *not* within any other sphere of power, such as sin, or the Law. Yet however reasonable this interpretation may seem, it is prudent not to press it, since there is nothing in the context to support it.^{p}

that you may belong to another: viz. the risen Christ. It is Christ the Lord under whose régime Christians live. Consequently nothing and no one else can be lord or hold sway over Christians; certainly not sin, and not even the Law, however good and holy in itself it may be (v. 12).

that we may bear fruit for God: it is life in and under Christ as Lord that produces the fruits of living that God wants to see. Living under sin

---

o Moule, 'A Note on Certain Datives', concludes that datives like this one are datives of relation.

p Among recent commentators, Wilckens II, p. 65, thinks both notes may be present, the second arising out of the first; Cranfield I, p. 336, thinks only the first is present.

most surely cannot do so (cf. 6$^{22f.}$), and Paul is about to argue that living under the Law cannot do so either (vv. 5–11).

5

While we were living in the flesh: as usual, 'flesh' is *sarx* (see the discussion at 1^3). The past tense shows that being 'in the flesh', *en tē(i) sarki*, is now left behind. Therefore *sarx* must be used in the bad sense of life apart from God, life based on something other than him. Physical aspects are included, but do not constitute the whole. Paul's terminology is confusing: in II Cor. 10$^{2f.}$ he drew a helpful distinction between living 'in the flesh', which is neutral and simply denotes living in this world under ordinary human conditions, and living 'according to the flesh', which is bad and denotes living for something other than God. Here, however, and in 8$^{4-9}$, there is no such distinction. 'In the flesh' and 'according to the flesh' are synonymous.

our sinful passions: in the light of the comments just made, these will include physical lusts but should not be limited to them. We may compare the 'works of the flesh' of Gal. 5$^{19-21}$, which include physical lusts, but also embrace wrong religion and especially wrong social relations.

aroused by the law: whether physical or not, how are our wrong desires stimulated by the Law? This appears to be a new idea in Romans, for 5^{20} ('Law came in, to increase the trespass') probably means that potential or implicit sin is turned into concrete acts of wrongdoing by the Law. More than that seems to be said in this verse. It is similar, perhaps, to the equally puzzling I Cor. 15^{56}, 'the power of sin is the law'. What does it mean?

(*a*) Perhaps Paul is talking about contra-suggestibility, the propensity some people have to react negatively to any directive. In this case the Law puts ideas into people's heads, and in effect leads them to sin. This is not true of everyone, and palpably not true of most things for anyone: few of us feel impelled to burglary because the Law forbids it. Moreover, many people are all too prone to be submissive to authority, and not in the least contra-suggestible. Of course, Paul could be generalizing from *one* aspect of *some* people's experience, but the idea seems slightly trivial, and in any case Paul does not seem to find some commands, like that to love (13$^{8-10}$), counter-productive.

(*b*) Some have thought that Paul is saying that the Law tempts people to use obeying it as a means to establish themselves as righteous before God (e.g. Cranfield I, p. 353), but there is no reason in Romans so far, or indeed elsewhere, to find this a convincing target for Paul.

(*c*) Perhaps this is a somewhat remote echo of Paul's own experience, when zeal for the Law led to his becoming a persecutor of Christians (Phil. 3^{6}; Gal. $1^{13f.}$), but there is nothing in the present context to support it. Indeed Paul's attitude may have been coloured by his experience, but this is to speculate.

(*d*) It is arguable that in vv. 7–11 Paul is concerned as in 5^{20} with the Law's propensity for turning implicit sin into explicit sins. There was sin before the Law ($5^{13f.}$), but it could not be identified or made concrete. Specific commands which must be either obeyed or disobeyed serve to bring latent sinfulness to a head, and result in transgression. We shall see that this works particularly well in the case of coveting, which most people would not even recognize as sinful until they hear and understand the command against it. This explanation can be found to fit at least most of the statements in $7^{7ff.}$, but does it fit this verse: 'our sinful passions, *aroused* by the law'?[q] The fit is not an easy one, if 'aroused' is the appropriate translation of *enērgeito*.

(*e*) However, *enērgeito* could equally well be translated 'were active', so that the sentence would run 'Our sinful passions were active, through the law, in our members to bear fruit for death.'[r] If we adopt this suggestion, it becomes easier to reconcile this verse with 5^{20} and $7^{7ff.}$, and explanation (*d*) becomes more plausible.

It is impossible to be dogmatic about all this. What we have to say about the rest of the chapter, and about the relation of sin to Law, has a crucial bearing on the way this verse is understood. Because of that, a combination of (*d*) and (*e*) is preferred.

6

dead to that which held us captive: as Käsemann points out (p. 190), the temporary guardian of Gal. $3^{23f.}$ (*paidagōgos*) has now become a jailer. The parallel with being under sin is striking, and once again we see that Paul universalizes human experience as if all, Jews but also Gentiles, had been under the Law as well as under sin.[s] It is extraordinary that a Jew should consider the Law a prison from which people need to escape; we

q Watson, *PJG*, pp. 152f., thinks that this point is a direct echo of the Genesis temptation and fall story, and is aimed at the Jewish community.

r This agrees with the way of taking the middle voice of the verb in Gal. 5^{6} and II Cor. 4^{12}. It avoids the causative connotation of 'aroused'.

s Cf. Sanders, *PLJP*, p. 72, who points out the similarity to the position in Galatians, where being under the Law is apparently equivalent to being under the *stoicheia*, 'the elemental spirits of the universe', 4^{3}.

need go no further than Ps. 119 for evidence of the common delight in the Law. Though it has been suggested (e.g. by Cranfield, I, p. 338) that only the Law's misuse, or its condemnation, can be regarded as imprisoning, there is no such qualification in Paul's language here. He does not explain, but in view of Ch. 6 it is reasonable to suppose that the Law is regarded in the light of its alternative, the life of freedom in Christ. Any régime or dominion other than that of Christ (and the Spirit, see Ch. 8) is seen as bondage, even if not perceived as such by those who live under it.

we serve not under the old written code but in the new life of the Spirit: literally, 'We serve in the newness of the Spirit and not in the oldness of the letter.' RSV rightly takes 'letter' to mean the written Law, the Law of Moses, and equally rightly gives 'Spirit' a capital letter. Paul is not arguing, as people sometimes do, that we should obey the spirit of the Law rather than its letter, i.e. that we should obey it with flexibility and common sense. That is not at issue here. The new life of the Spirit is shown quite clearly in Ch. 6, and will be shown in Ch. 8, to be life in the Holy Spirit, in Christ, under righteousness. Paul may introduce non-literal observance of the law about circumcision in 2[29], but here is nothing to show that he is doing that sort of thing here (nor in II Cor. 3[6]). As it stands in context, Paul's point is that it is the Spirit's régime under which the Christian serves God. This is not to imply that Christians no longer need bother about doing God's will: Ch. 6 alone is sufficient rebuttal of any such notion. It is also not to say that the Law and its contents are entirely abrogated, for we know from 13[8-10] that at least some things in it are emphatically not abrogated (cf. also 7[7]; 8[4]). What *is* abrogated is the ruling function of the Law. It is no longer the definitive criterion, the necessary and sufficient authority over life and behaviour. That role is now taken by the Spirit.

7[7-13]   THE LAW IS EXPLOITED BY SIN

[7]*What then shall we say? That the law is sin? By no means! Yet, if it had not been for the law, I should not have known sin. I should not have known what it is to covet if the law had not said, 'You shall not covet.' [8]But sin, finding opportunity in the commandment, wrought in me all kinds of covetousness. Apart from the law sin lies dead. [9]I was once alive apart from*

the law, but when the commandment came, sin revived and I died; ¹⁰*the very commandment which promised life proved to be death to me.* ¹¹*For sin, finding opportunity in the commandment, deceived me and by it killed me.* ¹²*So the law is holy, and the commandment is holy and just and good.*

¹³*Did that which is good, then, bring death to me? By no means! It was sin, working death in me through what is good, in order that sin might be shown to be sin, and through the commandment might become sinful beyond measure.*

If Paul was clear what he wanted to say in the rest of Romans 7, then it must be confessed that he failed to communicate that clarity to later readers. Few sections of any of his letters can have received so much scholarly attention with so little resulting agreement.

In the previous section he has seemed to place the Law in the same category as sin, as something from which Christians have escaped. Does this mean that the Law 'is' sin, or perhaps sin's fellow-traveller? Paul will not accept any such suggestion (vv. 7, 12), and like any good Jew maintains that the Law is holy. Yet he also wants to maintain that sin has exploited the Law (vv. 8–11), and, against the Law's own intention, this has led to death and not life (vv. 9, 10). The Law has thus become a victim, a view of it unprecedented in Paul's writings. As to how this exploitation happens, he offers no explanation, except in terms of the tenth commandment in the Decalogue, 'Thou shalt not covet' (v. 7). First he says that he would not 'have known what it is to covet' unless the Law had forbidden it. This is doubtless true, as coveting is not an *overtly* wrong thing, and is one to which, moreover, people often give much more respectable names. He then goes further and says that sin used the commandment to create covetousness in him. We are thus again faced with the possibility that Paul believed that a good and holy law could be perverted by sin and finally act as fuel for sin's fire.

Some have thought^t that the Law prompts sinfully self-centred people to use it in order to earn God's favour, so that obedience to it becomes little more than spiritual self-aggrandizement. This would indeed be a case of sin's exploitation of the Law, but there is no

---

t See the discussion in Wilckens II, pp. 8of.; Wilckens himself firmly rejects such a view.

evidence here (or elsewhere, in all probability) that Paul had ever thought Law-obedience to incur such a danger. Others have suggested that the Law prompts people to sin by putting ideas into their heads, a possibility we considered and rejected when discussing 7^5. What seems more likely is that it is his choice of the tenth commandment as a paradigm of sin's relation to the Law that controls a very great deal of the rest of the chapter, and this section in particular. No doubt he may have chosen it because covetousness was often regarded in Judaism as the seminal sin, from which all others sprang, and because it was identified as the sin by which Adam fell. This choice enables him in vv. 7–13 to make a fusion between the giving of the Law at Sinai and the giving of the command not to eat in the Garden of Eden. This choice, however, of a command against something which is not immediately recognized as sinful, gives force to the statement in v. 7 that he would not have known sin if the Law had not condemned coveting. Moreover, if we concentrate on this particular command, it is intelligible that he should say (v. 8) that 'sin finding opportunity in the commandment wrought in me all kinds of covetousness'. This is because it is very much worse (more sinful) to covet once coveting has been identified and forbidden, than to have unnamed longings for what other people possess. As we shall see in the next section, forbidding coveting does nothing to stop it; all it does is name it and make it wrong. Before we hear the command against it, we may well think that our longings are a passion for fairness, or merely recognize a resentment in ourselves that others are more successful or more fortunate or better than we are. The respectable names we give it, in other words, leave us on the side of virtue, not of sin. The commandment, therefore, while it does not *create* sinfulness, simply by naming it increases recognizable sinfulness. Right through Ch. 7, we shall argue that a concentration on covetousness as the paradigm of sin has led to statements which fit that particular sin well enough, but do not fit the relationship between the Law and sin in all respects.[u]

The question whether the same time is envisaged in vv. 14–25 as in this section will not be discussed until the introduction to that sec-

u For a more detailed defence of the case argued here, see J. A. Ziesler, 'The Role of the Tenth Commandment in Romans 7', *JSNT* 33, 1988, pp. 41–56.

tion. Here, all the verbs are in a past tense, and it is obvious that Paul
is not talking about Christian experience, but is looking back from a
Christian perspective at what was the position of men and women
before Christ. The question is whether in these verses he is talking
about his own personal experience, and generalizing from it (as also
in vv. 14–25); or whether he is using 'I' purely rhetorically, perhaps
not even including himself in the generalization; or whether he is
talking about the history of the human race in general and the Jewish
people in particular, using the model of Adam in the Garden of Eden.
Commentaries in English, even in recent years, have tended to
assume that there must be at least an element of autobiography.^v No
one supposes it is *only* autobiographical, but many think that even if
'I' is typical or rhetorical, it nonetheless includes Paul himself. It is
argued that statements like 'Wretched man that I am! Who will
deliver me . . .' and 'I do not understand my own actions . . . I do
the very thing I hate' are too pointed and even agonized to be only
concerned with other people, not oneself. Paul *feels* what he writes.
Moreover, as in v. 7 'You shall not covet' is presumably understood
to be addressed to all people including Paul, it is natural to suppose
that 'I' in the same verse and those following also includes Paul. If
we ask when Paul was ever alive apart from the Law (v. 9), then it
may be answered that this was before he was formally *bar mitzvah* (the
ceremony may be mediaeval, but the idea of becoming responsible
for obedience to the Law from the time of puberty is ancient).

On the other hand, especially since the work of W. G. Kümmel
(*Römer* 7), it has become common, especially in Germany, to take the
view that Rom. 7⁷⁻²⁵ is *not* a reflection of Paul's own experience. On
the contrary, 'I' is purely rhetorical and does not, as a matter of fact,
include Paul himself. Parallels to this state of affairs are to be found
in I Cor. 10^{29 b} and in numerous other passages both within and outside the NT.^w However, it seems that where 'I' is written in full (*egō*)
and is not merely the verbal suffix, and where it also occurs in positive

v See, for example, Bruce, pp. 147–50; Murray, pp. 248–55; Dodd, pp.
104–7. See also J. D. G. Dunn, 'Rom. 7, 14–25'.

w Kümmel, *Römer* 7, pp. 126–31. For a discussion of these passages see
Theissen, *Aspekte*, pp. 194–204. It is to Theissen that the criticisms that follow
are indebted.

statements and not in questions or conditional statements, and where finally those statements are in a past tense, it is very much more usual that the speaker is included in the typical or rhetorical 'I'. In fact no one would have doubted that Paul was including himself were it not for Phil. 3⁶ and for the sentence 'I was once alive apart from the law' in Rom. 7⁹.

Most of those who think this is not autobiographical now depend less on Kümmel's arguments than on the perception, now widely shared, that Adam and the story of his disobedience in the Garden of Eden are the model behind 7⁷⁻¹³, though not vv. 14–25.ˣ The pattern in Gen. 3 is the same as that here: innocence, command, transgression, death. Moreover, only of Adam could it be said that he was once alive apart from the Law (v. 9), i.e. before any commandment at all was given, and the reference to sin's deception (v. 11) looks very much like an allusion to Gen. 3¹³, where virtually the same verb is used for the serpent's deception of Eve. Against the objection that the command not to eat the fruit of the tree is hardly the same as the giving of the Law is the fact that before Paul there was a fusion of the two, with the command not to eat seen as the germ of the whole Law.ʸ Moreover both in Rom. 7 and in the Genesis story there is an emphasis on knowledge, and just as in Genesis the serpent is the agent of sin, so in Rom. 7 sin is a personified power. It seems, in short, overwhelmingly probable that the figure of Adam is to be detected behind this passage. In that case, how can 'I' include an element of autobiography?

x Kümmel rejected any Adamic reference, *Römer 7*, pp. 85ff. It is propounded persuasively by S. Lyonnet, 'L'histoire du salut selon le ch. 7 de l'épître aux Romains', *Bib* 43, 1962, pp. 117–51; also in ' "Tu ne convoiteras pas" ' in *Neotestamentica et Patristica*, FS O. Cullmann, Leiden: Brill 1962, and in *Les étapes du mystère du salut d'après l'Épître aux Romains*, Paris: Bibliothèque Oecuménique 8, 1969, pp. 212–37. See also Käsemann, pp. 193ff.

y The case is argued by Lyonnet in ' "Tu ne convoiteras pas" '; he also shows that there was a tradition according to which the tenth commandment was the essence of the Law. See also Feuillet, 'Loi de Dieu', pp. 32ff. On the fusing of the command not to eat with the Law, see *Shab.* 145b–146a; Ecclus. 17; Targum Neofiti on Gen. 1–3; Philo, *De spec. Leg.* iv, 84f. On the command against coveting as the essence of the whole Law, see IV Macc. 2.6; *Apoc. Mos.* 19.3; Philo, *De Decal.* 142, 150, 173; Targum Neofiti on Ex. 20¹⁷, and cf. Num. 11³⁴ and I Cor. 10⁶.

It can do so if, as Theissen proposes,[z] Adam is the model, but Paul himself as typical of all human beings is the subject. The story of Adam is the story of Everyman and Everywoman, but is still the story of Adam, with the result that there is a tension or oscillation in the passage between Adam and 'I'. Thus, while neither Paul nor we were 'once alive apart from the law', Adam was. On the other hand, the 'I' who speaks so agonizingly in v. 24 is not Adam, but Paul.

Yet there remains the strongest of all objections to allowing any autobiographical element, namely Phil. 3[6]. When Paul there writes of his Jewish credentials, he leaves no room for the tension and feeling of moral impotence that we find in Rom. 7, especially vv. 14–25. He boldly claims that he was 'as to righteousness under the law, blameless'. This is undeniably autobiographical, which seems to imply that Rom. 7 cannot be. The weakest aspect of the anti-autobiographical view is its proposal of a typical (or Adamic) 'I' which does not include Paul himself, or presumably his fellow-Jews who were also ardently Law-observant. The weakest aspect of the autobiographical view is the contrast with Phil. 3[6]. It may even, as some think, be decisive against it.[a] Yet it can be held that Phil. 3[6] reflects how Paul saw things before he was a Christian, while Rom. 7 shows how he sees them now from his Christian perspective. Perhaps he could indeed claim that to outward perception he kept the Law blamelessly, but now with his increased self-knowledge he recognizes that his inward desires were not blameless at all. This is the more plausible if, as we have suggested, it is the particular law against coveting that dominates what he says in Rom. 7.

Theissen[b] conducts a sort of psychological post-mortem on Paul, and suggests that in Rom. 7 we see a previously repressed conflict brought into consciousness. Many will doubtless feel that psychological analysis carried out on a figure from ancient history is apt to be dubious, and in any case is difficult to prove or disprove. At all events, if in Rom. 7 Paul is saying that he (as a typical human being) had trouble with his desires, and is using the tenth commandment as the vehicle of explanation, then he could also say in another context

z *Aspekte*, pp. 194–212.
a This appears to be the view of Sanders, *PPJ*, pp. 443, 479.
b *Aspekte*, pp. 231, 235ff.

that he zealously kept the Law (Phil. 3⁶).

Readers may be tempted to say that neither the case for auto-biography nor the case against it has won, and that neither should have the prize. Controversy continues unabated, and an agreed solu-tion to the identity of 'I' seems as far away as ever. Yet it does seem reasonable to propose that while Adam is the model for the passage vv. 7–13, and that while 'I' is to that extent typical or rhetorical, yet the subject is not Adam but Paul himself as an example. In other words, Paul is not excluded from 'I', but neither is he writing straight-forwardly about himself.[c]

ෆ෨

7

That the law is sin: except for 3³¹, mention of the Law for Christians up to this point in the letter has been largely negative. The apostle seems caught between believing that the Law is God-given (vv. 12–14), and thinking that Christians are now freed from it (vv. 1–6). If the Law can-not simply be classed with what is malign, like sin and sometimes *sarx*, then what is its place in a Christian scheme of things? The argument is far from straightforward, and the suspicion is raised that this was a problem which Paul could not satisfactorily solve.[d] If the Law is not in itself sinful, it is nevertheless connected with sin, and what follows deals with the connection.

if it had not been for the law, I should not have known sin: the most obvious meaning is not 'but for the law, I should not have sinned' but rather 'but for the law I should not have perceived my sin.' That this is the meaning is supported by 5¹³, 'sin indeed was in the world before the law was given, but sin is not counted where there is no law'. On the other hand, if the story of the fall of Adam in the Garden of Eden is in the background here, then Paul may be saying that the coming of the Law (here fused with the command not to eat) was the first occasion of sin. In view of the active nature of sin in vv. 8–11, it is possible that here too the power notion is included: the Law gives sin its opportunity.

c This is essentially to adopt Theissen's view, *Aspekte*, pp. 194–212, but cf. also Cranfield I, pp. 332–4; Althaus, pp. 73–5; Feuillet, 'Loi de Dieu', pp. 33–4.
d Räisänen's whole book, *Paul and the Law*, is a sustained attempt to show that at various points the treatment of the Law is not wholly consistent.

I should not have known what it is to covet if the law had not said, 'You shall not covet': we have already noted that in Jewish tradition coveting could be identified as the sin of Adam, and could also be regarded as the essence and origin of all sin. It is therefore not surprising that Paul takes it as his example. Once taken, it crucially affects what he says about sin and the Law. It is important to note that he does not say that he did not covet until the Law forbade him to do so; what the Law did was to make him aware of what coveting is, and that it is sinful. Longing of various kinds needs no prompting and is normally regarded as quite natural, nothing to do with morality. When people hear the tenth commandment, however, they know coveting for what it is. This argument works much better for the tenth commandment than for most others: one has only to imagine carrying through the argument of the passage in terms of the command not to kill, to realize how apt for Paul's purpose the tenth is.

Despite the arguments of R. H. Gundry,^e it seems unlikely that *epithumia* here means sexual lust rather than covetousness. In Gundry's view the whole of Ch. 7 arises from Paul's discovery of uncontrollable sexual urges within himself at the time of puberty, which coincided with his becoming *bar mitzvah*. It is true that the tenth commandment could be taken in a narrowly sexual sense, though it is not so taken in Ex. 20¹⁷ or Deut. 5²¹. Here, v. 8 tells against such an interpretation: 'sin . . . wrought in me all kinds of *epithumia*'. Moreover, in Paul's writings generally, there are only two places where *epithumia* has a strictly sexual reference: Rom. 1²⁴; I Thess. 4⁵. Elsewhere the reference is quite general.

Therefore we take it that the command is taken in the obvious way, against coveting, the urge to possess even at the cost of dispossessing one's neighbour, an urge which may well pass over into active scheming. It is this that the command does not create, but does expose. Cf. 5^{13, 20}.

8

sin, finding opportunity in the commandment: in the story of the temptation in the Garden of Eden, it was only when God had given the command not to eat of the one tree, that the serpent could have the opportunity to lead Adam and Eve into sin. The question remains how far this is generally true of men and women, especially in the light of the next

---

e 'The Moral Frustration of Paul before his Conversion: Sexual Lust in Romans 7: 7-25', pp. 228-45 of Hagner and Harris.

clause. Meanwhile, we note that sin, parallel to the serpent, appears as an active agent or power that is able to seize chances; it is more than a state of sickness or alienation. Cf. Introduction, 9.

wrought in me all kinds of covetousness: this seems to say that sin used the command to create covetousness where there had been none. Is this possible? Did the command put the idea into people's heads? Can they be taught to covet simply by hearing the command against coveting? It is possible that this is what Paul is saying, improbable though it sounds. However, if v. 7 is a true introduction to what follows, it is more likely that we should understand this statement as saying that implicit or potential sin is made actual by the command. The command does not create my longings, nor does it stop them. What it does is identify them. Then, when I continue with them, my state is so much the worse, for I now know that they constitute covetousness and that this is wrong. Coveting is bad enough when I do not know what it is. Once I do know, and go on coveting, my longings may properly be defined as sinful. In this sense the command leads to sin: my nameless longings become covetousness. Therefore sin 'wrought in me all kinds of covetousness'.[f]

There is nothing in this passage to suggest that the coming of the command leads to an impulse towards self-righteousness.

Apart from the law sin lies dead: if we follow the line of 5¹³f·, this does not mean that there was no sin, but means rather that sin was dormant, lacking the spark to set it off. In the Genesis story, the serpent cannot intervene until the command is given.

It is hard to know whether Paul is now generalizing about the Law as a whole, or still concentrating on the one particular law, that against coveting. In vv. 2, 3 the word *nomos* certainly denotes a particular law, or a particular aspect of the Law, and vv. 7f. up to this point have been about one law. Yet in v. 9a it is probable that the whole Law is meant by *nomos*. In this statement, the law against coveting is surely still in the foreground; there remains the possibility that the point is now being generalized. Cf. 5¹³: for sin to be counted, there needs to be Law.

---

f Cf. Wilckens II, p. 81: the Law gives sin its power. Theissen, *Aspekte*, pp. 225–7, takes seriously the contra-suggestibility explanation of the rise of sin through the Law, but also points out that a norm is needed before latent dispositions can gain direction and goal and become identifiable as sin.

9

I was once alive apart from the law: we have already noted the difficulty of taking this strictly autobiographically. No Jewish child was 'apart from the law': Jewish boys knew about it and were instructed in it long before they became officially responsible for its observance at puberty.ᵍ Yet a boy was 'exempt from the commandments' in the sense that he was not personally responsible for their observance, and this could be what Paul is saying here. On the other hand, in the light of 5¹³, it could be said that the reference is to the time before the giving of the Law on Sinai, but this does not fit with the fusion between Sinai and the command in the Garden, nor with 5¹⁴, 'death reigned from Adam to Moses'. The most likely reference is to the Adam story: death entered the Garden when the command was broken. Before that Adam was 'alive apart from the law' (Gen. 2¹⁶ᶠ·; 3¹⁹).

when the commandment came, sin revived and I died: in the light of the preceding verses, the commandment here is probably a fusion of the command in the Garden with the tenth commandment, a fusion we have already noted. 'I died' then refers to the death that followed breaking the command (Gen. 3¹⁹).

'Revived' is an unhappy translation of the verb *anezēsen*, because it implies that sin had previously been active but had become quiescent. This can hardly be what the passage means. Rather, sin 'sprang to life', a quite possible rendering: it fits the story of Adam, and it also fits the more general statements of vv. 7, 8. The command against coveting, by identifying and condemning innate desires, without doing anything to cure them, in fact produces sin in a now recognizable form. Once again we note that this argument works reasonably well, if somewhat obscurely, for covetousness, but it is hard to see it working for numerous other commandments (murder, for instance, or observing the sabbath). We thus have the sequence: dormant sin, command, active sin, death.

10

the very commandment which promised life: for life as the purpose of God's commandments see Lev. 18⁵; Deut. 30¹⁵⁻²⁰; *Pss. Sol.* 14². It is hard to detect any such promise in Gen. 2¹⁶ᶠ·, where there is only the threat of death if the command is disobeyed. If Paul is fusing the Genesis story with the Law-giving on Sinai, then here the emphasis is strongly on Sinai, not the Garden.

g See the references in Kümmel, *Römer 7*, pp. 81f., and Theissen, *Aspekte*, p. 253.

proved to be death to me: we now seem to have reverted to an emphasis on Adam, and the coming of death after the eating of the fruit, cf. v. 9. There could also be an allusion to Deut. 30¹⁵⁻²⁰, with its alternatives of 'life and good, death and evil' (v. 15). In any case Paul takes it for granted that sin and death belong together, as in 1³² and 5¹²⁻²¹; cf. also 7²⁴.

11

sin, finding opportunity in the commandment: see above on v. 8. The continued use of the singular 'commandment' (*entolē*) suggests that one particular commandment, the tenth, is still chiefly at issue.

deceived me: this is an unexpected word to find here. It is commonly suspected that it occurs because of the closely similar verb in Gen. 3¹³ LXX ('the snake tempted me', where the verb is *ēpatēsen*; here, in Rom. 7¹¹ it is *exēpatēsen*). We thus have another sign that the Adam story is the model for this passage.

12

the law is holy, and the commandment is holy and just and good: the argument since v. 7a has been that the Law is the occasion of sin. This does not mean that it is the cause of sin. On the contrary, the Law in the form of the tenth commandment has been exploited by sin. It is not sinful, but has been used by sin. As nowhere else in Paul, the Law is seen not as a stage in the divine process of salvation (cf. Gal. 3²³⁻²⁵) nor simply as an instrument to reveal what sin is. Instead, sin here feeds on the Law and increases itself. We have suggested that it is feasible to see it doing this in the case of the tenth commandment, though not in the case of many others. The nearest to an explanation that Paul comes is to be found in v. 13. Meanwhile, he reiterates that in itself the command not to covet is God-given (cf. also 13⁹), i.e. it is 'holy and just and good'. Probably 'the law is holy' refers to the whole Torah, of which the tenth commandment is representative, cf. above on v. 8.

13

Did that which is good, then, bring death to me: the human plight is not the fault of the Law or of any command within it, despite sin's exploitation. Paul uses his strongest denial, *mē genoito* (cf. above on 3⁴), against any suggestion that the Law is to blame. The fault is entirely that of sin.

in order that sin might be shown to be sin: once more the function of Law is to make sin perceptible and actual, not merely potential and implicit, cf. $5^{13, \ 20}$; 7^7. On the one hand this is good, as it enables symptoms to appear and thus the underlying and hitherto undetected malaise to be dealt with. At the same time it is bad, because in the process sin palpably increases.

might become sinful beyond measure: cf. 5^{20}. If we come to recognize something (like covetousness) as sinful, but do nothing to combat it, the effect is an increase of sin. [h]

7^{14-25} THE DIVIDED SELF

14We know that the law is spiritual; but I am carnal, sold under sin. 15I do not understand my own actions. For I do not do what I want, but I do the very thing I hate. 16Now if I do what I do not want, I agree that the law is good. 17So then it is no longer I that do it, but sin which dwells within me. 18For I know that nothing good dwells within me, that is, in my flesh. I can will what is right, but I cannot do it. 19For I do not do the good I want, but the evil I do not want is what I do. 20Now if I do what I do not want, it is no longer I that do it, but sin which dwells within me.

21So I find it to be a law that when I want to do right, evil lies close at hand. 22For I delight in the law of God, in my inmost self, 23but I see in my members another law at war with the law of my mind and making me captive to the law of sin which dwells in my members. 24Wretched man that I am! Who will deliver me from this body of death? 25Thanks be to God through Jesus Christ our Lord! So then, I of myself serve the law of God with my mind, but with my flesh I serve the law of sin.

Only a very bold commentator would claim complete understanding of the precise line of the argument in this section. There are changes of presentation from the previous passage, but the first person singular continues to be used. The most obvious change is that the verbs are no longer in a past tense but are now in the present. Is this significant? Again, the material is no longer built on the model of Adam in the

h Watson, *PJG*, pp. 154–5, offers an alternative explanation: sin as a power reproduces itself in human sinning and so becomes 'exceedingly sinful'.

Garden of Eden. Indeed, where there was an element of story in vv. 7–13, here there is an analysis of a divided self, reminiscent (whether Paul knew it or not) of one ancient tradition, best known in the words of Ovid, 'I see and approve the better things, but I pursue the inferior things.'[i] Most of the passage is an underlining of this sorry state of affairs, until in v. 25 Paul announces that there is release from it, through Jesus Christ our Lord. This announced, he then surprisingly returns to a restatement of the basic problem.

Although the notion of a divided self pervades the passage, it is presented in different ways. On the side of evil we have 'I' as 'sold under sin', or simply sin itself (vv. 13, 15, 16, 20), but we also have a law in 'my members' (v. 23) and 'my flesh' (*sarx*) under the control of sin (v. 25). On the side of wanting to do good, the side of hating evil, we have 'I' (vv. 15, 16, 18, 19, 20), 'my inmost self' (v. 22), the 'law of my mind' (vv. 23, 25), and even the law of God (v. 25). Up to v. 20 or even v. 21, there is a division within the person, but after that there is a conflict between different laws or norms. This conflict is not precisely the same as the ancient picture of the divided self so neatly drawn by Ovid. As a result, it is difficult to know exactly how the division is to be conceived.

The basic conflict may well be that of desires, especially if we give full weight to the fact that in vv. 7–13 the concern was with wrong desire, with covetousness. I cannot control my desires, which persist even when I wish they would not. Now this section is not formulated in conflict-of-desires terms, yet the problem of wrong desire not only introduces the passage (vv. 7–13) but may well conclude it (see below on 8^4).

A further difficulty arises from the fact that much of this passage does not work at all well for most of the Law: Paul himself says in Phil. 3^6 that he was 'as to righteousness under the law, blameless'. No doubt he and plenty of other people, then as now, managed to do quite well what God wanted in most respects. Did Paul (or Everyman

---

i *Metamorphoses* 7.19f. For a full account of this ancient tradition about inability to do what one knows ought to be done, and even wants to do, see Theissen, *Aspekte*, pp. 213–20. He also discusses the quite different ancient view that to know the right is to do it, so that at the root of defective action lies defective understanding.

or Everywoman) really have a conflict about keeping the sabbath, or about refraining from murder, or making graven images, or stealing? There have always been some people who have difficulty over things that others manage easily, but Paul is supposed to be presenting a human paradigm, not pleading a special case. We cannot call in aid that sort of inward infringement of commands familiar to us from reading Matt. 5²¹⁻⁴⁸, for there is nothing in Rom. 7 to suggest extending the Law in that way. So then, most people of whatever persuasion can keep most of the law under which they live, most of the time and without undue difficulty. What they cannot control are their desires, and these are the target of the command against coveting. There is thus a good case for supposing that throughout vv. 14–25 the tenth commandment is still Paul's concern. If he is generalizing from it, then we must confess that it is a precarious generalization.

The time reference of these verses is much disputed. Whether or not they include an element of autobiography, they cannot be solely autobiographical. They are typical, pointing to a human dilemma, but is it a dilemma of Christians, or a dilemma of people without Christ, whether Jews or pagans? Do these verses describe how it was, or how it is?

A. *For pre-Christian experience*

1. The preceding section, vv. 7–13, is certainly about life before Christ, and it is natural to assume the same of this section. We simply move from an Adam-model to a divided-self-model, in order to show that the Law cannot solve the human problem of how to do right.

2. For many commentators[j] the statements 'I am carnal, sold under sin' (v. 14), 'with my flesh I serve the law of sin' (v. 25), and even the cry 'Wretched man that I am, who will deliver me from this body of death?' are incompatible with the life of the Spirit to be set out in Ch. 8. It is not that there is expected to be no conflict in Christian life, but that these expressions suggest not so much conflict as defeat. Neither Ch. 6 nor Ch. 8 sits easily with the note of helplessness that is so strong here. It is sometimes replied[k] that the flesh-Spirit conflict

j E.g. Theissen, *Aspekte*, pp. 186f.; Althaus, pp. 79–81; Dodd, p. 108; Wilckens II, p. 86.

k As by Cranfield I, pp. 357f.; Feuillet, 'Loi de Dieu', p. 38; Dunn, 'Rom. 7, 14–25', pp. 260, 268f.

continues in Christians, and that it is commonly those who are most aware of God who are also most aware of their own sinfulness. This is true, but it is the notion of bondage expressed in 'sold under sin' that seems incompatible with the freedom that Christians have obtained according to the argument of Ch. 6.

3. There is nothing in Ch. 7 about Christ or the Spirit until we reach v. 25a, which is presented as the solution to the human dilemma. It is a natural presumption that up to that point Paul is talking about human beings without Christ and the Spirit.

4. The parallel with Ovid, *Metamorph.* 7.19f. and similar pagan accounts of the divided self (whether Paul knew them or not) may provide some slight support for the pre-Christian view.

5. While in 8$^{5-13}$ (and also Gal. 5$^{16-23}$) it is the essentially divine *Pneuma* (Spirit) that is opposed to *sarx* (flesh), in this passage it is rather the *nous* (mind), which may be taken to be a purely human faculty. Thus here the conflict is strictly within the human sphere, without that divine entry into the arena represented by *Pneuma*.

Of all these arguments, the second is the most cogent. Could Paul have said that the Christian is sold under sin? This is a difficulty that many find insuperable.

B. *For Christian experience*

1. According to Paul elsewhere (1$^{18-32}$), the human person apart from Christ is not divided at all, but is completely under the control of sin (cf. 3$^{9ff.}$; 6$^{17-20}$). It is the divided self that hates evil (7^{15}), as the undivided sinner does not. The advent of grace through Christ gives rise to the experience of division, because with the arrival of another power into the fray, sin no longer has things its own way.

2. To borrow a phrase from Martin Luther, the essence of the Christian's position is that of being *simul justus et peccator*, at once justified and a sinner, living between the Old and the New Ages, belonging essentially to the New (e.g. Rom. 6^{11}) but still existing in the Old (e.g. Rom. 6^{12}). In short, it is because Christians are anomalies with regard to the shift of the ages that they live in tension between being bound and being free, between being in the flesh and in the Spirit.[1]

1 This case is thoroughly argued by, among many others, Dunn, 'Rom. 7, 14-25', and Cranfield I, pp. 345f.

3. In v. 14 there is a change from the past tense to the present, and the natural inference to draw is that Paul has moved from what *was* (vv. 7–13) to what is (vv. 14–25), from past experience to present. This is reinforced by the fact that in vv. 7–13 sin appears to be invincible, while it is not in vv. 14–25. There it can be resisted, even if not with notable success. To all this it may be replied that if there is a fundamental change of situation represented by the change in verb tenses, it is surprising that it takes place so unobtrusively. Could it not be that Paul has slipped into the present because he has moved from story to analysis, and that the present is the natural tense to use for analysis?

4. In the structure of the letter, Chs. 5–8 are about the new life in Christ in its various aspects, and it would be strange if Ch. 7 were not about this, but about life without Christ. In other words it would be strange if 7$^{14-25}$ were a reversion to the situation left behind after 3^{21}. There is some force in this, but since 7$^{7-13}$ is undoubtedly about life without Christ, the supposed pattern has been broken in any case. The present passage could equally well be about life without Christ.

5. Perhaps the best piece of evidence for the Christian interpretation is the position of 7$^{25 b}$. If in vv. 14–24 we have an analysis of the human being without Christ, and v. 24a ('Thanks be to God through Jesus Christ our Lord') produces the solution, how can Paul in v. 25b revert to a restatement of the problem? How can he then say, 'I of myself serve the law of God with my mind, but with my flesh I serve the law of sin'? The answer suggested is that vv. 14–24 are about *Christian* experience, that v. 25a acknowledges that in the end Christ brings deliverance, and that v. 25b shows that meanwhile the division goes on. This is a weighty argument, and those who hold to the pre-Christian interpretation often have recourse to proposing that a marginal gloss has been inserted into the text, or that verses have become transposed.[m] There is no evidence in the MSS for either a gloss or a transposition, and most commentators are understandably reluctant to adopt either explanation in the absence of such evidence. Never-

---

m For the gloss explanation see R. Bultmann, 'Glossen in Römerbrief', *TLZ* 72, 1947, pp. 198f.; Leenhardt, p. 195; Käsemann, pp. 211f. For the transposition explanation see Dodd, pp. 114f.; very cautiously, Black, p. 108.

theless it must be admitted that there is another oddity at this point: 8^1 seems to interrupt the flow of thought, and 8^2 would follow naturally after 7^{25a}. It is also true that v. 25b comes oddly after v. 25a on *any* reading of vv. 14–25 (see below on v. 25). Nevertheless it is true that the position of v. 25b fits the Christian interpretation of the passage better than the pre-Christian.

6. 'The inmost self' (literally 'the inner man', *ton esō anthrōpon*) refers to the Christian person in II Cor. 4^{16} and Eph. 3^{16} and might be expected to do so here as well. Moreover, in this chapter (vv. 23, 25) the reason or mind (*nous*) is on the side of obedience to God, congruent with the renewed mind as the property of the Christian in Rom. 12^2 and Eph. 4^{23}. Therefore, it may be argued, in Rom. 7 we are talking about Christian experience. Unfortunately the matter is not quite as clear as that. 'The inner man' is a reasonably common expression in Hellenistic dualism, and in the case of II Cor. 4^{16} it is the context, not the expression in itself, that requires for it a Christian reference. Further, here the inner man is overpowered by sin, which is not the case in the passages in II Corinthians or Ephesians. In the end, this by no means negligible piece of evidence cannot be decisive.

In assessing the two sides of the argument, we may well be driven to conclude that in the face of such good but opposite cases, Paul's lack of clarity prevents a decision between them. Many of the arguments are less than conclusive, and whereas the position of v. 25b is a serious threat to the pre-Christian view, 'sold under sin' in v. 14 is an equally serious threat to the Christian view. Most commentators feel obliged to choose, though occasionally one suggests that, while Paul was fundamentally talking about the position without Christ, yet he showed an awareness that this situation did not abruptly cease at baptism but continued, though in a less crippling fashion.[n] The present commentary tentatively adopts the pre-Christian view: it is hard to believe that Paul could use such negative and uncompromising language of Christians as 'sold under sin'.[o] Nevertheless it is well to note that the struggle of the divided person is not the basic point of the passage, which is primarily concerned rather with the Law's in-

n This is the position of Feuillet, 'Loi de Dieu', pp. 38–40.
o This is in contrast to the view taken in Ziesler, *Meaning*, pp. 203f.

ability to deliver men and women from their moral problems. This may go some way towards explaining the lack of clarity already mentioned: Paul was focussing on the Law, not on the identity of 'I'. It is also well to remember that the passage is written from an avowedly Christian perspective; even if it is about pre-Christian experience, whether Jewish or universal, this does not mean that it seemed like this at the time.

ଏଉ

14
We know: who are 'we'? Once again Paul seems to assume that all his readers are, or have been, involved in the question of the Law. In fact, the personal history and experience of many of them may have been quite different (see above on vv. 1, 4).

the law is spiritual: the adjective 'spiritual' (*pneumatikos*) is a slippery one. It makes little sense in the context if it is taken as the opposite of 'material'. It must mean what it usually means in the NT, viz. 'belonging to and coming from God', for God is Spirit, and 'Spirit' is a regular way of denoting his activity.[p] As throughout the chapter, Paul continues to see the Law as in itself God-given. The trouble is not with it, but with sin's exploitation of it.

I am carnal, sold under sin: literally, 'I am fleshly (*sarkinos*), sold under sin.' 'Sold' reflects the metaphor of slavery: sin is the master, and I am the slave (cf. Ch. 6, where the pervasive point is deliverance from slavery). The Law is not the cause of the human problem, but its occasion. The causes are sin and *sarx*, as we have seen (on *sarx* cf. 1³; see also on 7⁵). It is my sin-dominated self, orientated towards anything but God, that causes me when faced by the divine command not to embrace it with joy and freedom, but to disobey it and prefer death to life. It is important that we grasp this understanding of *sarx* (flesh) as the sin-dominated self, for the gist of the passage is certainly not that the outward or physical is at war with the inward or spiritual, even if vv. 23, 25 could be misunderstood as pointing in that direction. The point is rather that the whole of me is errant, even while in my heart of hearts I know

p On *Pneuma* see above on 1³⁻⁴⁹, and Turner, *Words*, pp. 426–8; Hill, *Greek Words and Hebrew Meanings*, Ch. 6. On the interpretation of *pneumatikos* advocated here, cf. Cranfield I, pp. 355f.

what is right and even partly desire it. Moreover, the paradigm of sin that Paul adopted in v. 7 (*epithumia*, covetousness) is not concerned only with physical lusts, though naturally they are included, but with wrong desires of all kinds (v. 8). Paul's understanding of 'fleshly' life has already been outlined in Gal. 5^{19-21}, where it embraces wrong desires and attitudes in physical, religious, and social spheres. He will make the opposition between fleshly life (i.e. directed away from God) and spiritual life (i.e. directed towards God) more dramatically clear in Ch. 8.

15

I do the very thing I hate: all through this passage we have not only the question about the degree of autobiography that is present, but also the question about what in 'me' is divided from what. The heart of the dilemma is that 'I' can stand back from myself, observe and deplore the position I am in, but do nothing about it. 'I' am both subject and object of concern. This is simple enough to state, and in the end it may be all that Paul is saying. If so, it is unfortunate that his choice of words later on in the passage produces complications.

'Doing the thing I hate' is a common enough human experience that hardly requires a previous life in Judaism to give it poignancy.q We have noted that in most things for most people this is not true, but it is especially apt to be true in the matter of coveting, of controlling one's desires. In vv. 14–16, the fundamental opposition is between will and deed within me; in vv. 17–20 it is between me and sin.

16

I agree that the law is good: again, the particular law against coveting may be primarily in view, though Paul is probably generalizing from it. There is nothing wrong with the law. Yet, good and spiritual though it is, it cannot stop me from infringing the divine will, but rather increases my doing so (see on v. 13).

17

it is no longer I that do it, but sin: the opposition is now between me and sin. 'I' is now some sort of innate better self, even though as a whole I am 'sold under sin', with sin in control of me. Paul can hardly mean to disclaim all personal involvement when he says 'it is no longer I that do

---

q Cf. Theissen, *Aspekte*, pp. 213–23; Käsemann, pp. 200f. See also the words of Ovid quoted above in the introduction to the passage.

it', for it is still 'I' that need deliverance, v. 24. The next three verses elaborate this idea that I am not in control of myself, but that sin is.

18

nothing good dwells within me, that is, in my flesh: the alien power that has taken control of me is totally malign.

21

I find it to be a law: this law is not the Torah, nor any part of it, but simply 'a rule'; cf. the discussion of his general meaning for 'law' (*nomos*) at 3^{27}.[r] Paul may be making a deliberate play on words: *this* is the law that bothers us. Equivalent to a general rule, it is not the same as 'the other law' of v. 23, which is in fact the rule of sin, on which see below.

22

I delight in the law of God in my inmost self: on 'my inmost self' see above p. 194. The exact meaning of 'the law of God' is debatable. It could be the will of God in the broadest sense, or that will as expressed in the Torah.[s] At all events there is an opposition between the self that loves the divine will and the self that does not obey it. It is not a matter of the mind against the body, nor even of an external law against the inner self, for the delight in the law is inward.

23

I see in my members another law at war with the law of my mind: the way the conflict is expressed changes yet again, and is now a matter of opposing laws, not of 'I' against sin or *sarx*. Clearly enough the law that is at war with the law of my mind is the power of sin, and can hardly be the Torah. There seem to be so many uses of 'law' (*nomos*) in these verses that it is helpful to tabulate them:[t]

  (external) Law of God, v. 22   against law of sin, v. 23;
  (internal) law of mind, v. 23   against law in members, v. 23.
In v. 25, I serve the Law of God with my mind;
    I serve the law of sin with my *sarx*/flesh.
It is difficult to take 'law'/*nomos* consistently to denote the Torah

---

r See again Räisänen, *Torah*, pp. 119–47, especially p. 142.
s For the first, see Feuillet, 'Loi de Dieu', pp. 35, 42; for the second, Wilckens II, p. 90.
t Cf. Feuillet, 'Loi de Dieu', p. 41.

throughout these verses.[u] Something like 'norm', 'régime', or 'ruling force' is required, though no translation quite brings out the play on words.

What are these various laws? In the setting of the chapter, especially vv. 14–25, it is evident that 'the law of God' is his will, no doubt chiefly as expressed in the Torah. This is supported by 'the law of my mind', which, again in the light of the whole chapter, is not the mind as opposed to the body, but that urge towards the good that even pagans have, cf. 1^{19}; $2^{14, 15}$. It is the instinctive human assent to the divine will ($2^{14f.}$ again). 'The law of sin' and 'the law in my members' (v. 23) are evidently the same, and are that power of sin which perverts the Law of God and makes me do things which with 'my mind' or 'my inmost self' (v. 22) I do not wish to do. Once again, the basic picture of a divided self is not at all obscure, but complication arises from the varying terminology used to delineate it.

'My members' are my faculties, cf. above on 6^{13}. They naturally include sexuality, but are not limited to it, any more than covetousness in v. 7 is limited to sexual desire.

24

Wretched man that I am: cf. the somewhat similar lament over the human condition in the slightly later II(4) Esd. 7. 65–69, 116–26.

this body of death: the phrase encapsulates the plight from which the wretched man cries for deliverance. Literally it is 'from the body (*tou sōmatos*) of this death'. For *sōma* see on 6^6. It is possible that we should take it here in a strictly physical sense, thus lending support to the view[v] that the entire passage 7^{7-25} is concerned with the physical passion of lust. However, although the command quoted in 7^7 may be held to dominate the chapter, we have seen that this should not be taken narrowly as concerned with sexual lust. As we saw at 6^6, Paul could use *sōma* for the whole person; if that whole person is often viewed through the physical, this is hardly surprising. How else do we normally view

u See, however, Wilckens II, pp. 90f. On the other hand Räisänen, *PL*, pp. 52, 67, rightly points out that although generally in this part of Romans 'law' when unqualified is the Torah, in vv. 21–25 it is qualified by genitives, e.g. 'of sin', or by 'other', and when so qualified need not be the Torah. An expression like 'law of sin' can be applied to the Torah only with considerable ingenuity. Cf. *Torah*, p. 143.

v Cf. Gundry, 'The Moral Frustration of Paul before his Conversion', and *Sōma in Biblical Theology*, pp. 40, 139.

one another, or even ourselves? Yet the physical is not in contrast with the mental, emotional, and volitional, but represents and points to them. 'This body of death' is therefore the whole person living under sin and thus belonging to death, being indeed effectively already dead, cf. 8$^{6, 10}$.^{w}

25

Thanks be to God through Jesus Christ our Lord: there is more than one oddity about this. Not only does it come too early on the pre-Christian view of the passage (it ought to come at the end of the statement of the problem, i.e. at the end of v. 25), it also lacks any verb, and latches awkwardly on to the end of v. 24. What is needed is something like 'Thanks be to God, deliverance comes through Jesus Christ our Lord.' Yet this is not what we have. There are textual variants which, in answer to the question of v. 24, 'Who will deliver me?' read 'The grace of God through Jesus Christ . . .' These, however, look like attempts to provide a smoother reading; the text as we have it, despite its awkwardness, is to be preferred.

I of myself serve the law of God with my mind, but with my flesh I serve the law of sin: on the contrast see above on v. 23. On any view of vv. 14–25, it is odd to have the problem restated after the solution has been announced. It is therefore not surprising that some commentators (e.g. Käsemann, pp. 211f.) regard it as a gloss by a later hand, though once again there is no MS which lacks it. It is certainly easier to suppose that Paul restated the problem thus if the whole dilemma is a continuing Christian one than if it is one that is now past, but it is still strange. Right at the end of the treatment of the Law's powerlessness to heal the divided self we are given yet another way of formulating the division. There is some reason, then, to suspect that this is a gloss that has crept into the text at a very early stage.

8$^{1-17}$ DELIVERANCE FROM FLESH AND LIVING IN
         THE SPIRIT AS THE CHILDREN OF GOD

8 *There is therefore now no condemnation for those who are in Christ Jesus.* ^{2}*For the law of the Spirit of life in Christ Jesus has set me free from the law of sin and death.* ^{3}*For God has done what the law, weakened by the*

w On this see Dunn, 'Rom. 7, 14–25 in the Theology of Paul', pp. 269–71.

flesh, could not do: sending his own Son in the likeness of sinful flesh and for sin, he condemned sin in the flesh, ⁴in order that the just requirement of the law might be fulfilled in us, who walk not according to the flesh but according to the Spirit. ⁵For those who live according to the flesh set their minds on the things of the flesh, but those who live according to the Spirit set their minds on the things of the spirit. ⁶To set the mind on the flesh is death, but to set the mind on the Spirit is life and peace. ⁷For the mind that is set on the flesh is hostile to God; it does not submit to God's law, indeed it cannot; ⁸and those who are in the flesh cannot please God.

⁹But you are not in the flesh, you are in the Spirit, if the Spirit of God really dwells in you. Any one who does not have the spirit of Christ does not belong to him. ¹⁰But if Christ is in you, although your bodies are dead because of sin, your spirits are alive because of righteousness. ¹¹If the Spirit of him who raised Jesus from the dead dwells in you, he who raised Christ Jesus from the dead will give life to your mortal bodies also through his Spirit which dwells in you.

¹²So then, brethren, we are debtors, not to the flesh, to live according to the flesh – ¹³for if you live according to the flesh you will die, but if by the Spirit you put to death the deeds of the body you will live. ¹⁴For all who are led by the Spirit of God are sons of God. ¹⁵For you did not receive the spirit of slavery to fall back into fear, but you have received the spirit of sonship. When we cry, 'Abba! Father!' ¹⁶it is the Spirit himself bearing witness with our spirit that we are children of God, ¹⁷and if children, then heirs, heirs of God and fellow heirs with Christ, provided we suffer with him in order that we may also be glorified with him.

In a passage so strikingly reminiscent of Gal. 4 that it is possible that common tradition lies behind both passages, ˣ Paul sets out the alternative kinds of life: that in the flesh/*sarx*, marked by sin, death, and condemnation, and that in the Spirit/*Pneuma*, marked by life, peace, righteousness, and sonship. It is now amply clear that he envisages the two kinds of life as lived in different spheres of power which are mutually exclusive. It is only in the Spirit that men and women can be the sort of people and live the sort of life that God intends. Once again the general drift of the passage is much easier to grasp than some of the details.

x So Wilckens II, pp. 138–9.

Those who exist within the power of the Spirit go on living in this world, but not independently of God. Rather, they live under and for God and Christ, for the Spirit is now not only the agent of God, but also of Christ. Belonging to Christ and having the Spirit are the same. Thus life that continues here on earth cannot be ordinary, Godless life, but is that life in the Spirit of which the resurrection of Christ is the sign. So, the choice is between death and life, life that pertains not only to this world but also beyond it.

We ought not to think of alternative forms of enslavement (despite Ch. 6). On the contrary, life in the Spirit is life as the children of God, not as his slaves. Obedience is indeed still required, but it is the obedience of those who are in a special relationship with God, and who look forward to their full and final inheritance. The choice is thus clear: life centred in and empowered by God, or life centred in what is not God and so is powerless to please him.

෴

1
There is therefore: with what does 'therefore' (*ara*) connect? It can hardly be with 7²⁵ᵇ, and the suspicion that the last words of Ch. 7 are a gloss is thus reinforced. Probably it connects with 7⁶, so that vv. 7–25 are a parenthesis giving an account of what stands in the way of new life in the Spirit. 'Therefore' in any case is not explained by the mind-flesh division of 7²⁵ᵇ, and so, whatever we make of that, the argument to 8¹ runs either from 7²⁵ᵃ or from 7⁶.

now: we should give this its full force. It is not just a logical 'now', but a temporal one. *Now*, in the New Age of Christ and the Spirit, new life is available (cf. again 7⁶).

no condemnation for those who are in Christ Jesus: for 'in Christ' see above on 6¹¹. The first thing about those who belong to Christ, and who live within his sphere of power and authority, is that they are not condemned. On the contrary, they are acquitted, forgiven, reconciled (cf. 3²¹–5²¹). Having said this, for the rest of the section Paul is much more concerned with the continuing life of believers in the Spirit. It is important to notice that in a passage which is largely concerned with the Spirit, he can begin by talking about Christ and about being in him. Although being in Christ and being in the Spirit are the same from the point of view of the believers, this does not mean that Christ and the Spirit are simply identified. See further on vv. 9–11.

2

the law of the Spirit of life in Christ Jesus: despite some attempts to argue that 'law'/*nomos* here is the Law of Moses, now approached from the new perspective of faith in Christ and of life in the Spirit, it is much more likely that it means something like 'régime' or 'rule'. Those who argue the former case usually see the opposition in this verse as between obeying the Law as Christians in faith, and obeying it in order to achieve favour with God.[y] Here Paul is not, however, talking about different ways of keeping the Torah, but about different powers under which people may live.

'Spirit' has rightly been given a capital letter in RSV, for we are dealing with the Spirit of God himself. This is God's activity and power, evident from the creation of the world (Gen. 1^2), experienced by people like Saul (I Sam. $10^{6, 10}$) and the seventy elders (Num. $11^{24ff.}$), and to become much more widely experienced in the New Age (Joel 2^{28-29}). Indeed the New Age would be the age of the Spirit, as at Qumran (cf. IQS 4).[z] This Spirit gives life, as he always does in the Bible, going back to Gen. 2^7, but now 'in Christ Jesus'. With RSV, I take 'in Christ Jesus' with 'life' and not with 'has set me free' (against Cranfield I, pp. 374f.). This is the more natural connection, cf. v. 11. Being in Christ means life in the Spirit, a life which is also freedom.

has set me free from the law of sin and death: although it is possible that there is a reference to the Mosaic Law which led (cf. 7^{9-11}) to sin and death, it is more likely that there is a straightforward contrast with the reign of the Spirit. This reign of sin and death, opposed to that of the Spirit, is also a reign of *sarx*, as we are about to see. Being under the power of the Spirit spells deliverance from that oppression by sin and death which has dominated the letter since 5^{12}.

y See Hübner, *LPT*, pp. 144–7. Against such a view see Räisänen, *PL*, pp. 50–3. It is sometimes suggested that a general meaning such as 'rule/régime' is impossible for *nomos* (so Wilckens II, pp. 121f.), but this has now been answered by Räisänen's article, 'Sprächliches zum Spiel des Paulus mit NOMOS', pp. 119–47, of *Torah*. See especially p. 144.

z On Spirit/*Pneuma* especially in the OT and Judaism see E. Schweizer in *TDNT* VI. pp. 396–455; M. E. Isaacs, *The Concept of Spirit*, Heythrop College 1976; G. W. H. Lampe, *God as Spirit*, OUP 1978, Ch. 2; Turner, *Christian Words*, pp. 426–8; Whiteley, *Theology*, pp. 124–9.

3
God has done . . . what the law could not do: Paul does not make it altogether clear what the Law could not do, but we probably ought to take
this statement in the light both of v. 4 (where 'the just requirement of
the law' is 'fulfilled in us') and of 7^{14-25}, where the Law can point the
way, but cannot enable people to follow it. The previous chapter has
shown that there is even a sense in which the Law has increased sin, not
eliminated it.

weakened by the flesh: cf. $7^{14, 18, 25}$. Paul does not consider what the
Law might have done had it not been weakened by the flesh/*sarx*, i.e.
by the apparently innate human tendency to flee from God and his will.
Such speculation was doubtless not to his taste. As things are, knowing
God's will does not enable sinful human beings to do it. It is worth
observing that there is no hint here in Romans of the idea found in
Galatians (3^{19-26}) that the Law was a temporary divine expedient,
probably to prepare people for Christ by demonstrating the need for
salvation. Here, sin and flesh have rendered the Law useless as a way out
of the bondage under which men and women suffer. So what is it that
God has now done in order to replace sin by righteousness, bondage by
freedom, death by life?

sending his own son in the likeness of sinful flesh: for a possible reference to
Abraham's 'binding of Isaac', see on 8^{32}. An allusion to the Isaac story
is more convincing there than here. It is notable that in this chapter
Jesus is referred to as God's son almost as often as in the whole of the
rest of the letter: thrice in Ch. 1, once in Ch. 5, and thrice in Ch. 8. The
occurrence of 'own', whether or not we detect a reference to Isaac,
precludes the idea that Jesus is simply an emissary or obedient servant
of God. It must indicate some sort of special relationship.

'In the likeness of sinful flesh' could be held to mean that Jesus was
only apparently a real human being, in later terms a docetic Christ,
except for the fact that not only does Paul generally take it for granted
that Jesus was truly human, but also *needs* him to have been so if his
Adam-Christ antithesis is to work (5^{12-21}). Further, later in this same
verse he says that Christ 'condemned sin in the flesh', which presumably
means that he was in the flesh when he condemned sin. It is possible,
nevertheless, that there is some reservation about his humanness here,
arising from a conviction that this was not the whole truth about him. [a]

a So Cranfield I, pp. 579–82, after a long and lucid discussion of all the main
possibilities.

The more usual argument is that, if there is any reservation implicit in 'likeness', it is in relation to sin, not in relation to his being truly human: Jesus lived under the same conditions as we do, in the same network of human relationships, and within the same sinful structures of society, but he did not contribute to their sinfulness. [b]

There is another possibility. There may be no reservation implicit in 'likeness' (*homoiōma*) any more than there is in 5^{14} or 6^5: the meaning is straightforwardly that Christ came into the same conditions of human life as the rest of us. That, according to Christian belief, he was nonetheless sinless is taken account of in the rest of the verse, but at this point it must first be established that his conditions of life were just like ours.

Part of the difficulty of this phrase is related to the meaning here of *sarx*, 'flesh' (see above at 1^3). In the light of what follows up to v. 13, it is most natural to take it here to mean life without God, life centred in something other than God, and how could a sinless Christ have entered into that? On the other hand it is possible that this meaning of *sarx* does not take over until v. 4, and that in v. 3 'flesh' is simply those human conditions and relationships in which Christ did enter. It may seem difficult to propose a different meaning for the same word in successive verses, yet one meaning easily slides into the other. That is to say that we start with *sarx* used in a neutral sense for mere ordinary humanity (with a reference to sin in order to show that this is the realm in which sin operates). Then, from v. 4 *sarx* becomes the realm of sin without qualification. [c] Probably, therefore, Paul is saying that Christ lived under normal human and sinful conditions, with the one exception that he did not share the sin of those conditions, but rather condemned it and provided a way to overcome it, cf. vv. 3d–4.

and for sin: literally, 'concerning sin' (*peri hamartias*). If this translation is correct, then Paul is saying that God sent his son in order to deal with sin, without being any more specific. It is possible, however, that this is a technical expression meaning 'as a sin-offering' (cf. Lev. 9^2; 14^{31}; Isa. 53^{10}; Ps. 40^6) so that we have what amounts to a repetition of the

b So Wilckens II, p. 126; Barrett, pp. 155–6; Bruce, pp. 160f.; Robinson, p. 94, and many others.

c See, however, Jewett, *Terms*, pp. 148–53, for the view that *sarx* is used in the same way throughout, and that Christ is 'made to be sin' in the same sense as in II Cor. 5^{21}.

expiatory use of *hilastērion* in 3²⁵. [d] Though it is impossible to be certain about it, this interpretation cannot be ruled out. In any case we have the problem of what it means to say that Christ was a sin-offering, and in effect we are brought back to our earlier discussion about the meaning of *hilastērion* and of sacrificial terminology in general when applied to the death of Christ. Therefore whether we take *peri hamartias* to allude to the sin-offering or to be much more vague, we are doubtless right to see a tacit reference to the cross; yet are we to think in representative, substitutionary, or participatory terms? [e] See the discussion on 3²⁵.

he condemned sin in the flesh: startlingly, God's way of dealing with sin is first of all to condemn it! There are two questions here.

(*a*) Is Paul saying that Christ condemned sin-in-the-flesh, or that Christ-in-the-flesh condemned sin? It can hardly be the former, because that would be tautological: what other kind of sin is there? Ideas of the angels' sinning spiritually in heaven can scarcely be imported into the text without some clue that they should be. For Paul, sin and flesh/*sarx* go together so naturally that to talk about sin-in-the-flesh is otiose. Much more probably the clause says that Christ, when in the flesh, condemned sin, either by his sinless life or by his death. Commentators usually detect a double reference, i.e. both to his life and to his death, influenced partly by the whole context and partly by *peri hamartias*, 'for sin'. [f]

(*b*) Is it explicable that Paul should begin talking about what God achieved in sending his son by talking about condemnation? Surely sin was quite sufficiently condemned before the coming of Christ; one has only to read the Law and the Prophets. Perhaps we could say that sin was shown up in an even starker and more terrible light than before by the life and especially the death of Christ. The more immediate explanation, however, must be in terms of the verse that follows (v. 4): the condemnation Christ brought was a necessary step towards release and

d. On this possibility see Wilckens II, pp. 126–8; Käsemann, p. 216. That the sin-offering was aimed precisely at the sort of unwilling sin depicted in Rom. 7 is argued in detail by N. T. Wright, 'The Meaning of *peri hamartias* in Romans 8.3', pp. 453–9 of Livingstone, *Studia Biblica 1978 III*.

e Sanders, *PPJ*, pp. 466f., thinks that even in this verse Paul's understanding of the cross is participatory, i.e. we die with Christ. This is certainly supported by the nearest discussion of the cross in the letter, in Ch. 6.

f See Cranfield I, pp. 382f.; Wilckens II, pp. 126–8; Käsemann, p. 217; Sanday and Headlam, p. 194; Murray, pp. 281f.

recovery. We needed to know the truth about our condition before we could accept the remedy. In the same way, 1^{18}–3^{20} with its thoroughly negative view of the human condition has the positive purpose of preparing for the healing of that condition provided by Christ.

4

in order that the just requirement of the law might be fulfilled: this is the end God had in view, that we should at last be empowered (by the Spirit) to do what the Law requires. But what is that?

(*a*) Paul could be saying that the Law, presumably all of it, can now at last be kept by Christian believers, whereas formerly it could not. After all that has been said in Ch. 7 about dying to the Law, this sounds very strange indeed. It remains surprising, even if we think that while in Ch. 7 Paul was talking about dying to the Law as a way of salvation, here he is talking about its being kept by those who, in the Spirit, have no misconception of it as a means of earning salvation.^{g} This view is not easy to support from the text. It must be said that usually 'the just requirement of the law' is understood more in terms of doing God's will than in terms of literal keeping of the whole Torah. This is chiefly because we know, even from within Romans itself, that Paul could sit loose to some requirements of the Law, such as circumcision and probably sabbath-keeping (cf. 2^{29}; 14$^{5, 14}$).

(*b*) There could be a tacit reference to the summary of the Law in terms of love, cf. 13$^{8-10}$; Gal. 5^{14}. This is a widely-held interpretation of the clause, favoured at least partly because it is implausible to suppose that Paul really wanted all Christians to keep all the Law.^{h} Even more widely-held is the view that it is essentially the moral law, or the moral parts of the Law, that we should understand as now kept by Christians.^{i} In both these views, Paul is talking about something other than the Law, the whole Law, straightforwardly understood. Neither view can be deemed impossible, nor even implausible, yet there is nothing in either text or context to point to such a concentration on love in particular or the moral law in general. To that extent, these interpretations are unsatisfactory.

g For such a view see Hübner, *LPT*, pp. 146f.; Cranfield I, pp. 383–5. Bruce, pp. 161–3, refers to the hope of a new heart, a new inwardness, which makes the doing of God's will at last a possibility, in terms of Jer. 31$^{33f.}$; Ezek. 36$^{26f.}$.

h See Wilckens II, pp. 128–30; Robinson, p. 95.

i E.g. by Lagrange, p. 195; Michel, pp. 251f.; Schmidt, pp. 137f.; see also Cranfield I, p. 383f., though compare his view on (*a*).

(c) The word normally used in LXX for the requirements of the Law is *dikaiōmata*, a plural for the commands collectively. Here, however, we have the singular *dikaiōma*, which we should expect to denote one particular command of the Law. If we suspect that turning to the command to love is unwarranted here, then it may be right to turn back to 7^7 and the command against coveting (the command to love will not be mentioned until 13^{8-10}). Moreover, if we are right in understanding 7^{7-25} as focussed on the tenth commandment as the paradigm of the Law, then it would be natural for Paul here in 8^4 to return to where he began, now that he is propounding the solution to the problems raised through the command not to covet. In short, it is plausible to suppose that 'the righteous requirement of the law' is that tenth commandment which has pervaded the discussion since 7^7.[j] We know that though Paul did not regard circumcision and some other items of the Law as binding for all Christians, he did so regard the command against coveting, within the overall requirement to love (13^{8-10}). Perhaps, therefore, in maintaining that believers are now enabled to obey this particular commandment, he is not saying anything for or against obedience to other commandments, except in so far as 7^{1-6} has said that Christians are free from the Law as a régime. At any rate *this* command stands, and can now be kept.

Apart from maintaining a unity of presentation from 7^7 onwards, the interpretation suggested avoids having Paul mean something different from what he says, such as referring to the love command, or the moral law, or even those parts of the Law which do not separate Jews from Gentiles.[k] It also softens the contradiction between being dead to the Law in 7^6, and being enabled to keep it as never before in 8^4. Again, such a focus on the command against coveting, which is primarily to do with desires and inwardness, is especially appropriate to 8^{1-11}, which is concerned with inwardness also, and with the hidden basis of life.

There remains the matter of the requirement's being 'fulfilled in us' (*plērōthē en hēmin*). In the Greek Bible, both OT and NT, 'to fulfil the law' in the active is very unusual, and even more so in the passive. The

---

j For a more detailed account of this interpretation, see J. A. Ziesler, 'The Just Requirement of the Law (Romans 8:4)', *Australian Biblical Review* XXXV, 1987, pp. 77–82. See also now Watson, *PJG*, pp. 156f., though he takes the tenth commandment strictly sexually.

k On this last proposal see Sanders, *PLJP*, pp. 98f., 101–3, and cf. Dunn, 'The New Perspective on Paul', pp. 95–122. Räisänen, *PL*, pp. 28, 67, 113–15, thinks that 'the just requirement of the law' is 'the law as interpreted by Paul the Christian'.

Law was normally observed or kept or simply done, but not fulfilled. The expression in the active with Jesus as subject does occur in Matt. 5^{17}, but there it is highly likely that at least some note of eschatology is present, some note of things having now been brought to fruition and consummation. It seems natural to detect the same note here, with the passive reflecting the fact that Paul is talking not about what believers do, but about what is done in and through them by the Spirit.

in us, who walk not according to the flesh but according to the Spirit: as in 6^4, 'walk' is here the common biblical word for ordinary daily living. On flesh/*sarx* see at 1^3 and 8^3, and for Spirit/*Pneuma* see at 1^3 and 8^2. If 'flesh' was ordinary humanness in v. 3, then now it is certainly used negatively for human life without God at its centre. Thus for the first time in this letter it is set in that explicit opposition to Spirit that is already found in Gal. 5$^{16-25}$ and II. Cor. 10^3, an opposition that is not between material and non-material aspects of the person, but between life centred in something other than God, and life centered in and empowered by him. However, because the Spirit was characteristic of the New Age, there is also an opposition between the two ages. For the equivalence of being in the Spirit and being in Christ see on 8^1. Those who belong to Christ have a new basis for life, God himself, so that walking according to the Spirit means a complete change of belonging, direction, and empowerment.

5

set their minds: the orientation and 'mind-set' of each sort of life are in diametrical opposition to those of the other. This confirms that Paul is not talking about different parts of the same person, but about alternative directions, cf. Gal. 5$^{16-23}$. It is because of this emphasis on mental set that reference is often made to Jer. 31$^{33f.}$ and Ezek. 36$^{26f.}$, where the prophets talk of a new heart, a new inwardness. Whether or not Paul is deliberately alluding to these passages, the congruence is obvious.

6

to set the mind on the flesh is death: what does this mean?

(*a*) It could mean that if we set our minds on what is merely human, the only and entirely natural end is death.

(*b*) It could mean that death is the punishment for a life dominated by sin and *sarx* (cf.: 6$^{21, 23}$, and Wilckens II, p. 130).

(*c*) Perhaps the point is that the *sarx*/flesh kind of life is in itself really a death, in that it excludes God (cf. vv. 7, 10).

It may be that asking these questions is to ask for more precision than Paul offers: whether it comes intrinsically, or as a divine punishment, or as a natural termination, the fleshly life leads to death.

to set the mind on the Spirit is life and peace: the Spirit is the source of life almost by definition (cf. Gen. 1²), and here the context shows that it is life for God, not just natural life, that is at issue. Peace, in the biblical tradition, is not just the absence of hostility, but something like total well-being. The Spirit thus gives a rich quality of life (cf. above on 5¹).

7

the mind that is set on the flesh is hostile to God: this is the essential thing about it. We have here what virtually amounts to a definition of *sarx* as it is used in these verses.

it does not submit to God's law: since its whole orientation is away from God, it is hardly surprising that *sarx*-life does not place itself under his will. What is a little surprising is the occurrence here of 'law'/*nomos*: does it refer to God's will in general, or to the Mosaic Law in particular? The thrust of the passage is towards doing God's will, not towards defining it, yet it would be helpful to know what is the field of reference of *nomos*. The most immediate possibility is a reference back to 7²⁵ and 'the law of God' there, but we have seen some reason to suspect a gloss in the second part of that verse. Reference here could be to the tenth commandment, as suggested for v. 4, or it could be quite unreflective use of *nomos* for the divine will, whether or not focussed in the Torah (cf. I Cor. 9²¹). The last seems most likely, but there is insufficient evidence to come to a firm conclusion.

8

those who are in the flesh cannot please God: 'in the flesh' (*en sarki*) obviously cannot mean 'in this human life', as v. 9 shows. Rather, the phrase is synonymous with 'according to the flesh' in v. 4,[1] and so means life that is apart from God.

9

you are not in the flesh: if the expression had meant ordinary human life, those addressed plainly would have been 'in the flesh' (*sarx*). More than

---

1 See Jewett, *Terms*, p. 153, and the brief discussion above at 7⁵, on how the two expressions are sometimes equivalent and sometimes not.

any other, this verse shows that 'flesh' must refer to an orientation of life, that which is the opposite of being in the Spirit. Although in principle flesh and Spirit are mutually exclusive spheres of power, in practice there may be incomplete transfer from one to the other so far as any given individual is concerned. As a consequence, in v. 11 the resurrection is still seen as future for Christians. Compare Gal. 5²⁵, where after setting out the two sorts of life, in the flesh and in the Spirit, Paul still finds it necessary to say 'If we live by the Spirit, let us also walk by the Spirit.'

you are in the Spirit if the Spirit of God really dwells in you: there is probably no effective difference between being in the Spirit and having the Spirit in oneself. Being within the power of God is not different from having the power of God in oneself. The variety of expression presumably arises from rhetoric. [m]

the Spirit of Christ: there are not two different Spirits. The Spirit of Christ is the Spirit of God. This must mean that Paul sees Christ as having conveyed the life and activity of God, so that now the Spirit is defined by Christ. That in turn means, at least in functional terms, that Christ and God are equally represented by the same Spirit. This is not to say that Christ and God are straightforwardly identified, but it is to imply that they are inseparable in terms of activity. It is not surprising that the church rapidly came to use divine language of Christ, for once the Spirit is seen as the Spirit of Christ, a movement in that direction has decisively begun. [n]

. . . does not belong to him: having the Spirit and being Christian are the same thing. The Spirit is thus not a highly desirable extra to Christianity, but the heart of the matter. [o] This is evidently so when we recall that in this passage Paul is talking about alternative ways of living, 'according to the flesh' and 'in/according to the Spirit', of which only the second is Christian. Compare also the two, and only two, ways of being human in 5¹²⁻²¹, the Adam way and the Christ way.

---

m So Sanders, *PPJ*, p. 462, agreeing with Bultmann, *Theology* I, p. 208f. See also Moule, *Origin of Christology*, p. 58, and Dunn, *Baptism in the Holy Spirit*, p. 148. Dunn argues for a meaning something like 'I am assuming, of course, that the Spirit of God really is dwelling in you', i.e. that you really are Christians.

n See Isaacs, *Concept of Spirit*, pp. 113ff.; Dunn, *Jesus and Spirit*, pp. 318ff.

o Cf. Dunn, *Baptism in the Holy Spirit*, pp. 95, 148f.

10

if Christ is in you: this is an unusual formulation, though cf. Gal. 2²⁰.
Normally we are in Christ, not he in us. Most likely it is because Paul
can move so easily from Spirit-language to Christ-language and back
again, and because he has just been speaking of the Spirit's dwelling in
believers, that he can now use this unaccustomed expression. If the
Spirit can be in us (v. 9), then it follows that Christ can be also, however awkwardly this fits with the 'in Christ' formula (on which see
above at 6¹¹). Throughout, the subject is life in the New Age and in the
power of the New Age, whether expressed in terms of Christ or of the
Spirit.

your bodies are dead because of sin: there are two inseparable difficulties
here, the meaning of 'dead' and the meaning of 'bodies'. We must
leave open the possibility[p] that Paul's rhetoric has lead him into
obscurity, and that in order to provide a neat contrast to the second half
of the statement, about 'your spirits', he comes out with something that
is well-nigh unintelligible. Nevertheless it may be possible to make
some sense of what results. 'Dead' may mean destined for death, or else
separated from God. On the other hand, it may mean 'having died with
Christ' (cf. 6⁶, and Wilckens II, p. 133). 'Bodies' in this context most
probably means whole persons, not just physical persons, as dominated
by sin.

We therefore have here one of two things:
either a statement that the sin-directed person is doomed to die;
or a statement that the sin-directed person has already died (with
Christ), in agreement with Ch. 6.
Of these two, in the light of the whole passage, the second is preferable.
What is most unlikely is that here, quite contrary to his usual practice,
Paul is talking about two parts of the human being, one of which (body)
is dead because it is sinful, and the other of which (spirit) is alive because
it is righteous. Substituting 'destined for death' for 'dead' does little to
alleviate that improbability. We are still in the realm of orientations of
the whole person.[q] This view being rejected, either of the other two
explanations is possible, and if the dying-with-Christ one has a slight
edge, it is because it fits with a leading Pauline theme.

p As suggested by Sanders, *PLJP,* p. 42.
q See also Robinson, p. 98; Jewett, *Terms,* pp. 290, 296f. Cranfield I, pp.
389f., however, takes the expression to be a reminder that Christians are as
mortal as other people.

your spirits are alive because of righteousness: in the Greek it is not 'your spirits' but 'the spirit' or even 'the Spirit' *(to de Pneuma).* Quite possibly, therefore, Paul is not saying that the spirits of his readers are alive, but that the Spirit, the Holy Spirit, is *life.*ʳ The Spirit then is life, i.e. is life-giving, 'because of righteousness'. This cannot be because of the believers' own righteousness; that would be thoroughly un-Pauline. It must be because of that divine saving righteousness spoken of in 1¹⁷ and 3²¹, ²², unless 'because of righteousness' is purposive, referring to the human righteousness which the Spirit effects.ˢ Either way, living for sin ends in death, whether it be natural death or death with Christ, while living for God leads to life, life not only in the present time but for ever.

11

he who raised Christ Jesus from the dead will give life to your mortal bodies also: this confirms that the best interpretation of v. 10 is in terms of Ch. 6. This is because we now have an explicit reference to the resurrection, and we know from Ch. 6 that Paul thinks of Christians as rising with Christ. Moreover, the bodies that in v. 10 were destined for death are now destined for life. This again makes the best sense if we take 'bodies' *(sōmata)* to be whole persons rather than to imply a strictly physical resurrection, especially in the light of Phil. 3²¹ and I Cor. 15³⁵⁻⁵⁴, where human destiny is transformation, not physical resuscitation. The future tense in this verse is important: Christ has been raised by God, but believers have not yet been raised. What they have instead is the assurance that they will be raised, an assurance which comes from the knowledge that the Spirit of life is already at work within them. They already have something of the life whose fullness they can confidently expect, cf. II Cor. 1²² and 5⁵, where the Spirit is the guarantee of what is to come, and Rom. 8²³, where the Spirit is the first-fruits of the resurrection.

12

we are debtors, not to the flesh, to live according to the flesh: i.e. to live for something other than God, cf. above on vv. 4ff. Why should Paul write of not being 'debtors' to the flesh? The translation is not altogether illuminating: what is at stake is *obligation.* We are under obliga-

---

r Wilckens II, pp. 132f., takes it to refer to the Holy Spirit, though as active in believers, and so do Cranfield I, p. 390; Barrett, pp. 154, 159; Bruce, p. 164; Käsemann, pp. 214, 224.

s As in Ziesler, *Meaning,* pp. 168, 204.

tion only to God, it is to him we belong and him alone, and so there cannot be any conflicting obligations.

13

put to death the deeds of the body: out of context, this could mean that life in the Spirit consists in mortifying the physical. In context, however, it means nothing of the sort, though it must be confessed that Paul's terminology is confusing. Most of this verse is a recapitulation of vv. 5 and 6, with 'body'/*sōma* used as an equivalent to 'flesh'/*sarx* there.ᵗ The meaning is therefore 'Get rid of the actions of the self as at present constituted', cf. 6¹²ᵇ.

you will live: this may well mean the life of the future, life after natural death.

14

sons of God: in Ch. 6 the Christian life was depicted as one of service, even of slavery, to God. In 6¹⁹ we saw that Paul showed some embarrassment about such language. We now see why it is inadequate to designate Christians slaves of God, for in fact they are children of him. In Ch. 4 believers were children of Abraham in so far as they shared his faith, but now for the first time in the letter they are more than that: they are children (sons) of God.

15

the spirit of slavery . . . the spirit of sonship: it is not that there are two spirits, one of which Paul's readers have received, and the other of which they have not. It is rather that the Spirit they have received is one that creates not slaves but sons (and, by implication, daughters). The reason for the hesitation in 6¹⁹ is now fully apparent. To call Christians the servants or slaves of God is only half the truth.ᵘ The difference between slaves and sons has nothing to do with obedience. A good son was just as bound to obey his father as a good slave was obliged to obey

t Some Western MSS do in fact read *tēs sarkos*, 'of the flesh' (D and G among others), but this is usually seen as an attempt at clarification. See Jewett, *Terms*, pp. 158f., 290, 297. He thinks Paul chooses *sōma* to indicate that old and new existences are both 'somatic', in some sense embodied. Cf. Cranfield I, p. 395; Käsemann, p. 226.

u On the possibility that there is an allusion here to the escape from slavery in Egypt at the exodus see J.-M. Cambier, 'La liberté du spirituel dans Romains 8.12–17', in Hooker and Wilson (pp. 205–20), p. 209.

his master, something that ought not to be overlooked by those whose picture of sonship is more permissive or sentimental. Nor is the difference here stated in terms of intimacy, as it is in John 15^{15}.^{v} On the contrary Paul sees the difference in terms of future destiny: a slave does not enter into an inheritance, but a son does, v. 17.

The word for sonship is the same as that translated 'adoption' in v. 23 (*huiothesia*). There it is still awaited, but here it is already enjoyed (on the discrepancy see at v. 23). The word comes from Hellenistic vocabulary, not from the OT or Jewish tradition. Nonetheless Paul's choice of it may allude to the election of Israel as God's son, as in 9^4.^{w}

'*Abba! Father!*': much is sometimes made of this abrupt incursion of Aramaic. *Abba* is the Aramaic, of which 'Father' is the translation. In a text addressed at least partly to people who spoke no Aramaic, its presence calls for explanation.^{x} Even if too much has sometimes been made of it, it remains remarkable.

(*a*) It is a term of address naturally used within a family context, capable of bearing the connotations of human affection and intimacy.

(*b*) It occurs in Mark 14^{36} in Jesus's prayer to God in the Garden of Gethsemane. It is commonly held to reflect his special sense of intimacy with God. Sometimes it has been argued that applying such an intimate word to God was unknown before the gospel tradition, and that therefore it is a sure characteristic of the historical Jesus. It has been suggested that it originally stood in the Lord's Prayer (cf. Luke 11^2, where the simple address 'Father' occurs), but there is certainly no hint of the contents of that prayer here.^{y}

(*c*) The contribution of Paul, here and in Gal. 4^6, is to extend the use of the *Abba*-address from Jesus to Christians, who thus join the Son in being sons, and learn to speak to God as he did.

(*d*) It is not now to be regarded as an incontrovertible fact that this word was never used in address to God before Jesus and the NT. Though it was not common in religious (e.g. liturgical) contexts, it was not altogether without precedent.^{z}

v 'No longer do I call you servants/slaves, for the servant/slave does not know what his master is doing; but I have called you friends, for all that I have heard from my Father I have made known to you.'

w See Wilckens II, p. 136 and n. 547; Cranfield I, pp. 397–8.

x See especially J. Jeremias, *New Testament Theology* I, ET SCM Press 1971, pp. 36f., 61–8.

y Cf. Wilckens II, p. 137; Käsemann, p. 228.

z For evidence, see Vermes, *Jesus the Jew*, pp. 210–13.

(e) Nevertheless, its importance here and in Gal. 4⁶ does not lie in its being unprecedented, nor even in its presumed echo of the tradition behind Mark 14³⁶. What matters for our understanding of this passage of Romans is that the cry is evidence that those who live in the Spirit are children of God, who belong to him and obey him as men and women who are within his family by adoption.

(f) The retention of an Aramaic term in letters to people many if not most of whom would know no Aramaic suggests that the cry had become known and used well beyond the Palestinian church in which it presumably originated. We may compare the use of another Aramaic/Hebrew term, 'Amen', which has survived many centuries and many changes of language.

16

the Spirit himself bearing witness with our spirit: in view of the context, we should have expected to hear that addressing God as *Abba* is not something we arrive at naturally, nor just by echoing a liturgical tradition, but is made possible only by God himself, through the Spirit. Being a child of God is not an immediately recognized natural fact, like having arms and legs, but needs to be disclosed by God into whose family we have been adopted (v. 15). At least apparently, this is not what Paul says. He appears to say that there are two spirits, God's and our own, which agree with each other that we are God's children. It is almost as if God confirms what we ourselves already sense. Can this be right? There are three main possibilities of interpretation.

(a) Perhaps Paul *is* saying that when we learn from the Holy Spirit that we are children of God, this strikes a chord in our own human spirit, giving us a feeling of having come home.[a] The difficulty with this is that it so poorly fits the context, especially v. 15: apart from the present verse we certainly get the impression that our status as God's children is quite unexpected and gratuitous. Moreover, the idea that divine and human spirits come to an agreement in the matter is decidedly odd.

(b) Some commentators point out that the verb 'bearing witness with' (*summarturei*) could be translated 'bearing witness to', so that God's Spirit bears witness not *with* but *to* our spirit, that we are God's chil-

---

[a] So Robinson, p. 100; somewhat similarly Black, p. 119, who refers to the importance in biblical tradition of having *two* witnesses.

dren.^b This is without doubt a straightforward and attractive interpretation that may very well be correct.

(c) A rather more complicated alternative is that, as Spirit, God is
both outside us and within us, standing over against us yet active inside
us. 'Our spirit' is then not a natural organ or faculty of our own, but
ourselves as acted upon by God. If this understanding of the Spirit
underlies this verse, then God's Spirit bearing witness with our spirit
means that God, who is both within and beyond us, affirms that we are
his children.^c

Either of the last two interpretations is to be preferred to the first,
and it is difficult to choose between them. Perhaps the last has a slight
edge, because it follows the more natural meaning of the Greek verb
(which occurs in the NT only here and in 2¹⁵; 9¹), 'bearing witness
with', but does not at the same time suggest the difficult idea of a divine-
human consensus.

17

heirs: the notion of inheritance goes back in the OT to the story of
Abraham (Gen. 12²; 17⁴⁻⁸; 18¹⁸; 22¹⁶⁻¹⁸) and the land that his descendants would inherit (17⁸). The promised land idea took on great
prominence in the story of the exodus and the wanderings in the
wilderness. Here, however, there is nothing about a land, and even the
reference to Abraham is no more than an allusion. Christians are heirs
of glory which will follow their sufferings (cf. the end of the verse).
That is, they will enter into the splendour and presence of God him-
self (on 'glory'/*doxa* see above at 1²³; 3^{7, 23}). All this still lies in the
future: Christians are heirs, not possessors, as their present suffering
demonstrates.

---

b So Cranfield I, p. 403. Wilckens II, pp. 137f., thinks that as in I Thess. 5²³,
'our spirit is the human organ of receptivity to the divine witness, or even just
receptivity itself; in that case Paul is in effect saying simply that God bears
witness to us.

c So Jewett, *Terms*, pp. 198f.; Käsemann, pp. 228f.; Schweizer, *TDNT* VI.
pp. 425, 436.

¹⁸*I consider that the sufferings of this present time are not worth comparing with the glory that is to be revealed to us.* ¹⁹*For the creation waits with eager longing for the revealing of the sons of God;* ²⁰*for the creation was subjected to futility, not of its own will but by the will of him who subjected it in hope;* ²¹*because the creation itself will be set free from its bondage to decay and obtain the glorious liberty of the children of God.* ²²*We know that the whole creation has been groaning in travail together until now;* ²³*and not only the creation, but we ourselves, who have the first fruits of the Spirit, groan inwardly as we wait for adoption as sons, the redemption of our bodies.* ²⁴*For in this hope we were saved. Now hope that is seen is not hope. For who hopes for what he sees?* ²⁵*But if we hope for what we do not see, we wait for it with patience.*

²⁶*Likewise the Spirit helps us in our weakness; for we do not know how to pray as we ought, but the Spirit himself intercedes for us with sighs too deep for words.* ²⁷*And he who searches the hearts of men knows what is the mind of the Spirit, because the Spirit intercedes for the saints according to the will of God.*

²⁸*We know that in everything God works for good with those who love him, who are called according to his purpose.* ²⁹*For those whom he foreknew he also predestined to be conformed to the image of his Son, in order that he might be the first-born among many brethren.* ³⁰*And those whom he predestined he also called; and those whom he called he also justified; and those whom he justified he also glorified.*

³¹*What then shall we say to this? If God is for us, who is against us?* ³²*He who did not spare his own Son but gave him up for us all, will he not also give us all things with him?* ³³*Who shall bring any charge against God's elect? It is God who justifies;* ³⁴*who is to condemn? Is it Christ Jesus, who died, yes, who was raised from the dead, who is at the right hand of God, who indeed intercedes for us?* ³⁵*Who shall separate us from the love of Christ? Shall tribulation, or distress, or persecution, or famine, or nakedness, or peril, or sword?* ³⁶*As it is written,*

'For thy sake we are being killed all the day long;
we are regarded as sheep to be slaughtered.'

³⁷No, in all these things we are more than conquerors through him who loved us. ³⁸For I am sure that neither death, nor life, nor angels, nor principalities, nor things present, nor things to come, nor powers, ³⁹nor height, nor depth, nor anything else in all creation, will be able to separate us from the love of God in Christ Jesus our Lord.

The present time is characterized by suffering, perhaps not unexpectedly in view of the dawning of the age of the Messiah.^d This section takes up and expands the theme of 5²⁻⁴. In their sufferings, which are presumably to be understood in terms of opposition and even persecution,^e Christians are signs for the whole world that the present universal decay, wickedness, and suffering are but a stage in a divine process which is moving towards freedom and renewal. That this is the assured outcome is demonstrated by those who already have the Spirit, a mark of the New Age, and so both a foretaste and a guarantee of what is to come. It is true that these Christians are so weak that they cannot even pray as they ought to, but even in this the assistance of the Spirit is a promise of the glorious future. God's ultimate intention is clear and cannot be finally frustrated. He has chosen for himself a people, who belong to his Son Jesus Christ, and they know that just as they have already found favour with him solely by his own gracious decision, so they are securely destined for his presence and his splendour.

Therefore, whatever now seems to militate against them will fail to destroy their fundamental belonging to him; the sending of Christ is evidence that God has a primordial purpose which must come to fruition, and those who belong to him are assured that they have a place in that purpose. The conclusion of the passage (vv. 31–39) is strongly rhetorical; sufferings are not removed, but even in the midst

d See Wilckens II, p. 148, on the expectation of Messianic sufferings, also Dale C. Allison, *The End of the Ages has Come*, Fortress Press 1985 and T. & T. Clark 1987, Ch. 2. See, however, the scepticism about this as an established idea in the NT period represented by Beker, *Apostle*, p. 146, and E. P. Sanders, *Jesus and Judaism*, SCM Press 1985, pp. 124, 130.

e On this see J. S. Pobee, *Persecution and Martyrdom in Paul*, JSNT Supp. 6, Sheffield Academic Press 1985, pp. 111f.

of them believers are not overcome by them. This is because belonging to Christ involves sharing his resurrection life as well as his dying. If God accepts them and Christ pleads for them, what does it matter who accuses or condemns them? Indeed there is nothing in heaven or on earth that can stand between them and the love of God that has been demonstrated in the person of Jesus Christ, not now nor in the future. They are and they will be totally secure in that love.

⁎

18

glory: for *doxa* see above on v. 17, also on 1 23. This is what is hoped for, confidently expected because of God's constancy (cf. v. 20 on hope). It is a sharing in the radiancy and bliss of God himself. It remains a hope, not a present possession, cf. v. 17, also 5 2.

19

the creation waits with eager longing: 'creation' (*tēs ktiseōs*) is here probably the whole created universe and not just, indeed not specially, the human part of it.[f] This is made almost certain by vv. 21-23. An allusion to Gen. 3 17-18 is quite likely: at the present time the created universe, animate and inanimate, lacks the peace and perfection which God intended for it. It will recover them only at the End, when there will be –

the revealing of the sons of God: these are those who believe in and belong to Jesus Christ, cf. vv. 14-17. Their true nature and status are at present obscured, but at the End these will become obvious. Nevertheless, for those with eyes to see, even now they constitute a sign of hope. On their destiny see also vv. 29-30; I Cor. 15 20, 23; Phil. 3 20-21.

20

the creation was subjected to futility . . . by the will of him who subjected it in hope: it is taken for granted that the created world is not at present free to be its true self. This is because it is unwillingly under bondage, and is therefore meaningless, futile. The question is, by whom has it been placed under bondage?

[f] For the various interpretations that have been offered of 'creation', see Wilckens II, pp. 152f.; Cranfield I, p. p411f. They rightly contend that Christians are not included.

(a) The immediately obvious answer is, by Satan, who has deprived the world of its character as the place of human peace and well-being. This would echo the story of the serpent in the Garden of Eden (Gen. 3¹⁻⁵), though in that story it is not the serpent directly who deprives the man and the woman of their blissful environment. It would, however, agree with Paul's depiction of humanity as under malign power until the divine power supervenes, as it is tantamount to being under sin. Nevertheless it is hard to find any modern commentator who takes this view, mainly because another view seems much more likely.

(b) It is occasionally suggested[g] that by his first disobedience, Adam was the one who subjected the world to futility. This is generally doubted, on the grounds that in the Genesis story this does not quite seem to be the role of Adam.

(c) The great majority of commentators agree that the one who subjected the world to futility was God himself, and for several reasons.

(i) Only God could subject it 'in hope' (on which see below).

(ii) If there is some reference to the Genesis story here, as there probably is, then it is important that in that story it is God who does the subjecting (Gen. 3¹⁷⁻¹⁸, and cf. the curse in vv. 15–16).

(iii) The absence of any stated agent for 'it was subjected' makes one suspect that this is a divine passive, i.e. having God as the implicit agent. As often, desire to avoid anthropomorphism or simply the wish not to take God's name lightly has led to this indirect way of talking about the divine action.[h]

It is most likely, then, that the third view is correct, and that it was God himself who subjected the world to futility but with the long-term objective of restoration ('in hope'). We may compare the exemplifications of the wrath/*orgē* in 1¹⁸⁻³². On 'hope' (*elpis*) see above at 4¹⁸: in the end, there is an assurance that God's beneficent purpose will be fulfilled.

21

the creation itself will be set free from its bondage to decay: however strange it may be to modern ears, this almost certainly means exactly what it

---

g Among recent commentators see O'Neill, p. 141; Robinson, p. 102. Wilckens II, p. 154, provides a detailed examination of this view, and rejects it.

h Among commentators who think God is the agent of subjecting are Cranfield I, p. 414; Leenhardt, p. 220; Sanday and Headlam, p. 208; Althaus, p. 93; Black, p. 122; Bruce, pp. 172f.; Käsemann, p. 235; Murray, p. 303; Wilckens II, p. 153.

seems to mean. The whole created world will undergo a transformation and restoration. This reflects a traditional Jewish hope to be found both within and outside the OT: see Isa. 65^{17}; *I Enoch* $45^{4f.}$; 72^1; IQS 4^{25}; IQH 11^{13-14}.[i] Whether such statements were originally taken literally is hard to say, but it seems likely that they were eventually so taken. Certainly there was a hope of a cosmic redemption, involving both nature and humanity, a new heaven and a new earth. Not only the man and the woman, but the Garden itself will enjoy restoration, a restoration which will match 'the glorious liberty of the children of God', cf. vv. 19, 23.

22

the whole creation has been groaning in travail: this is introduced as if it were already known, and there does indeed seem to be evidence that it was a familiar idea not only in Jewish circles (cf. on v. 21) but also in Hellenism.[j] In this expectant travail, Christians participate.

23

we ourselves, who have the first fruits of the Spirit: probably, 'the first fruits constituted by the Spirit'. The Spirit is thus both the beginning and the guarantee of the promised glorious future, just as it is the *arrabōn*, the deposit on and first instalment of that future in II Cor. 1^{22}; 5^5; Eph. 1^{14}. Nevertheless the future remains future, even for those who have the Spirit and are thus the forerunners of the renewal of creation. They too 'groan', suffer with longing, as they wait –

for adoption as sons: it is strange that we should now hear of waiting for adoption (*huiothesia*), since Paul has said in v. 15 that Christians have already received a Spirit of adoption. One explanation of this anomaly is that 'adoption as sons' is an intrusion here, and that Paul originally wrote simply 'waiting for the redemption of our bodies'. There is considerable MS support for omitting *huiothesia*, including that of our earliest witness for this verse, 𝔓 46 and the important Western MSS D and G. However, scribes would more readily omit it because of its apparent conflict with v. 15 than add it gratuitously to a text which originally lacked it, or so many scholars think.[k]

i See Davies, *PRJ*, pp. 37–9.
j See the material cited in Wilckens II, pp. 149–50; also Cranfield I, p. 416.
k P. Benoit argues for the omission of the phrase in ' "We too groan inwardly as we wait for our bodies to be set free" (Romans 8:23)', pp. 40–50 of *Jesus and the Gospel* II, ET Darton, Longman and Todd 1974.

If we reject the idea of a textual intrusion, how do we explain the anomaly? The best answer is that living as they do between the times, in an 'already' and also a 'not yet', Christians can be seen as both having received and still awaiting their adoption. In v. 15, they are said to have received 'the Spirit of adoption', in its character as first fruits, as guarantee and first instalment, but not the full and complete reality of adoption itself. That awaits the consummation.

the redemption of our bodies: if, as often, 'bodies' (in Greek singular, *tou sōmatos hēmōn*) are our whole selves, including but not limited to our physical selves, then this is somewhat similar to Phil. 3²¹ and I Cor. 15⁴²⁻⁵⁰. That is, as a part of the renovation of all creation, our whole selves too will be transformed, not by release *from* the physical in Gnostic fashion, but by redemption *of* our total embodiment. To judge by what he says elsewhere, Paul does not envisage a strictly physical resurrection, that is, a resuscitation of our physical persons just as they have been: 'flesh and blood cannot inherit the kingdom of God', I Cor. 15⁵⁰. Rather is there transformation and a new and appropriate embodiment, cf. I Cor. 15³⁵⁻⁵⁰; II Cor. 5¹⁻⁵; Phil. 3²¹. It is the whole of creation, including our embodiment, that needs renewal and that receives it; compare this verse with 7²⁴; 8²¹, and also 8¹¹.[1] It is unlikely that *only* the transformation of the physical is at stake here, because adoption as sons and redemption of bodies appear to be equated.

24

in this hope we were saved: we saw at 4¹⁸ that hope in the Bible commonly has two notable characteristics: it is grounded in the nature and reliability of God, not on human probabilities, and secondly is therefore assured and not doubtful. 'Saved' (see on 1¹⁶) both in Paul and in the NT generally usually refers to the future consummation of God's beneficent purposes, very often at the End of this present Age. Thus, when Paul says that we *were* saved, the statement is immediately qualified by the introduction of 'hope' (*elpis*). The salvation already given is anticipatory, proleptic, and not yet consummated. NEB not inaccurately translates, 'For we have been saved, though only in hope.' Yet although the mention of hope enters a reservation, the consummation is not in doubt: it is merely not yet a reality. As throughout this passage, there is a tension between the 'already' and the 'not yet', an eschatological

[1] See Jewett, *Terms*, pp. 298f., 457; for a heavily physical interpretation, see Gundry, *Sōma in Biblical Theology*, p. 44.

tension which is brought out both in the rest of v. 24 and in v. 25. By definition, the object of hope lies in the future, yet it is assured, and that is what matters.

It would be possible to translate 'we were saved *by* hope', but as this is without parallel in Paul's writings it is extremely unlikely to be correct.

26

the Spirit helps us in our weakness: what weakness? The most obvious answer is that it is the weakness inherent in our 'not yet' situation, and that the difficulty of prayer (see the middle part of the verse) exemplifies this. On the other hand Käsemann (pp. 239–41) suggests that the whole verse is about speaking with tongues, glossolalia, which the Romans, like the Corinthians, think is praying in the Spirit, but which Paul here characterizes as a deficiency, 'weakness'. 'The sighs too deep for words' are then literally the inarticulate cries of glossolalia, and the whole verse is an attack on the practice, which is interpreted as a mark of the immaturity of the Roman congregations. This interpretation of Käsemann's cannot be ruled out as impossible, though if that is the meaning it is hardly made clear. Indeed, it can be argued that it is highly unlikely that Paul would suddenly insert a discussion of glossolalia without giving precise indication that he was doing so, and without any preparation for it. Moreover, there is no other evidence that it was a problem in Rome.

It is more probable, therefore, that 'our weakness' is the 'not yet' position of Christians. In that situation, the Spirit anticipates the future by enabling them to pray, probably 'what to pray for' rather than 'how to pray'. This is the more natural rendering of the Greek. The Spirit vivifies everything for Christians, even their prayers: 'spiritual' life too needs to be guided and enriched by the Spirit of God.

the Spirit himself intercedes for us: in the light of the preceding, it is more likely that this means 'pray on our behalf' rather than simply 'pray for us'.

sighs too deep for words: literally, 'unspoken/unspeakable groanings' (*stenagmois alalētois*). We have noted that Käsemann thinks these are glossolalia: it is only while we still do not know how or what to pray that tongues are appropriate.[m] The RSV translation reflects the view of

m See pp. 239–41, and also his *Perspectives on Paul*, pp. 127ff. For counter-argument, see Wilckens II, p. 161 (glossolalia does not fit the over-all argument of vv. 26–27) and Cranfield I, p. p. 422.

most commentators that we should understand Paul to be saying that the prayers which the Spirit helps us to make are beyond articulation, perhaps because they concern that unseen hope (vv. 24–25) for which it is impossible to find words.[n] The word translated 'sighs' (*stenagmois*) is the same as that for the sigh or groan of creation in v. 22, and for the sigh or groan of those who have the first fruits of the Spirit, but still await full sonship in v. 23. This certainly lends support to the view that we are not dealing with glossolalia, but with the frail attempts of Christians to reach out in their prayers to what lies ahead and beyond. There is debate about whether *alalētois* means 'unspeakable', i.e. ineffable (cf. Black, p. 123), or 'unspoken' (cf. Barrett, p. 168) because they do not need to be put into words. Either way, this is not a very appropriate adjective for glossolalia.

27

he ... knows what is the mind of the Spirit: whether the words are unspoken or unspeakable, unformulated or unable to be formulated, God understands the thoughts that are implicit. Only God understands God, and it is God through his Spirit who is at work in these inarticulate prayers, cf. I Cor. 2$^{10-11}$.

because the Spirit intercedes for the saints: we note three things.

(*a*) We see from the RSV margin that instead of 'because' we could translate 'that' (the Greek *hoti* is ambiguous). 'That' is in fact to be preferred: the Spirit's intercession is not the reason for God's knowing the mind of the Spirit, but its exemplification.

(*b*) 'Intercedes' could be either the Spirit's praying on behalf of the saints, or praying for them.[o]

(*c*) 'The saints' are God's people, and here they are those who belong to Christ, cf. on 1^7; 6^{19}.

28

in everything God works for good with those who love him: there is some textual disagreement in this verse, resulting in varying translations.

(*a*) Most MSS read the text represented in the King James Version, 'All things work together for good for those who love God.' This could be taken to imply that they do so by some sort of automatic providence.

---

n So Wilckens II, pp. 160–1.
o Cf. the intercession of angels in Jewish tradition, Wilckens II, p. 162 and nn. 714, 715.

This notion is not in accordance with usual biblical thought which is rather, according to most commentators, that *God* is able to bring good out of all things.

(*b*) This may well explain why a relatively small number of MSS, but including the important early MS 𝔓⁴⁶, have 'God makes everything work for good for those who love God.' In spite of the awkwardness of the repeated 'God', this reading probably arose in order to avoid what we might call evolutionary optimism, and in order to emphasize eschatological hope instead. It is not that things in themselves combine to be good, but that God can bend them to his purposes. However, against this reading, it is not likely that scribes would omit a reference to God when it stood in the text, and so it is hard to see the (*a*) reading as having developed out of the (*b*). This solution therefore looks like an attempt at theological clarification.

(*c*) Thus the first reading is to be preferred. Nevertheless, it is improbable that the subject of 'work together' is 'all things'; rather, although the word does not appear in the Greek, 'God' is to be understood as the subject. In other words, RSV brings out the meaning well. It may be added that it is even possible that 'the Spirit' is the one who makes things work together for good, to judge by the preceding context.ᴾ

who are called according to his purpose: God's people, the elect, are not those who have some special inside knowledge (*gnōsis*), but those who love him. There may well be a reference back to v. 18 with its mention of the sufferings of God's people. In these sufferings, they are assured that God will finally bring good out of evil. They are those who have the Spirit, who are the children of God, and who have been called by him (the 'elect').

29

those whom he foreknew he also predestined: we are now brought face to face with the difficult and historically controversial doctrine of election, which will recur up to the end of Ch. 11. More will be said about it as 9–11 proceed, but some comments must be made now in connection with both the present and the following verses.

(*a*) It is probably automatic for us to take it for granted that divine predestination and free human choice are incompatible. Either we have

p On this see M. Black, 'The Interpretation of Romans viii 28', pp. 166–72 of *Neotestamentica et Patristica* (FS O. Cullmann), Leiden: Brill 1962. For detailed discussion of the textual problem see Cranfield I, pp. 425–8.

free choice, or God determines all that happens, and in particular determines the sort of response we make to him. There is evidence in Jewish sources that for Israel, on the contrary, the two were compatible: human responsibility (and freedom) and divine decision could go hand in hand. q From one point of view, the choice is that of human beings; from another point of view, their salvation is secure because they are part of the invincible divine purpose. Paul never works out the connection, but there is no doubt that for him divine predestination did not rule out human freedom.

(b) There is a strong possibility that, because of the way in which he introduces v. 28 ('we know'), and because of the tight formulation of points in series, Paul is using and adapting already known traditional material in vv. 28–30. r He is not so much making a point about election as using it to reassure his readers who are beset by persecution. They did not need to be anxious about the final outcome, because that is in the hands of God.

(c) Chapters 9–11 confirm that Paul is concerned not with the salvation or damnation of individuals, but with the choice of a people to further his purposes. 'Those who love God' (v. 28) *are* the elect, the people chosen (cf. Deut. 6⁵; 7⁹) first in order that they should be like Christ ('conformed to the image of his son'), secondly in order that they should be the precursors of a renewed creation (vv. 21, 22), and thirdly in order that God should be able to 'have mercy upon all' (11³²).

(d) The nature of election is that it is entirely in the gift of God, and has nothing to do with the worthiness of the people elected. It is thus closely connected with justification, the notion that it is always strictly by God's grace that people become and remain the people of God, the bearers of his purposes.

(e) 'Foreknew' amounts to the same thing as 'elected', for in the OT when God 'knows' people it means that he has chosen them, as in Gen. 18¹⁹ (Abraham), Amos 3² (Israel), or Jer. 1⁵ (Jeremiah). s Presumably he *fore*knew them because his election was prior to anything else, including their response.

(f) 'Predestined' is almost a synonym for 'foreknew', but is used to

q See Sanders, *PPJ*, pp. 446–7; G. F. Moore, *Judaism in the First Centuries of the Christian Era: The Age of the Tannaim*, Cambridge, Mass.: Harvard University Press, 3 vols., 1927–30, Vol. I, pp. 454–9; Whiteley, *Theology*, pp. 89–98.

r So K. Grayston, 'Election in Romans 8,28–30', in F. L. Cross (ed.), *Studia Evangelica* II, pp. 574–83.

s See Grayston, 'Election', pp. 582f.

introduce the outcome of election ('to be conformed . . .'). The use of this word in the English translation must not lead us to suppose that Paul was concerned, as some later thinkers were, to discuss the eternal damnation of some souls and the eternal salvation of others, before they were born. He is talking about God's choice of a people for his purposes. To a degree this is in line with a good deal of Jewish tradition; what is new is that for Paul God's people now embraces Gentiles and Jews without discrimination, so long as they respond in faith to God's grace in Jesus Christ. Cf. Chs. 4 and 9–11.

to be conformed to the image of his son: Adam was made in the image of God (Gen. 1²⁷), but failed to be a true son (Rom. 5¹²⁻²¹). Christ, on the other hand, is the true son, and those who belong to him are also the true children of God (8¹⁶, ¹⁹, ²¹, ²³). Christ was not to be an isolated instance, but the forerunner of many sons and daughters, 'the first-born among many brethren'. 'Image' (*eikōn*) and 'glory' (*doxa*) tended to be used interchangeably when referring to the nature of humanity,ᵗ so that it is not surprising that those who are to be 'glorified' (vv. 17, 18, 21, 30) are also to bear the image of Christ. Bearing his image is being like him and representing him. It is not clear when this happens: it could be at baptism, cf. 6³, ⁵ and Phil. 3¹⁰; it could be at the End, as in I Cor. 15⁴⁹; or it could be a continuing process, as in II Cor. 3¹⁸ (cf. Wilckens II, pp. 163f.).

30
those whom he predestined . . . : this verse summarizes what Paul is saying. God's eternal purpose leads to his call; it is not an idea that has only recently entered the divine mind! Moreover, Paul now states explicitly what has been implicit, that those who are God's people are such purely by his grace in justification, cf. (*d*) in the discussion of v. 29 above.

those whom he justified he also glorified: since glorification surely lies in the future (cf. vv. 17, 18, 21), why does Paul here put the verb into the past tense? If Paul is adapting traditional material of a liturgical sort, perhaps it was already in the past (aorist) in the source, and he simply retains it. Perhaps it is in a past tense to complete a neat series of such tenses (cf. Wilckens II, p. 165). In any case, if the glorification of his

---

ᵗ There was much talk of the glory of Adam in Jewish tradition, cf. Scroggs, *The Last Adam,* pp. 26–7. For the connection of the two words in Paul, see I Cor. 11⁷; II Cor. 3¹⁸; 4⁴.

people is the divine intention, then it may be regarded as certain, as good as done, the more so as there is an anticipation of it in the Spirit, cf. v. 23. God's decree that his people are to be glorified, to share his nature and presence, has already gone out. Indeed the full reality is yet to come, as the other references to glory in the chapter show, but there is still a strong element of certainty, which illuminates the note of assurance in what now follows.

31

What shall we then say to this: in this verse and those that follow, we seem to scent something like a judicial process with charge and counter-claim. This is not uncommon in the Bible, cf. the forensic settings in Zech. 3 and in the book of Job.[u]

If God is for us: that God is on the side of his people, not in any static way but in what he does (cf. Ps. 23⁴; 56⁹, ¹¹; 118⁶⁻⁷), is demonstrated in what follows as well as in what has preceded. The consequence is that any opposition to such a people is finally insignificant.

32

He who did not spare his own son: cf. above on v. 3. It is possible that we have here a reference to the *Akedath Isaac,* 'the binding of Isaac', re-garded in some Jewish circles as the perfect sacrifice. Abraham was willing to surrender to God even the son who was incomparably dear to him. The fact that the sacrifice was not carried through in Gen. 22 is not to the point: Abraham's intention and willingness were what mattered.[v] Not only 'his *own* son' but also the word 'spare' may be held to reflect Gen. 22¹², ¹⁶ LXX. If such an allusion is rightly to be perceived, then the death of Christ is seen as the fulfilment of the most complete sacrifice Judaism knew.

will he not also give us all things with him: cf. the promise of future glory in v. 17, and compare a similar promise in I Cor. 3²¹⁻²³.

[u] It is sometimes argued that here too Paul is using traditional material, cf. Käsemann, p. 247, for vv. 31–2 especially, and Wilckens II, pp. 171–2, for vv. 31–9. In any case Paul has adapted the material for purposes of his own.

[v] On the *Akedah* in general and its relevance to the NT teaching about atone-ment, see N. A. Dahl, 'The Atonement – Adequate Reward for Akedah?', in *Neotestamentica et Semitica* (FS M. Black), ed. E. E. Ellis and M. Wilcox, T. & T. Clark 1969, pp. 15–29. See also Wilckens II, p. 173 and n. 772.

33

Who shall bring any charge . . . : the punctuation of vv. 33–34 is disputed.
Once more we may recall that in the original autographs there was no
punctuation and that what we have in modern texts and translations is
the work of editors. In this passage, editors must try to make sense of a
somewhat puzzling sequence. Perhaps NEB is right, and every item in
these verses is a question:

> Who shall bring any charge . . .? God who justifies?
> Who condemns us? Christ Jesus who died?

If this is correct, then the second and fourth questions plainly expect the
answer 'No', and are tantamount to denials.

Many commentators[w] take the first and third items as questions, and
the second and fourth as statement-answers, while RSV has question,
answer, question, and further question, the last obviously expecting a
negative answer. Whatever punctuation is adopted, it is surely to be
accepted that the second and fourth items are responses to the first and
third.

34

Christ Jesus who died: from here to the end of the verse, the string of
relative pronouns suggests that Paul may be quoting traditional con-
fessional material. The very condensed character of the statements
endorses this.

who is at the right hand of God: this reflects Ps. 110[1], which is quoted or
alluded to in the NT more than any other verse of the OT.[x]

who indeed intercedes for us: Paul usually expresses Christ's present activity
in terms of what the Spirit does, rather than in terms of his own direct
action. In his own *persona*, as it were, Christ is at the right hand of God,
and intercession is what he does there. Compare also Heb. 7[25]; I John 2[1].
In Rom. 8[26-27], however, intercession in believers' hearts is carried out
not by Christ directly, but by the Spirit. Needless to say, the Spirit is
seen as the agent or vehicle of the activity of Christ, cf. 8[9].

w E.g. Cranfield I, pp. 437f.; cf. also RV and the Nestlé Greek text.

x Further on the use of Ps. 110[1], see *inter alia* B. Lindars, *New Testament
Apologetic*, SCM Press 1961, pp. 45–51 and *passim*; W. R. G. Loader, 'Christ at
the Right Hand – Ps. cx.1 in the New Testament', *NTS* 24. 2, 1978, pp. 199–217.

35

Who shall separate us from the love of Christ: the context virtually requires us to understand this as Christ's love for us, not ours for him.

persecution: this list of woes likely to afflict Christians may be evidence that the Roman church was undergoing persecution even as Paul was writing. It may also refer back to the troubles that led to the expulsion of the Jews by Claudius (see Introduction, 1(*b*)(iv), when the Jewish community may have been in a turmoil over the messiahship of Jesus. On the other hand Paul may be generalizing from his own experience of opposition and danger (cf. II Cor. 11²³⁻²⁷), and be simply reminding his readers that they are under constant threat.

36

As it is written: the quotation is from Ps. 44²² (43²³ in LXX). This psalm was used with reference to the death of the martyrs for Judaism in II Macc. 7. Paul had plenty of models from recent Jewish history of suffering for the sake of Yahweh. The Roman Christians too are to be neither surprised nor abashed when suffering strikes them.

37

in all these things: their victory comes not be escaping such sufferings and perils, but by living through them with endurance by the help of God (cf. 5³⁻⁵).

more than conquerors: the Greek verb *hupernikōmen* is intensive, and so the meaning is victory by a wide margin, with plenty to spare.

38-39

It is disputed how far these verses contain reference to supernatural powers rather than earthly or abstract opponents. Paul simply lists them in pairs, without any indication of categorization. Only 'nor powers' breaks the pairing, in itself perhaps an indication that Paul is throwing in everything he can think of that might be seen as inimical to his readers' discipleship and security in faith. Although it has been claimed that all these opponents are within the range of normal human experience, it is more likely that there is a mixture of human and earthly with supernatural forces.^y While in v. 35 Paul has listed strictly natural phenomena that may threaten discipleship, he now moves to a list which is more cosmic, even though probably not every item in it is supernatural.

38

neither death nor life: i.e. nothing at all in human experience.

nor angels, nor principalities: plainly angels cannot be seen here as the ministers of God. As they are at least a possible threat to Christian existence, they must be evil powers. The 'principalities' (*archai*) could be human rulers, as they usually are in the NT, and in LXX as well as in Philo and Josephus. However a 'spiritual power' meaning also occurs and is found here by many commentators, especially in the light of its pairing with 'angels'.

nor things present, nor things to come: nothing that happens now or will happen in the future can separate the Roman Christians from God's love.

nor powers: this item destroys the neat run of pairs, as of course does the final 'nor anything else in all creation' in v. 39. Like *archai*, 'powers' (*dunameis*) is ambiguous. In LXX the word is used mainly for earthly forces, but in the NT, apart from its frequent use for miracles, it mostly denotes spiritual forces of some kind, good or bad. The powers here are obviously evil.^z

39

nor height nor depth: it is sometimes suggested that these are astrological forces, zenith and nadir, or zenith and abyss.^a A much more immediate

y For argument against supernatural malign powers here as elsewhere in the NT, see Carr, *Angels and Principalities*, pp. 112–14. The more usual scholarly view that a belief in intermediate hostile powers was common in Paul's day, and held by Paul, is given a thorough defence in Wink, *Naming the Powers*, see pp. 47–50 for this passage. Wink sees a belief in a continuum of power, in which human/earthly and supernatural forces were not sharply distinguished.

z On *archai* and *dunameis* in NT, LXX, Philo, Josephus, and much other literature, see the succinct account in Wink, *Naming the Powers*, Appendices I and III.

a So Käsemann, p. 251. See the comments in Cranfield I, p. 443. Carr, *Angels and Principalities*, pp. 15–18, 113, argues that fatalistic astrology was an issue only from the second century, but see now Tester, *History of Western Astrology*, Chs. 2 and 3, for much earlier popularity.

source of the opposing terms is Ps. 139^8: whether we go up to heaven or down to Sheol (the abode of the dead, in the nether regions), God is still to be found. [b]

nor anything else in all creation: the very vagueness may well confirm that Paul is not being precise about differentiating sorts of powers. In rhetorical fashion he is throwing together the things that may imperil his readers' discipleship, and the result is a rather odd agglomeration. Straightforward things like life and death, and powers like *archai*, will all fail to come between us and the love of God. The destiny of God's people is assured: this is the practical meaning of being foreknown and predestined, vv. 28–30.

in Christ Jesus our Lord: cf. the very similar closing formulae at 5^{21}; 6^{23}; 7^{25a}. The chapter-divisions correspond to the natural divisions in Paul's presentation unusually well. Yet these formulae are more than pious flourishes. The lordship of Christ is at the heart of the argument in all these chapters, as he is the new sphere of power into which Christians have moved and in which they live. Those who are accepted by God, in Christ, to be within his people, live under the lordship of Christ, and this is the crucial thing about them. That this is the crucial thing about the people of God, however, raises the question of Israel, for God already *has* a people, a very ancient one. To the problem of how Christians are related to that people, the problem of Christians and Israel, Paul must now turn. This is not least because it is also the problem of the reliability and trustworthiness of God.

9$^{1-18}$ IF GOD'S WORD IS RELIABLE, WHAT IS THE
             POSITION OF HIS ANCIENT PEOPLE?

9 *I am speaking the truth in Christ, I am not lying; my conscience bears me witness in the Holy Spirit, ²that I have great sorrow and unceasing anguish in my heart. ³For I could wish that I myself were accursed and cut off from Christ for the sake of my brethren, my kinsmen by race. ⁴They are*

b So Wilckens II, p. 177; Cranfield I, p. 433. Wink, *Naming the Powers*, pp. 49–50, finds the clue to the meaning in *I Enoch* 18$^{3, 11}$, in height and depth as the top and bottom of the pillars supporting the heavenly firmament.

Israelites, and to them belong the sonship, the glory, the covenants, the giving of the law, the worship, and the promises; ⁵to them belong the patriarchs, and of their race, according to the flesh, is the Christ. God who is over all be blessed for ever. Amen.

⁶But it is not as though the word of God had failed. For not all who are descended from Israel belong to Israel, ⁷and not all are children of Abraham because they are his descendants: but 'Through Isaac shall your descendants be named.' ⁸This means that it is not the children of the flesh who are the children of God, but the children of the promise are reckoned as descendants. ⁹For this is what the promise said, 'About this time I will return and Sarah shall have a son.' ¹⁰And not only so, but also when Rebecca had conceived children by one man, our forefather Isaac, ¹¹though they were not yet born and had done nothing either good or bad, in order that God's purpose of election might continue, not because of works but because of his call, ¹²she was told, 'The elder will serve the younger.' ¹³As it is written, 'Jacob I loved, but Esau I hated.'

¹⁴What shall we say then? Is there injustice on God's part? By no means! For he says to Moses, 'I will have mercy on whom I have mercy, and I will have compassion on whom I have compassion.' ¹⁶So it depends not upon man's will or exertion, but upon God's mercy. ¹⁷For the scripture says to Pharaoh, 'I have raised you up for the very purpose of showing my power in you, so that my name may be proclaimed in all the earth.' ¹⁸So then he has mercy upon whomever he wills, and he hardens the heart of whomever he wills.

In the letter up to this point we have seen that God has called for himself a people composed of both Jews and Gentiles, and that on the human side entry into this people is solely on the condition of faith. ᶜ This multi-racial people is the heir to the promises made to Abraham (Ch. 4), and is a people that exists 'in Christ'. It is in itself an anticipation of the renewal of the whole creation (Ch. 8). All this raises a problem that may seem remote from modern readers who have hundreds of years of almost entirely Gentile Christianity as part of their corporate history, but it is a problem that was acute for someone

ᶜ On the connection between 9–11 and the rest of the epistle, see Introduction, 7.

like Paul who was a Jew as well as a Christian. The problem is this: if
entry into the people of God is solely by faith, and for Jews and
Gentiles equally, what happens to the special position of Israel in the
purposes of God? Does justification by faith imply God's rejection of
Israel? Put another way, if historical Israel was the recipient of God's
promises to Abraham (vv. 4–5), and if God has now rejected her in
favour of a new and multi-racial people, does that not impugn the
faithfulness and reliability of God?[d] Paul cannot accept that 'the word
of God has failed' (v. 6), so he must now begin to find a solution to
the problem that does not leave him with a God who changes his
mind.

He starts with a lament over an Israel that has not accepted Jesus
Christ. Although he has just said in 8^{39} that nothing can separate us
from the love of God in Christ, he now declares that he would be
ready to undergo such a separation if that would do anything to
retrieve Israel for Christ. The passage is obviously rhetorical, and is
not to be taken as a serious proposal. Yet it demonstrates the sharpness
of the problem: how can it be solved? In Ch. 11 he will allow the
hope that in God's long-term strategy, Israel's present rejection will
ultimately lead to her full reinstatement. In Ch. 10 he will argue that
it is because of her own disobedience to the word of God in Jesus
Christ that she is outside the people of God as now understood. In
this chapter, however, he in effect solves the problem by redefining
Israel. Having taken it as an axiom that the word of God cannot fail,[e]
he proceeds to show that true Israel always has been a group within
Israel, and it is the former for which the term 'Israel' should be reserved. This means not only that true Israel is narrower than historical,
racial Israel, but also that it is capable of becoming broader by the
admission of Gentiles. The reason is that Israel is a matter of calling,
not of racial descent: the line of the people of the divine promise ran
through Isaac and not Ishmael, though both were sons of Abraham,
through Jacob and not Esau, though both were sons of Isaac and
Rebecca, and through Moses in the face of Pharaoh's opposition.

d This is often seen as the root question of 9–11, cf. Dahl, *Studies*, Ch. 8, 'The
Future of Israel', especially p. 143; also Wilckens II, pp. 181–2.

e See the parallels between this chapter and 3$^{1-7}$ as set out in Williams,
'Righteousness', p. 280.

Being Israel has always been a matter of calling and promise; it has always been the result of God's grace, and never an automatic, racial thing. It is inevitable that the selection of some to carry forward the purpose of God has meant the rejection of others. In short, the people of God has never been straightforwardly identifiable with Israel racially understood, nor is it now. Moreover, throughout the story God's sovereign freedom to choose has never been subject to human interrogation. Even opposition, like that of Pharaoh and the Egyptians to the children of Israel, can become means of demonstrating the power and purpose of God. The ultimate aim is the universal acknowledgment of the divine glory, by all peoples, both Jewish and Gentile, as the rest of the argument will show.[f]

אאא

1

I am not lying: this section of the letter is marked by an argumentative style, and it begins with an outburst of rhetoric.[g] For all that, it is thoroughly personal.

my conscience bears me witness in the Holy Spirit: for 'conscience' see on 2¹⁵. Here it stands almost as an independent entity which, when illuminated by the Spirit, can combine with Paul himself (v. 2) to provide the two witnesses required by the Law to establish any important matter (cf. Deut. 17⁶; 19¹⁵; Num. 35³⁰; Matt. 18¹⁶; II Cor. 13¹; I Tim. 5¹⁹; Heb. 10²⁸).

2

that I have great sorrow: the subsequent verses show that this is sorrow over the rejection of Jesus Christ by the generality of Jews. There is a strong possibility that Paul introduces his attitude with such surprising emphasis in v. 1 because it had in fact been questioned by opponents who accused him of lightly turning his back on his own national and religious heritage.[h] On the contrary, he maintains, far from turning his back on his own people he looks towards them with great grief.

---

f For a recent and extended discussion of the problems of the whole of 9–11 see Räisänen, 'Geistigen Ringens'.

g On Paul's technique of argument here and throughout these chapters, see Siegert, *Argumentation*.

h See Davies, *JPS*, p. 137; Campbell, 'Freedom', p. 28.

3

For I could wish that I myself were accursed: note the vivid contrast to
$8^{38f.}$. The wish cannot be fulfilled. This may be a deliberate echo of the
willingness of Moses to be blotted out for the sake of Israel (Ex. $32^{31f.}$;
Num. 11^{15}), or even of the self-offering of Jesus Christ (5^8; 8^{32}). It is not
difficult, however, to find parallels for such a readiness to give oneself
up for the sake of others, and it is possible that Paul's readers would have
understood the statement simply as an expression of warm human feeling. In that case there would be detected no particular reference to
Moses.[i] It is in any case clear that the defection of his fellow-Jews, as he
sees it, is not just a theological problem for Paul to solve, but a matter of
intense personal distress.

'Accursed' (literally *anathema*) originally meant 'devoted to destruction', but by now had become a formula of excommunication.[j]

my kinsmen by race: literally 'my kinsmen according to the flesh', i.e.
'my fellow-Jews'. There may be an oblique reference to the belief that
as a Christian Paul now has a new family, that of the body of Christ,
'the sons of God' of $8^{15-17, \, 23}$.

4

They are Israelites: Paul is shortly to redefine Israel, but at this point, as
again at $11^{7, \, 25f.}$, he uses the designation they use of themselves.[k]
Although we might have expected the apostle to list Israel's privileges
in the traditional concrete terms of the Holy City, the land, and the
Temple, he enumerates them rather in more abstract terms.

the sonship: this is the only place in the NT where 'sonship' (*huiothesia*,
translated 'adoption' in 8^{23}; cf. also 8^{15}) refers to Israel. It does not occur
in LXX at all. Nonetheless the notion of Israel as God's son is not
unusual, cf. Ex. $4^{22f.}$; Jer. 31^9; Hos. 11^1; *Jub.* 2^{20}. We saw in Ch. 8 that
being God's sons was a matter of grace, and was never an automatic
thing; still less was there ever in Jewish circles any idea that Yahweh in

---

i Munck, *Israel*, pp. 12f., 29f., argued for not only a Mosaic reference, but also
one to Paul's understanding of himself as a significant eschatological figure in
parallel to Moses. This is denied by Siegert, *Argumentation*, p. 121. For discussion
of contemporary understanding of self-sacrifice see Hengel, *The Atonement*.

j For details, see Cranfield II, p. 457.

k Cf. Cranfield II, pp. 460f.; Campbell, 'Freedom', p. 28 and n. 9.

some sense fathered Israel, as gods do father peoples in some mythologies.

the glory: this is presumably a reference to the *Shekinah*, the bright cloud that both revealed and veiled God's presence with Israel in the wilderness and in the Temple. See Ex. 16^{10}; 24^{16}; 33^{22}; $40^{34f.}$; Isa. 6^3; Heb. 9^5; I Cor. $10^{1f.}$.

the covenants: for the use of the plural see Wisdom 18^{22}; Ecclus. $44^{12, 18}$; II Macc. 8^{15}. The covenants in which Paul shows most interest are those on Mount Sinai (Ex. 19^5; $24^{1ff.}$; for Paul see especially Gal. $4^{24ff.}$) and with Abraham (Gen. $15^{17ff.}$; $17^{1ff.}$; for Paul see especially Rom. 4 and Gal. $3^{6ff.}$). It is, however, the Abrahamic covenant to which he refers more positively and more frequently.

There is a major problem of consistency when this verse is compared with vv. 6–23. Here, God's covenants seem to be unambiguously with the whole of historical Israel (and in 11^{11-36} once again salvation for the whole of Israel remains a possibility). Yet in 9^{6-23} the promise and therefore the covenant is restricted to a selected group within Israel, to theological rather than historical Israel. Certainly the meaning given to 'Israel' varies from place to place within 9–11, but it is usually possible to sort out the terminological tangle. The real problem is the place of 'all Israel' in the purposes of God: does it, or only a smaller group within it, serve as the focus of the divine plan? Perhaps we should see 9^{4-5} as what ought to be the case in Jewish estimation, 9^{6-23} as what is in fact the case in the divine estimation, and 11^{11-36} as God's resolution of the discrepancy. Perhaps we ought to accept with Räisänen that we have here an issue with which Paul was still wrestling and for which he had found no more than tentative solutions. If so, it is understandable that those solutions are not altogether consistent with one another.[1]

the giving of the law: despite what has been said about dying to the Law ($7^{1ff.}$), the giving of the Torah[m] remains one of the privileges of historical Israel.

[1] H. Räisänen, 'Paul's Conversion and his View of the Law', *NTS* 33, 1987, (pp. 404–19), pp. 410, 417. See also and especially 'Geistigen Ringens', pp. 2930–6.

[m] Despite Cranfield II, pp. 462f., not the Torah in itself, but its granting to Israel: so Käsemann, p. 259, and Munck, *Israel*, pp. 31f.

the worship: presumably in the Tabernacle during the wanderings in the wilderness, and in the Temple in Jerusalem. In the Mishnah, *Aboth* 1^2, we find a saying of Simeon the Just, 'By three things is the world sustained: by the Law, by the (Temple-) service, and by deeds of loving-kindness.' No Jew believed that only in the Temple and its cult was God to be found, yet it was believed that his presence was concentrated and especially active there (cf. Solomon's prayer in I Kings 8^{22-30}). It is the more noteworthy that in the only other passage where Paul uses this word (*latreia*), it is not for the Temple cult but for the service of Christians in ordinary life, Rom. 12^2.

and the promises: probably the reference is primarily to the promises to Abraham, Gen. 12^7; 13^{14-17}; 17^{4-8}; 22^{16-18}; cf. Rom. 4^{13-22} and Gal. 3^{16-29}. We come thus to the nub of the problem, to be raised more directly in v. 6, that God's word or promise cannot fail, yet appears to have done just that. Being the people of God seems to have passed from historical Israel as the children of Abraham, to a mixed body consisting of some Jews and many Gentiles.

5
to them belong the patriarchs: Abraham, Isaac, and Jacob.

of their race, according to the flesh, is the Christ: this is one of the very few places where Paul stresses the messiahship of Jesus in traditional terms, though cf. 1^3. It is clear that he does consider it important that Jesus is the Messiah, the fulfilment of specifically Jewish hopes.

God who is over all be blessed for ever: this is a notorious crux in Romans, because the last part of the verse can be punctuated in two different ways, giving two strikingly different meanings. Once more we are reminded that Paul used no punctuation, and that editors have to decide which of the two meanings is appropriate here, and consequently which punctuation to insert.

(*a*) If we punctuate as in RSV, with a full stop after 'the Christ', the ascription of blessing is made to God.

(*b*) If, however, a comma is placed after 'Christ', the rest of the sentence must run 'who is God over all, blessed for ever'. On this punctuation, Christ is then unambiguously identified with God.

Although it can be argued that syntactically (*b*), which identifies Christ and God, is to be preferred, many scholars nevertheless find (*a*), the punctuation adopted by RSV, more appropriate. This is because, while elsewhere Paul ascribes divine functions to Jesus Christ, he nowhere says that he *is* God without qualification.[n] Some scholars, finding the issue impossible to settle, have favoured another possibility:

(c) There is a conjectural emendation which replaces 'whose' for 'who' (*hōn ho* instead of *ho ōn*). The effect is to put at the end of the enumeration of the privileges of the Jews, 'whose is the God blessed for · ever'. The question of the relation of Christ to God thus does not arise at all.[o]

Our choice is therefore between a plausible emendation, which is unfortunately not supported by the MSS, a natural syntax with unusual christology, and a reading which raises no theological problems but which involves a change of subject between 'Christ' and 'God' (a change which would normally be marked by an adversative particle, such as *de*, but is not so marked in this case). The whole point is decidedly moot, and although conjectural emendation can be over-bold, there is a good deal to be said for it in this instance.

6

it is not as though the word of God had failed: this denial is central to the whole argument of these chapters, which may well be seen as an extended attempt to grapple with the problem it raises. One way of dealing with it Paul does not adopt: he does not simply transfer God's promises, including that to Abraham, from historical Israel to the Christian church. The later Gentile church may have found it possible to make such a transfer, but not Paul. Moreover, a conclusion that Paul finds totally unacceptable is that the promises have lapsed, for that would imply that God does not keep his word. Instead of saying the promises have been transferred, or have lapsed, Paul tries to show that God's word is not compromised by what has happened. Justification by faith, and with it the admission of Gentiles into the people of God without further condition, does not run counter to the promise ('word', *logos*) of God nor to his trustworthiness. On the contrary, his view is

[n] For (b) see, e.g. Munck, *Israel*, p. 32; Sanday and Headlam, pp. 233–8; Siegert, *Argumentation*, pp. 122f.; Cranfield II, pp. 465–70. For (a) see, e.g. Wilckens II, p. 189; Käsemann, pp. 259–60; V. Taylor, 'Does the New Testament Call Jesus God?', *Exp T* LXXIII, 1961–62, pp. 116ff.; Dodd, p. 152.

[o] This emendation is mentioned by Dodd, and tentatively proposed by Robinson, p. 112; Black, p. 130. Barrett, p. 179, thinks little of it, but declines to decide between (a) and (b).

that it is only justification by faith that properly coheres with promise, and that to see God's people in racial terms is to deny promise.

not all who are descended from Israel belong to Israel: we now begin the crucial redefinition of 'Israel'. In distinction from what he says in Ch. 11, he now apparently denies to historical Israel as a whole the covenant blessings listed in vv. 4–5 (for the discrepancy see the comments on v. 4). His point is that if being Israel, the people of God, is a matter of the divine choice, and is to continue to be that, then it cannot also be a matter only of natural lineal descent from Abraham. Up to v. 23 this is treated only as selection within Israel; thereafter we learn that God calls people not only from within historical Israel but from outside it as well.

7
'*Through Isaac shall your descendants be named*': the promises to Abraham never have been to him and to *all* his line (cf. Gal. 4²¹⁻³¹). The line runs not through Ishmael, the natural child, but only through Isaac, the child of God's promise and Abraham's faith (Gen. 18¹⁰; 21¹²; cf. also 15⁵, ⁶).

8
it is not the children of the flesh who are the children of God: this reinforces the point made in v. 7, but it also echoes Rom. 4, where the true descendants of Abraham are those who share not his race necessarily, but his faith, and Rom. 8, where God's children/sons are those who have received the Spirit of sonship (v. 15).

9
'*Sarah shall have a son*': Gen. 18¹⁰.

11
though they were not yet born and had done nothing either good or bad: God's selection within the descendants of Abraham has nothing to do with moral worth, and everything to do with the divine sovereignty. Not Esau but Jacob was the instrument God chose to carry forward his purpose. This is not to make a value-judgment on either of them. It is worth noting that in the case of the sons of Rebecca, nothing is said about promise and response. See Gen. 25²¹ᶠᶠ·. Nevertheless the second half of the verse shows that Jacob is seen as the one called and chosen by

God; being of the direct and legitimate line of Abraham, as both Esau and Jacob were, is not enough.

12

'*The elder will serve the younger*': Gen. 25^{23}. Paul does not say that either Ishmael or Esau fall outside the mercy and concern of God, but only that the line of being the people of God runs in each case through the other brother. We need to remember that the whole drift of the passage is God's consistency in working through a selection within Israel, not through historical Israel as a whole. Racial descent is not enough: promise, or call, and (in the case of Abraham) faith are decisive.

13

'*Jacob I loved, but Esau I hated*': Mal. 1$^{2-3}$. We have seen in v. 11 that this has nothing to do with moral worth, but rather concerns the choice of a people for the divine purposes. 'Love' and 'hate' therefore should be understood not as divine *liking* for the one and dislike for the other, but as choice of the one over the other.p Of course this involves rejection, but that problem Paul will take up in Ch. 11. Moreover it must be remembered that Jacob and Esau stand for the two *nations* of Israel and Edom, cf. again Gen. 25^{23}, and Edom was Israel's traditional enemy, cf. Ezek. 35$^{1-15}$. To interpret this passage as if it concerned the fate of particular persons is to miss the point. q

14

Is there injustice on God's part?: cf. 3^5, where a similar question is met as here with Paul's emphatic denial, *mē genoito*, 'not on your life'. From here to v. 29 Paul again employs the rhetorical device of the diatribe (see Introduction 1(*b*) (i)), arguing with a hypothetical partner, which is not to deny that real discussion with opponents may lie in the background. What precisely is the charge of divine injustice that Paul rejects? Perhaps he faces the claim that his argument is putting the covenant itself in question, or perhaps he fears that his account of God's dealings in vv. 6–13 may make God seem arbitrary. Whatever the

---

p On this cf. Cranfield II, p. 480. If there is any hint of predestination here, it is strictly focussed on the progress of God's saving activity within the process of history, not on the fate of individuals, cf. Wilckens II, pp. 196–7; Käsemann, p. 265.

q On it as concerned with peoples, cf. Munck, *Israel*, pp. 38, 42, 48; Leenhardt, pp. 249f.; Campbell, 'Freedom', p. 29.

exact nature and source of the charge, its answer depends on 9–11 as a whole; here he makes the immediate reply only that God's sovereignty is absolute, even in his mercy. Cf. below on v. 17.

15

'*I will have mercy on whom I have mercy* . . .': Ex. 33^{19}. The words of God to Moses come after the incident of the golden calf, so that Paul's use of them is not at odds with their original application. Despite Israel's lack of deserving, God shows his mercy to them because of his purposes in election.[r] No external factors condition the activity of God.

16

it depends not on man's will or exertion: it would be too much to read into this passage the doctrine of justification by faith. Faith does not come into the picture at all in the case of Jacob, and Paul is not talking about justification by faith as opposed to works. Rather is he stressing that in election all that matters is what God chooses to do to further his purposes.

17

'*I have raised you up for the very purpose of showing my power in you*': Ex. 9^{16}.[s] 'I have raised you up' must mean 'I have caused you to appear on the stage of history' or something of the sort. Pharaoh is to be seen not just as an individual, but as a representative of the Egyptian people, just as Esau represents Edom (cf. Ex. 14^{17}). The Egyptians and their opposition are needed to enable God to win a victory for Israel.

so that my name may be proclaimed in all the earth: we need to remember the issue with which the chapter began, and also the direction in which it is heading. The opposition of Pharaoh and the Egyptians, by being gloriously overcome by God at the exodus, served to publicize ('proclaim') his power to all nations. In the same way, in Paul's day the opposition of some Jews will serve, because of the consequent turning to the receptive Gentiles, the universal proclamation of the Christian gospel (11$^{11ff.}$).

How does Pharaoh fit in with the theme of selection within historical

r Cf. Hanson, *Technique*, pp. 157f., and Leenhardt, pp. 252f.; Cranfield II, pp. 483f.

s On the difference between Paul's quotation and LXX see Siegert, *Argumentation*, pp. 129f.; Cranfield II, pp. 485–7.

Israel that has dominated the preceding verses? In fact he represents not a continuation of that theme, but a new move: just as selection of Israel-within-Israel was for the divine purpose, so was Pharaoh, though on the negative side as a foil for the power of God. Now we see what that purpose is: it is the proclamation of God's name everywhere. To this, not only the figure of Pharaoh but the other figures, too, have been leading.

18

he hardens the heart of whomever he wills: it is a common enough OT idea that opposition to God or to his people is God's own action (cf. Ex. 4^{21}; 7^3; 9^{12}; 10$^{20, 27}$; 11^{10}; 14$^{4, 8, 17}$, for the hardening of Pharaoh's heart). Paul shows no interest in the human motives of the Egyptians, but is concerned only with the overarching divine purpose and with the demonstration of God's power, whether in the events of the exodus or in the coming of the gospel of Christ (cf. 1^{16}). No interest is shown in the eternal fate of Pharaoh either: we cannot read into this passage the 'destruction' of v. 22 (cf. Cranfield II, p. 489). Moreover, Paul appears to find no difficulty in having God exploit an evil for a good purpose. All he does here is offer the explanation of a divine hardening for the fact that many within historical Israel have refused to accept Jesus Christ. In Ch. 10 he will blame Israel's own obduracy, and in Ch. 11 raise the hope that hardening is only temporary, but in the meantime there is no lightening of the picture.

9$^{19-29}$ GOD'S SOVEREIGN FREEDOM
AND THE REMNANT

^{19}*You will say to me then, 'Why does he still find fault? For who can resist his will?'* ^{20}*But who are you, a man, to answer back to God? Will. what is moulded say to its moulder, 'Why have you made me thus?'* ^{21}*Has the potter no right over the clay, to make out of the same lump one vessel for beauty and another for menial use?* ^{22}*What if God, desiring to show his wrath and to make known his power, has endured with much patience the vessels of wrath made for destruction,* ^{23}*in order to make known the riches of his glory for the vessels of mercy, which he has prepared beforehand for glory,* ^{24}*even us whom he has called, not from the Jews only but also from the Gentiles?* ^{25}*As indeed he says in Hosea,*

> 'Those who were not my people
> I will call "my people",
> and her who was not beloved
> I will call "my beloved".
> ^{26}'And in the very place where it was said to them, "You are not my
>   people",
> they will be called "sons of the living God".'
> ^{27}And Isaiah cries out concerning Israel: 'Though the number of the sons
> of Israel be as the sand of the sea, only a remnant of them will be saved; ^{28}for
> the Lord will execute his sentence upon the earth with rigour and dispatch.'
> ^{29}And as Isaiah predicted,
> 'If the Lord of hosts had not left us children,
> we would have fared like Sodom and been made like Gomorrah.'

It looks as if Paul is not altogether sure that he has adequately answered
the question of v. 14 about injustice on the part of God, for v. 19
virtually repeats it. He then returns to finding an answer, using the
well-known OT image of the potter and the clay, arguing that what
is crucial is the purpose of the potter. The question may be in terms
of deserving, but the answer is in terms of purposes. The important
thing about pots is how they are intended to be used, so that any talk
about the rights of bits of clay is irrelevant. Once again Paul is talking
not about individuals but about peoples, and it is to be noted that in
the similar Jer. 18^{6-10} the talk is also clearly about peoples.

As Paul sees it, God's purpose is to have a people which is composed of Jews and Gentiles together (in v. 24 the Gentiles are mentioned for the first time in this chapter). In order to create such a
people, God uses negative as well as positive forces. Thus, just as
Pharaoh was used by God as a negative force at the exodus, so the
unbelieving Jews are used by him in bringing about his newly multi-
racial people (cf. $11^{11f.}$, 14^f). In practice this means that many who
have not been considered part of the people of God must now be so
considered, while some who have been thought of as within that
people, can no longer have their membership sustained. Quotations
from Hosea are used to establish the first point, the inclusion of the ·
Gentiles, and from Isaiah to show that although many Jews are not
now to be included in God's people, nevertheless a 'remnant' is still

there and is still faithful to the purposes of God. There is no question that a Jewish Israel is to be replaced by a new and Gentile Israel. Historical Israel has not been rejected *en masse* (any more than historical Israel *en masse* has rejected Jesus Christ). As there has always been election for God's purposes not of a racial grouping as such but of a particular line within that grouping, so now the promises to historical Israel continue but apply to only some within it, and to Gentiles as well. ᵗ

If the divine election necessarily has the corollary that some people are not elected, this rejection is to be seen not only as temporary (cf. $11^{25f.}$) but also as arising from the needs of the divine strategy, not from divine value-judgments. That election is in accordance with deserving has already been ruled out in $9^{11, 14f.}$.

ℵℷ

19

'*Why does he still find fault? For who can resist his will?*' : cf. the comments above on 3^{5-6}. Surely, if hardening, like showing mercy, is a matter of the divine will, there can be no human responsibility in the affair?

20

who are you, a man, to answer back to God? : one question is met by another, which aims to show that the first question is not legitimate, cf. v. 14. The immediately following piece about the potter shows that Paul's point is not that God is arbitrary, but that everything happens in accordance with consistent purposes. The now famous cry, 'But the trouble is that man is not a pot' ᵘ and will insist on asking why the responsibility should not be borne by God and not by himself, is thus understandable but misses Paul's point. Pots are for uses, and uses determine what is made. God needs a Moses, but he also needs a Pharaoh in the furtherance of his plans (v. 17). It is precisely because Paul is talking about the divine plan in history that it is impossible for human beings to criticize or assess the divine justice. God's plans are in

t On the idea of the remnant within Israel, which Paul uses but does not invent, see the useful brief treatment by R. E. Clements, ' "A Remnant Chosen by Grace" (Romans 11.5)', Ch. 8 of Hagner and Harris.

u Dodd, p. 159; cf. also Robinson, p. 116.

his hands and in his alone, cf. Isa. 29¹⁶ for a similar use of the potter and clay figure in the context of the divine purpose.

To be fair to Dodd and to others who find this passage a low point in Pauline thought, the argument is vulnerable to misunderstanding. Paul does write as if human beings were both passive instruments of God and yet also blameworthy, see especially v. 22b. We may perhaps say[v] that while objectively Pharaoh and the rejected part of historical Israel may serve God's ultimate ends, subjectively they do not. God may use for positive purposes their negative response to him, but negative that response remains and is not to be excused. Yet this is an argument that Paul does not mount. He simply assumes that God's judgment is just, and concentrates on the long-term strategy which is within the sovereign freedom of God who is not capricious, but *is* in charge of the movement of history.

21

the potter: for the use of this figure in Jewish tradition see Isa. 29¹⁶; 45⁹⁻¹³; Jer. 18⁶⁻¹⁰; Job 10⁸⁻⁹; Wisdom 15⁷. The use for which pots are made is stressed in Wisdom, and the application of the analogy to God's purposes in relation to Israel or humanity in general has parallels in Isaiah and Jeremiah. Paul is clearly using an idea that would have been familiar to those versed in Jewish Scripture.

22–24

What if God . . . : there are two major difficulties with these verses taken together, their correct translation and their seeming inconsistency with v. 21.

(*a*) The translation difficulty centres on the participle 'desiring' (*thelōn*, v. 22). Is it causal, so that the sentence runs 'What if God, because he desires to show his wrath . . .?' or is it concessive, resulting in 'What if God, although he desires to show his wrath and make known his power, nonetheless has endured . . .?' The causal interpretation is now most often favoured[w] although the concessive was often preferred by older commentators,[x] in particular because it seems to agree better with 2⁴. Käsemann, however (pp. 270f.), has argued that the participle is neither causal nor concessive but modal, and that the rendering

v With Siegert, *Argumentation*, pp. 133f.

w E.g. Barrett, pp. 184, 189f.; Cranfield II, pp. 492–4; Murray II, pp. 33–5.

x E.g. Sanday and Headlam, p. 261; Dodd, p. 159; Leenhardt, p. 258; more recently Black, p. 134f.

should be 'with the purpose'. The difference in effect between this and the causal view is not great. The issue in the end is whether God's endurance of the vessels of wrath is in spite of his will to manifest his wrath and power, as a kind of check on them, or whether it is because of that will, so that the endurance is an outworking of his wrath and power.

(b) This leads us to the problem of meaning, and in particular to the question of the divine consistency. Why should God be spoken of as having to be patient with (or endure) 'vessels of wrath' – nations and groups of people that oppose his purposes – when it was his decision to create or mould them in the first place? A suggestion by Siegert may be helpful:[y] he proposes that v. 24 is the apodosis to the protasis of v. 22. The sentence then runs, 'If God, wishing to show his wrath . . . endured with much patience the vessels of wrath, *this was* in order to make known the riches of his glory for the vessels of mercy . . .' In other words, God needed the negative forces like Pharaoh, however much he disliked them in themselves, in order to bring about the positive result that accorded with his plan. This in effect repeats the idea of v. 17. Siegert's syntactical suggestion involves taking *kai* ('and/even/also') in an unusual but not impossible way as the introduction to the apodosis of a conditional sentence.

However, the divine consistency remains a problem. Granted that God needed negative elements, it is still to be asked why they should be condemned as such. Paul seems to be saying that God's need of them does not imply his endorsement of them; even useful negative elements are still negative. The opponents of God's people, and those who now decline to remain his people, will *despite themselves* be used, like Pharaoh, to carry forward the divine saving strategy. Later, in Ch. 11, Paul will hold out a prospect of reconciliation even for them, but here the picture is not softened in the least. Those who oppose God are here totally negative forces.

vessels of wrath made for destruction: on 'wrath'/*orgē* see at 1^{18}. It is probable that the vessels of wrath are here the unbelieving Jews, for which in v. 17 Pharaoh was an analogy. If this is right, we have here an anticipation of the view to be expounded in Ch. 11 that it is the Jews' rejection of Jesus Christ that has led to the mission to the Gentiles, and so to the increasing implementation of God's plan for a people composed of both Jews and Gentiles. Basically, Paul is seeing what has

[y] *Argumentation*, pp. 132f., 136.

happened as all part of the divine intention. That the rejecting Jews are now faced with the divine judgment ('of wrath made for destruction') is an idea found also in I Thess. 2^{16}. If that judgment, there as in the present passage, is taken to be the final one, then the endurance of the vessels of wrath during the delay is in order to allow for the spread of the gospel.[z]

also from the Gentiles: up to this point there has been only selection within Israel, and the exploitation of the opponents of God for his goals despite themselves. Even in his harshest criticisms of the majority of historical Israel, Paul expresses no doubts that God's promises to Israel still stand, nor that God's grace to her continues.[a] Now we have the point up to which the argument has been leading, namely that the people of God's calling is not to be constituted solely of Jews.

25

'*Those who were not my people I will call "my people"* . . .': we have here an adaptation of the text of Hos. 2^{23}.[b] In Hosea the words have to do with the lapse and return of the northern kingdom of Israel, but as Paul uses them they concern the incoming of the Gentiles; unlike the Israelite northerners, they have never previously been God's people. The effect of this quotation, and of that in v. 26, is to give Scriptural backing for 'also from the Gentiles' in v. 24.

26

in the very place: the quotation now is from Hos. 1^{10}, a passage to which there is an allusion also in I Peter 2^{9-10}.[c] In Hos. 1^{10} the place is Palestine. Here, perhaps, the meaning is less clearly geographical: it may be simply to do with the new universal reality, the Christian people. It is possible, however, that there is a stress on geographical place, especially as the Greek includes 'there' (*ekei*) before 'they will be called', and this may be Paul's own addition to the quotation. If such a stress on place is to be understood, then the place may well be the city of Jerusalem.[d] Munck proposes that the purpose of the collection, cf.

z On this see Munck, *Israel*, pp. 62–71.

a See Dahl, 'The Future of Israel' in *Studies*.

b For details see Lindars, *New Testament Apologetic*, pp. 242f.

c On the different ways in which the passage is used in Romans and I Peter see Richardson, *Israel*, p. 173.

d As argued by Munck, *Israel*, pp. 12, 72; see also his *Salvation*, Ch. 10.

$15^{25ff\cdot}$, was to signal that the last days were at hand, when the Gentiles would stream to Zion (Jerusalem) to join the people of God, and that this was why Paul was taking with him to Jerusalem representatives of the Gentile churches. It was also why he was determined to go in spite of the evident danger, and further why the collection loomed so large in the later stages of his missionary work (see 15^{31}; I Cor. 16^{1-4}; II Cor.. 8^{1-5}; 9^{13}).

27

only a remnant of them will be saved: Isa. 10^{22-23}. In Isaiah, this is a condemnatory passage. Paul, however, uses it to console and reassure: at least a remnant will be saved, and that by the mercy of God, cf. v. 29. This idea of a remnant which has been running through the passage since v. 6 now receives explicit expression. It shows that the focus is not on the rejected nor on what happens to them, but on the remnant that is faithful. If not all racial Israel is true Israel, nevertheless there is an element within it that is true to its calling. God's word has not failed, v. 6.

28

the Lord will execute his sentence upon the earth: once again as in vv. 20–24 we have the strange combination of a divine purpose which can exploit even human opposition, and human responsibility with its consequent liability to judgment. God is responsible for what has happened, yet human beings are to be blamed for it. Theologically this combination is a puzzle, but it is hardly without parallel, cf. Matt. 18^7, 'For it is necessary that temptations come, but woe to the man by whom the temptation comes!' In the meantime, it looks as if Israel is not derelict, yet continues only in a remnant, the rest being under God's condemnation. Later (11^{26}) we shall come across a wider hope for historical Israel.

9^{30}–10^{13} WHAT ISRAEL HAS MISSED AND THE GENTILES HAVE FOUND

30 What shall we say, then? That Gentiles who did not pursue righteousness have attained it, that is, righteousness through faith; 31but that Israel who pursued the righteousness which is based on law did not succeed in fulfilling that law. 32Why? Because they did not pursue it through faith, but as

if it were based on works. They have stumbled over the stumbling stone,
[33]*as it is written,*

> '*Behold, I am laying in Zion a stone that will make men stumble,*
> *a rock that will make them fall;*
> *and he who believes in him will not be put to shame.*'

IO *Brethren, my heart's desire and prayer to God for them is that they may be saved.* [2]*I bear them witness that they have a zeal for God, but it is not enlightened.* [3]*For, being ignorant of the righteousness that comes from God, and seeking to establish their own, they did not submit to God's righteousness.* [4]*For Christ is the end of the law, that every one who has faith may be justified.*

[5]*Moses writes that the man who practises the righteousness which is based on the law shall live by it.* [6]*But the righteousness based on faith says, Do not say in your heart, 'Who will ascend into heaven?' (that is, to bring Christ down)* [7]*or 'Who will descend into the abyss?' (that is, to bring Christ up from the dead).* [8]*But what does it say? The word is near you, on your lips and in your heart (that is, the word of faith which we preach);* [9]*because, if you confess with your lips that Jesus is Lord and believe in your heart that God raised him from the dead, you will be saved.* [10]*For man believes with his heart and so is justified, and he confesses with his lips and so is saved.* [11]*The scripture says, 'No one who believes in him will be put to shame.'* [12]*For there is no distinction between Jew and Greek; the same Lord is Lord of all and bestows his riches upon all who call upon him.* [13]*For, 'every one who calls upon the name of the Lord will be saved'.*

We are still with the question of who are God's people and on what basis, but now turn to the effect of the coming of Jesus Christ on the constitution of that people. If 9^{1-29} has set out the problem, and if Ch. 11 deals with the application of the solution, 9^{30}–10^{21} is the solution itself.[e] We begin with the issue of righteousness, a multi-faceted term which here seems to mean something like 'life as God's people'. This is what historical Israel apart from the faithful remnant has missed, and what those Gentiles who have turned to Christ in faith have found. Israel missed it because of her mistaken belief that it depended on Law (the Torah), and the Christian Gentiles found it

e See Munck, *Israel*, pp. 78f.

because of their correct recognition that it depends on faith, as in the case of Abraham. Those who rejected the way of faith, open as it is equally to Gentiles as to Jews, have done so because they failed to acknowledge Jesus Christ as the key to life as the people of God. Paul desperately longs for them too to be included (cf. 9^3) and recognizes their religious zeal, but believes that they are looking for life under God in the wrong place. Only those who have faith in Christ can enter and belong to the people of God, for Christ is the fulfilment of what the Law was aiming at.

Under the Sinaitic covenant, Israel believed that life consisted in adhering to the Law which was freely accessible to them as a revelation of the divine will. Even more accessible, however, is the new life as God's people, based as it is simply on faith in Christ. There is no need to search heaven for it, because Christ has come, nor search the nether regions for it, because Christ has been raised from the dead. The source of this life is close at hand, is heard about in Christian preaching, and it is a life that is entered wherever there is faith in. Christ crucified and risen. Having the Law cannot any longer be a crucial matter, for it separates Jews from Gentiles and there can be no such division in God's people which is constituted solely by faith, a faith which is equally open to Jews and Gentiles. Similarly, the divine gifts that follow faith are equally to be granted to Jews and Gentiles.

ജ

30
What shall we say, then?: here and in 8^{31}, this common Pauline question (cf. 3^5; 4^1; 6^1; 7^7; $9^{14,\ 19}$) introduces not an objection or a false view to be answered, but a resumé of a case.

pursue: athletic imagery runs through vv. 30–32. The non-starters have won the race.[f]

righteousness: the correct way to understand this term (*dikaiosunē*) is debated here as much as anywhere (see on 1^{17}; $3^{5,\ 21}$).
　(*a*) Some, like Cranfield (II, pp. 506f.), think that it is equivalent to

---

f On the use of such imagery here, see Badenas, *End*, pp. 101f.

justification, but we have seen that this is an unlikely meaning for it. In any case at this stage of his argument Paul is dealing with the maintenance of Israel's existing status as the people of God, not with how they might gain it for the first time. Further, 'righteousness based on law' in Judaism was not the means of entry into, but the manner of living within, the covenant.[g]

(b) It is possible that Paul is here talking about *God's* saving righteousness, but this does not naturally fit the language of pursuit. God's saving righteousness is his own activity, or even his fidelity to his promise to Abraham[h] and human beings can scarcely pursue that.

(c) It is certainly out of the question that morality, pure and simple, is at stake here. Paul has not been talking about morality more than very marginally indeed; in any case he argued in Ch. 2 that Gentiles who lack the Law nevertheless often obey the will of God rather better than the Jews who have the Law.

(d) The interpretation adopted here is that righteousness is life under God of his covenant people, life in all its ramifications, its privileges, its duties, and its general character.[i]

through faith: cf. v. 32, and 3^{22}. One cannot press Paul's logic too hard in this verse. When he says that the Gentiles did not pursue righteousness, he can hardly mean that at no point and by no means did they do so; their having faith is tantamount to their pursuing life as God's people. Perhaps 'formerly' should be understood in the first half of the verse: 'Gentiles who formerly did not pursue righteousness have now attained it, that is righteousness through faith.'

31

Israel who pursued the righteousness which is based on law: literally, they pursued 'the law of righteousness' (*nomon dikaiosunēs*), an unexpected expression. How should we take it?

(a) What we might have expected is 'the righteousness of law', i.e. the righteousness that is based on keeping the Law (the Torah), which is how RSV takes it. Cranfield (II, p. 507) not unreasonably criticizes this as rewriting Paul's sentence for him. If he had wanted to say this he could have done so. If despite this criticism we follow RSV, then Paul is saying that Israel did not succeed in finding righteousness because they

g See the argument of Sanders, *PPJ*, and especially pp. 493ff.

h This is the argument of Williams, ' "Righteousness" '.

i See again Sanders, *PPJ*, pp. 493ff.; Ziesler, *Meaning*, especially pp. 36–43.

mistakenly thought it was a matter of Law-obedience, whereas in fact it is a matter of faith.

(b) Some commentators propose that 'the law of righteousness' is the righteous Law, the Law whose aim, goal, or content is righteousness.[j] Then to say that Israel failed to fulfil it is either to draw on 2^{27} where Israel is so charged, or more commonly to say that she failed because she approached it legalistically, in the wrong spirit of seeking to earn merit.[k] The former is possible, but the latter is most unlikely: Paul does not say that Israel failed to fulfil it in the right way, but that she failed to fulfil it at all.

(c) Perhaps it is a mistake to take 'law' here as prescription. It could be that, as in 3^{31}, it is the Law in its character as promise that is at stake, the Law that in Gen. 15^6 promises righteousness to faith.[l] This would mean that throughout vv. 30–33 the topic is not keeping the commands of the Torah but receiving its promises. It would amount to an echo of Ch. 4. Israel failed to arrive at the Law by missing its promise-character and in particular by not accepting Jesus Christ. This interpretation takes *ouk ephthasen* to mean not 'did not succeed in fulfilling' but 'did not arrive at', which is probably a more accurate translation in any case. As a proposal it is by no means impossible, though as the most recent discussion of the Law (in Ch. 7) has been to do with it as prescription rather than as promise, one would have expected some indication of the change of aspect. There is such an indication in 3^{31}: the reference to Law there is at once followed by the discussion of Abraham and Gen. 15^6 in Ch. 4.

(d) We may therefore prefer the view that 'law of righteousness' means a 'leading-to-righteousness-law', and that when Paul says Israel 'did not succeed in fulfilling that law' (literally 'did not arrive at the law') he is not saying that they did not keep the Law. He is instead saying that in their pursuit of the goal of righteousness they failed to find the Law that would lead to it. They were bound to fail, because such a Law did not exist. It is faith and not keeping the Law that leads to righteousness, to life as God's people. Although travelling by a different route, this interpretation ends up at much the same place as (b) above.[m]

j E.g. Williams, ' "Righteousness" ', p. 283; Barrett, *Essays on Paul*, pp. 139–42; Lagrange, p. 249.

k So Barrett, op. cit.; Cranfield II, pp. 507f.

l See Badenas, *End*, pp. 103–5.

m Cf. Siegert, *Argumentation*, p. 142, for the suggestion that 'law' (*nomon*) is a metonymy for the goal of the Law, namely righteousness.

32

they did not pursue it through faith but as if it were based on works: if the interpretation of v. 31 just given is correct, then the trouble with Israel is not that she has kept the Law in the wrong way, 'legalistically', when she ought to have kept it by faith. Those who think this seem to understand that Israel kept the Law in order to earn God's favour thereby. It is extremely hard to find evidence that Paul elsewhere attacked Israel for this, or that Israel was vulnerable to such an attack. [n]

If we reject this interpretation, what alternative is there? We can take 'it' to represent, as in v. 31, not the Law, but righteousness, and it is this that is fundamentally a matter of faith, not of keeping the Law. This has been argued in Ch. 4, and is crucial here because of the concern in this passage to establish that the people of God is now equally open in its membership to Jews and Gentiles. That membership therefore cannot depend on Law-observance, but does depend solely on faith which Gentiles can have just as Jews can. In a word, Israel's understanding of righteousness was too narrow, in that it applied only to Jews, but also (as v. 33 shows) in that it did not allow for Christ who would fulfil the promises to Abraham and open up the people of God to all who had faith in him. [o]

33

'*I am laying in Zion a stone that will make men stumble . . .*': a mixture of Isa. 28[16] (cf. also 10[11] below) with Isa. 8[14]. [p] The quotation shows that the faith mentioned in v. 32 is not faith in general, but specifically faith in Christ. In effect, the stone over which Israel has stumbled is the same stone that the Christian Gentiles have taken as their foundation. Whether this stumbling occurred in the rejection of the historical Jesus, or in the failure to respond to the Christian preaching of people like Paul himself, is not clear. Certainly 'he who believes in him' in 10[11] refers to one who has Christian faith, and it is to be presumed that it does so here too. It is therefore likely that the 'rock' in this verse is Christ, and not the Torah, as has been suggested. [q]

n This view of Israel's fault, however, is held by many commentators, e.g. Barrett, *Essays on Paul*, pp. 141ff.; Cranfield II, pp. 509f. It is now opposed not only by Sanders, *PPJ*, throughout, but by Wilckens II, p. 213 and n. 952; Watson, *PJG*, p. 165; Räisänen, *PL*, pp. 174f.

o Cf. Badenas, *End*, p. 107.

p There is a similar conjunction in I Peter 2[4, 6–8], where it is more explicitly christological. For details see Barrett, *Essays on Paul*, pp. 143f.

q Barrett, *Essays on Paul*, p. 144.

10.1

saved: Greek *eis sōtērian.* As usually in Paul and the Bible in general, this refers to the consummation, the ultimate destiny in this instance of historical Israel for which Paul longs, cf. $9^{1ff.}$. For *soteria*/salvation see on 1^{16}. At present historical Israel as a whole is not gathered into God's newly multi-racial people, but Paul continues to long for that to happen and in 11^{26} formulates a hope that it will.

2

they have a zeal for God: there may here be an oblique reference to Paul's own zeal for God as a Pharisee, which nonetheless led him to reject Christ and persecute the church, Gal. 1^{14}; Phil. $3^{5–6}$.

but it is not enlightened: it lacks understanding of the will of God. If we take the stumbling of $9^{32f.}$ to refer to the rejection by the Jews of Jesus during his lifetime, then being without enlightenment here has the same reference, one that is quite common in Acts ($2^{23, 26}$; $3^{13, 14, 17–21}$; $4^{10–11, 27–28}$; $13^{26–31}$).[r] If the stumbling of $9^{32f.}$ is about failure to perceive the word of God in the preaching about Christ by Paul and others, then that may be the reference here as well.

3

being ignorant of the righteousness that comes from God: more precisely than in v. 2, we learn what it is that Israel does not perceive. Then what is this righteousness that comes from God?

(a) It could be the same as God's righteousness to which they did not submit, in the last part of the verse. The precise wording is different: 'the of-God-righteousness' (*tēn tou theou dikaiosunēn*) in v. 3a, but 'the righteousness of God' (*tē(i) dikaiosunē(i) tou theou*) in v. 3c. Despite the difference, it is possible that Paul is saying that the Jews did not submit to the righteousness of God, being ignorant of it, and being satisfied with their own righteousness. God's righteousness in v. 3c is surely God's own saving activity, seen in his promises to and through Abraham, and now to be seen in the formation of his people as multi-racial, through Jesus Christ.[s]

> [r] This is the view of Munck, *Israel*, p. 81. Cf. also I Cor. 2^8; Luke 19^{44}; 23^{34}.
> [s] Cf. Williams, ' "Righteousness" ', pp. 282–4. Badenas, *End*, pp. 109f., sees the expression as virtually equivalent to Christ, so that the refusal of submission is the same as the stumbling of $9^{32f.}$; see also Wilckens II, p. 220. Badenas points out that each time Paul speaks of the righteousness of God in this letter, it is in connection with the inclusion of the Gentiles in the people of God, p. 102.

(b) It is possible, however, that while in v. 3c it is God's own saving righteousness that is meant, in v. 3a it is life as God's people, in accordance with his will and intention, life therefore based on faith in Jesus Christ. If so, there is a movement within the verse:

from ignorance of the sort of righteousness God wants (3a)
through the wrong sort of righteousness (3b)
to submission to the saving righteousness of God (3c).

Either of these alternative interpretations is feasible; both make sense in the context. Despite the slight difference in wording between 3a and 3c, it is marginally easier to take them as referring to the same thing than to give them substantially different meanings. On balance therefore it is just preferable to adopt the first: being ignorant of the righteousness of God, they failed to submit to it.

seeking to establish their own (righteousness): many commentators have assumed that this is a matter of accruing merit before God and so having a righteousness which is not a gift from God, but a claim upon him. Put simply, it is to earn God's favour and a place among his people. Paul must reject this because it denies grace and faith and readily leads to self-righteousness. Precisely this was what was wrong with much Jewish piety.[t] Once again we must record grave doubts whether this was Paul's charge against the Jews, and whether Jewish teachers held any such view (see the discussion at 3^{20}). Building up merit was a concern of the Reformers, but there is remarkably little evidence that it was Paul's. In any case, in this section of the letter Paul has been discussing Jewish rejection of Christ, and so it is much more likely that 'their own righteousness' here means something like 'their own version, not God's, of what constitutes life as his people'. A large part of their misunderstanding of righteousness was that they left no room for faith in Jesus Christ as the essential requirement, cf. 9^{30-33}. However, the larger context indicates that another and closely related thing was also wrong with their understanding of righteousness: it really allowed room only for Jews. If righteousness is by keeping the Law, then there is no place for Gentiles. On the other hand life as God's people that is based on faith is open to Jews and Gentiles equally. It is their failure to understand this that leads to 'their own righteousness' being condemned

---

t See for example Barrett, *Essays on Paul*, pp. 146f.; Black, p. 138; Bruce, p. 201.

here; it is in effect 'their own righteousness, Christ-rejecting and for Jews only'.[u]

4

Christ is the end of the law: in the Greek 'end' is *telos*, which could mean termination, or purpose, or completion/fulfilment. Is Paul saying that Christ brings the Law to a full stop, is he saying that Christ was all along the purpose of the Law, or is he saying that Christ is its completion and perfection? These questions are endlessly debated, and dogmatism is quite out of place, but a few points may clarify the issues.

(*a*) It is important to decide how to take 'law'/*nomos*: if it is the Law in its character as promise (cf. 3^{31}), then it would be natural to see Christ as the fulfilment of that promise, as the one to whom the Law was pointing.[v] On the other hand if 'law' is the Law as prescription, as defining righteousness, there is a better case for seeing Christ as bringing that to a termination, though it could still be held that Christ was the fulfilment of what the Law was aiming at, *viz.* making it possible to live as God's people.[w]

(*b*) It is sometimes suggested that Paul was inclined to the view that with the coming of the Messiah, the Law as it had been was now at an end, and would be replaced by a new messianic Torah. Reference is often made to the work of W. D. Davies, though he himself is cautious about it. If such a view is represented in the present verse, it follows that 'end' means termination, even if the notion of fulfilment is not too far away. There is in Paul, however, little support for any idea of a new messianic Torah, and it would be precarious to allow the notion to be the key to Rom. 10^4.[x]

(*c*) One interpretation that can now be discarded is that *nomos* is really 'legalism', the use of the Law to erect one's own righteousness before God, and that it is this of which Christ is the termination. See the discussions above at 3^{20} and 10^3.

u See Räisänen, *PL*, p. 174, and *Torah*, pp. 74f.; Sanders, *PLJP*, p. 38.

v So for example Rhyne, *Faith Establishes the Law*, Ch. IV and p. 110; Badenas, *End*, especially pp. 114–18.

w For the first, see for example Räisänen, *PL*, pp. 53–6; for the second Cranfield II, pp. 515–19. It is often difficult to distinguish between the latter view, and an interpretation of the Law as promise.

x The crucial work is W. D. Davies, *Torah in the Messianic Age and/or the Age to Come*, *JBL MS* 7, 1952. There is a useful summary of the discussion with good bibliography in Badenas, *End*, pp. 28, 187–8.

(d) Powerful support for taking *telos* to mean 'goal' or else 'completion' has come from the work of R. Badenas who has argued that in the Greek of the day, the overwhelmingly dominant use was positive, to mean purpose, fulfilment, or completion. This evidence cannot be lightly set aside, so that while a 'termination' meaning may not be impossible, it has now been rendered much less likely by the exhaustive study of Badenas (*End*).

(e) Some scholars not unreasonably point out that fulfilment carries with it the notion of supersession, so that even if we accept 'goal' or 'completion' as the meaning of *telos* here, the Law can hardly go on playing the role it has done.[y]

It remains difficult to interpret this statement with confidence. The immediate context in Ch. 10 rather argues for a termination meaning: the basis of righteousness, of being God's people, is not now the Law which divides Jews from Gentiles, but Christ and faith in him, available to Jews and Gentiles alike. Nonetheless the evidence amassed by Badenas is weighty, and we probably ought to accept that Christ is seen here not so much as the negation of the Law as the one to whom it points, the one in whom it finds its completion.

that every one who has faith may be justified: literally, 'for righteousness for every one who believes'. The RSV rendering of *dikaiosunē/* righteousness by 'justified' must be questioned. This is not only because it is not the usual meaning of *dikaiosunē*, but also because Paul is talking not about means of entry into the people of God, but about what constitutes life as that people, not about what God does in order to have a people, but about what men and women must do in order to remain as his people. The answer is what it has always been, namely to be righteous, but righteousness now is based on faith in Jesus Christ, not on keeping the Law. Justification also depends on faith, but that is not the issue here. We may thus paraphrase the verse, 'Christ fulfils the aim of the law, namely to lead to life as God's people, and he does this for all those who believe in him.' This is why so many Gentiles who do not have the Law have found righteousness, and why so many of historical Israel who do have the Law have failed to find righteousness.

5

Moses writes: Lev. 18[5]. Paul is about to interpret an OT passage in the light of Christ, as he does also in Ch. 4; cf. the closely similar Gal. 3[12].

[y] See, e.g. Leenhardt, p. 266; Campbell, 'Christ the End', pp. 76f.

The covenanters of Qumran likewise interpreted the OT in the light of their own times and their own circumstances.

the man who practises the righteousness which is based on the law shall live by it: when he quotes Lev. 18⁵ in Gal. 3¹² Paul contrasts righteousness based on Law with righteousness based on faith, and it is natural to assume that he makes the same distinction here. In the present statement he then simply accepts the common Jewish assumption that life as the people of God basically consists in observing the Law. What follows in vv. 6–8 thus aims to show that if the one is readily accessible, the other (righteousness by faith) is even more accessible in Jesus Christ. However there are difficulties about this.

(*a*) He quotes the Torah in support of both righteousness by Law and righteousness by faith.

(*b*) If we take Christ as the goal or fulfilment of the Law (v. 4), then we should expect this verse to lead on to righteousness based on faith, rather than to stand in contrast with it.

It is therefore sometimes now suggested that there is no contrast here between a Law-righteousness and a faith-righteousness. Instead, properly understood Law-righteousness *is* faith-righteousness.ᶻ This view accords well with much in the passage, though the word 'But' (*de*) at the beginning of v. 6 then needs to be taken transitionally rather than adversatively. This is quite a possible if not the most natural way to take it. Much will obviously depend on how we take 'the righteousness which is based on law' not only here but also in 9³¹ (see above).

Both interpretations make acceptable sense, and as on 10⁴ dogmatism is perilous. Yet on balance the more traditional explanation seems preferable, if only just: if we give *de* in v. 6 its full meaning of 'but', and take the Law-righteousness of this verse as standing in contrast to the faith-righteousness of v. 6, we are in line with the general drift of this section of the letter. The climax comes in v. 12, with the reminder of there being no distinction between Jew and Greek, picking up the theme of much of Ch. 9 that God's people is multi-racial. The core of the difficulty is that righteousness by Law as Paul believes God intended it, *was* for Jews and Gentiles alike and was by faith (Ch. 4). Israel unfortunately understood it as specific to the Jews and as dependent upon observance.

z See Campbell, 'Christ the End', p. 77, for whom vv. 5–6 show how Christ is the goal of the Law; Badenas, *End*, pp. 119–33, after a full discussion concludes that Paul means to say that righteousness by faith is taught by the OT.

The disagreement in interpreting Paul at this point is a disagreement about which reading of righteousness-by-Law we should take, that of God (as it were) or that of the Jews.

6

the righteousness based on faith says: is this a mere personification, a rhetorical flourish, or does it mean something like 'the faith-interpretation can also quote the Torah'? At all events faith here is specifically faith in Jesus Christ, and 'righteousness based on faith' is that life as the people of God which depends on him, and on the human side is received by faith.

Do not say in your heart . . .: Paul now annotates an edited version of Deut. 30^{12-14}, omitting all the references to Law-observance. The opening words may be an echo of Deut. 9^4. There has been much discussion of Paul's use of the passage from Deuteronomy, a use which seems highly arbitrary to modern readers. Nevertheless if Paul believes (v. 4) that Christ is the fulfilment of the Law, then he may also see him as the fulfilment of what the OT says about the Law, so that it is proper to make Deut. 30^{12-14} refer to him. Moreover it appears that there was already a tradition which identified the Torah in the passage with Wisdom; Paul may have taken the further step of identifying Wisdom with Christ.[a]

The Deuteronomy passage maintains that the commandment (i.e. the Law' is by no means remote or esoteric: there is no need to send someone up to heaven or across the sea to find it. On the contrary it is in Israel's mind and heart, and the people both know it and can do it. If the righteousness based on Law is thus accessible, how much more is that based on faith. Of course, if we take vv. 5ff. as not contrasting two sorts of righteousness, but take it that the righteousness based on Law when properly understood *is* the righteousness based on faith, then there is no 'how much more' about it. Then the Deuteronomy passage straightforwardly shows the accessibility of the Christ/faith righteous-

---

a See Suggs, ' "The Word is Near You" ', endorsed by Dahl, *Studies*, p. 148; cf. also M. Black, 'The Christological Use of the Old Testament in the New Testament', *NTS* 18, 1971–72, pp. 1–14 at pp. 8f., for a not dissimilar treatment in the Neofiti Targum; Badenas, *End*, pp. 129f. A comparison is often made with OT exegesis at Qumran, e.g. by Wilckens II, p. 225; Käsemann, p. 284; Cranfield II, pp. 523f.

ness on Paul's view, cf. above on v. 5.[b] However this does not seem the more natural way to take the passage.

'*Who will ascend into heaven?*' (*that is, to bring Christ down*): cf. Deut. 30¹². The source of righteousness is Christ who has come and does not need to be sought, cf. I Cor. 1³⁰; Phil. 2⁶⁻⁸. Alternatively, bringing Christ down may refer not to the incarnation, but to the coming again (e.g. I Thess. 4¹⁶), so that as Christians have the 'word' (v. 8), there is no need to bring Christ down again from heaven (so Käsemann, p. 288).

7
'*Who will descend into the abyss?*' (*that is, to bring Christ up from the dead*): cf. Deut. 30¹³. The point is clear enough: it is the risen Christ who is the source of righteousness, cf. Phil. 3⁹⁻¹⁰, and not a dead prophet. There is a difficulty about Paul's quotation, in that LXX speaks not of the abyss, which is presumably the abode of the dead, but of (going across) the sea. Has Paul altered the quotation, and if so why? We cannot be sure that his Greek OT was precisely the same as ours, so he may not have altered it at all. The word for 'abyss' (*abusson*) usually means 'deep waters', but it can also mean '*the* Abyss', i.e. Sheol, the dwelling place of the dead, as it does in Ps. 71²⁰ (LXX 70²⁰). Its ambiguity thus enables Paul to keep to a respectable Greek version of the Deuteronomy passage and at the same time make a reference to the story of Jesus. Whether this was a happy accident or whether Paul deliberately chose *abusson* to achieve the effect is impossible to determine. This is the first reference in the NT to the tradition that after the crucifixion Jesus descended into Hades/Sheol.[c]

8
The word is near you . . . (. . . the word of faith which we preach): cf. Deut. 30¹⁴, where the word is the commandment. Whether we take it that this is in continuity with the Law rightly understood, or in contrast with the Law wrongly understood, we now come to the crux of the matter. The righteousness based on faith is readily and universally available wherever the preaching of Christ is heard.

9
if you confess with your lips that Jesus is Lord: inward response is not

b See Badenas, *End*, pp. 126–33.
c On the point of vocabulary see Cranfield II, p. 525.

enough and overt acknowledgment is needed, but to whom? It is possible that confession before the authorities is meant, such as Paul's conceivable need to confess his allegiance to Christ before the Sanhedrin during his projected visit to Jerusalem, and the need for all Christians to refuse to recant when brought up before Roman authorities. [d] There may even be a deliberate allusion to the title 'lord' (*kurios*) assumed by Roman emperors. It is more commonly supposed, however, that 'Jesus is Lord' was *the* primitive Christian declaration of belief, cf. I Cor. 12³; Acts 16³¹. This may have been in a baptismal setting. [e]

The ascription of this title to Christ Jesus is extremely common in Paul and in many other parts of the NT, and its precise effect is much disputed. When quoting the OT, Paul uses it for Yahweh, in Christian terms for God the Father, but when writing freely, he uses it for Christ. How far this involves ascribing divinity to Christ in the same sense that Yahweh is divine is a moot point. Its occurrence in an Aramaic rendering in I Cor. 16²² suggests that as a title for Christ it was very early, and that it did not simply arise in Hellenistic circles to counter the 'many lords' of pagan cults (cf. I Cor. 8⁶). Certainly Paul can transfer to Christ some OT statements about Yahweh (e.g. Phil. 2¹⁰), but equally he seems to draw back from equating Jesus Christ with God purely and simply, though see the discussion at 9⁵. However, although it is exceedingly difficult to determine how Paul conceives the relation between Christ and God[f] it is not nearly so difficult to grasp what the relation between Christ and believers is conceived to be. Lords have servants, and so Christ the Lord is to be served by Christians (cf. 1¹). 'Jesus is Lord' is therefore an acknowledgment of belonging and of submission. Conversely, lords are protectors of their servants, and so the confession also implies that Jesus will care for his own.

believe in your heart that God raised him from the dead: for the connection between the resurrection and the lordship of Christ see also 14⁹ (and see Acts 2³¹⁻³⁶). The word that is preached (v. 8) thus moves from the mouth of the preacher to the heart of the hearer, and thence to the mouth of the hearer.

d The view of Munck, *Israel*, pp. 88–9.

e See Badenas, *End*, p. 133 and notes; Cranfield II, pp. 527f.

f For further discussion see Cranfield II, pp. 527–9; Dunn, *Christology in the Making*; C. F. D. Moule, *The Origin of Christology*, pp. 35–46; Vermes, *Jesus the Jew*, Ch. 5. The issues are summarized in Ziesler, *PC*, pp. 33–9.

you will be saved: as usual in the Bible and in Paul in particular, salvation is in the future, at the consummation of God's purposes for the world and men and women within it. See on 1^{16}.

10

man believes with his heart: however strange it may seem to modern Western ears, 'heart' (*kardia*) in the Bible is not exclusively or even especially used for emotion and sentiment, but can refer to intellect, will, or the inner self in general, as it does both here and in v. 9.[g]

and so is justified . . . and so is saved: the literal translation of the verse is 'For what is believed in the heart leads to righteousness (*dikaiosunē*) and what is confessed with the mouth leads to salvation.' There is reason to think that RSV translates *dikaiosunē* mistakenly here, and that Paul is talking about righteousness and not about justification. The topic is not God's transfer of men and women into his people by faith, for which 'justified' would be appropriate, but what constitutes life as that people, as from 9^{30} onwards. Of course the answer is 'faith', just as it is for justification. At the end, this life as God's people will be vindicated and endorsed by him so that, if belief and confession go hand in hand, the final outcome is salvation.

11

'No one who believes in him will be put to shame': Isa. 28^{16} (already cited in 9^{33}) with the addition of *pās*, 'no one'. This addition may be small, but it is highly significant in that it underlines the universality of God's people, with no distinction between Jew and Gentile. This has been a continuing thread in the argument since 9^{24} at least: if it is faith that constitutes God's people, then neither belonging to a particular race nor observing the Torah can also be a requirement. For 'shame' see on 1^{16}; the meaning here is probably 'will not be left in the lurch, will not be failed (by God)'.

12

there is no distinction: the familiar point is reiterated. Jews and Gentiles are equally eligible to be within Israel as it is now defined. We are also reminded that the fundamental theme is not the salvation of this individual or that, but which peoples or races are eligible for the divine favour.

g See J. Behm, in *TDNT* III, especially pp. 608–14.

Just as there was no distinction of race in the universality of sin. (3²²ᶠ·), so there is none in the possibility of ultimate salvation.

all who call upon him: in the OT this is a formulaic expression for anyone who is a supplicant or devotee of Yahweh (cf. the quotation in v. 13). It is also far from uncommon in paganism. But who is 'he', the Lord on whom they call? In the quotation that follows, the Lord is Yahweh, and we could assume that he is the Lord here as well. On the other hand, in v. 9 we had the confession 'Jesus is Lord', and so Jesus Christ could be the Lord here. As it is not an OT quotation, we should normally expect the Lord to be Christ. On the other hand, this verse is obviously under the influence of the quotation that immediately follows, which reinforces the case for identifying the Lord as Yahweh. Further, a theme since 9¹ has been *God's* sovereign freedom in calling his people. It is this last which perhaps just tips the balance in favour of taking 'Lord' here, rather unusually, as referring not to Jesus but to Yahweh. ʰ

13
'*every one who calls upon the name of the Lord will be saved*' : Joel 2³², LXX exactly. If the majority of commentators are to be followed, this is an instance (like Phil. 2¹⁰) where Paul transfers to Christ language that in the OT is used of God. In any case the quotation serves to underline the universality of God's purposes.

10¹⁴⁻²¹   ALL HAVE THE OPPORTUNITY TO HEAR THE MESSAGE, BUT NOT ALL RESPOND

¹⁴*But how are men to call upon him in whom they have not believed? And how are they to believe in him of whom they have never heard? And how are they to hear without a preacher?* ¹⁵*And how can men preach unless they are sent? As it is written, 'How beautiful are the feet of those who preach good news!'* ¹⁶*But they have not all heeded the gospel; for Isaiah says, 'Lord, who has believed what he has heard from us?'* ¹⁷*So faith comes from what is heard, and what is heard comes by the preaching of Christ.*

ʰ Not only in this verse but also in v. 13 commentators usually equate 'Lord' with Jesus Christ, see e.g. Cranfield II, p. 532; Black, p. 139; Sanday and Headlam, p. 291; Leenhardt, pp. 272f.

¹⁸*But I ask, have they not heard? Indeed they have; for*
> *'Their voice has gone out to all the earth,*
>> *and their words to the ends of the world.'*

¹⁹*Again I ask, did Israel not understand? First Moses says,*
> *'I will make you jealous of those who are not a nation;*
>> *with a foolish nation I will make you angry.'*

²⁰*Then Isaiah is so bold as to say,*
> *'I have been found by those who did not seek me;*
>> *I have shown myself to those who did not ask for me.'*

²¹*But of Israel he says, 'All day long I have held out my hands to a disobedient and contrary people.*

This section is sometimes given the heading 'That Israel does not Believe is her own Fault' or something of the sort. Yet it is not until v. 19 that Israel is specifically mentioned, and vv. 14–18 appear to be more generally concerned with the need for the message to be heard, with the fact that opportunity for hearing it has been given, and with the fact that despite this not all have responded to it in faith. It may be that Israel in particular is the unresponsive audience throughout, yet she is not named until v. 19.[i] If not from v. 14, then certainly from v. 19, Israel – despite ample opportunity to hear and respond – has declined to embrace faith in Jesus Christ, while others have embraced it. Elsewhere Paul presents this failure as part of the long-term divine providence (9^{17}, and especially $11^{11f., 14f., 26, 31f.}$) but there is nothing of that here. It is simply Israel's own fault. So here is another answer to the problem of Israel's rejection of Christ, and to the consequent problem of God's apparent rejection of her. She has brought it upon herself. How this is congruent with the notion of the remnant, the selection within the election, or with the idea of the divine hardening, all in Ch. 9, is not explained. The next chapter will show that all this is not the end of the matter, and that even the 'hardened' and the unresponsive may be saved in the End.

❧

---

[i] Watson, *PJG*, pp. 166f., sees the passage as defending Paul's Gentile mission. Cranfield II, p. 533, thinks that in view of the whole context, 9^{30}–10^{21}, the Jews are probably intended throughout.

15

'*How beautiful are the feet of those who preach good news*': Isa. 52⁷, closer
to the Hebrew than to LXX.ʲ The quotation is used to answer the
questions of vv. 14–15a; people cannot call upon one in whom they do
not believe, nor believe in one of whom they have not heard, nor hear
of one who has not been proclaimed. But Christ *has* been proclaimed,
and the Isaianic quotation is transferred from good news about restoration from captivity to good news about Jesus Christ. ᵏ If we take it that
'the Lord' in vv. 12 and 13 is Yahweh, then it is the more likely that this
section up to v. 18 concerns the Gentile mission, for only the Gentiles
could be plausibly said not to have called upon, nor even known of,
Yahweh. If, on the other hand, 'the Lord' is Christ, then these verses will
be about Jews as well as Gentiles. In any case, the message of Christ *is*
the message of Yahweh as it ought to be understood, in Paul's Christian
view.

16

'*Lord, who has believed what he has heard from us?*': Isa. 53¹. Scripture
confirms that many will not respond, whether they be Jews or Gentiles.

17

So faith comes from what is heard . . .: this virtually repeats v. 14, and also
recapitulates the three main items of Isa. 53¹, faith, the message, and the
Lord who sends.

the preaching of Christ: what is this? It could be preaching about Christ
by Paul and other apostles; it could be the preaching that Jesus himself
did; or it could even be the word of the exalted Lord. 'Preaching' is
literally *rhēma*, 'word'.ˡ It is impossible to be sure which is meant, but
in any case the point is that there has been opportunity for response.

18

'*Their voice has gone out to all the earth . . .*': Ps. 19⁴. This is to show that
what was said in v. 17 is true, and that the opportunity to hear has been

---

j Nevertheless Paul's wording may presuppose LXX, as is argued by Wilckens
II, pp. 228f.

k For evidence that some Rabbis also transferred it to the Age of the Messiah
see Käsemann, p. 294; Cranfield II, p. 535.

l On the possibilities see Munck, *Israel*, p. 94; Käsemann, p. 295; Cranfield
II, pp. 536f.

universal. On the face of it this is an extraordinary exaggeration. Paul surely must have known that there were innumerable people who had not heard the Christian gospel! There are several possible solutions to this conundrum.

(*a*) Paul is arguing *a fortiori*. That is, he is saying that if other nations have had the opportunity to hear, how much more has Israel (cf. v. 19). The point is rhetorical, and does not imply a sober claim that every single individual or even every single nation has heard the Christian message.

(*b*) Paul is simply saying that the message is universal in character, and uses this quotation rhetorically to make the point.

(*c*) As in 15¹⁹ (on which see below), Paul is speaking in a representative fashion, meaning that all regions in his world had been evangelized, but not that every single individual or sub-group had heard the preaching.^m

There is doubtless something in all these solutions, but (*a*) has the advantage that it explains the link between vv. 18 and 19.

19

did Israel not understand: as at the beginning of v. 18, there is a double negative (*mē . . . ouk*) which, in the introduction to a question, has the effect of implying a positive answer. If Israel understood, then why did she not respond? The answer is threefold, and is conveyed by three quotations.

(*a*) Deut. 32²¹, in v. 19, which suggests that Israel has been set aside in favour of another nation. This roughly corresponds to Rom. 9¹⁴⁻²⁹, though it is more negative about the place of Israel as a whole than we find in the latter Pauline passage.

(*b*) Isa. 65¹, in v. 20. This stresses not the rejection of Israel but the gathering of the Gentile nations, again in rough correspondence to Rom. 9¹⁴⁻²⁹.

(*c*) Isa. 65², in v. 21. This shows that what has happened arose from Israel's disobedience to the call and purpose of God. It is now that we have a clear indication that Israel is to blame for her rejection. This note is not as dominant throughout the section as is sometimes thought, but it is undeniably present.

In vv. 18–21 we thus have more than one explanation for Israel's rejection: it is in God's plan, *and* it is Israel's own fault.

m For (*a*) see Wilckens II, p. 230; Cranfield II, pp. 537f. For (*b*) see Sanday and Headlam, p. 299. For (*c*) see Munck, *Israel*, pp. 96–8.

A FAITHFUL REMNANT
                    NEVERTHELESS STILL EXISTS

11 *I ask, then, has God rejected his people? By no means! I myself am*
an Israelite, a descendant of Abraham, a member of the tribe of Benjamin.
²God has not rejected his people whom he foreknew. Do you not know what
the scripture says of Elijah, how he pleads with God against Israel? ³'Lord,
they have killed thy prophets, they have demolished thy altars, and I alone
am left, and they seek my life.' ⁴But what is God's reply to him? 'I have
kept for myself seven thousand men who have not bowed the knee to Baal.'
⁵So too at the present time there is a remnant, chosen by grace. ⁶But if it is
by grace, it is no longer on the basis of works; otherwise grace would no
longer be grace.

⁷What then? Israel failed to obtain what it sought. The elect obtained it,
but the rest were hardened, ⁸as it is written,
    'God gave them a spirit of stupor,
    eyes that should not see and ears that should not hear,
    down to this very day.'
⁹And David says,
    'Let their feast become a snare and a trap,
    a pitfall and a retribution for them;
    ¹⁰let their eyes be darkened so that they cannot see,
    and bend their backs for ever.'

The argument now faces explicitly the question that has been implicitly present more or less constantly since 9¹: has God rejected
Israel? The answer is that he has not. The idea of a remnant (9²⁷) is
taken up again, and use is made of the story of Elijah's experience
after the contest with the priests of Ba'al on Mount Carmel. As then
so now, there is a remnant which has faith. In this part of the chapter,
the answer to the question is what we should expect after reading
Ch. 9, that Israel's rejection is only partial. In vv. 11–27 the further
answer is that the rejection is only temporary, and finally in vv. 28–
37 the whole issue is set within an ineffable long-term divine purpose.

It was suggested that in 9²⁷ the remnant idea was used positively to
indicate that there is at least a remnant. That positive use is even more
clear here, and the OT quotations underline the importance of the

idea for the argument. It remains true that the majority have been 'hardened' (cf. 9$^{14-18}$), but a minority which includes Paul himself has not. The divine purpose which always did work through an Israel within Israel, continues with that part of her, the remnant, which has responded in faith. The promises to Abraham have not failed, but at least in the meantime are being channelled more narrowly. God's election is, as it has always been, a matter of grace, and the remnant has rightly met that grace with faith, not supposing that election could ever be a matter of human achievement.

ಐಐ

1

has God rejected his people? By no means: the question begins with *mē*, signifying that the answer expected is 'No'. This is further emphasized by the strong denial *mē genoito*, 'Not in the very least', cf. on 3^4. Despite what has been said in 10$^{18-21}$, Israel *in toto* has not been rejected by God.

I myself am an Israelite: the chosen instrument of the mission to the Gentiles himself comes from historical Israel, is in good standing and has a respectable pedigree. As long as there are Jews like him who are also Christians, it cannot be held that God has rejected his ancient people. The confidence found in passages like I Sam. 12^{22} and Ps. 94^{14} that God will never forsake his people, is still justified.

It is reasonable to deduce from these words of Paul's about himself that those whom he addresses are in the main Gentile Christians. We should otherwise have expected him to say something like 'we ourselves are Israelites'.

2

his people whom he foreknew: cf. on 8^{29}. Foreknowledge implies election or calling, and not just advance information. For God to 'know' Israel is for him to elect them and regard them as his people. He cannot now default on that commitment to them.

Elijah: here taken as a representative remnant figure.[n] He is used, however, differently from the figures of Isaac and Jacob in Ch. 9. There it

[n] See again Clements, ' "A Remnant Chosen by Grace" ', on the remnant ideas in the Bible.

was a matter of divine selection within historical Israel; here it is a matter of there having been apparently only one Israelite who remained faithful to God despite temptation to apostasy.

3

'. . . *I alone am left, and they seek my life*': cf. I Kings 19$^{10,\ 14}$, here paraphrased. Elijah was a fugitive after winning the trial of the strength of their respective gods with the prophets of Ba'al. It is possible that a deliberate parallel is being drawn between Elijah's confrontation on Mount Carmel and the confrontation with the Jewish authorities that Paul expects when he goes up to Jerusalem.º

4

'*I have kept for myself seven thousand men . . .*': I Kings 19^{18}. In fact Elijah was far from being the only faithful one left; there was a considerable remnant with him.

5

at the present time there is a remnant, chosen by grace: cf. 9^{11}. The remnant, the Israel within Israel, always has been chosen by God's grace. For Paul, this remnant consists of those who have responded in faith to God's grace in Jesus Christ.

6

if it is by grace, it is no longer on the basis of works: we have now moved away from the position (10^{21}) that Israel's rejection of Jesus Christ was simply by her own free choice. Here, those who have not rejected him have been deliberately chosen by God, as an act of grace further to that of the covenant itself. It is not that those who have responded are better in character, or better keepers of the Torah, than the rest. If that were so, God would be dealing with people on the basis of their merit, and that is incompatible with his dealing with them on the basis of grace, which is by definition free and not deserved. The covenant had always been understood as being by the divine grace (cf. Deut. 7$^{6ff.}$; Rom. 9^{11}), and the gathering of the newly multi-racial people of God is on the same basis.

o So Munck. *Israel*, p. 109.

7

Israel failed to obtain what it sought. The elect obtained it: what is 'it'? As in 9$^{30ff.}$, it is presumably righteousness, the life of the covenant people. As there also, Israel as a whole failed to find it. The elect who did find it could be the Gentiles who came to have faith in Christ; this would continue the parallel with 9$^{30ff.}$. However, since in the present context we are dealing with the idea of a remnant within Israel, it is more likely that the elect here are those Jews who, like Paul himself, have come to accept Jesus Christ, cf. vv. 5, 7b. ᵖ

but the rest were hardened: cf. Pharaoh in 9^{18}. The verb used here is different, but the idea is the same, and in both places we find the divine passive, with God as the implied agent in hardening. The idea that those who reject Christ or fail to understand him do so because of a divine hardening of their hearts is a not uncommon one in the NT: see John 12^{40}; Mark 3^5; 6^{52}; 8^{17}; II Cor. 3^{14}; Eph. 4^{18}. It is possible that Isa. 6$^{9f.}$, which is quoted in John 12^{40}, is the background passage for all or most of these. Somehow, even human rejection or failure to understand is within the divine purpose. Here, as with Pharaoh in 9^{18}, that is certainly the case, though Paul does not explain how the same rejection can be both culpable (10$^{18-21}$) and the result of God's action.

8–10

as it is written . . . : Isa. 29^{10} (cf. 6^{10}); Deut. 29^4; Ps. 69$^{22f.}$ (cf. 35^8). Passages from Law, Prophets, and Writings are thus invoked to make the case against Israel. It is probable that detailed applications should not be looked for, though it has been suggested that in v. 9, for example, there is an attack on the Jewish cult. ᑫ The lack of understanding of the bulk of Israel is clearly in view, and with that their rejection, cf. v. 7; 9$^{14ff.}$.

11$^{11-24}$ ISRAEL'S REJECTION IS NOT FINAL

^{11}*So I ask, have they stumbled so as to fall? By no means! But through their trespass salvation has come to the Gentiles, so as to make Israel jealous.*

p So Wilckens II, p. 238; Barrett, pp. 209f.; Sanday and Headlam, p. 313.
q Cf. Käsemann, p. 302; Wilckens II, p. 239. Cranfield II, pp. 551f., is sceptical of any precise reference.

^{12}Now if their trespass means riches for the world, and if their failure means riches for the Gentiles, how much more will their full inclusion mean!

^{13}Now I am speaking to you Gentiles. Inasmuch then as I am an apostle to the Gentiles, I magnify my ministry ^{14}in order to make my fellow Jews jealous, and thus save some of them. ^{15}For if their rejection means the reconciliation of the world, what will their acceptance mean but life from the dead? ^{16}If the dough offered as first fruits is holy, so is the whole lump; and if the root is holy, so are the branches.

^{17}But if some of the branches were broken off, and you, a wild olive shoot, were grafted in their place to share the richness of the olive tree, ^{18}do not boast over the branches. If you do boast, remember it is not you that support the root, but the root that supports you. ^{19}You will say, 'Branches were broken off so that I might be grafted in.' ^{20}That is true. They were broken off because of their unbelief, but you stand fast only through faith. So do not become proud, but stand in awe. ^{21}For if God did not spare the natural branches, neither will he spare you. ^{22}Note then the kindness and the severity of God: severity toward those who have fallen, but God's kindness to you, provided you continue in his kindness; otherwise you too will be cut off. ^{23}And even the others, if they do not persist in their unbelief, will be grafted in, for God has the power to graft them in again. ^{24}For if you have been cut from what is by nature a wild olive tree, and grafted, contrary to nature, into a cultivated olive tree, how much more will these natural branches be grafted back into their own olive tree.

We have already been given hints (e.g. 10^1; 11^1) that the rejection of Israel by God, consequent upon her rejection of Jesus Christ, is not to be considered final. It now becomes clear that the rejection is only one move in a long process, and that it is temporary as well as partial. Because Israel has rejected Jesus Christ, the Christian mission has turned to the Gentiles, and they have responded in large numbers, so that Israel as a whole is now obliged to see Gentiles within the people of God, in effect in their place. Doubtless they do not see it in that way themselves, but in Paul's view this is what the reality is. He hopes and believes that this will have the effect of making them at last turn to Jesus Christ, and enter the people of God as God wants it to be (or, from another point of view, re-enter it). This is not a hope for a remnant, but for all Israel. In the divine strategy, their rejection was to lead to the incoming of the Gentiles, and this has happened in fact. Paul looks for a further move in that strategy when those who are not now in the remnant will join those who are. That will be like another resurrection. Meanwhile, the remnant can be regarded as the foretaste of that full restoration. Just why it is supposed that seeing Gentiles within the Christian community will prompt non-Christian Jews to join them, is hardly clear. It may be connected with the hope that the Gentiles would stream to Zion in the Last Days (e.g. Isa. 2^{2f.}); the Jews should see that this is now happening through the Christian mission.

Meanwhile, those Gentiles who are now within the people of God through faith in Christ must not despise historical and unbelieving Israel, for Israel is like an olive tree. Some of the branches of that tree have become unproductive and must be pruned (unbelieving Israel), while shoots from an uncultivated olive (Gentile Christians) are grafted in. Nevertheless, the original branches are not finally thrown away, and the hope is retained that in the end they too will be grafted back into the tree. The newly ingrafted (Gentile) branches must not assume that their position is invulnerable: if they prove unfruitful they too will be pruned. So, the tree continues to flourish, and the main point is that it is an old tree which has been injected with new life, not an altogether new tree. Israel is very old, but its composition must now be seen to depend not on race, nor on keeping the Torah, but on grace and faith, i.e. on divine generosity and human response. Belonging to Israel is thus a possibility for Gentiles as much as for Jews.

❧

11

stumbled: cf. 9^{32-33}. Despite all that has been said in 9^{30ff.}; 10^{19f.}, and in 11^{7-10}, we must not think that stumbling is to be equated with total collapse. It is not. Indeed historical Israel (as distinct from the true Israel, the remnant, or the Israel within Israel) is in trouble, but the trouble is not necessarily mortal.

through their trespass salvation has come to the Gentiles: it is clear that Paul is giving a theological interpretation to historical events. What has happened is that the Jewish mission, in relative terms at least, has failed; as a consequence the church has turned to the Gentile mission. This is a picture which is repeatedly painted by the author of the Acts of the Apostles. Of course neither that author nor Paul himself ever gives that as the reason for the Gentile mission, for both base that mission in a divine call (Gal. 1^{16}; Acts 1^8; $10^1–11^{18}$). Presumably the important aspect of the historical situation was that the much greater success of the Gentile mission rapidly led to a correspondingly greater concentration of the primitive church's limited resources to it, rather than to the comparatively ineffective Jewish mission. All this is largely inferential, but something of the sort is required to explain Paul's statement.

to make Israel jealous: this may well refer back to 10^{19} (and so to Deut. 32^{21}), and to trying to show historical Israel what she is missing. The argument seems strange: if most of historical Israel have rejected the Christian message, and with it the Christian community, why should they be jealous of Gentiles who accept the one and enter the other? The most plausible explanation is that Paul is tacitly adapting a Jewish expectation that at the End the Gentiles would come in large numbers to Zion to join Israel there (see Isa. $2^{2f.}$; $25^{6f.}$; $60^{3f.}$; Jer. 16^{19}; Micah $4^{1f.}$; Zech. 14^{16}; Ps. $22^{27–29}$).[r] If the Jews can only perceive that this is what is now happening, but in reverse so that the Gentiles are gathering in advance of many Jews, then they may be moved to join in the great event that so far has been taking place without them.

12

if their trespass means riches for the world: we again have Paul's view that Jewish rejection has led to the Gentile mission. As in the previous verse, their trespass is plainly their refusal to accept Jesus Christ. It is just possible that the Greek *paraptōma* should be translated literally as 'false step' rather than 'trespass', in line with its etymology and with the metaphor of stumbling (v. 11).[s]

how much more will their full inclusion mean: lest we should suppose that the mission to the Gentiles is not for their own sake, but only to provoke the Jews to jealousy, we now learn that the restoration of Israel as a whole will even further enrich the Gentiles. 'Their full inclusion' (*to*

r On this see further Munck, *Salvation*, pp. 47f., also *Israel*, p. 133; Wilckens II, p. 255 and n. 1145; also Tob. 13^{13}; $14^{6f.}$.

s See the rather sceptical discussion of this possibility in Cranfield II, pp. 555f.

plērōma autōn) must surely mean that the majority of Israelites, who are at present outside the multi-racial and Christ-centred people of God, will eventually be gathered in. Whether this means that every single Israelite will be included is less certain. It could mean a successful completion of the Jewish mission and the consequent belief of the bulk of Israel, not just the remnant, but without specifying whether this means 'absolutely all' or simply 'most'.[t] Since 9¹, and even since Ch. 4, Paul has seen true Israel as a remnant or a selected group within historical Israel, but it is now evident that he has not relinquished the hope that at the End the remnant and historical Israel may become identical. Neither here nor in 11^{25ff.} does he explain how he envisages this happening.

13

I am speaking to you Gentiles: this remark is important in that it indicates that the aim of the argument is to make the Gentiles understand their place in the divine saving history, the long-term plan for the human race. This place is not to be an alternative to or replacement of God's ancient people, but rather to be within Israel as God always intended it to be.

I magnify my ministry: or, 'I make the most of the significance of the Gentile mission, which is my particular concern.' Munck may be right when he says that Paul believed himself, as the apostle to the Gentiles, to have a key role in the divine plan of salvation.[u] When he takes the collection from the Gentile churches up to Jerusalem, accompanied by representatives of those churches, that will be the sign that the Gentiles are coming to Zion, and therefore that God's purposes are approaching their consummation, cf. above on v. 11.

14

in order to make my fellow Jews jealous: cf. on v. 11. However highly Paul rates his Gentile mission, this does not in the least imply a renunciation of concern for historical Israel.

---

t For the latter, view, see Munck, *Israel*, pp. 119f.; for the former, Sanday and Headlam, p. 322, and Cranfield II, pp. 557f., who also gives a useful discussion of *plērōma* here.

u Israel, pp. 121f. He cites also Rom. 15^{15f.}; I Cor. 9^{15ff.}; Gal. 2⁷⁻⁹; Col. 1^{24f}; Eph. 3²⁻¹¹.

and thus save some of them: it is only here that Paul gives himself any role in the mission to and the redemption of historical Israel.^{v} In 15$^{17f.}$, for example, his mission is directed strictly to the Gentiles. Even here, of course, his role is indirect, but it is nonetheless crucial to God's strategy as he conceives it.

Yet why is the hope only that 'some of them' may be saved? We need to remember that for the moment he is speaking only of his own part in the mission of the church; his hope is that at least some Jews, seeing the success of the Gentile mission, will perceive what they are missing and turn to Christ. Later in this chapter (v. 26) we learn of his wider hope that within the divine providence all Israel will be saved, but this is not necessarily to be as a result of his own ministry.

15

the reconciliation of the world: for 'reconciliation' see at 5^{10}. It is probably too much to detect here the sort of cosmic reconciliation we find in Col. 1^{20}; Paul is more likely talking of the reconciliation to God of the human world. The point of vv. 11f. is thus recapitulated: Jewish rejection has led to Gentile acceptance of the Christian gospel.

what will their acceptance mean but life from the dead: cf. v. 12. Paul maintains the hope that racial Israel will become co-extensive with the remnant, that even those who now reject Christ will finally become part of Israel as now defined.

It is impossible to be sure what is the meaning of 'life from the dead' here.

(*a*) It could be a reference to the general resurrection. The End will come, with resurrection as part of it, when all Israel is gathered in, cf. v. 26.^{w}

(*b*) It could just possibly refer to a universal awakening of Christian faith.^{x}

(*c*) Because resurrection usually has an eschatological nuance, (*a*) is preferable to (*b*). Nevertheless it is also probable that there is a reference to the olive-tree figure which is about to be introduced, and to the

---

v As pointed out by Sanders, *PLJP*, p. 184.

w So Davies, *JPS*, p. 133. Munck, *Israel*, pp. 126f., finds precision impossible, but thinks Paul must be referring to events just before or during the Second Coming.

x Sanday and Headlam, pp. 325f., discuss this view but reject it in favour of an eschatological one.

branches which have been cut off but may yet be restored. If so, Paul is saying that the restoration of Israel amounts to the resuscitation of what has died (cf. Ezek. 37, and 'can these bones live?').

Suggestion (*c*) means that it is Israel's life from the dead that is at issue. Suggestion (*a*) means that it is life from the dead for everyone, Gentiles as well as Jews. In the immediate context, a concentration on the restoration of Israel seems more likely than one on the general resurrection. Therefore (*c*) is preferred.

16

If the dough offered as first fruits is holy, so is the whole lump: if the fundamental point is not difficult to grasp, how the figure works is more of a problem. The offering of part of something to God signifies that in principle all of it belongs to him. The argument then seems to be[y] that what has been representatively consecrated to God cannot for ever remain opposed to him or separated from him. The remnant is therefore the sign that eventually all of what is properly God's, i.e. all of historical Israel, must join in being the people of God as now gathered around Jesus Christ. The relevant OT passage (Num. 15$^{17-21}$) does not, however, say that the offering sanctifies the whole lump, nor does Philo (*Spec. Leg.* I, 131–44); it could be argued that the offering rather frees the rest for secular use, and that would not help Paul's argument here at all. Cranfield (II, pp. 563f.) points out, on the other hand, that in the analogous Lev. 19$^{23-25}$ the offering of first fruits from a tree removes from the remaining fruits their 'uncircumcised' character. It is thus reasonable to follow Lagrange (p. 279) in taking it that the rest of the dough, the lump, would be regarded as blessed and purified.

A more substantial difficulty lies in determining just who are the first fruits.

(*a*) They could be the patriarchs, especially Abraham (see Ch. 4, and 9$^{6-13}$).

(*b*) They could be the Jewish Christians of the time of Paul's writing, i.e. the remnant (cf. 9^{27}; 11$^{5, 7}$).

(*c*) In I Cor. 15^{23} Jesus Christ is the first fruits, but such an identification here could be made only with the greatest difficulty.

(*d*) Ruling out (*c*), perhaps we should take it that Paul is not here making a sharp distinction between the true Israel of old and true Israel now, and that both (*a*) and (*b*) are to be included among the first fruits.[z]

y Cf. Dahl, *Studies*, p. 151.
z So Dahl, *Studies*, p. 151.

A reference to the patriarchs is supported by v. 28, and one to the present remnant is supported by vv. 1f. In the context a reference to contemporary Jewish Christians is more natural, but 'root' in the second half of the verse suggests beginnings, and thus the patriarchs.[a] The evidence points in both directions, and we are thus given grounds for concluding for both (a) and (b): as the remnant are the true children of Abraham because they rely on God's undiscriminating grace (11[6]; cf. 9[30]–10[4]) to Jew and to Gentile alike, the first fruits are a timeless fusion of ancient patriarchs and contemporary remnant.

if the root is holy, so are the branches: this figure suggests beginnings and fulfilment, and is the more important because it leads into the crucial figure of the olive tree. The latter dominates this part of the argument and may even dominate the Pauline view of the relation between Israel and the church, not to mention the relation between Jews and Gentiles within the church. In this part of the verse the reference must surely be to the patriarchs as the root. We thus have a stress on the continuity of God's dealings: if the Fathers belonged to God, so do their descendants, despite the fact that in the meantime most of them have rejected their place in God's plan. Perhaps the chief point is that even a pruned Israel has kept its place in the divine strategy.[b]

This notion of the people of God, however constituted, as an olive tree, is not new. See Jer. 11[16], where Israel as such a tree is under judgment and in danger of destruction. Paul is less radical: only some of the branches are in danger, not the whole tree.

17
if some of the branches were broken off: i.e. if some Jews have refused to acknowledge Jesus Christ and so refuse to be within the multi-racial people of God defined in terms of faith in him. The passive verb 'broken off' lacks a stated agent, from which we infer that this is a divine passive, so that God is the implied agent. *God has now rejected them.*

you, a wild olive shoot: the Gentiles are still being addressed (cf. v. 13) and are identified as cuttings from the wild olive. This is the same species as the cultivated olive and does bear fruit, though they are small and

a See also Käsemann, p. 308; Wilckens II, p. 246 and nn. 1101, 1103; Munck, *Israel*, p. 127.
b See Richardson, *Israel*, p. 129.

hard and not to be compared with what comes from a cultivated tree. [c]

were grafted in their place: one sometimes reads that this shows that Paul was a townsman who did not understand the cultivation of trees and that no one grafts wild olive shoots into a cultivated tree. Alternatively one may read that Paul knew it to be an impossible and even absurd procedure, but talks about it in order to show the sheer grace of God's allowing Gentiles into his people. Both views appear to be mistaken. The ancient expert on horticulture and arboriculture, Columella, gives a careful description of just this process in the care of olives (*De Re Rustica* V 9, 16f.), used to re-invigorate an old, exhausted or diseased tree. In the case of certain trees, such a process is still used in modern arboriculture.

The effect in the case of the olive was two-fold: first, the ingrafted shoot was enabled to bear true olives because it was now part of a culti-vated tree; secondly, the vigour of the ingrafted wild shoot had a posi-tive effect on the tree itself. Indeed, the latter was why the grafting was undertaken. It seems to be agreed on all sides that the cultivation of olives was so basic a part of Paul's environment that anyone with eyes to see ought to have known something about it. If so, then Paul would have known not only that such ingrafting was done, but also that it was done in order to re-invigorate the tree.

It therefore appears that in using this analogy Paul is saying to Gentile Christians: 'Do not think that you have replaced the old tree (Israel), and do not get above yourselves. You may have taken the place of some branches, and indeed by God's grace you serve to give renewed vigour to the tree, but you still depend on that tree for your life.' Against the interpretation thus suggested stands the usual way of taking v. 24 and 'contrary to nature', for which see below, where it is argued that it is not the grafting process in itself that is contrary to nature.

to share the richness of the olive tree: RSV here opts for the only one of several variant readings which omits the word 'root' (*tēs rhēzēs*). The omission has the support of the oldest MS, 𝔓 [46], and of important West MSS (including D and G). It certainly makes for a smoother sen-tence. In itself this is suspicious, since scribes were more likely to have made things easier than harder. It is widely thought, therefore, that the

[c] On this, and on the whole question of Paul's use of the olive tree figure, see A. G. Baxter and J. A. Ziesler, 'Paul and Arboriculture: Romans 11.17–24', *JSNT* 24, 1985, pp. 24–32.

best text is one of those that include 'root', probably 'to share the root, the richness of the olive tree', which is supported by 𝔑 and B.[d] Thus, although the ingrafting will re-invigorate the tree, that tree has not lost its basic value, and will in turn enrich the new branches.

18

do not boast over the branches: the Gentile Christians are not to be complacent, nor contemptuous of historical Israel in that they are now within God's people while many of the latter are not. In the first place, they too are vulnerable and can easily be pruned if they prove unfaithful and so unfruitful (vv. 20–22). In the second place, it must be remembered that they replace not the whole tree but only some of the branches; they belong to an ancient tree and depend on it for life just as as natural branches do (v. 18b). Although, as we have seen, Paul and his readers would doubtless know that ingrafting was done to invigorate the tree, this must not give the new branches ideas of their own superiority. The boasting is clearly of one group over another, and not at all boasting of one's merit before God.[e]

it is not you that support the root, but the root that supports you: even though they serve to give new vigour to the tree, their dependence on the root remains. They need the tree as a whole for their existence as fruitful branches.

21

neither will he spare you: remaining within the tree, the people of God, is on the human side strictly a matter of faith. Not only could old branches (the majority of historical Israel) be pruned; so too can the newly ingrafted Gentile branches, if their faith is not maintained.

23

the others, if they do not persist in their unbelief, will be grafted in: at this point, any feasible arboriculture has been left behind, and the naturalness of the figure breaks down. Nevertheless it is vital for Paul to include in the figure the idea of vv. 11–12, that the rejection of Israel is not final, and that the hope remains, against all apparent probability,

d See Metzger, p. 526; Cranfield II, p. 567; Wilckens II, p. 247.

e Cf. Räisänen, *PL*, p. 173: the boasting is a communal and not a soteriological matter.

that historical Israel as a whole will again be within the people of God. The remnant and historical Israel will then be the same.

24

grafted, contrary to nature, into a cultivated olive tree: RSV implies that it is the process of grafting that is contrary to nature. We saw on v. 17 that this was not so, and that Paul and his readers would almost certainly have known that it was not so. The grafting of wild olive shoots into a cultivated but ailing tree was a normal procedure. Then what is 'contrary to nature' (*para phusin*)? Surely it is the belonging: by nature (*kata phusin*) you belonged to the wild olive, but now you are grafted into the cultivated olive to which you did not belong naturally. Moreover there is no point in Paul's saying earlier in the verse that the wild olive is 'by nature' a wild olive: of course it is! Throughout the verse the expressions 'by nature' and 'contrary to nature' attach to the notion of belonging. The whole of v. 24a should, in the light of this, be translated:

> For if you have been cut from the wild olive to which you naturally belong, and have been grafted into the cultivated olive to which you do not naturally belong . . .

In short, once again those who were not God's people have become God's people, cf. 9^{25}.

will these natural branches be grafted back: see above on v. 23. It is remarkable that Paul concludes his use of the figure of the olive tree by reiterating his concern for the salvation of Israel. Indeed, if the view we have taken of the procedure of grafting is correct, from one angle the whole Gentile mission serves to promote the reinvigoration of Israel, with the hope that even the fruitless branches (those lacking faith in Jesus Christ) will be reinstated. Paul is very far from seeing a predominantly Gentile church as the replacement of historical Israel.

II$^{25-36}$ THE COMPLETION OF THE DIVINE STRATEGY

^{25}*Lest you be wise in your own conceits, I want you to understand this mystery, brethren: a hardening has come upon part of Israel, until the full number of the Gentiles come in,* ^{26}*and so all Israel will be saved; as it is written,*

'The Deliverer will come from Zion, he will banish ungodliness
from Jacob';
²⁷'and this will be my covenant with them when I take away their
sins.'

²⁸As regards the gospel they are enemies of God, for your sake; but as regards election they are beloved for the sake of their forefathers. ²⁹For the
gifts and the call of God are irrevocable. ³⁰Just as you were once disobedient
to God but now have received mercy because of their disobedience,³¹ so they
have now been disobedient in order that by the mercy shown to you they also
may receive mercy. ³²For God has consigned all men to disobedience, that he
may have mercy upon all.

³³O the depth of the riches and wisdom and knowledge of God! How un-
searchable are his judgments and how inscrutable his ways!

³⁴'For who has known the mind of the Lord,
or who has been his counsellor?'
³⁵'Or who has given a gift to him that he might be repaid?'
³⁶For from him and through him and to him are all things. To him be glory
for ever. Amen.

There now draws to its close the long section of the letter concerned
with the faithfulness of God, and arising from that with the relation
between the Israel of the ancient promises and the church of Jesus
Christ. We now have an answer to the question 'Who are the people
of God?' It is not a simple answer. Probably the analogy of the olive
tree has given it as clear an expression as we are going to get. In the
present section of the letter the Gentile Christians are still being
addressed, and Paul begins by warning them once more against boasting over the unbelieving Jews, against feeling spiritually superior to
them. It is true that at present most Jews are recalcitrant, but in the
divine strategy this is only the first move; the second move is the
successful mission to the Gentiles, and the third move is the final
salvation of historical Israel as a whole. In the end, all Israel will be
gathered in, their sins forgiven and God's ancient promises fulfilled:
God does not go back on his word. Their present refusal to accept the
Christian message, and with that their disobedience to God and
failure to enjoy the divine mercy, are all temporary. Once again Paul
appears to be reflecting on history, on the way in which the Christian

preaching has succeeded among the Gentiles much more than among the Jews. He is reflecting, however, against a background of confidence in the faithfulness or consistency of God, and therefore of hope that historical Israel will be restored to her appointed place in the people of God.

Finally, the apostle breaks into a paean of praise to God for his inscrutable ways that always tend towards life and mercy. This may indicate that Paul himself cannot see how this final ingathering of the Jews will happen; he therefore simply asserts that all things are in God's hands, and may safely be left there.

~~~

25

wise in your own conceits: as translated, this is unnecessarily obscure. Literally it is 'clever in yourselves', referring to that propensity for feeling above themselves in relation to the Jews to which Paul has already referred in 11$^{18f.}$.

I want you to understand this mystery: in Paul's writings, 'mystery' (*mustērion*) is not esoteric in the sense that it is disclosed only to a select few. Rather is it something that has hitherto been hidden in the divine purposes, but now has become open to human view. In this instance, the content of the mystery is clear enough from the context: it is that the 'hardening' which led the Jews as a whole to reject Jesus Christ is no more than an intermediate stage in the divine plan. It is to be limited not only in extent (cf. the remnant), but also in time, see vv. 25b–26. The salvation of all Israel depends on the ingathering of the Gentiles, which in turn depends on the recalcitrance of the majority of the Jews. The argument is thus partly historical, partly theological, and as the use of the word 'mystery' hints, partly intuitive. Rightly interpreted, the contemporary situation shows the divine strategy effectively at work. The rest of v. 25, and vv. 26–32 as well as vv. 11–16, attempt to spell this out.[f] Elsewhere in Paul's letters 'mystery' has different connotations, but always denotes something hitherto hidden and now disclosed by God. See 16$^{25f.}$; I Cor. 15^{51}; also I Cor. 2$^{1, 7}$; 4^{1}; 13^{2}; 14^{2}; Col. 1$^{26, 27}$; 2^{2}; 4^{3}.

[f] On *mustērion* see further Wilckens II, pp. 253f.; Cranfield II, pp. 573f.; Munck, *Israel*, pp. 131f.

until the full number of the Gentiles come in: see above on II^{11}. Paul is making an important reversal of a Jewish expectation: instead of the hope that at the End the Gentile nations would join Israel in Zion (Jerusalem), Paul suggests that it is when the Gentiles are first gathered in that Israel will join them. This is a theological complement to the historical perception of the success of the Gentile mission in comparison with the mission to Israel. In God's plan, contrary to expectation, the Gentiles must come first, and *then* the Jews.

Then what is 'the full number of the Gentiles' (literally, 'the fullness – *plērōma* – of the Gentiles')? Is it every single non-Jew, or some pre-determined number, or what? In some apocalyptic writings[g] there is a precise number to be saved before the Last Judgment, and all that goes with it, can take place. In those instances, however, the word is *arithmos* and not *plērōma*, and while it is not impossible that the same notion is to be found here, it is also possible that there is nothing so precise. 'The full number of the Gentiles' could be simply the Gentiles as a whole, without any specific number implied; the concentration could be on the completion of a missionary task rather than on questions of whether all, most, or only many individual Gentiles are to 'come in'.[h]

26

and so all Israel will be saved: contrast I Thess. 2$^{14-16}$, where 'God's wrath has come upon them at last'. However, the Thessalonians passage may well refer to a punishment already meted out to Israel within history,[i] and in any case the hope expressed in the present passage must represent Paul's more mature and considered position. Whatever has been said in Ch. 9 or Ch. 11 about an Israel within Israel, and about a remnant, there still emerges this confidence that at the end of the day Israel as a whole will be saved. 'Saved' presumably means what it normally means in the Bible and in Paul (see on I^{16}): the final act in the divine drama when everything is accomplished and God's people are gathered to be with him for ever. Is this to be in heaven or on earth? It is impossible to be sure, and perhaps it hardly matters. Certainly in vv. 26f. Paul uses OT passages (Isa. 59$^{20f.}$; 27^9) that speak of the restoration of Zion (Jerusalem), and another (Jer. 31^{33}) which could be understood to do so, but how strictly we take the reference of such quotations is not straightforwardly decided. It may be that all we can legitimately infer is that

g II (4) Esd. 4^{36}; *II Apoc. Bar.* 23$^{4, 5}$; Rev. 6^{11}; 7^4; 14^1.
h See Munck, *Israel*, pp. 133f. See also Rom. 15^{19}; Col. 1^{25}; II Tim. 4^{17}.
i So Räisänen, *PL*, p. 263.

God's purposes will be consummated, but that how and where must be left vague.

There are, however, two much more pressing questions.

(a) What is meant by 'all Israel'? Is it literally every single Jew, or only the vast majority of Jews without being dogmatic about every last man, woman and child? Is it a pre-determined number within Israel (cf. v. 25 and 'the full number of the Gentiles)? As there is no doubt about the salvation of the remnant, we can hardly be talking here about a minority within Israel. It is also a near-impossibility that 'all Israel' is the newly defined multi-racial Israel, for in vv. 25f. we are clearly concerned with races, with peoples. When Paul says 'all Israel' we therefore take it that he means 'all Jews'. If we try to press the question harder, and discover whether this is all Jews without any exception whatsoever, then we shall receive no answer. All we can say is that the argument requires that historical Israel as a whole will come in.ʲ Paul surely cannot be saying merely that rather more Israelites than at present will come in. *Both* parts of historical Israel, those now in the remnant and those not, will find salvation.

(b) How will they be saved: by finding faith in Jesus Christ or without doing so?

(i) It has been suggested that, as Paul never states that they will become Christians, he allows for the possibility that somehow at the End God will bring together those who have followed two different tracks to being his people: the track taken by the remnant and by the believing Gentiles, the Christian track; and the track of historical Israel, relying on God's grace in his ancient covenant with them.ᵏ This suggestion avoids any theological antisemitism, but is scarcely congruous with Paul's argument, and in particular with his argument towards the end of the olive-tree passage. There, the broken-off branches were grafted back in precisely when they no longer persisted in their lack of belief, i.e. when they too came to faith in Jesus Christ. It is too much to suppose that Paul sees God as having two strategies, one for repentant

j See F. Hahn, 'Zum Verständnis von Römer 11.26a', Ch. 18 of Hooker and Wilson, especially pp. 229, 233f. Wilckens II, pp. 255f., cites *m. Sanh.* 10.1, 'All Israelites have a share in the world to come', followed by a list of exceptions.

k So most notably K. Stendahl, *Paul among Jews and Gentiles*, Fortress Press and SCM Press 1977, p. 4. See the criticism in Sanders, *PLJP*, pp. 194f. and 205 n. 88. The double-track view is also rejected by Hahn, 'Zum Verständnis', and in the very careful treatment by Davies, *JPS*, pp. 140–3, who notes that vv. 11 and 14 become very difficult to interpret on this view.

branches and one for unrepentant branches, cf. also vv. 26f., 31. If that were the case, why should repentance matter?

(ii) All the way from 9⁶, being the people of God has been a matter of grace and not one of being racially in Israel, and it would be very odd if at the End there were a reversal to the latter. In some undefined fashion, therefore, Paul holds the belief that at the End the Jews who do not belong to the remnant will be moved to 'jealousy', and repent.

'*The Deliverer will come from Zion*': the Deliverer could, as in Isa. 59²⁰, be Yahweh himself, but it is much more likely that he is Christ, as in I Thess. 1¹⁰ (cf. also Rom. 7²⁴).

27
'*and this will be my covenant with them*': see Isa. 27⁹, and probably also Jer. 31³³. Israel's repentance and return are presumably the same as their not persisting in unbelief (v. 23).

28
they are enemies of God: who is hostile to whom? Is God their enemy, or are they his? It is impossible to distinguish the two, because they are both rejecting God in Christ, and being rejected by God as a result, cf. 9²², ²⁷, ³⁰⁻³³; 10³, ²¹; 11⁷f., ¹⁵, ¹⁹, ²², ²⁵. In the light of the parallel with 'beloved' (by God) later in the verse, some element of God's opposition to them is difficult to avoid.

for your sake: 'you' here are obviously Gentile Christians. There is nothing really new in this verse, which is a restatement of the point made in 11¹¹f., ²⁵, that the rejection of Christ by the majority of Jews has in the event led to the Gentile mission and its notable success. As in 9¹⁴ff., God's purposes run not only through those who endorse them, but also through those who oppose them.

as regards election they are beloved for the sake of their forefathers: their descent from the patriarchs, Abraham in particular, remains a fact. Despite all that has been said in Ch. 4 about the true children of Abraham being those who have a faith like his, and in Ch. 9 about selection within the elect people, and in this chapter about the remnant as the true Israel, Paul has still not given up his concern for racial Israel (cf. 9¹⁻⁵). Although physical, racial descent from Abraham is not the condition for being God's people, Paul still sees historical Israel as loved by

God and within the divine purpose. It may be illogical that he does, in the light of all that has been said since 9⁷, but in the last resort Paul cannot believe that God washes his hands of the majority of the Jews.

It has sometimes been held that 'for the sake of their forefathers' is an echo of a Jewish doctrine of merits, so that Paul is saying that, although the present generation cannot produce sufficient merit before God, the fathers had enough and to spare, and for their sake God looks with grace and favour upon present-day recalcitrant Israelites.[1] It is, however, very unlikely that in the time of Paul there was any notion of transferred merits at the Judgment, and it is moreover clear from the context (v. 29, cf. Käsemann, p. 315) that Paul is talking quite straightforwardly about the blessings given and promises made to the fathers, cf. 9⁴ᶠ·. Taken together, vv. 28–29 say that God's love, seen in his dealings with the patriarchs and especially with Abraham whom God called, remains constant and is not deflected even by the recalcitrance of many Jews.

30–31

Just as you once were disobedient: the basic argument, still addressed specifically to Gentile Christians, is repeated. The sequence runs:

Gentiles were disobedient (not within God's people);
Jews were obedient (were God's people);
Jews became disobedient (rejected Jesus Christ);
God therefore through the church turned to the Gentiles;
Gentiles believed and received mercy (entered God's people);
Jews will be prompted to return and receive mercy (re-enter God's people).

The second item in the sequence is implicit, but not articulated.

they also may receive mercy: some MSS add 'now' (*nun*), 'may now receive mercy'. A second 'now' in the verse is clumsy, and is not included by some good and early MSS, such as 𝔓 ⁴⁶ and A. Yet it very clumsiness may suggest that it did originally stand in the text and was removed by scribes with an eye for style. MSS that have it include ℵ and B. Against RSV, there is probably more to be said for its inclusion

---

[1] See Dodd, pp. 178f.; Davies, *PRJ*, pp. 272f.; Barrett, p. 225; Ziesler, *Meaning*, p. 150. It is now clear that this whole question must be approached with extreme caution, cf. Sanders, *PPJ*, pp. 183–98.

than for its omission.^{m} It is hardly an issue of major importance.

32

God has consigned all men to disobedience, that he may have mercy upon all:
for the first half of this statement, see 1^{18}–3^{20}, and for the second half see
3^{21}–5^{11}. If the sequence set out in the comment on vv. 30–31 is correct,
then Paul believes that all people, Jews and Gentiles, go through or start
from a phase of disobedience, but only in order that God's mercy may
come upon them all in the end. This leaves an obvious loose end,
namely those Jews who did respond to the preaching of Jesus as Christ.
When were they disobedient? The only answer can be that although at
times in this whole argument Paul can talk about individuals (perhaps,
for example, when dealing with branches that have been broken off in
11^{19ff}.), he is usually talking about peoples and groups. Common sense
tells us that not all Jews were disobedient; nevertheless historical Israel
as a whole was disobedient to the Christian message, and therefore as a
whole has declined to be within the people of God as it is now defined.

It is important to note that here obedience and disobedience are not
matters of ethics, but concern being or not being God's people. Least of
all is Paul talking about individual morality. This is one reason why it is
inappropriate to ask if Paul is putting forward the theory that in the end
all men and women, all individuals, will be saved. He is neither affirm-
ing that nor denying it. He is talking about the responses of *peoples*,
Jews and Gentiles respectively. Nevertheless it is important to reiterate
that at the end of this long discussion from 9^1, Paul sees the divine
purpose as embracing not just a few Jews here and there, but the people
of historical Israel as a whole.

The argument is now complete, and the case has been made. God is
faithful, and the only proper response is that of praise to him, vv. 33–36.

33

O the depth . . .: this cry of wonder begins a catena of OT quotations,
perhaps together with allusions to pagan insights, which should be taken
as the outburst of rhetoric that it is, and not as further argument. God's
purposes and ways are far beyond any human ability to fathom, but
they are always beneficent and he is always God and Lord. It is possible
that this outburst betrays Paul's consciousness that he has not really
found a complete solution to the problem of Israel in history, and here
confesses that what he has said can be no more than a provisional at-

---

m So Metzger, p. 527; see also Cranfield II, pp. 585f. Wilckens II, pp. 261f,
tends to favour omission.

tempt.[n] Yet there is a good deal in Jewish literature that breathes the same air as these verses, and it is quite natural that in the end Paul should fall back in awe before the ineffability of God.[o]

34

'*For who has known the mind of the Lord*': Isa. 40^{13} LXX. See also I Cor. 2^{16}, and there may be an echo of Job. 15^8.

35

'*who has given a gift to him*': this cannot be identified as a direct quotation, but recalls Job 41^{11}, and also perhaps Job 35^7. It can hardly be accidental that the last few chapters of Job are quoted from in these verses, for they constitute probably the most sustained praise of the · greatness of God to be found in the OT.

36

from him and through him and to him are all things: cf. I Cor. 8^6. Although there are Hellenistic and especially Stoic parallels to this (see Cranfield II, p. 591), it is often and rightly pointed out (e.g. by Michel, p. 285) that Paul is not discussing the nature of things in an analytical fashion, but is rather talking about the way in which God acts in history and has now acted decisively in Jesus Christ.

12^{1-21} HOW THE PEOPLE OF GOD LIVE

12 ¹*I appeal to you therefore, brethren, by the mercies of God, to present your bodies as a living sacrifice, holy and acceptable to God, which is your spiritual worship.* ²*Do not be conformed to this world but be transformed by the renewal of your mind, that you may prove what is the will of God, what is good and acceptable and perfect.*

³*For by the grace given to me I bid every one among you not to think of himself more highly than he ought to think, but to think with sober judgment, each according to the measure of faith which God has assigned him.* ⁴*For as in one body we have many members, and all the members do not have*

n See Richardson, *Israel*, pp. 126f.
o Cf. the treatment of this theme in Wilckens II, pp. 270f.

*the same function, ⁵so we, though many, are one body in Christ, and indivi-
dually members one of another. ⁶Having gifts that differ according to the
grace given to us, let us use them: if prophecy, in proportion to our faith;
⁷if service, in our serving; he who teaches, in his teaching; ⁸he who exhorts,
in his exhortation; he who contributes, in liberality; he who gives aid, with
zeal; he who does acts of mercy, with cheerfulness.*

*⁹Let love be genuine; hate what is evil, hold fast to what is good; ¹⁰love
one another with brotherly affection; outdo one another in showing honour.
¹¹Never flag in zeal, be aglow with the Spirit, serve the Lord. ¹²Rejoice in
your hope, be patient in tribulation, be constant in prayer. ¹³Contribute to
the needs of the saints, practise hospitality.*

*¹⁴Bless those who persecute you; bless and do not curse them. ¹⁵Rejoice
with those who rejoice, weep with those who weep. ¹⁶Live in harmony with
one another; do not be haughty, but associate with the lowly; never be con-
ceited. ¹⁷Repay no one evil for evil, but take thought for what is noble in the
sight of all. ¹⁸If possible, so far as it depends upon you, live peaceably with
all. ¹⁹Beloved, never avenge yourselves, but leave it to the wrath of God; ·
for it is written, 'Vengeance is mine, I will repay, says the Lord.' ²⁰No, if
your enemy is hungry, feed him; if he is thirsty, give him drink; for by so
doing you will heap burning coals upon his head.' ²¹Do not be overcome by
evil, but overcome evil with good.*

The theological and historical arguments are now essentially over,
and Paul turns to what it means in everyday terms to live within
God's multi-racial Christian people. It is not that he turns to ethics for
the first time, for that has already been his concern at important points
in the letter (see, for example, Chs. 6 and 8). It is only now, however,
that he begins to treat questions about how one lives, in a concrete
and detailed fashion. It is also now that the letter becomes much more
diffuse, and the tight structure that is a marked feature of so much of
the argument of Romans becomes much less evident. As elsewhere in
the letter, in this and subsequent chapters the concern is less indivi-
dualistic than corporate: how should the community live? In vv. 1–2
we have a summary of the nature of the new Christian existence: it is
living as a perpetual sacrifice of oneself to God, being inwardly
changed so as to belong to the new reality, and so as to exist solely for
God and his will. In vv. 3–13 this new life is treated in terms of the

church, the new community, within which people with differing gifts nonetheless live together as members of one body. It is note-worthy that all the gifts listed and discussed are community-orientated Those gifts that could lead to rivalry are not mentioned. There is to be no sense of superiority or inferiority, for each serves in his or her own way, and above all each is to love the other. At v. 9 Paul turns from the differing gifts to what is required of all Christians, and here love heads the list.

It is likely that much of this material had already become tradi-tional, but Paul bends it to his own purposes in his concern both for the theological centre of Christian behaviour (in the service of God, empowered by the Spirit), and for the specific needs of the church, such as offering hospitality and helping the poor. In v. 14 he moves beyond the Christian community to life in the larger world, though it is possible that in v. 16 he returns to intra-mural Christian relation-ships. He counsels the Roman Christians to foster a forgiving spirit towards those who oppress and oppose them, and a sensitive harmony together with absence of pretentiousness. The return to concern about attitudes towards oppressors suggests that this may have been a serious problem for the church. The advice given is uncompromising: they are to go on loving, and must never allow themselves to be pro-voked into retaliation. They must counter the evil inherent in oppres- . sion, not add to it. Judgment is God's business, and only in his hands may it safely be left.

The chapter has a somewhat miscellaneous appearance, but it is clear that at its centre is love, and much of it is a working out in particular cases what the 'good' of v. 2 means.

తింది

1
I appeal to you therefore, by the mercies of God: to what does 'therefore' *(oun)* refer, or in other words on what is the appeal based? It may be that the reference is back to the statement about the divine mercy in 11^{30-32}, and that Paul now moves to the consequences of that mercy in daily life. Yet it is to be noted that with this verse we move into a new section of the letter as it is usually analysed, from the body-middle to the paraenesis (see Introduction, 6). We should therefore expect that

what now follows is consequent not just on a few nearly contiguous verses, but on the drift and concerns of the letter as a whole. 'The mercies of God' are thus all that has been said up to this point, while 'therefore' means 'in the light of the whole preceding argument'. It is on the basis of God's goodness and grace that Paul makes his appeal for good living, and only on that basis (cf. $6^{12ff.}$).

to present your bodies: it has been argued that 'bodies' (*sōmata*) here are our physical selves only, and that the offering of the mind and the inward self follows in v. 2.[p] It is more commonly supposed that 'bodies' here are persons, or selves, or perhaps more precisely persons in that network of relationships to other persons and institutions that characterizes ordinary life.[q] In view of 'spiritual worship' later in the verse which, whatever it means precisely, is certainly inward rather than purely physical and external, it is preferable to take 'bodies' here in a wider than physical sense. 'Your selves, in their concrete embodiment in relation to the world' is probably as close as we can get to a satisfactory rendering.[r] How the selves or persons offer themselves is explained in v. 2, which is thus not the other half of the self-offering (inward to match outward), but its amplification.

a living sacrifice: there is a good deal of cultic, or sacrificial language in this verse. 'Present', 'living', 'holy', and also 'acceptable' are all from that realm.[s] The obvious meaning of 'a living sacrifice' is one that does not die in the process. Its sphere of offering is not a temple, but everyday affairs. This is the sacrifice to be brought by Christians, replacing the offerings they were accustomed to bring to their pagan temples, and in the case of Jewish Christians, fulfilling the sacrifices offered in the Jerusalem Temple. There may well be an allusion back to Rom. 6 and to dying with Christ: there too in the obvious sense the believer does not die, or at least not yet, but is nonetheless truly a sacrifice and so the property of God, holy and acceptable to him.

p See Gundry, *SOMA*, pp. 34–6, though he does see *sōma* as 'the place and means of concrete activity in the world'.

q See Whiteley, *Theology*, pp. 37f.; E. Best, *One Body in Christ*, SPCK 1955, pp. 215–21; E. Käsemann, *New Testament Questions of Today*, SCM Press 1969, Ch. 9 and especially p. 191. There is a valuable summary of the history of research in Jewett, *Terms*, pp. 201–50.

r See Käsemann, p. 327; Wilckens III, pp. 3, 6.

s For the detailed evidence see Newton, *Purity*, pp. 70f.

your spiritual worship: the Greek *logikēn latreian* is elusive mainly because of the excessive richness of possible backgrounds, especially to *logikēn/* 'spiritual'. No one is sure how the expression ought to be understood, though there is little doubt that 'worship' rather than 'service' is the appropriate word with which to translate *latreian*.

(*a*) The most immediate Hellenistic background to *logikēn* is in Stoicism, where it refers to the all-pervasive Reason that relates human beings to the divine. As in the Hellenistic enlightenment, it can thus be used to express a contrast with popular and excessively outward cultic worship.[t] What Paul says would thus be understood by people raised in Hellenism.

(*b*) Although the adjective *logikos* does not occur in LXX, the OT not infrequently makes it plain that the sacrifice acceptable to God is not a purely outward one, but one which is both outward and inward, or even one where the inward is all that there is, see for example Isa. 1$^{11-20}$; Hos. 6^6; Amos. 5$^{21-24}$; Ps. 51^{17}; 69$^{30f.}$; Ecclus. 35$^{1f.}$. Often a proper manner of life within human relationships is the offering preferred to the strictly cultic, and this is very much what we find here too.

(*c*) If we take it that the worship of the people of God as now defined in terms of Christ and his Spirit, and as non-racial, stands as a replacement or fulfilment of the Temple-cult, then it is plausible to see here a reference to such 'spiritual worship'.[u] It is true that Paul uses not 'spiritual' (*pneumatikēn*) but 'reasonable' (*logikēn*), yet this could be because of its existing and on the whole apt connotations for those reared in Hellenism.

Certainly the sort of worship that is advocated is one which is not merely outwardly cultic, but embraces the whole of life. This does not exclude cultic occasions and observances, but requires that they be continuous with the sacrificial offering of life. This offering is of the whole person in all human relationships and connections, within the New Age, the Age of the Spirit: we find references to this New Age in 12^2 and in 13$^{11-14}$, thus giving these two chapters an eschatological frame. In short, although it is impossible to pinpoint the sense of *logikēn*,

[t] See Käsemann, *NT Questions*, p. 190. It is not unknown in Philo, *Spec. Leg.* I, 277, cf. 272, where it refers to the disposition of the 'rational spirit' of the person making a sacrifice. See Wilckens III, pp. 5f., and Cranfield II, p. 602, for the use in Hellenistic Judaism apart from Philo.

[u] See Newton, *Purity*, pp. 70–2; also earlier B. Gärtner, *The Temple and the Community in Qumran and the New Testament*, SNTSMS 1, CUP 1965, pp. 73, 75, 85.

suggestion (c) is attractive, because of its excellent coherence with those NT passages which speak of Christians as a new Temple, e.g. Phil. 2$^{17f.}$; Rom. 15^{16}; cf. I Peter 2^5; Eph. 2$^{20-22}$.

2

Do not be conformed to this world but be transformed: 'world' is *aiōn*, 'age', and so we are dealing with the shift of the Ages. Christians are seen as belonging to Christ in the dawning of the New Age, even if in practical terms they must go on living in 'this present evil age'. To the latter they do not belong, and must not live as if they did, cf. Rom. 8; II Cor. 5^{17}.

In English 'conformed' and 'transformed' are cognate; in Greek they are not, the first employing the root *schēma* and the second the root *morphē*. It has been suggested, for example by Sanday and Headlam (p. 353), that in the case of 'conformed' we should think of the outward form in contrast with the inward reality, but that in the case of 'transformed' we should think of the outward form as expressive of the inward reality. While such a distinction between the two roots can exist in Greek, it is often lacking, as it is in Phil. 3^{21}, where the *schēma* root occurs in just the sense alleged to be properly that of *morphē*. In any case, it is hardly to be supposed that Paul is rejecting only outward conformity to this present Age.^{v} We may therefore take it that the two roots are used simply to provide vocabulary variation, and that in talking of being conformed or transformed Paul is talking about the totality of belonging, inward and outward, to one Age or the other.

by the renewal of your mind: the essential change in belonging is inward and invisible. Yet the following verses and chapters show that it does not remain only inward, but is worked out in ordinary living.

For Paul the mind (*nous*) is not in itself perfectly good nor the source of good, but needs change and renewal, cf. 7$^{23, 25}$. According to the line of interpretation adopted for Ch. 7, the mind that is set against the *sarx*/flesh is still an aspect of the man or woman without Christ and his Spirit.^{w}

you may prove what is the will of God: 'prove' is used here in the sense of 'discover in order to carry out'. Though the verb *dokimazō* can mean

---

v For a full discussion of the question see Cranfield II, pp. 605–8.

w Determining what Paul – or anyone else – means by 'mind' is extraordinarily difficult. See Jewett, *Terms*, pp. 358–90, who suggests that in 12^2 *nous* is 'a constellation of thoughts and assumptions', p. 385.

'approve' as well as 'prove' or 'test', in the present context it is more likely to mean learning to discern the will of God, though indeed it must then be put into practice.

what is good and acceptable and perfect: the RSV alternative translation, which attaches these adjectives to 'the will of God', is not to be preferred. It is no doubt 'the good and acceptable and perfect will of God' that the Christian learns and obeys, but the Greek syntax is better understood as conveying that the believer comes to discern what the will of God is, namely that it is good and acceptable and perfect.

3
by the grace given to me: is the apostle appealing to the Romans simply as one Christian who has received grace speaking to others (cf. I Cor. 1⁴), or is he appealing rather to the special favour granted to him when called to be an apostle (cf. 1⁵; 15¹⁵ᶠ·)? As he seems to be making a claim to authority here, it is more likely that the second is the correct interpretation. Nevertheless it is true that the grace which made him an apostle was but a special case of the general grace by which all men and women can become Christians. He does not seem to maintain a sharp distinction between the two, cf. 12⁶.

not to think of himself more highly than he ought to think: warnings against boasting over other people are not infrequent in this letter. See 11¹⁸, ²⁰, ²⁵, as well as 11¹³ᶠ·, and earlier 2¹⁷ᶠᶠ·; 3²⁷; 4².

to think with sober judgment: 'sober judgment' is *sōphronein*, which is one of the cardinal virtues in contemporary ethics as also in Hellenistic Judaism. ˣ It stands for balance, clarity of vision, and good sense. The Romans are thus urged to see things, and especially to see themselves, as they really are, not blinded by undue concern for themselves nor by an inflated opinion of themselves. Excessive self-concern ruins good sense and good judgment.

the measure of faith: this unusual expression recurs in slightly different form in v. 6. Here it is *metron pisteōs*, there it is *tēn analogian tēs pisteōs*, but what does it mean?
  (*a*) Here it could mean the fruits of faith, such as charismatic powers, so that Paul is advising his readers to think of themselves in relation to

ˣ See Wilckens III, p. 11; Käsemann, p. 332.

their actual gifts, and not to have an unrealistic view of them. This is improbable, as it would open the door to the possibility that those with more impressive gifts could value themselves more highly than others, which is precisely what Paul seems to be trying to guard against, cf. vv. 4f.

(b) The measure of faith could be the capacity for faith, of which some have more than others. There is a case to be made for this in the light of 14^1-15^{13} with its concern for both the strong and the weak in faith.ʸ This could be an anticipation of that discussion and the way in which Paul pursues it. The faith of some Roman Christians allows them to eat meat without qualms, while the faith of others does not. Neither side must condemn or despise the other. This suggestion has the merit of fitting well with the verse's thrust against boasting, and it must be a possible option. However, it has two drawbacks. The first is that we are required to interpret the present verse in the light of something that will not be articulated for quite some time, and that is a questionable procedure in explicating a letter presumably designed to be read aloud and therefore resistant to cross-references. The second is that it implies the sort of ranking of faith which sits oddly in this context.

(c) If 'faith' is *the* Faith, the objective reality which we call Christianity, then Paul is saying that they must measure themselves against a rule to which they are subject. This is not, however, the most usual meaning of faith in Paul's letters, and moreover does not fit the statement that 'God has apportioned to each a measure of faith'.

(d) Somewhat similarly, if we take a different and more usual meaning of faith, namely the human response to Christ, Paul could be saying that the guiding-line is provided by that faith. All are recipients, so none has any room for conceit (so Cranfield II, p. 615).

None of these interpretations leaps to the eye as obvious. There is an attractiveness to (b), but on the whole (d) raises the fewest problems.

4

as in one body: the modern reader, though naturally not the original Roman reader, is inevitably reminded of I Cor. $12^{12ff.}$. There are obvious similarities: in both passages, membership of the one body involves mutual dependence on people's differing contributions. Nevertheless there are also differences, most notably that it is not said in this passage that the body is the body *of* Christ, but rather that believers are one body *in* Christ (v. 5).

ʸ See Minear, *Obedience*, p. 84.

The figure of the body is a natural one to use, and it may require no special explanation. Nonetheless scholars have detected in it, especially here and in I Cor. $12^{12ff.}$, the influence variously of Stoicism, eucharistic practice, Rabbinic speculations, and Gnosticism. These proposals can be given no more than summary treatment here.[z]

(*a*) In Stoicism the commonwealth of the human race was seen as like a body; perhaps Paul's innovation was then to see the church as a body *in* or *of* a named individual, Christ.

(*b*) In eucharistic language (see I Cor. $10^{16f.}$) sharing in Christ's body at the table of the Lord leads into *being* his body. This may have created the idea, and at the least must have reinforced it. The latter is more probable: the fact that in I Cor. 10 Paul can make the logical leap from 'sharing in' to 'being' the body, without any explanation, does tend to suggest that the idea was already familiar to his readers. After all, there is never any suggestion that sharing in the blood leads to being the blood.

(*c*) There was talk among some Rabbis about the gigantic body of Adam as already containing all the souls that would one day exist on earth. Perhaps the body of the new Adam also contained all those who believed in him. Even if we discount the knotty problem of whether the Rabbinic idea was early enough to have influenced Paul, there is still the problem that the cases are not really parallel, for the souls were in Adam only before they were born, only as potentialities.

(*d*) In later thought of a Gnostic type, the Redeemer figure was thought of as gathering all the redeemed into himself to complete himself, thus restoring the primal unity. Once again, however, there are serious problems. The problem of dating in this case is acute: such a Gnostic idea is almost certainly to be placed at a time much later than that of Paul. Further, for Paul those who are in Christ's body by no means lose their individual identity, as those in the Gnostic Redeemer seem to do.

In short, there is no shortage of rough parallels, but there is none which is close and convincing enough to be taken as the explanation of Paul's language. All we can say with confidence is that for him the church is a body, with all the variety and interdependence but also all the unity that a body has. That body is within the sphere of power and lordship of Christ: it is his. Indeed, if we exclude from consideration passages outside Romans, what is said here is relatively straightforward:

z For detailed accounts, see Jewett, *Terms*, pp. 227–50; Best, *One Body in Christ*, pp. 83–95; Davies, *PRJ*, pp. 55ff.

the body that believers form is *in* Christ, i.e. it exists under him (cf. for 'in Christ' above at 6^{11}).

At all events, the point of v. 3 is reinforced. Christians are to think of themselves as neither more nor less important than others. Christ is the Lord, and all his servants/members are equally vital to the healthy functioning of the Christian body.

6

Having gifts: in the Greek there is no indicative verb, and so RSV has added *let us use them* in order to make a proper sentence. 'Gifts' (*charismata*) are strictly 'grace-gifts', not natural endowments. All Christian life is the result of the divine grace and thus charismatic, but it must be seen within the mutuality and discipline of the whole body, the church.

prophecy: this is usually taken to be inspired but intelligible speech, unlike glossolalia (speaking with tongues), which is inspired but not intelligible to all. These matters are given extended treatment by Paul in I Cor. 12–14.[a] It is noteworthy that prophecy is the only gift that is included in every list of gifts. It is spontaneous, directed to a particular situation, and – to judge from I Corinthians especially – is of particular value because it builds up the community of faith. See I Cor. 12^{10}; 13^2; $14^{3, 6, 22, 26, 30, 31}$; I Thess. 5^{20}. It is not particularly to do with foretelling the future, though an element of that may sometimes be included, cf. Acts 11^{28}. It does not by-pass the prophetic speaker's own consciousness, for the understanding of both speaker and hearer is engaged.

in proportion to our faith: cf. the discussion on v. 3 above. It was noted that this expression is similar, but not identical to the expression used there. Are we to understand them as synonymous?

(*a*) If they are synonymous, and if we were right in tentatively adopting explanation (*d*), then in both passages the meaning is that what is thought or said must be in accordance with the guiding-line of faith, i.e. response to Jesus Christ. Here, prophecy is then not a matter of 'anything goes', as long as the speaker claims inspiration. Rather, there must always be the relationship to Christ as the controlling factor in what is said. Contrast I Cor. 12^3,

[a] On prophecy see especially D. Hill, *New Testament Prophecy*, Marshall Pickering 1979, pp. 8f., 119, 127 and *passim*; Cranfield II, pp. 619–21; Dunn, *Jesus and the Spirit*, pp. 227–33.

no one speaking by the Spirit of God ever says, 'Jesus be cursed'.

(b) If we do not take it for granted that the two expressions are synonymous, then the present passage could be saying that prophecy must always be in relation to 'the faith', i.e. firmly within in the Christian tradition. The difference between this and (a) is slight.

(c) Again if we reject the synonymity of the two expressions, this could be saying that the prophet must never go beyond the particular faith he or she has for the task of prophecy. That is to say, he or she must not go beyond the confidence that it is God who is really speaking through the prophecy. When that confidence is missing or lapses, the speaker should refrain or cease from speaking. Within the context, this seems the most plausible of the available interpretations. [b]

7

service: the Greek *diakonia* can be used almost as widely as its English equivalent for service of many sorts, cf. I Cor. 12^5, but especially for apostolic ministry, Rom. 11^{13}; II Cor. 4^1; 5^{18}; 6^3; Acts $1^{7, 25}$; 20^{24}; 21^{19}. It can also be used for specific service to the needy, for poor relief, as in Rom. 15^{31}; I Cor. 16^{15}; II Cor. 8^4; $9^{1, 12, 13}$; 11^8; Acts 6^1; 11^{29}; 12^{25}. The more general meaning is unlikely here. After all, in their various ways prophets, teachers and exhorters also serve. Presumably, therefore, it is relief of people in material need.

in our serving: as in v. 6, something like 'let us use it' the 'gift' is implied. That is to say that in vv. 6–8, the point is 'If that is your gift, use it; if that is the task God has given you, do it.'

teaching: how does this differ from prophecy? Probably in that the teacher does not claim special divine inspiration but transmits and expounds the tradition to be found in the OT, in whatever was known about the life and teaching of Jesus, and in Christian catechetical materials, cf. Rom 6^{17}; 16^{17}; I Cor. 4^{17}; Acts 5^{28}. [c]

b As proposed by Dunn, *Jesus and the Spirit*, pp. 211f. He thinks that in v. 3 as well Paul is talking about confidence in charismatic roles, so that both expressions carry the same meaning.

c See Dunn, *Jesus and the Spirit*, pp. 236–8, who points out that nevertheless teaching is seen as a charismatic activity.

8

exhortation: as this could be any sort of encouragement, it is hard to distinguish it from prophecy, with which it must have overlapped. It may have included some connotation of 'return to order'[d] based both on the gospel and on the actual needs of the hearers.

he who contributes, in liberality: it is unlikely that this is a repetition of 'serving' in v. 7, for in such a tightly packed passage unnecessary verbosity would be incongruous. It probably refers to the source of the funds for poor relief rather than their distribution (cf. among others Cranfield II, p. 624).

'In liberality' (*en haplotēti*) may not be the best rendering. The most natural meaning is 'simply, sincerely, whole-heartedly', though 'without ulterior motive' is also possible. If Paul is talking about the distribution of funds rather than their source, then 'with integrity' is appropriate. If he is talking about their source, then 'without ulterior motive' may be best.

he who gives aid, with zeal: at first sight 'he who gives aid' is a strange rendering, for *proïstamenos* most naturally means 'the one who presides', as in I Thess. 5^{12}; I Tim. 5^{17}. If we accept such a meaning here, then Paul is talking about the leader of a local church, perhaps a house-church. It can even be held[e] that it refers to the comparatively wealthy and socially prominent person who is in a position to offer protection to those members of the church who are otherwise weak and vulnerable. Nevertheless, the context is that of aid to the needy, and therefore the most likely reference is to the person who is in charge of the administration of that aid.[f] If so, it is hardly surprising that this person is to act with diligence or zeal.

he who does acts of mercy: this is one more reflection of the social-service aspect of the primitive church's life. It is likely that now things like care of the sick, the aged, and those in prison, are at stake as well as financial assistance.

with cheerfulness: even perhaps 'without grumbling', as is suggested by Wilckens (III, p. 16).

It is to be noted that of the seven gifts to be exercised within the church (vv. 6–8), five are of a practical, caring character. Thus both the

d So Hill, *NT Prophecy*, p. 128, quoting H. Schlier.
e Michel, p. 300; Cranfield II, pp. 626f.
f Thus Lagrange, p. 300; Leenhardt, p. 312; cf. again Cranfield II, p. 626.

service of v. 7 and the love which is about to be mentioned in v. 9, are to be expressed in concrete actions of concern.

9

Let love be genuine: hitherto in Romans, love (*agapē*) has been God's love ($5^{5, 8}$; $8^{35, 39}$). As elsewhere in Paul's letters, human love for others is the appropriate response to that divine love, cf. Rom. 13^{8-10}; 15^{30}; I Cor. 13; Gal. 5^{22}. Here, the exhortation to love is the centre point of the whole passage; its centrality has been implicit since v. 1, and what now follows can naturally be seen as love's outworking both within the Christian community (vv. 9–13) and beyond its boundaries (vv. 14–21). This love is to be no pretence, but the real thing.

hate what is evil, hold fast to what is good: if this verse is a kind of heading, with what follows as an expansion of it, then it is plausible to see it as a reflection of the 'two ways' theme common in the ancient world and in early Christianity. A choice has to be made, and the Christian should know how to make it.

With these two commands we begin a series that runs intermittently up to v. 19, constructed in a somewhat unusual way: participles are used as imperatives. That is to say, in this verse we have literally 'hating what is evil; holding fast to what is good', and the majority of the commands in the rest of the chapter are expressed by the same participial means. More regular ways of conveying commands are, however, found in vv. 14, 15, 16, and 19, but they are outnumbered by the participles. This is now widely held to be evidence of an underlying Semitic tradition, for in post-biblical Hebrew, ethical codes could be expressed in this way. This was not true of fundamental codes like the Decalogue, nor of individual *ad hoc* commands, but it was sometimes true of codes that gave systematic and standardized commands for situations that needed something more detailed and practical than the Ten Commandments, for instance.[g] If this is correct, then Paul is using material much

---

g This use of the participial imperative was established by D. Daube in an Appended Note to E. G. Selwyn's *I Peter*, pp. 467–88, and then in *The New Testament and Rabbinic Judaism*, University of London, Athlone Press 1956, pp. 90–7, 102f. The difficulty that vv. 14ff. appear to contain echoes of the commands of Jesus, which are hardly appropriate to a generalized and subordinate code, has been met by C. H. Talbert, 'Tradition and Redaction in Romans XII.9–21', *NTS* 16, 1969–70, pp. 83–94. He argues that an originally Semitic code was modified in Hellenistic Christianity before it reached Paul.

of which originated in Judaism, but which had become traditional in the church. This last supposition is strengthened by the fact that in vv. 14ff. some of the material is similar to some that we know as part of the Sermon on the Mount in Matthew, but is used by Paul without any acknowledgment. This is not surprising if his immediate source is church tradition.

10

brotherly affection: the members of the Christian community are to show one another the same deep affection (*philadelphia*) that is found in a family.

outdo one another in showing honour: cf. Phil. 2^3; I Cor. 12$^{22-26}$. This appears to mean that one should honour others above oneself, not just as much as oneself. Behind it may be the idea that it is particularly the weaker members of the church who should be treated with special respect.[h]

11

serve the lord: some Western MSS, including D and G, have instead 'serve the time'. This represents *kairō(i)*, 'time', as against *kurio(i)*, 'Lord', and is presumably reflected in Charles Wesley's line 'to serve the present age, my calling to fulfil'. Though serving the time (or age) need not be taken as opportunism, and could mean something like serving in love during the time of eschatological crisis, nevertheless 'Lord' undoubtedly gives a smoother reading. In itself this may make us suspect that later scribes have changed an original 'time' to the easier 'Lord', but . the position is complicated by the fact that the variation could have arisen because, when abbreviated as they sometimes were, the two words are easily mistaken for one another. Many critics therefore opt for 'Lord', which makes the smoother sense.

12

be patient in tribulation: the word for 'tribulation', *thlipsis*, very commonly refers to the opposition and persecution faced by Christians in an unbelieving and hostile world. See Rom. 5^3; 8^{35}; II Cor. 1^{4,8}; 6^4; Phil. 4^{14}; I Thess. 3^{3,7}; cf. Matt. 13^{21}; 24^9; John 16^{33} etc. While such a reference is not invariable, it fits well enough here. Christians are to

---

h On this, as on the whole passage, see V. P. Furnish, *The Love Command in the New Testament*, Abingdon Press and SCM Press 1973, pp. 102–8.

endure ('be patient' is too weak a translation) because of their hope, their confident assurance, in God's ultimate providence and victory. This is cause for joy, cf. Phil. 3^1; 4^4; I Thess. 5$^{16f.}$.

13

the needs of the saints: the saints are fellow Christians, cf. 1^7. The immediate reference is thus to the church's meeting the needs of the poor among its own members. There may, however, be a particular reference to the Christians in Jerusalem, 'the poor among the saints' of 15^{26} or 'the saints' of 15^{25}. If so, then we have here an allusion to the collection for the Jerusalem church, but the probability is not great.

hospitality: to modern readers this may sound banal. In the early church, however, hospitality was vitally important. Unless someone offered a room, the church could not meet at all; it was long before there were church buildings as such, and longer still before they were common. Moreover, a wandering apostle like Paul himself was constantly in need of board and lodging. In short, the church could not function without hospitality, and this is why it appears so often in lists of virtues, e.g. Heb. 13^2; I Tim. 3^2; Tit. 1^8; I Peter 4^9; I Clem. 1^2.

14

Bless those who persecute you: 'practise hospitality' is literally 'pursue hospitality' (using the verb *diōkō*). The same verb also means 'persecute', as it does here, so that in successive verses we have it used in first its good and then its bad sense. It may be that this indicates that the material has been put together not only thematically, but also sometimes by association of key words. It may also be, however, that this is a deliberate play on words: 'hospitality is the pursuing you practise, unlike the pursuing you suffer.' Together with v. 12, this is one of the very few indications that at this time the Roman church was apt to face persecution. Paul may be merely raising the possibility.

Here, at the beginning of a sub-section which looks beyond the church to life in the wider world, we meet the first of a series of what appear to be echoes of Matt. 5–7. For this verse compare Matt. 5$^{43-44}$, and cf. Luke 6$^{27-28}$. Paul gives no hint that he is quoting words of Jesus. If he knew that this was what he was doing, it is strange that he does not say so, as that would certainly have added force to his exhortation. It is therefore possible that he is quoting a piece of common Christian ethical tradition without knowing that it could be attributed to Christ himself.

15

Rejoice with those who rejoice, weep with those who weep: cf. I Cor. 12^{26};
Ecclus. 7^{34}. Has Paul now returned briefly to behaviour within the
church? Cranfield (II, p. 642) suggests that this is about an understanding sharing in all the joys and sorrows of ordinary men and women,
whether Christian or not, without at the same time accepting their
standards of what is good and what is bad.

16

Live in harmony with one another: while this is a defensible rendering of
the Greek, equally possible is 'have a common mind' or even 'have a
common aim' (cf. 15^5; II Cor. 13^{11}; Phil. 2^2; 4^2). As in 15^5, Paul is
clearly here talking about relationships within the church, yet in the
context, which is concerned with the relation of the church to the wider
human community, it is possible that Cranfield (II, p. 643) is right to
suggest that Paul sees Christian harmony as part of the church's offering
of itself to the world.

do not be haughty: literally, 'do not set your minds on high things'. The
RSV translation is probably apt. An alternative suggestion, that it means
'do not set your minds on exalted things, such as the more spectacular
charismata' is less likely in this context, concerned as it is with the
church in the world. It would have fitted better in vv. 10–13.

associate with the lowly: cf. Prov. 3^7 LXX. As the RSV alternative
rendering has it, this could be 'give yourselves to humble tasks (or
ways)'. However, in both LXX and NT the adjective in question,
tapeinos, is nearly always used of people, so it is probably used the same
way here. Christians are not to be over-fond of seeking out the great
and influential of this world.

17

Repay no one evil for evil: there is to be no thought of revenge for in-
juries or injustices. Once again Matt. 5 (here vv. 38–42, cf. Luke 6^{29})
comes to mind, but see also Jer. 18^{20}; Prov. 17^{13}; I Thess. 5^{15}; I Peter 3^9.
We are now certainly back with the relation of the church to the
world.

take thought for what is noble: cf. Prov. 3^4 LXX, and see also below on
v. 20. The book of Proverbs is a strong influence on this teaching against
revenge. Perhaps 'noble' is a slightly unhappy translation, as it could

imply a striving for privilege. The Greek is *kala*, 'good things', and there can be no doubt that for Paul the will of God defines what is good, especially that will as it is disclosed in Jesus Christ (cf. v. 2).

18

so far as it depends upon you, live peaceably: in effect, though it takes two to make peace, ensure that on your side there is no hostility towards anyone, and that includes those against whom you may be tempted to seek vengeance. Cf. Mark 9^{50}; Matt. 5^9.

19

never avenge yourselves: cf. Matt. 5^{44}.

but leave it to the wrath of God: 'of God' does not appear in the Greek but is inserted by RSV to indicate that the wrath is the final accounting by God at the Judgment, as often (cf. Rom. $2^{5,\,8}$; 5^9; I Thess. 1^{10}; for wrath/*orgē* see on 1^{18}). It may seem that Paul is telling his readers not to take vengeance into their own hands, but to leave it to God who can do it much more effectively than they can. Such a sentiment is not unknown among people who suffer oppression, or even individual hostility, and we cannot automatically rule it out here. Nevertheless it is at least equally possible that Paul is saying that judgment is God's business, not theirs, and they must not presume to anticipate his action, whatever it may be, on the Day of Judgment. The same idea is found at Qumran, IQS $10^{17f.}$; CD 9^{2-5}; cf. *TGad* 6^7. In other words it is a matter of not infringing upon the divine prerogative, rather than of ensuring harsher and more effective judgment.

'Vengeance is mine, I will repay, says the Lord': this quotation from Deut. 32^{35} tends to support the interpretation just given. Vengeance is God's affair, and must be left to him.[i] That there will be vengeance is not denied, yet this invocation of it comes in a context of non-retaliation and love from v. 14 onwards.

20

No: the Greek is *alla*, 'but', which we should expect to be adversative, drawing a contrast between the note of divine vengeance in v. 19 and that of longsuffering and forgiveness in the present verse. The difficulty

[i] For OT and later Jewish material on the divine recompense see Wilckens III, p. 25f.

about taking *alla* so is that it would be unusual, to say the least, to have two OT quotations in contradiction.[j] It is possible, therefore, that *alla* is not adversative, but continues the theme of not presuming upon the divine prerogative. On the other hand it is possible that the two quotations do not contradict one another even if *alla* is adversative: the Romans are to leave vengeance to God, and for their own part to be kind and forgiving.

'if your enemy is hungry, feed him . . . for by so doing you will heap coals of fire upon his head' : Prov. 25$^{21f.}$ LXX. It has been suggested that behind this quotation from Proverbs lies an Egyptian ritual in which hot coals, presumably in some sort of dish, really were piled on the head of someone who had done wrong, as a sign of repentance. If there is an allusion to this both in Proverbs and in Romans, then the idea is that generous treatment of an enemy will lead him or her to repentance and thus achieve reconciliation. In this case the coals of fire do not represent punishment of a more devastating character than mere mortals could ever inflict, but stand for repentance brought about by generous and loving treatment. To Christians this is an attractive suggestion, and fits the gentler way of taking v. 19. The problem is that it requires us to assume that Paul knew the supposed Egyptian ritual allusion in Prov. 25$^{21f.}$, and that seems to ask rather a lot.[k] The issue turns also to some extent on whether *alla* is adversative. We may now sum up the possibilities.

(*a*) Whether knowingly or not, Paul catches the spirit of the Egyptian ritual, and contrasts generosity and love with the desire for vengeance. Vengeance and judgment are God's affair and not ours, and it should be borne in mind that he is a God of mercy (11^{32}). This interpretation is aided if *alla* is taken adversatively, to mean something like 'on the other hand'.

(*b*) Christians must not anticipate the Judgment of God, which may be the more severe because of their forbearance in the meantime. This

j See K. Stendahl, 'Hate, Non-Retaliation, and Love', *HTR* LV, 1962, pp. 343–55 at p. 346.

k For the Egyptian interpretation see W. Klassen, 'Coals of Fire: Sign of Repentance or Revenge?' *NTS* 9, 1962–63, pp. 337–50. For the view that even here Paul is simply talking about deference to God's judgment, and that he could scarcely have known of the Egyptian background, see Stendahl, 'Hate, Non-Retaliation, and Love'. For his interpretation, Klassen relies considerably on the sequence of thought in the passage.

is to take *alla* non-adversatively, to mean 'for' or some such, and it is to ignore the possibility of allusion to an Egyptian repentance ritual.

It is natural for many readers to feel uneasy about (*b*) because it imputes to God a less generous attitude than is commended to men and women, but this uneasiness does not mean that we can rule out the possibility that it is what Paul is saying. It can scarcely be denied that such an attitude is to be found in the book of Revelation at a somewhat later date. The exegetical problem is not easily solved, but perhaps just – and only just – (*a*) is to be preferred, because of the final statement in v. 21 that evil is to be overcome by good.

THE CHRISTIAN AND THE STATE

13 *Let every person be subject to the governing authorities. For there is no authority except from God, and those that exist have been instituted by God. ²Therefore he who resists the authorities resists what God has appointed and those who resist will incur judgment. ³For rulers are not a terror to good conduct, but to bad. Would you have no fear of him who is in authority? Then do what is good, and you will receive his approval, ⁴for he is God's servant for your good. But if you do wrong, be afraid, for he does not bear the sword in vain; he is the servant of God to execute his wrath on the wrongdoer. ⁵Therefore one must be subject, not only to avoid God's wrath but also for the sake of conscience. ⁶For the same reason you also pay taxes, for the authorities are ministers of God, attending to this very thing. ⁷Pay all of them their dues, taxes to whom taxes are due, revenue to whom revenue is due, respect to whom respect is due, honour to whom honour is due.*

This is one of the most contentious passages in the whole letter. Paul says, or appears to say, that Christians must give to the state unconditional obedience because it has been established by God, without any qualifications about the constitution and behaviour of that state. It is a passage that has had a critical role in the history of Christendom, being invoked by those who wished to maintain the Christian duty of obedience to the state. Conversely, it has been seen as problematic by those who wished to challenge the state's authority, in whole or in part, in the name of Christian faith and obedience. What, for example, were Christians in Nazi Germany to make of such teaching?

If we grant (as some scholars do not grant) that 'the governing authorities' in v. 1 are straightforwardly civil powers and earthly governments, Paul seems to want to uphold the existing political situation, because governments are possessed of God's authority, and so men and women must submit to them. There is no place for anarchy. It is possible, on the other hand, that Paul is talking not about government in matters of high and potentially controversial policy, but rather about what we call local government. As it stands, the text does not demand such a limitation, though we shall see that it cannot be ruled out.

There have been suggestions that this passage is a later insertion,[1] only awkwardly connected to what surrounds it, but as it stands it forms part of an interesting sequence:

outworkings of love (12^{14-21});
the Christian and the state (13^{1-7});
love as the crux of the Law (13^{8-10});
the nearness of the End (13^{11-14}).

If it does belong where we now have it, then the sequence does affect out understanding of the passage.

(a) The general Christian commitment to love ($12^{9, \ 14-21}$; 13^{8-10}) is not limited to treatment of other Christians, nor even to how opponents are dealt with, but includes being responsible members of civil society. It includes an acceptance of, and a willingness to live within, that ordering of society which God himself has given. It excludes anarchy, and it excludes a flight from the actual, concrete conditions of human social organization. In other words, Christians are not in heaven yet. They accept the ordering of society as being under God, though whether this entails accepting everything that the political power does and demands, is quite another question.

(b) Though there is nothing in vv. 1-7 about the nearness of the

---

1 For the view that 13^{1-7} is a self-standing Pauline insertion see Michel, p. 312; that it is a non-Pauline insertion, see O'Neill, pp. 207-9, and cf. the more complex position of Munro, *Authority in Paul and Peter*, pp. 56-67. On such views see the discussions of Wilckens III, pp. 30f., and Cranfield II, pp. 651f.

End, any more than there is about love, vv. 11ff. are a reminder that such subjection to the civil power is only provisional and that the End is in prospect. If the form of this world is passing away, one does not try to change it, but lives within it as it is, knowing that its days are numbered.

In its context, then, this passage enjoins living out Christian existence in the world as it is, but it does not propound any theory of the state. It should not be taken to say more than it does. Nevertheless, because it seems to say that Christians' political obedience should be unquestioning, and because many readers not surprisingly find such an idea abhorrent, we need to probe a little deeper into how Paul's original readers would have understood it.

(i) The idea that power comes from the people, or ought to do so, would not have seemed an obvious one to Paul or his contemporaries. Moreover, at this time very few of his readers would have been Roman citizens, in all probability, and they were therefore removed from political power and responsibility. Submission to the civil power was their only feasible course.

(ii) There was the option of armed revolt, and rumblings of Jewish revolt may already have been perceptible in Palestine. It may thus have been important for the Roman Christians not to be tarred with that brush if they were to survive at all. It is just possible that some Christians were responding to the Lordship of Christ by rejecting all human lordship, including that of the Roman state; if so, Paul tells them that they are wrong, and that the existing political situation is the God-given framework for their Christian life.

(iii) Paul's teaching here stands within a Jewish tradition of adopting a positive attitude to the established authorities, the alternative to which was seen as chaos and anarchy. See for example *Aboth* 3.2:

> R. Hanina the Prefect of the Priests said: Pray for the peace of the ruling power, since but for the fear of it men would have swallowed up each other alive.

See also Prov. 24^{21}; Ecclus. 17^{17}.[m] The same idea is found elsewhere in early Christianity, cf. I Peter 2^{13-17}; I Tim. 2^2; Tit. 3^1.

---

[m] For further material see Käsemann, pp. 354f.; Wilckens III, p. 33.

(iv) It has been argued that the language of this passage is not that of the theory of the state, but that of Hellenistic administration.[n] Thus we have to do with how the routine processes of government impinge upon ordinary people in everyday situations, such as paying taxes, v. 7.

(v) It is often pointed out that up to this stage in the history of the church, the Roman state tended to be seen as a protection against popular hostility, but that the time would come when the state itself was perceived as the major threat. Then the attitude towards it would change, as it has in the book of Revelation. What Paul would have said in that altered situation we do not know, though he could scarcely have allowed for any infringement of the Lordship of Christ.

At all events, the apostle does here see the reality and role of the civil authority as positively to be welcomed by Christians, even though the talk is all of ordering by God, with no mention of Christ. The power of the magistracy to punish wrongdoing is presented as an expression of the divine wrath/*orgē*, as an aspect of God's pressure towards the good. So, as part of their concrete existence in this world, Christians must pay their taxes without question.

৯৫৯

1

be subject: the verb *hupotassesthō* is not precisely the same as 'obey', but rather means 'accept the claims of, submit to'. At this point Paul is not talking of obedience to this or that regulation, but of the orders of society within which it is necessary to live, and within which God is to be served. There is no indication that he is alluding to Mark 12^{13-17} and parallels ('Render to Caesar the things that are Caesar's, and to God the things that are God's', v. 17).

the governing authorities: all commentators agree that these include political powers, in particular the Roman state. There has in the past, however, been some debate about whether Paul and his readers conceived there to be angelic forces behind such earthly powers, rather as if Uncle Sam and John Bull really existed and were the super-powers

---

n See the summary of the meanings of the Greek terms in Käsemann, pp. 353f.

behind the American and British states. Whatever the arguments for detecting such superhuman powers in other NT passages, there is now a consensus that they are not in view here.° Among the reasons for this consensus may be mentioned first that in 8³⁷ᶠᶠ. such powers are hostile, and it would be very strange if Paul were here advising the Romans to submit to them. Moreover, if it is correct that the language here is that of Hellenistic administration,ᴾ then it hardly fits to introduce ideas of celestial or infernal powers. In short, in this passage we are dealing with power as it is experienced in the ordinary run of life, not with the mythology of the state.

those that exist have been instituted by God: that is, they are part of the divine provision in creation. There is nothing in vv. 1–7 about Christ, nor about the realm of redemption. Yet we must remember that Paul now looks at everything, creation included, from the perspective of the lordship of Christ. We must also note that this passage is to do with the attitude of Christians. Despite the absence of any mention of Christ, we therefore take it that 'God' here has a Christian colouring.

All the same, it is important that the state is discussed in God-language rather than Christ-language. The state is not part of the New Age, nor does Paul envisage its being re-made to Christian specifications. It is part of the present Age, in which Christians and non-Christians co-exist. It is also part of God's provision, and the implication of the verse is that all human powers must rule by the licence and under the supreme authority of God. They are not independent powers alongside the divine power.

2

the authorities: Roman officials.

o The literature is considerable, but for the 'angelic' view see especially O. Cullmann, *The State in the New Testament*, ET SCM Press 1957, pp. 93–114; with important modifications, C. D. Morrison, *The Powers that Be*, SCM Press 1960; against the whole idea, Carr, *Angels and Principalities*; defending it, but not for the present passage, Wink, *Naming the Powers*, especially pp. 45–7; similarly C. E. Arnold, 'The "Exorcism" of Ephesians 6.12 in Recent Research', *JSNT* 30 1987, pp. 71–87.

p Käsemann, pp. 353f., using the work of A. Strobel, 'Zum Verständnis von Röm 13', ZNW 47, 1956, pp. 67–93: *exousiai tetagmenai* (v. 1) are leading Roman officials; *leitourgos* (v. 6) is something like a civil servant; *archē* (v. 3) is municipal authority, and so on.

those who resist will incur judgment: whose judgment, that of the state or that of God? In view of v. 4, where the judicial sanctions of the magistracy are seen as agents of the divine wrath/*orgē*, there is probably a double reference here, but the future tense suggests that we should think of the divine Judgment as at least an important element (cf. Wilckens III, p. 33). We do not know whether some Roman Christians were in fact resisting, or were thinking of resisting, the decrees of the state, perhaps by withholding taxes, or whether Paul was speaking hypothetically and generally. There is no evidence of Christian civil disobedience in Rome.

3

rulers: municipal authorities (see note on v. 1).

are not a terror to good conduct, but to bad: Paul must be assuming that they keep within their divinely given role. The time came when rulers, including municipal ones, were very much a terror to good (Christian) conduct, though in other matters no doubt they were usually on the side of good conduct. Unlike the book of Revelation, Paul does not take such a possibility into account. All he is saying is that good citizens need and welcome the protection of law and order; it is the criminal who fears that protection and finds it a threat.

4

it does not bear the sword in vain: in general terms, the reference is clearly to the power of life and death held by the judiciary. The precise image, unfortunately, is elusive. Cranfield (II, pp. 666f.) points out that at this time the term *ius gladii*, 'law of the sword', was used only in military contexts. It is therefore possible that we should think of the ability of the army to suppress rebellion, rather than of capital punishment in a civil setting. Yet this does not fit the general atmosphere of local and civil administration at all well. Probably we can with confidence find no more here than a reminder of the state's power of enforcement.

he is the servant of God to execute his wrath on the wrongdoer: 'he' is the one who is in authority (v. 3), i.e. the Roman official. The fact that he is the servant of God, within the ordering of society ordained by God, does not mean that he is consciously co-operating with God. It rather means that objectively, whatever his own intention or understanding, he does carry out God's will for society.

He 'executes his (God's) wrath': the word rendered 'executes' is literally 'is an avenger', but it can mean no more than carrying out the decisions of the administration. Yet it is plain that in doing so, he also carries out the divine judgment (wrath/*orgē*, see above on 1^{18}). In the Greek it is simply 'to execute wrath on the wrongdoer', but as the official is the servant of God in the matter, and as in Paul 'the wrath' is normally God's wrath, it is presumably God's here and in v. 5 too. It is thus God's judgment on evil, which belongs to the Last Judgment (cf. 2^5), but which can be foreshadowed in various ways in the present (see also $1^{18ff.}$). Thus the divine pressure towards good and against evil which will be complete at the End is also exemplified in the processes of law and order of a civilized state. It is, for example, part of that divine pressure that if I defraud my neighbour I shall bring down on my head the condemnation and punishment of the civil power.

5

one must be subject: cf. v. 1. As there, we are dealing with life within the given structures of society. Anarchy is ruled out.

not only to avoid God's wrath: 'God's' is absent from the Greek and has been inserted by the translators, as also in effect in v. 4. The same clarifying addition has been made in 5^9; 12^{19}. The fact that four times the translators have felt it necessary to make the addition 'of God' or something equivalent, tends to give credence to Dodd's view discussed at 1^{18}, that 'the wrath' is to be understood as working almost impersonally as cause and effect in a moral universe. We saw that there was more to be said than this, yet the almost regular absence of 'of God' from the Greek is striking. At all events it is clear that the call to submission has more behind it than the authority of the state in itself.

but also for the sake of conscience: on 'conscience' (*suneidēsis*) see above at 2^{15}. In this verse it is not a manifestation of the wrath, as if the pangs of conscience were part of the divine judgment on wrongdoing, yet it is closely associated with it. We saw that in popular morality conscience was usually retrospective, operating as a judgment on what had been done or said, but it is not at all certain that Paul always used it in that way. Here it may be prescriptive, giving direction about what ought to be done, and not only retrospective. q If it is, then Paul is saying that

q See M. Thrall, 'The Pauline Use of *SUNEIDĒSIS*', NTS 14, 1967–68, pp. 118–25.

submission to the rules of civilized living in community is something
they all know quite well they ought to offer, even without (or in addition to) their awareness that this is the divine ordering of things.

6

you also pay taxes: the tax in question (*phoros*) is either a poll tax or a
land tax, but in any case a direct one. Did early Christians debate
whether they, who recognized Christ alone as Lord, ought to pay taxes
to Caesar? Mark 12¹³⁻¹⁷ and parallels may indicate so. At any rate,
whether the point was questioned or not, Paul is quite certain that their
being citizens of a New Age does not absolve the Roman Christians
from their civic duty in this matter. Probably this was where submission
to the governing power most closely affected them, and it is even possible that payment of taxes is the main point of the whole of 13¹⁻⁷.

the authorities are ministers of God: cf. on vv. 1, 4. In the first instance they
represent earthly power, but in the last analysis they represent God's
provision of an orderly society.

7

Pay all of them their dues: literally, 'Pay all of them what you owe them'.
The next verse begins 'Owe no one anything except to love one
another'. Does this indicate that pieces of exhortatory material have
been joined artificially, by key-words, or does it suggest that payment
of taxes is a corporate aspect of unrestricted love for one another? The
context of 13¹⁻⁷ makes the latter at least a possibility.

revenue: this (Greek *telos*) is a toll or customs duty.

respect to whom respect is due: 'respect' is literally 'fear' (*phobos*) and we
may have a reference back to vv. 3f. and fear for those in authority.
Moreover, if respect/fear is taken to be greater than 'honour', then we
could have a gradation of attitudes to greater and lesser civic or state
personages. It could be merely a rhetorical pairing, in effect saying the
same thing twice to drive it home. There is a yet further possibility (so
Wilckens III, pp. 38f.) that as in I Peter 2¹⁷, a distinction is being made
between fearing God and honouring the emperor (or his representatives). See also Mark 12¹⁷ and parallels, where one must render to
Caesar what is Caesar's and to God what is God's. It is thus quite possible
that we have an echo of the exceedingly common Jewish stress on the

need to fear or be in awe of God, e.g. Ps. 2^{11}; 5^7; Prov. 1^7; Jer. 32^{40}; Jonah 1^{16}.

honour to whom honour is due: see the previous note. In the context, we may take it that they are to be honoured not because of who they are, but because they bear their authority under God.

13^{8-14} LOVE, THE LAW, AND THE PASSING AWAY
OF THIS AGE

⁸*Owe no one anything, except to love one another; for he who loves his neighbour has fulfilled the law.*⁹ *The commandments, 'You shall not commit adultery, You shall not kill, You shall not steal, You shall not covet,' and any other commandment, are summed up in this sentence, 'You shall love your neighbour as yourself.'* ¹⁰*Love does no wrong to a neighbour; therefore love is the fulfilling of the law.*
¹¹*Besides this you know what hour it is, how it is full time now for you to wake from sleep. For salvation is nearer to us now than when we first believed;* ¹²*the night is far gone, the day is at hand. Let us then cast off the works of darkness and put on the armour of light;* ¹³*let us conduct ourselves becomingly as in the day, not in revelling and drunkenness, not in debauchery and licentiousness, not in quarrelling and jealousy.* ¹⁴*But put on the Lord Jesus Christ, and make no provision for the flesh, to gratify its desires.*

The centre of Christian obedience is love, cf. 12^{9-10}. If we are right to see this love as partly exemplified in submission to the structures of organized society, we now also see it as summing up what the Torah, the Law, was aiming at. Paul twice (vv. 8, 10) says that love is the fulfilment of the Law, and further that loving one's neighbour as oneself sums up the Law (v. 9). He cites four of the five commandments in the second half of the Decalogue, all of them concerned in one way or another with relationships with one's neighbour. He adds that other commandments also are summed up in the love-commandment, which is taken from Lev. 19^{18}. He does not cite the command to love God.

It is not immediately obvious what he means when he says that the love-commandment fulfils and sums up the Law. Such summaries of the Torah were far from unknown in Judaism, but they were used to lead into the keeping of the whole Law, not as a substitute for it, and it is impossible to suppose that this is what Paul is aiming at. We cannot suppose, for instance, that he is saying that obedience to the love-command will lead to obedience to the law about circumcision, or to the food laws. Perhaps the least unsatisfactory solution is that the command to love represents the realization of the goal of the Law. That is to say, what the commands in the second half of the Decalogue and commands like them were intended to achieve, is now to be understood as having been brought to full and final expression in the command to love. This does not mean that it leads to the observance of every single command in the Torah. We need to note that it is love and not the Law that is the primary concern of the passage; if we truly love one another, we shall in effect carry out what the Law requires, at least in so far as it is to do with social relationships.

Paul now turns to the nearness of the End. Presumably his readers were familiar with the conviction, for it appears quite abruptly. It is used to reinforce the demand for good living which has already been expressed through the love command. The proximity of the End and the love command together require Christians to live as men and women who already belong to the coming Day of light, within the sphere of the Lord Jesus Christ. What belongs to the old Day must be rejected, even though in vv. 1–7 Paul's readers were told to accept the political and social structures of that Age.

ဢၕ

8
Owe no one anything: in v. 7 we saw that the cognate noun 'debts' (*opheilas*, RSV 'their dues') was used for giving the civil authorities their appropriate acknowledgment. Here, the only debt is to be that of mutual love. 'Have no debts except that of love' is the idea; such debts can never be fulfilled.

except to love one another: it is not altogether clear whether we are now concerned with love within the Christian community, or with love for all men and women. In the light of the quotations from the Ten Commandments which follow, and which give examples of what love is, it seems much more likely that love is not here restricted to relationships between Christians. For example, it can hardly be refraining from stealing only from fellow-Christians that is an expression of love.

for he who loves his neighbour has fulfilled the law: 'neighbour' is literally 'the other' (*ton heteron*), i.e. any other person. For what is meant by love as fulfilling the Law, see below on v. 10. Paul now begins his attempt to relate the teaching about love to the Jewish inheritance of the Torah.

9

The commandments: we have noted that the four commands from the Decalogue are all taken from the second table, those dealing with human relationships. Oddly, the ninth commandment, not to bear false witness, is omitted. Some MSS do have it, but this is almost certainly in conscious or unconscious assimilation to Ex. 20^{16} and Deut. 5^{20}. In any case Paul is not trying to be exhaustive, as 'any other commandment' shows. As it stands, this last phrase is unqualified, but it is scarcely possible to take the lack of qualification seriously. The apostle cannot be saying, for example, that the command to circumcise infant males is included in the love command. Such things, together with such laws as those concerning the Temple, are not in view at all.

It is doubtless no more than a curiosity that Paul reverses the order of the sixth and seventh commandments.

are summed up in this sentence, 'You shall love your neighbour as yourself': Lev. 19^{18}. The idea that the Law can be summed up in a few commandments, or even only one, is well-known in Judaism. The most famous instance is the saying of R. Hillel (*b. Shab.* 31a),

> What is hateful to you, do not do to your neighbour: that is the whole Torah, while the rest is commentary on it. Go and learn.

In the gospel tradition too we have the famous summary of the Law in terms of love in Mark 12^{28-31}; Matt. 22^{34-40}; Luke 10^{25-28}. Here, however, as in the similar Gal. 5^{14}, there is no mention of the love of God, which is the first of the twin commands to love in the gospel passages (quoting Deut. 6^5). This must cast doubt on whether Paul knew this gospel tradition.

317

What does it mean for Paul and his readers that the love-command-ment sums up commandments like those in the second table of the Decalogue, and how widely ought we to cast our net for command-ments that are summed up? In the Jewish summarizing tradition, as in the example just quoted from R. Hillel, it is clear that the one command (or the few commands) encapsulates and includes all the rest. It does not replace them. Our difficulty in the case of Paul is that we know he does not consider all the commands of the Law to be still obligatory for all Christians. If he is consistent, he cannot be saying that the whole Law flows logically from this one commandment. We need think only of Rom. 4, where being the people of God no longer rests on circumcision as a necessary condition. Moreover, not only has he in Ch. 7 spoken of dying to the Law, in $14^{14, 20}$ he will effectively contradict the necessity of distinguishing between clean and unclean foods, and this is quite inconsistent with holding that the love-command implies the whole Law. It is therefore impossible to believe that when he says that the commandments are summed up in the command to love, he is saying what the Rabbis said.[r] He makes no explicit distinction between ritual and moral commands (an elusive distinction in any case), nor between commands that apply to all peoples and those that apply to Israel alone. Perhaps all that we can say with confidence is that the love-command sums up commandments of the Law *of the sort cited in this verse*. This is reinforced if we accept that the primary concern of the passage is to explain love, not to deal with the question of the Law. Those who love will be keeping the Law in relevant respects, even if that was not what they set out to do.

10

love is the fulfilling of the law: we now return to the question first raised at v. 8; in what sense does loving *fulfil* (*plēroun* in v. 8; *plērōma* in v. 10) the Law? Neither in LXX nor in NT is 'fulfil' the normal word to use for obeying the commandments: The only reasonably clear instance in LXX is I Macc. 2^{55}, and apart from the present two verses, in the NT there are possible instances only in Rom. 8^4; Gal. 5^{14}; Matt. 5^{17}, but in all these it is debatable whether the meaning is straightforwardly 'carry out, obey'. It is much more likely, therefore, that the meaning is that the Law *culminates* in love (cf. Wilckens III, p. 68), that the goal of the Law is reached in love. There is thus an eschatological colouring to these

r On these differences see further Sanders, *PLJP*, pp. 95, 99; Räisänen, *PL*, pp. 33-42; Wilckens III, pp. 68f.

statements in vv. 8 and 10: 'fulfilment' should be given its full value as implying completion.

This is consistent with the view that the Law as a régime is finished, and has been 'died to' (7^{1-6}), and with the fact that some parts of the Law (for example, food laws) are now regarded as things about which Christians may differ (Ch. 14). It also shows, on the other hand, that Christians are by no means absolved from obedience to everything that is in the Law. What love means in practice is exemplified in commands of the Law like those in the second half of the Decalogue: if I love my neighbour as myself I do not steal, commit adultery, and so on.

Finally, the relation of the love-command to specific laws in the Torah helps us to see why love can be commanded. How can anyone, even God, command an emotion? The answer is that in the biblical writings love is not just an emotion, but a pattern of acting as well. It is how we behave towards one another.

11

you know what hour it is: literally, 'knowing the time/season', another instance of the participial imperative. This refers to the divine time-table, which Paul believes to be so far advanced that the End must be near.

to wake from sleep: in effect to be watchful, vigilant, ready for the End when it comes. Cf. Phil. 4^{4-7}; I Thess. $5^{1-11, 23}$.

salvation: for this (*sōtēria*) see above at 1^{16}. It is not primarily individual acceptance with God, but the cosmic consummation of the divine purposes. For the people of God, this will mean life with him for ever, but for the whole creation it will mean the end of everything as we know it, and the coming of a new heaven and a new earth.

nearer to us than when we first believed: 'first' is not in the Greek, and is added by RSV in order to indicate that the aorist (punctiliar past tense) is ingressive, i.e. it refers to the beginning of belief.

12

the night is far gone: 'night' stands for the Old Age, which in Paul's view is rapidly dying. The 'Day', the New Age, is about to dawn. In Jewish circles, talk of a cosmic End is mostly post-OT, though see Dan. $8^{17, 19}$; $11^{35, 40, 45}$. For the nearness of the End cf. *II Apoc. Bar.* 82^2. The use of night and day, or light and darkness, for the two ages is so natural as to need no explanation. It is found especially richly in the literature of Qumran, e.g. the so-called *War Scroll*, 'The War of the Sons of Light against the Sons of Darkness', IQM.[s] For Paul and his readers, the passing of the night means that the time of anomaly is coming to an end, and that there will soon be a cessation of the tension that arises from living between the Ages. Although there has been little in the letter until now that is clearly concerned with the consummation, Paul has obviously not discarded that belief which is so prominent in the Thessalonian letters. There he focusses on how it will affect those still living as well as those who have died in the meantime, and on what it will be like. Here, we are merely reminded that an End is coming and coming soon, with nothing said about the role of Jesus Christ in that cataclysmic event. See above on 11^{26} and on salvation as belonging to the End at 1^{16}.

Let us then cast off the works of darkness and put on the armour of light: this is the language of Christian catechesis, of baptismal instruction and preparation, in which converts were urged to get rid of old habits, goals, and practices, and to adopt new ones appropriate for Christians. It is commonly thought that a context in baptismal preparation is indicated by the reference to dressing and undressing, not only here but also in other NT passages, cf. Col. 3^{8-12}; Eph. 4^{22-25}; I Peter 2^1; James 1^{21}.[t] Here it is noteworthy that not just new clothes, but armour is to be donned (cf. I Thess. 5^8), for there is a fight to be won.

13
let us conduct ourselves becomingly as in the day: the list of things to be avoided by those who belong to the imminent new Day is quite conventional, and need not imply anything about the habits or character of the Roman Christians. We cannot, for example, deduce from this verse that they were greatly given to drunkenness, though it is possible that there is an oblique allusion to what went on in the evenings in Roman taverns.[u] The list is not exhaustive, but stands for all bad actions.

14
put on the Lord Jesus Christ: this forms a contrast with the second half of

s For details see Wilckens III, pp. 76f.; Cranfield II, p. 682.
t See further Selwyn, *I Peter*, pp. 393-400.
u See Wilckens III, p. 77 and n. 413.

the verse with its 'make no provision for the flesh'. Putting on Christ is therefore living under him as Lord, as opposed to living under the flesh/ *sarx* which, as often, does not mean the purely physical, but rather living apart from God (see above at 1³). Its desires thus include not only licentiousness but also jealousy (v. 13). Putting on the Lord Jesus Christ is an image which is enriched by the armour image of v. 12, as well as by the 'in Christ' language, cf. on 6¹¹. We therefore have the notion of protection here as well as that of lordship: cf. the partial parallel in Gal. 3²⁷, 'as many of you as were baptized into Christ have put on Christ'. He is not only the Lord of the Roman Christians, but also the power under whom and by whom they exist.

14^{1-23} THOSE WHO EAT MEAT AND THOSE
             WHO WILL NOT

14 *As for the man who is weak in faith, welcome him, but not for disputes over opinions. ²One believes he may eat anything, while the weak man eats only vegetables. ³Let not him who eats despise him who abstains, and let not him who abstains pass judgment on him who eats; for God has welcomed him. ⁴Who are you to pass judgment on the servant of another? It is before his own master that he stands or falls. And he will be upheld, for the Master· is able to make him stand.*

⁵One man esteems one day as better than another, while another man esteems all days alike. Let every one be fully convinced in his own mind. ⁶He who observes the day, observes it in honour of the Lord. He also who eats, eats in honour of the Lord, since he gives thanks to God; while he who abstains, abstains in honour of the Lord and gives thanks to God. ⁷None of us lives to himself, and none of us dies to himself. ⁸If we live, we live to the Lord, and if we die, we die to the Lord; so then, whether we live or whether we die, we are the Lord's. ⁹For to this end Christ died and lived again, that he might be Lord both of the dead and of the living.

¹⁰Why do you pass judgment on your brother? Or you, why do you despise your brother? For we shall all stand before the judgment seat of God; ¹¹for it is written,

'As I live, says the Lord, every knee shall bow to me,
and every tongue shall give praise to God.'

^{12}*So each of us shall give account of himself to God.*

^{13}*Then let us no more pass judgment on one another, but rather decide never to put a stumbling block or hindrance in the way of a brother.* ^{14}*I know and am persiaded in the Lord Jesus that nothing is unclean in itself; but it is unclean for any one who thinks it unclean.* ^{15}*If your brother is being injured by what you eat, you are no longer walking in love. Do not let what you eat cause the ruin of one for whom Christ died.* ^{16}*So do not let what is good to you be spoken of as evil.* ^{17}*For the kingdom of God does not mean food and drink but righteousness and peace and joy in the Holy Spirit;* ^{18}*he who thus serves Christ is acceptable to God and approved by men.* ^{19}*Let us then pursue what makes for peace and for mutual upbuilding.* ^{20}*Do not, for the sake of food, destroy the work of God. Everything is indeed clean, but it is wrong for any one to make others fall by what he eats;* ^{21}*it is right not to eat meat or drink wine or do anything that makes your brother stumble.* ^{22}*The faith that you have, keep between yourself and God; happy is he who has no reason to judge himself for what he approves.* ^{23}*But he who has doubts is condemned, if he eats, because he does not act from faith; for whatever does not proceed from faith is sin.*

Throughout 14^1–15^{13} the nature of the problem is a major question. Paul's advice to do nothing that would cause offence to one's neighbour shows close similarities to his advice in I Cor. 8 and 10, where the issue was whether or not Christians could legitimately eat food that had previously been offered in pagan sacrifices, and if so under what circumstances. Here, however, the position is not so clear, because Paul never says that the meat in question has been offered in idolatrous worship, and never uses the word *eidōlothuta* ('things offered to idols') that is so important in I Corinthians, cf. 8$^{1, 4, 7, 10}$; 10^{19}. Again, there is nothing in I Cor. 8, 10 about the observance of certain days nor about abstinence from wine, as there is here (vv. 5, 21). There has consequently been much effort to identify a group which could plausibly have been represented in the Roman church and which exhibited these three traits: abstinence from wine, abstinence from meat, and observance of certain days.[v] There is no shortage

[v] There are particularly full accounts of the possibilities in Michel, pp. 419–21; Schlier, pp. 403–6; see also Käsemann, pp. 367f.; Cranfield II, pp. 690–8.

of groups that might fit more or less, but none that fits entirely comfortably or so obviously as to exclude other possibilities.

(a) The most obvious solution is that the abstainers were Christians who were anxious to keep the Torah in such matters as observance of the Sabbath (and perhaps other holy days), as well as in avoiding forbidden foods and meat not killed in the prescribed way.[w] Thus they would not be vegetarians properly speaking, but people who abstained from meat when they suspected its provenance. If we ask why they did not simply go to a Jewish butcher, the answer may be either that such butchers would not serve Jewish Christian customers, or that we have to do with occasions when strictly observant Christian Jews were eating in the houses of the more permissive.[x] Wine is a problem, for the Jews were not normally teetotallers unless they were Nazirites (Num. 6$^{1ff.}$; Judg. 13$^{4f.}$), though they might abstain for a particular reason and for a limited time, such as for a penitential exercise (*TRub.* 1.10; *TJud.* 15.4). There were indeed sectarian groups like the Therapeutae in Egypt, described by Philo, *Vit. Contempl.* 37, who abstained from meat and wine and were strict about observance of the Sabbath, and it is conceivable that groups of Jews influenced by such practices existed in Rome and had contributed Christian converts in significant numbers. Yet we have no evidence of this.

(b) On the other hand it is conceivable that abstention had nothing to do with Judaism or the Torah, but rather reflected the ascetic and vegetarian movement represented by the Orphics and Pythagoreans. Meat would be avoided because eating it involved consuming the life or soul of the animal, and wine because it attacked the human mind and made intercourse with the divine more difficult. Days, on such a view, would perhaps be lucky and unlucky days. It is hard to imagine, however, that Paul would have been so tolerant of such views and practices. Yet it is not impossible that pagan ascetic influences were at work, and some scholars[y] suspect that the abstainers were some sort of syncretistic, probably Judaeo-Gnostic, group. It must be said that there is in Romans no hint of a group with a tendency to the sort of

---

w See e.g. Minear, *Obedience*, pp. 8–17.

x See Watson, *PJG*, p. 95; Cranfield II, p. 695.

y E.g. Barrett, pp. 256–9; Althaus, p. 138; Käsemann, pp. 365–69.

speculations characteristic of Gnostics, unless we can detect such a group behind 16[17-20].

(c) Further, there are some who argue[z] that this passage does not reflect the Roman situation at all. Indeed Paul may have little or no knowledge of that. Rather is he generalizing from his Corinthian experience, which is why the advice given here is so similar to that in I Cor. 8, 10. Like the two previous chapters, this passage could be addressed to any church, anywhere, but happens to be addressed to Rome. Against this, most readers suppose that the extended treatment given to the question of abstention, together with 15[14] which does suggest that Paul knew quite a lot about the situation in Rome, means that the passage is directed to a specific and known issue in Rome. On this view, at 14[1] we have a shift from more generally applicable ethical advice to the specific.

(d) On the whole, the best case can be made for the view that the problem in Rome was very similar to that in Corinth (or at least that Paul assumes the two issues are the same). The mention of wine may be merely a hypothetical parallel, thrown in for the sake of the argument, or it may be evidence that in Rome, as later in Palestine (m.AZ 2.4, 7; 5.2: note that Abodah Zarah is concerned with idolatry), pious Jews and perhaps some Gentile Christians would not drink wine produced by pagans, for fear that at the vintage or later it had been used in pagan rites, and so was 'libation-wine'. It has also been pointed out[a] that there are instances in Jewish literature where the pious who found themselves in a pagan environment abstained from both meat and wine for fear of contamination, i.e. through cultic use. If this is the correct interpretation of the reference to wine in 14[21], then it reinforces the idol-meat interpretation of 14[2ff.]. As for days, the best suggestion is probably the most obvious one, namely that what is meant is the Sabbath, perhaps together with other Jewish holy days. It is fair to observe that throughout the passage only meat is spoken of as a problem. Days in vv. 5–6 may well be a parallel case to aid the solution, not part of the problem, and wine is not discussed as an

z Like R. J. Karris, in Ch. 6 of Donfried, *Debate*; cf. also Furnish, *The Love Command*, pp. 115ff.

a By Watson, *PJG*, p. 95. He adduces in evidence Dan. 1[8-16]; Judith 12[1-4]; Esth. 14[17] LXX; Josephus *Vit.* 14.

issue. All the problem-language is directed to the question of meat, so that only of that can we be sure it was a problem.

So then, if we hold that this passage is, like I Cor. 8, 10, about meat offered to idols, we can understand why it is so dangerous for the abstainers to succumb to pressure and eat. Paul fears that in succumbing they would trip over a stumbling-block, be injured, and finally be ruined as Christians, so that the 'work of God' is destroyed ($14^{13, 15, 16, 20, 21}$). Such strong language and such dire danger makes sense if, like the Corinthians (I Cor. $8^{4, 7-13}$), the 'weak' who ceased to abstain did so, not because they had come to believe that idols were nothing and the meat therefore meat and nothing more, but in the conviction or suspicion that idols did represent reality and that by eating they were continuing some attachment to their previous cult. For them to eat would be to confess that Christ was not the only Lord, and thus to be 'ruined'. To be sure, Paul says none of this in Rom. 14, but something like it explains his language and his fear. The language of clean and unclean (v. 14) fits this explanation, though it fits other explanations as well.

While the Corinthian abstainers were probably ex-pagans, those in Rome were probably a mixed group. On the argument just outlined, ex-pagans are obvious members, as they were the people who would suspect that eating perpetuated their attachment to pagan cults. Nevertheless pious Jews would also fear that eating meat offered to idols implied such an attachment, cf. the so-called Apostolic Decree of Acts $15^{20, 29}$; 21^{25}, and see also Rev. $2^{14, 20}$. It is likely, then, that the division between eaters and non-eaters did not correspond to the division between Jewish- and Gentile-Christians, but cut across it.

There are two major objections to the interpretation here offered.

(a) If this is about meat offered to idols, why does Paul not use the term *eidōlothuta* as he does in I Cor. 8, 10? It is certainly odd that he does not. Perhaps it was a term being used in the debate within the Corinthian church, but not in that in Rome, and so Paul picks it up and uses it in the Corinthian letter, but not in the Roman. In any case the absence of this term is not sufficient reason to reject a solution that fits in other respects.

(b) Perhaps a more serious objection is that 15^{7-13} is without doubt about the need for Jewish- and Gentile-Christians to accept one another, and is also commonly taken to continue the issue between the 'weak' and the 'strong'. This would mean that the abstainers were at least mostly Jews. However, it is not self-evident that 15^{7-13} is the conclusion of the idol-meat discussion. It is as likely that the strong and the weak issue is concluded at 15^6 with its little doxology, and that 15^{7-13} is the conclusion of the whole of the ethical advice from 12^1 onwards. From 15^{14} Paul moves into concluding remarks and a discussion of his travel plans, and so vv. 7–13 can plausibly be taken as the conclusion of the whole ethical section of the letter, not as the conclusion of the strong and weak part of it.[b]

Despite these two objections, therefore, it remains reasonable to suppose that the issue in 14^1–15^6 is that of meat offered to idols. As for the way in which Paul deals with the issue, that is not easy to disentangle, any more than in the partial parallel in I Corinthians. Yet some things are clear enough.

(i) There is to be no passing of judgment by the weak, nor any contempt of the weak by the strong.

(ii) The overriding principle is service of and devotion to Christ.

(iii) While people must follow the light they have, they must not do so in isolation from one another, nor in lack of consideration for the effect on others of their own practice. Some of these matters recur in the sections that follow.

Indubitably the words 'weak' and 'strong' are anything but neutral: who would not rather be strong than weak? So, in using them Paul signals his own position, and this remains so even if he has taken the terms over from some of the disputants. He appears to use them without question. 'Weak' may, however, be a term imported from the Corinthian dispute (I Cor. 8^{7-12}), with 'strong' added as a foil to it. If so, to be strong is to be strong in faith, in the sense of being convinced that the grace of Jesus Christ is all that matters, that idols have no reality as gods, and that the history of the meat one eats (or indeed the observance of certain days as especially holy) is unimportant in comparison with that grace. To be weak in faith is correspondingly to be still partly under the influence of one's past, whether Jewish or

[b] Not a few scholars concur in seeing meat offered to idols as the issue in 14^1–15^6, e.g. Bruce, pp. 244f.; Wilckens III, pp. 79ff.; Schmidt, pp. 226f.; Jewett, *Terms*, p. 45.

pagan, and therefore still subject to scruples that relate to that past.
Even though Paul counsels tolerance, and has a deep concern for the
'weak' Christian's existence before God, it is obvious that he himself
finds these scruples to be matters of very subordinate importance.

තිටි

1

weak in faith: there is no indication in this chapter or the succeeding one
that being weak in faith has anything to do with justification by faith.
It is not that the weak are not quite sure that faith alone really is sufficient for acceptance with God. 'Faith' here is something like confidence, or assurance. If the interpretation of the whole passage that has
just been advanced is correct, the weak lack the confidence that would
give them the ability to eat knowing that no harm could come to them
as a result. Compare the person in I Cor. 8 whose conscience is weak
because of a lack of assurance that the idols have no power over meat
sacrificed to them.

welcome him: it is quite possible that we should imagine a setting in
someone's house, where a guest at a Christian gathering may not be
able to eat whatever is offered. The admonition to welcome such a person may therefore be quite concrete. It is important to note that among
the poor the eating of meat was comparatively rare, and occurred
chiefly on festal occasions or in the homes of the well-to-do. So much
was this so, that the very idea of meat may have had cultic associations
for the worse off. [c]

not for disputes over opinions: the meaning of the Greek (*mē eis diakriseis
dialogismōn*) is uncertain. It could mean 'not in order to pass judgment'
or 'not to have debates about his scruples'. In any case, it is clear that the
person is to be welcomed without either such ulterior motive, and the
differences of view are to be tackled pastorally, with concern for the
person.

2

the weak man eats only vegetables: as noted in the introduction to the

[c] See Meeks, *Urban Christians*, pp. 69, 98; G. Theissen, *The Social Setting of
Pauline Christianity*, ET T. & T. Clark 1982, pp. 125–9.

passage, it is by no means certain that the reference is to strict vege-
tarianism, something known among some Hellenistic groups, e.g. neo-
Pythagoreans, but not normal in Jewish circles. It is perfectly possible
that abstinence from meat was only on particular occasions, such as
when a group of Christians met for a meal and some of them were uncertain about the provenance of the meat provided by the host. Except
for those who had access to a Jewish butcher, it may well have been the
case that Christians who had scruples about eating meat that might have
been offered in pagan sacrifices, were in practice vegetarians.

3
Let not him who eats despise him who abstains: in any situation where some
people have a more permissive attitude than others, an attitude of contempt towards the more strict (or at the least mild raillery) is likely to
arise. In this case, the contempt is presumably because the weak are not
liberated from their past sufficiently to be convinced that its history
cannot contaminate the meat (on the assumption that it was meat
offered to idols that was the basic issue).

let not him who abstains pass judgment on him who eats: again, such condemnation of the permissive by the strict is prone to arise wherever
there is such disagreement about practice. Yet it is particularly likely if
the non-eaters think the eaters are implicitly compromising with
paganism.

4
Who are you to pass judgment . . .: this must be addressed to the weak.
Christ is the Christians' Lord, and he alone can pass judgment. He has
sole rights in the matter, and no one can usurp them.

his own master: the Greek word is *kurios*, normally translated 'lord', and
in Paul's letters normally denoting Christ, except where the OT is being
quoted, when it denotes Yahweh. See on 10^9.

the Master is able to make him stand: as the context is that of judgment,
the standing may be at the Last Judgment (cf. e.g. Ps. 5^5; 140^3; Mal. 3^2;
Rev. 6^{17}). The argument is about answerability, which is not to one
another, but to the servant's Lord or Master. It is also possible, however,
that the reference is more generally to perseverance as a Christian in this
life.

5

One man esteems one day as better than another: why? Paul gives us no clue. There are two main interpretations.

(*a*) Paul is talking about the Sabbath, perhaps together with other Jewish holy days.

(*b*) He is referring to pagan propitious and unpropitious days, a distinction perhaps based on astrology. Compare Gal. 4¹, though there too it is not immediately obvious whether the reference is pagan or Jewish. In Col. 2¹⁶ the Sabbath is included among days that some observe and some do not, and about which there is dispute, but many think that in Colossae there was some sort of Judaeo-Gnostic mixture. There is no real evidence of that here.

In view of Paul's tolerant attitude here and in v. 6 towards the observance of particular days, they are unlikely to have been pagan. There is a further suggestion that these were the days on which the more strict fasted, cf. *Did.* 8¹, where Christian fasts are to be on different days from the fasts of 'the hypocrites'. This could, however, be regarded as a particular form of one or other of the two basic explanations already given. In all, the Sabbath explanation seems probable.

Let every one be fully convinced in his own mind: we noted in the introduction to the passage that the matter of days seems to be adduced as a parallel case that is not, or not still, a problem. It can rather be taken as a model of how the question of eating is to be approached. The parallel is not fully worked out, and does not need to be (cf. below on v. 6). If, as we suppose, Paul is talking primarily about the Sabbath, it is striking that he approaches it in a much less polemical way than that in which he tackles circumcision in Galatians. Is this because the context is less polemical? Or is it because to insist on the circumcision of Gentile Christians is to compromise the sufficiency of Christ, while allowing Jewish Christians (and perhaps others) to continue observing the Sabbath does no harm to anyone, unless they demand that others join them? Certainly there is no hint in Rom. 14 that those who did observe days were censorious or aggressive, just as there is no hint that non-observers of days regarded observers with contempt. To repeat what was said in the introduction to the passage, while there clearly was difference of practice in the matter of special days, there is no indication at all that this gave rise to problems in the community.

6

He who observes the day, observes it in honour of the Lord: this fits Jewish days much better than pagan ones, about which it is hard to imagine Paul saying any such thing. We note (cf. the comment on v. 5) that the parallel with eating is incomplete: Paul does not go on to say, 'he who ignores the day, ignores it in honour of the Lord'. The question of days is touched on only briefly, and Paul rapidly returns to the question of eating meat, the real focus of concern. There is a heavy stress in this verse on practice, whatever it is, as being in honour of the Lord, in continuity with the spirit of v. 4. As long as the Lord is honoured, one way or the other, diversity of practice may be accepted in the matter of food, just as it is in the matter of the observance of days. In other words, the matter of days is offered as part of the solution to the problem of food, not as an addition to it.

9

that he might be Lord both of the dead and of the living: this almost rhetorical statement sums up the essentially simple argument from v. 5 onwards: Christ is Lord. This means that no one and nothing else can determine the behaviour of Christians. In life and in death believers are his, whose lordship rests on his dying and rising again, cf. 10^9; Phil. 2^9; Acts 2^{36}.

10

Why do you pass judgment on your brother . . . why do you despise your brother: in the light of v. 3, we must take it that it is the weak who judge, and the strong who despise.

11

it is written: the first few words come from Isa. 49^{18}, but the body of the quotation is from Isa. 45^{23}, which is used also in Phil. 2^{10-11}.

'As I live, says the Lord . . .': although 'Lord' (*kurios*) has in the passage until now referred to Christ, it is more likely that here it refers to God. In quotations *kurios* normally retains its OT reference to Yahweh, and in any case here in vv. 10–12 the context is God's, not Christ's, role as Judge. [d]

shall give praise to God: the Greek (*exomologēsetai*) could also mean

d See e.g. Cranfield II, p. 710. However, Wilckens III, p. 85, thinks there may be a mixture of christology and theology here.

'confess'. In any case, it is the acknowledgment of him as divine Judge that is the point.

12

each of us shall give account of himself to God: if the passage ended here, we could reasonably conclude that Paul simply counsels mutual acceptance of differing practices. What I do is my own responsibility before God, and no one else's. The passage does not end here, but goes on to stress that one must do nothing that could imperil one's neighbour's integrity and security as a Christian. This is not a modification of the principle stated in this verse: it runs counter to it. In practice we either follow the light we have, or we act in love and consideration for our neighbour. At least in the case of the non-abstainers, it is impossible to follow both principles at once. This verse must therefore be regarded as only the first step towards an answer; a principle is stated, but it is only provisional. The real guide to what to do is about to come.

13

never to put a stumbling block or hindrance in the way of a brother: although the first part of the verse, forbidding judging, is presumably addressed to the weak, this part must be directed to the strong. Nowhere in the passage is there any suggestion that the weak's scruples could be a stumbling block in the way of the strong. How the strong's non-abstention could be a stumbling block to the weak is never explained, not even in vv. 20–21. It is assumed that the reader will understand. This is a prime reason for adopting the idol-meat interpretation, for on most if not all other theories it is easy to see how differences of practice could · cause disagreement, but not so easy to see how eating could be a stumbling block (*skandalon*), could *threaten* the abstainers. Paul fears that the non-eaters may give up their abstention under pressure from the others, and if they do, their very Christian existence is endangered, as the strong's is not. This is why, rather audaciously, we have suggested importing an explanation from I Cor. 8$^{7-12}$: the weak are not in their hearts convinced that it is safe to eat the meat, and suspect that if they eat they will at least implicitly be taking part in the pagan cult. If they eat under such circumstances, they are in effect mixing their lordships and their worships, thus turning their backs on Jesus Christ as sole Lord.

14

nothing is unclean in itself: Paul here reflects the distinctively Jewish use of *koinos*, 'common', for what is ritually unclean (in v. 20 he uses

katharos, 'clean', which was not distinctively Jewish terminology).[e]
This remarkable statement undercuts the whole distinction between
clean and unclean foods on which Paul, like all other observant Jews,
had been brought up. Modern readers inevitably think of Mark 7[14-23];
Luke 11[41]. Yet there is no reference here to such passages. 'I know and
am persuaded in the Lord Jesus' simply means 'I am convinced as a
Christian'.

In itself the use of *koinos* does not determine the nature of the objections to eating meat raised by the weak. It does not even make it certain
that the objections were Jewish in origin. It could be merely Paul's
Jewish way of putting things, though it may give a slight edge to some
sort of Jewish explanation and makes it plausible that the abstainers
included at least some Jewish Christians. It certainly, however, fits the
idea that meat offered to idols is in question in this chapter (and cf. IV
Macc. 5[2]; 7[6]; Acts 15[20], for food offered to idols as unclean). It would
also fit the view that the meat was rejected because it did not conform
to the food laws, but this seems to be excluded by other statements,
especially those about creating a stumbling block and ruining those for
whom Christ died (vv. 13, 15, 20, 21).

it is unclean for any one who thinks it is unclean: objectively there may be
nothing the matter with it, but subjectively, to the eater, it may be unclean, and for the purposes of this argument that is what matters. Cf. on
v. 13, and see I Cor. 8[4ff.].

15
cause the ruin of one for whom Christ died: this is strong language, and
shows that it is in their Christianity, not in their Jewishness or even in
their neo-Pythagoreanism, that the weak are vulnerable, if they compromise their beliefs and eat. It is hard to see how such language would
be called for on any other interpretation of the passage than that which
sees meat offered to idols as the central issue. If the weak understand
their eating as implicitly consenting to pagan worship, then the danger
could be expressed in such extreme terms.

The message is, despite v. 12, not to deny a major truth about love
for one another for the sake of another truth, that each of us is entitled
to our own opinion, so long as God is served.

e See the articles in *TDNT* III by F. Hauck and R. Meyer, pp. 413–31;
789–809.

16

do not let what is good to you be spoken of as evil: probably this is simply to say that what is good (the freedom of the strong) can, but must not, become regarded as bad when it leads to the compromise and ruin of the weak (v. 15). Other suggestions have, however, been made: that what is good is here the gospel of Christ itself, or the state of salvation, or even the kingdom of God.[f]

17

the kingdom of God: this is nothing like as common an expression in Paul's writings as it is in the Synoptic Gospels, though see I Cor. 4^{20}; 6$^{9, 10}$; 15$^{24, 50}$; Gal. 5^{21}; I Thess. 2^{12}; Col. 1^{13}. In some of these the time-reference is uncertain, but the future tends to predominate, the kingdom being what believers will inherit. In this passage, therefore, Paul may be talking about the life of heaven, which has nothing to do with eating and drinking, but is characterized by righteousness and so on. However, it is possible that the reference here is not future but present, akin to the Rabbinic 'taking upon oneself the yoke of the kingdom', which means accepting the practical obligations of being the people of God.[g] Such a present reference is made more likely by v. 18, which clearly is about serving God in the present time.

righteousness: for an observant Jew, righteousness (*dikaiosune*) would without doubt include obeying the Torah in one's diet. For Paul, here as usual in the letter its precise meaning is elusive (though see above on 1^{17}; 3$^{5, 21}$; also 9$^{30f.}$; 10$^{3-10}$). Yet it is clear enough that it is not defined by the Torah, for it is in contrast with concern over matters of diet. Together with peace and joy (cf. Gal. 5^{22}), it is the gift of the Holy Spirit. It may thus be that, without further details being given, it is the life of God's people that is made possible by the Spirit, and so has something of the character of the divine life.

20

Do not, for the sake of food, destroy the work of God: as in v. 15, the danger of which Paul writes is so serious that the weak may be destroyed *as Christians*. Once more we need something like I Cor. 8$^{4, 7-12}$, to explain the language. Once more, therefore, food offered to idols is the best

---

f See Wilckens III, pp. 92ff.; Cranfield II, pp. 715–17; Käsemann, pp. 376f.

g See the materials in Sanders, *PPJ*, pp. 85f.; see also *m. Aboth* 3.5, where the yoke of the Law frees one from other yokes.

candidate for the matter at issue. Those who eat against their conscience really may be effectively destroying their Christian discipleship by mixing their worship of the God of Jesus Christ with that of pagan deities.

Everything is indeed clean: the word for 'clean' is here *katharos* and its opposite is *kakos* and not *koinos* as in v. 14, but the same point is being made.

21

it is right not to eat meat or drink wine: we saw in the introduction to the passage that abstention from wine may have been brought into the discussion simply as a hypothetical parallel, perhaps suggested by the mention of food *and drink* in v. 17.[h] Yet someone, somewhere must have abstained from wine, or it would be an unconvincing parallel. While there were teetotal pagan groups, regular total abstinence by Jews was rare. Of course there could have been a teetotal Jewish group in Rome of whose existence we otherwise know nothing, yet as we saw in the introduction to the passage, the most obvious explanation is that there were some who abstained from wine for fear that it was libation-wine, so that abstention from wine and from meat were for the same reason. It may not be otiose to repeat that there is nothing in this chapter to suggest that abstention from wine was a community issue in the same way that abstention from meat was.

It is to be noted that the verbs 'eat' and 'drink' are aorist infinitives, the use of the aorist implying that we are concerned not with a general habit but with a particular occasion. If so, Paul is presumably not advising the strong to give up meat and wine altogether; rather is he advising them to abstain on those occasions when eating or drinking could cause problems for other people. This again fits well with the advice he gives in I Cor. 8, 10.

that makes your brother stumble: some MSS, including the notable B and D, expand this verse to read 'or to offend or to weaken (him)'. It is likely that the text as implied by RSV is more correct, and that the expansion was made by copyists who recalled I Cor. 8^{11-13}.[i]

22

The faith that you have: as in v. 1, there is good reason to think that faith here is Christian confidence or assurance. In effect, he is saying 'you are

h See Cranfield II, p. 725; Jewett, *Terms*, p. 44.
i So Metzger, p. 532; Wilckens III, p. 95f.; Cranfield II, p. 725 n. 1.

quite sure that there is no pagan power in the meat, and you are not endangering your exclusive devotion to the one God by eating it. This is between you and God.'

no reason to judge himself for what he approves: it would be lamentable if one had to condemn oneself for doing what one was quite convinced was legitimate and right (i.e. eat meat), but had discovered to have done terrible harm to someone else.

23

whatever does not proceed from faith is sin: this has been taken to mean that all actions by non-Christians, however virtuous they may seem, are in fact sinful.^{j} Surely, however, this statement must be kept within its context. Paul is still talking about eating or not eating, and faith is still the assurance or even good conscience about which he began to write in v. 1. The person who goes beyond that assurance, and eats in the conviction or suspicion that it is wrong to do so, sins. To make of this a general principle that all actions that do not proceed from Christian faith are sinful, is more than perilous: it is absurd. Every day all Christians do innumerable things which cannot sensibly be said to spring from their Christian faith, including large numbers of routine and quite unreflective things, not to mention the equally innumerable good things done by people who have no Christian faith. Paul himself acknowledged that in Ch. 2. It is worth adding that 'sin' here is used without any of the power-connotations that we found, for example, in 3⁹, and simply means wrongdoing.^{k}

15$^{1-13}$ THE HEALTH OF THE COMMUNITY UNDER GOD

15 *We who are strong ought to bear with the failings of the weak, and not to please ourselves; ²let each of us please his neighbour for his good, to edify him. ³For Christ did not please himself; but, as it is written, 'The reproaches of those who reproached thee fell on me.' ⁴For whatever was*

j See the useful discussion in Cranfield II, pp. 728f.

k The ascription of praise that in RSV comes at 16²⁵⁻²⁷ is inserted here by some ancient MSS. On the whole question of its placing, see Introduction 4, especially (*b*) (ii).

written in former days was written for our instruction, that by steadfastness and by the encouragement of the scriptures we might have hope. ⁵May the God of steadfastness and encouragement grant you to live in such harmony with one another, in accord with Christ Jesus, ⁶that together you may with one voice glorify the God and Father of our Lord Jesus Christ.

⁷Welcome one another, therefore, as Christ has welcomed you, for the glory of God. ⁸For I tell you that Christ became a servant to the circumcised to how God's truthfulness, in order to confirm the promises given to the patriarchs, ⁹and in order that the Gentiles might glorify God for his mercy. As it is written,

'Therefore I will praise thee among the Gentiles,
    and sing to thy name';
¹⁰and again it is said,
'Rejoice, O Gentiles, with his people';
¹¹and again,
'Praise the Lord, all Gentiles,
    and let all the peoples praise him';
¹²and further Isaiah says,
'The root of Jesse shall come,
    he who rises to rule the Gentiles;
    in him shall the Gentiles hope.'
¹³May the God of hope fill you with all joy and peace in believing, so that by the power of the Holy Spirit you may abound in hope.

In the discussion about eating meat in Ch. 14, Paul has shifted the debate away from the area of right and wrong, permissible and impermissible. He has dealt with it instead in terms of pastoral care for one another, and in terms of the health and upbuilding of the whole community. He now underlines this and generalizes it, and does not again refer specifically to the meat issue. Our primary concern must be for one another and not for ourselves, just as Christ was concerned for us and not for himself. The line of argument is not very clear in detail, but the overall preoccupation with the well-being of the church is obvious enough. The Scriptures provide the community with strength and hope, and Paul calls upon God to give it harmony and peace, in order that its praise of him may be with one voice.

It is likely that at v. 7 the apostle moves into a conclusion of the

whole section of ethical and practical advice that began at 12¹, and so
'welcome one another' picks up the similar plea from 14¹, but extends
its reference. The advice in Ch. 12 and Ch. 13 cuts across the division
between Jewish and Gentile Christians, and we have seen that the
same is probably true of Ch. 14 as well. Nevertheless much of the
letter has been concerned with the implications and dangers of just
that division, and it is therefore natural that at the close of this long
section of ethical advice we should be reminded that God has accepted
both Jews and Gentiles into the same Christian community. Consequently, they should be eager to accept one another. Together,
enabled to do so by God himself, they should unite in praise and in
hope.

 споен

1
We who are strong: once again Paul betrays where his sympathies lie.
It is extraordinary that he can use such prejudicial language in a passage
that is aimed at reconciliation, mutual respect, and at the accommoda-
tion of the strong in their practice to the susceptibilities of the weak.

ought to bear with the failings of the weak: the word rendered 'bear with'
(*bastazein*) means not so much 'put up with, endure' as 'give help with,
do something to assist with'.[1] It is doubtful if RSV really brings his
meaning out. Paul is recapitulating in a sentence what he has argued in
the preceding chapter. The strong do not just follow their own conscience, but take careful account of the needs and vulnerability of the
weak.

3
as it is written: Ps. 69⁹ LXX. This psalm is also used elsewhere in the
NT in connection with the suffering and death of Jesus, e.g. Mark 15³⁶;
Luke 23³⁶; John 19²⁹; Rev. 13⁸.[m] Paul almost never takes exemplary
material from the life of Jesus; here too he rather quotes the OT, as so
often applying it not to the life but to the death of Christ. Further, he
uses it not to expound the meaning of the cross, but to set the self-giving

l See the long footnote in Cranfield II, p. 730.
m See Hanson, *Technique*, pp. 15f.: those who insulted Christ, insulted God
though without realizing it. On the use of the psalm passage in general see
Lindars, *New Testament Apologetic*, pp. 98–108.

of Christ as the pattern for Christians' loving willingness to give themselves for others, cf. Phil. 2$^{6-8}$.

4

whatever was written in former days: this is an explanatory digression. In a modern text it would be in parentheses or appear in a footnote, but Paul had access to neither device. He is justifying his use of the psalm by saying that Christians rightly use what we call the OT for encouragement and instruction in the present time.

we might have hope: for hope/*elpis* see above at 4^{18}. The Scriptures lead to the confidence that the support God has given his people will continue to be given, and that as a consequence the future of the church is safe with him.

5

May the God of steadfastness and encouragement grant you to live in such harmony: as a result of the confidence expressed in v. 4, the church on earth may invoke God's help to create the harmony and mutual acceptance necessary to her life and well-being.

7

Welcome one another: this echoes 14^1. It either shows that we are continuing with the issue introduced there, so that the division dealt with in Ch. 14 is between Jewish and Gentile Christians, or it is a device which echoes that earlier verse in order now to apply it to the general question of division. In the second case, we do not need to assume that Ch. 14 is primarily about Jewish and Gentile Christians. As vv. 7–13 bring the sections of ethical and practical advice to a close, it seems more likely that we now leave the matter of food, and turn back to the division that dominated the letter up to the end of Ch. 11.

as Christ has welcomed you: our acceptance of one another is a reflection of Christ's unconditional acceptance of us. This is not just a recapitulation of what was said in 14$^{1-12}$, for there mutual acceptance was only a provisional principle. Paul went on to argue that the strong should be prepared to modify their practice in order to avoid injuring the weak. The present verse does not, therefore, fit very neatly with the outcome of the discussion in Ch. 14 about eating and not eating, and this reinforces the suspicion that this section is not about that, but is more general advice.

8

Christ became a servant to the circumcised: Christ was a Jew, a member of the circumcised people of God, and it is important that he became a servant to them. Why? Because God's reliability ('truthfulness') is at stake, cf. 3^4; 9^{1-5}; $11^{1ff.}$. God has not turned his back on his ancient people, cf. Ch. 11.

9

and in order that the Gentiles might glorify God for his mercy: see again Rom. 4, 9–11. The promises to Abraham are fulfilled not only within historical Israel, but also among the Gentiles who have faith in Christ. The Gentile church is thus an heir, and not a usurper of those promises. God has in Christ widened, but not contradicted, his dealings with Abraham and his descendants; indeed in Paul's view the wider application was implicit from the beginning, see again Chs. 4, 9–11. Now, when the body of the letter is complete, and Paul is making a transition to the long closing section consisting of a mixture of personal matters and rather general admonitions, there again surfaces the issue which has occupied so much of the epistle. That issue is the relation between God's Christian people and his ancient one.

As it is written: four OT passages are quoted, Ps. 18^{49}; Deut. 32^{43}; Ps. 117^1; Isa. 11^{10}. They are used to underline the scriptural basis for the hope that not only the descendants of Abraham humanly speaking, but also those Gentiles who have faith (v. 13), will receive God's mercy and be within his people.

15^{14-33} PAUL'S PLANS AND THE PURPOSES OF GOD

[14]*I myself am satisfied about you, my brethren, that you yourselves are full of goodness, filled with all knowledge, and able to instruct one another.* [15]*But on some points I have written to you very boldly by way of reminder, because of the grace given me by God* [16]*to be a minister of Christ Jesus to the Gentiles in the priestly service of the gospel of God, so that the offering of the Gentiles may be acceptable, sanctified by the Holy Spirit.* [17]*In Christ Jesus, then, I have reason to be proud of my work for God.* [18]*For I will not venture to speak of anything except what Christ has wrought through me to win*

obedience from the Gentiles, by word and deed, [19]*by the power of signs and wonders, by the power of the Holy Spirit, so that from Jerusalem and as far round as Illyr'icum I have fully preached the gospel of Christ,* [20]*thus making it my ambition to preach the gospel, not where Christ has already been named, lest I build on another man's foundation,* [21]*but as it is written,*

'They shall see who have never been told of him,
    and they shall understand who have never heard of him.'

[22]*This is the reason why I have so often been hindered from coming to you.* [23]*But now, since I no longer have any room for work in these regions, and since I have longed for many years to come to you,* [24]*I hope to see you in passing as I go to Spain, and to be sped on my journey there by you, once I have enjoyed your company for a little.* [25]*At present, however, I am going to Jerusalem with aid for the saints.* [26]*For Macedo'nia and Acha'ia have been pleased to make some contribution for the poor among the saints at Jerusalem;* [27]*they were pleased to do it, and indeed they are in debt to them, for if the Gentiles have come to share in their spiritual blessings, they ought also to be of service to them in material blessings.* [28]*When therefore I have completed this, and have delivered to them what has been raised, I shall go on by way of you to Spain;* [29]*and I know that when I come to you I shall come in the fulness of the blessing of Christ.*

[30]*I appeal to you, brethren, by our Lord Jesus Christ and by the love of the Spirit, to strive together with me in your prayers to God on my behalf,* [31]*that I may be delivered from the unbelievers in Judaea, and that my service for Jerusalem may be acceptable to the saints,* [32]*so that by God's will I may come to you with joy and be refreshed in your company.* [33]*The God of peace be with you all. Amen.*

With the transition to the closing part of the letter now made, the rest of this chapter is a mixture of travel plans looked at in the light of the divine purposes, and implicit exhortation to the Roman church, becoming explicit at the end with the reference to Paul's impending visit to Jerusalem. He justifies his having written to them so frankly by pointing to his commission as God's agent in bringing the Gentiles to him as an offering. In this commission he has seen notable success, but only because God himself has been working through him. He makes the astonishing claim that the preaching of the Christian message has been completed throughout an enormously wide area, and always in virgin territory. He has aimed always to break new ground, and not to water where another has planted. The dimensions of this task have hitherto prevented his visiting Rome, but the time has now arrived when he can look forward to doing so on his way to Spain. Meanwhile, he must go to Jerusalem to deliver the proceeds of his collection: this seems to have been important theologically as well as financially. If its immediate purpose is to relieve the needs of the poor Jerusalem Christians, it also has the ecumenical aim of enabling the Jerusalem church to share the monetary resources of the Gentile churches, just as the latter have received benefit from the spiritual riches that have come to them from Jerusalem. The Jewish and Gentile churches are thus bound together in interdependence. Yet there may be further significance, for Paul, in bringing the gifts of the Gentiles to Jerusalem. He may see it as representing the flocking of the Gentiles to Zion at the End.

The section closes with an appeal for the prayers of the Roman Christians, first that Paul may survive the dangers inherent in his Jerusalem visit, and secondly that the church there will be prepared to accept the gift of the Gentile churches. There is evidently some doubt that they will. Finally, if all goes as he hopes, he will soon be with them.

※

14

I myself am satisfied about you: as we saw (Introduction 1), it is debated how far Paul wrote Romans to answer the needs of the Roman church, which he knew well enough for this to be feasible, and how far he wrote out of a pre-occupation with the needs of his mission as a whole, and to enlist the help of the Romans (whose situation he may have known hardly at all). This verse gives some modest support to the first view: it appears to imply that he was reasonably well-informed about them, and was encouraged by what he knew (cf. 1⁸).

16

in the priestly service of the gospel of God: the terminology of this verse is strongly redolent of that of the Temple.[n] Indeed the word rendered

n See Wilckens III, p. 118; Cranfield II, p. 755f.

'minister' (*leitourgos*) is so often used of a Levite in the OT (LXX) that Paul may be saying that he is a Levite in the Christian cult, with Christ himself as the priest. Yet this is hardly made plain in the verse, and it may be a mistake to try to pin down too precisely the reference of the cultic language. At all events we see here an example of the transfer of Jewish cultic language to the Christian community, which must therefore hold much the same place within the Christian world as the Temple has held within Judaism. o

the offering of the Gentiles: in the Christian version of the cult, the Gentile Christians are an offering to God, analogous to (or even, perhaps, a replacement of) the sacrificial offerings in the Temple. This increases the suspicion already gained from Ch. 11 that Paul sees the coming of the Gentiles into the (Christian) people of God as the fulfilment of the hope that in the last days they would stream to Zion (cf. on 9^{26}). p Taking the collection to Jerusalem would thus be a highly significant action. Even if this interpretation is rejected as lacking solid justification in the text, it is still the case that the substantial success of the Pauline mission in bringing Gentiles into the people of God is seen as enormously important in the history of God's dealings with his people and with humanity in general.

18

I will not venture to speak of anything except what Christ has wrought through me: there are two things this could mean.

(*a*) Paul is not qualified, nor does he intend, to speak of any other branches of the Christian mission, but only of that in which he has himself been engaged.

(*b*) More probably, in the light of the stress in the verse on what God has done, he is saying that he does not want to speak of what he has done as if it were his achievement. Rather is it what God has done by means of him. q

19

by the power of signs and wonders: this is a rare indication within his own letters that Paul's ministry was accompanied by miracles, though see

o See also on $12^{1f.}$; also Phil. 4^{18}; Newton, *Purity*, p. 72.

p See Munck, *Salvation*, Ch. 10; Richardson, *Israel*, pp. 145f.; Sanders, *PLJP*, p. 171.

q So Käsemann, p. 393; Wilckens III, pp. 118f.; Cranfield II, pp. 757f.

II Cor. 12^{12}. In Acts, on the other hand, it is a more commonly mentioned feature, e.g. 13^{4-12}; 14^{8-10}; $16^{16-18, \, 25-34}$; perhaps most notably of all, 19^{11-20}.

from Jerusalem and as far round as Illyricum I have fully preached the gospel of Christ: Illyricum is part of modern Yugoslavia, and there is no record anywhere of Paul's having preached there. This is then a source of puzzlement in this verse. It is possible that Illyricum is regarded as the western limit of the eastern part of the Roman Empire, so that Paul is claiming to have covered it as a whole, apart from Italy and the west. This, however, only serves to pinpoint an even greater source of puzzlement: could Paul really claim to have preached everywhere in such a vast area? Plainly he could not; the idea is so absurd that it cannot be what he is saying. The most likely explanation is that he is claiming to have covered the area in a representative fashion, going to the chief centres, from which the gospel could then spread into the surrounding country.[r]

20

lest I build on another man's foundation: Paul has aimed always to be the pioneer. In accordance with this, he must intend to evangelize not Rome but Spain, and v. 24 makes it clear that it is indeed Spain that is his goal, and that Rome is but a staging-post. It is true that 1^{15} gives a decidedly different impression: on the problem of reconciling the two passages see Introduction 1(*a*). From the present passage it is plain that he expects to visit Rome at least primarily to make it a forward base for his Spanish mission, cf. v. 24, and not for its own sake. Moreover, it is obvious from Ch. 16 (assuming that it was originally directed to Rome) that there are already Pauline Christians there: see vv. 3–4, and perhaps also vv. 2, 5, 7, 8, 9, 13. Because of this, and perhaps also because Rome, as the capital of the empire, could be regarded as a special case, Paul exhibits no embarrassment over any inconsistency between preaching the gospel to the Romans (1^{15}) and avoiding building on someone else's foundation.

21

as it is written: Isa. 52^{15} LXX is quoted to underline his sense of vocation to be a pioneer preacher.

r See Wilckens III, p. 122; Cranfield II, p. 762; Sanders, *PLJP*, p. 186, who rightly points out that even so it remains a hyperbolic claim.

22

This is the reason why I have so often been hindered from coming to you: cf. 1^{13}, where no reason for the hindrance is given. What has hindered him? One could argue that he had been hindered by Satan (cf. I Thess. 2^{18}), or by God (on the grounds that God is usually the implied agent when a passive verb is left without a stated agent). Nevertheless neither of these is plausible here, for it is plain enough from 'This is the reason' (*Dio*) that he has simply been too pre-occupied with the programme outlined in vv. 19–20.

23

I no longer have any room for work in these regions: why ever not? Surely there must have been large numbers of towns and villages left which had not been evangelized. We can only speculate, but the best guess is that in the terms suggested for v. 19, he has completed what he regards as the pioneer work, and it is time to leave the development of it to others.

24

as I go to Spain: did he ever get there? It seems unlikely, unless we adopt the theory that after being in prison in Rome he was released, conducted further missionary work, and then was again arrested, and finally was executed. The only real evidence for this is *I Clem.* 5$^{6-7}$, where it is said that Paul 'reached the limits of the west', which could well mean Spain. It is to be suspected, however, that Clement is simply echoing this verse, and assuming that Paul was able to carry out his intention.

be sped on my journey there by you: 'be sped by' (*propemphthēnai*) often means 'be escorted by'. Käsemann (p. 398) is probably right to suggest that Paul is hoping for practical help which would include the provision of companions to act as escorts and guides.

25

I am going to Jerusalem with aid for the saints: cf. v. 31; also I Cor. 16^1; II Cor. 8$^{19f.}$. The saints are usually just ordinary Christians (see on 1^7), but it is obvious that here they are the Jerusalem Christians in particular. Strangely, there is no request that the Romans should participate, except by praying that the money may be accepted, v. 31. The reason for this must presumably be that the collection was taken up specifically from Pauline churches, of which Rome was not one. If there was a conflict between the Pauline version of Christianity and the more traditionally

Jewish Christianity of Jerusalem, the Roman church was outside it, but its prayers for and its endorsement of the ecumenical enterprise would be the more vital.

At all events, the collection loomed large enough on Paul's horizon . for him to defer his westward plans while he took it in person to Jerusalem. If it were merely a matter of poor relief, someone else could have taken it. Moreover, we know from I Cor. 16^3 and II Cor. 8^{19} that he took a sizable party with him to deliver the money, as representatives of at least some of the churches that had given it. All this serves to confirm that for Paul it was a crucial ecumenical matter.[s]

26

contribution: Greek *koinonia*, which usually means 'sharing/participation'. Here, as in II Cor. 8^4 and 9^{13}, it is virtually a technical term for the collection. We may see the beginnings of Paul's enterprise of gathering money for Jerusalem in Gal. 2^{10}, at the end of his account of the so-called Jerusalem Council, 'only they would have us remember the poor, which very thing I was eager to do'.

the poor among the saints at Jerusalem: although 'the poor' (*hoi ptōchoi*) had by this time in some Jewish writing become more or less a synonym for the godly and pious, who were often also the oppressed and the economically deprived,[t] the term is here to be taken literally. The collection was for the poor *among* the Jerusalem saints.

27

the Gentiles have come to share in their spiritual blessings: i.e. in things to do with their faith. Christianity, and that includes Pauline Gentile Christianity, has Jewish roots and Jerusalem is its home town, cf. 15^6 and also 9^5; 15^{8f}. We may also think of 11^{17-24}, where the Gentile Christians are grafted into a Jewish tree. In the things that matter most, the Gentiles are deeply in debt to the Jews, but this does not mean that the debt must remain only on one side. The collection is a sign and expression of mutual belonging, though not of dependence.

[s] See above on 9^{26} and 15^{18} for the possibility that it was even more than this. We should note that Watson, *PJG*, pp. 174–6, thinks the collection was not an ecumenical gesture, but an attempt to persuade Jerusalem to recognize the legitimacy of the Pauline churches. It would be surprising if there were not some element of such a hope.

[t] See E. Bammel in *TDNT* VI, pp. 888–915.

28

When therefore I . . . have delivered to them what has been raised: literally, 'When therefore I . . . have sealed to them this fruit'. This expression is puzzling, though 'fruit' is evidently the proceeds of the collection. 'Sealed to them' may imply some formal handing over, with the giving of a receipt of some sort, or with the attestation of witnesses. At least some kind of ceremonial occasion seems needed to account for the rather high-flown language.

29

I shall come in the fulness of the blessing of Christ: some later MSS expand this to read 'in the fulness of the blessing of the gospel of Christ'. The weight of the MSS is against such an expansion, which may have been influenced by the mention of the gospel of Christ in v. 19. The difference in meaning is scarcely of importance.

30

the Lord Jesus Christ . . . the Spirit . . . God: it is sometimes noted that in passages like this (see also v. 16) we have the materials which later led to the doctrine of the Trinity.[u] The consequences of talking about God in a threefold way soon began to emerge, but this passage pre-dates such developments, and it would be anachronistic to read into it a trinitarian view of God.

to strive together with me: although it is possible that this is an allusion to Jacob's wrestling with God (Gen. 32[24ff.]), neither the verb (*sunagōnizes-thai*: occurring nowhere else in NT or LXX) nor any of its cognates is used in that story in LXX. It is more likely, therefore, that Paul is simply using a very vivid image for strenuous prayer in which he wants the Roman Christians to join him.[v]

31

that my service to Jerusalem may be acceptable: Paul's call for strenuous prayer is not only for his own safety, but also for a favourable reception for the collection. Obviously this is in some doubt, despite the arrangement made according to Gal. 2[10], and it suggests a deterioration in relations between the Pauline and Jerusalem churches. It is a fact that Acts very strangely gives no more than the barest hint that there ever was a

u So Barrett, pp. 275, 279.
v So Cranfield II, p. 777, against Black, p. 177.

collection (24^{17} implies it, without using the word *koinōnia*), despite its importance to Paul and despite Luke's own ecumenical tendency. There is therefore a distinct possibility that in the event it was not accepted and that Paul's fears were justified. ^{w} If Jewish scruples did indeed have this result, then because the rejection was such a painful episode, Luke's passing the whole matter over in silence is understandable. ^{x}

16   CLOSING GREETINGS AND A WARNING

16 *I commend to you our sister Phoebe, a deaconess of the church at Cen'-chre-ae,* ^{2}*that you may receive her in the Lord as befits the saints, and help her in whatever she may require from you, for she has been a helper of many and of myself as well.*

^{3}*Greet Prisca and Aquila, my fellow workers in Christ Jesus,* ^{4}*who risked their necks for my life, to whom not only I but also all the churches of the Gentiles give thanks;* ^{5}*greet also the church in their house. Greet my beloved Epae'netus, who was the first convert in Asia for Christ.* ^{6}*Greet Mary, who has worked hard among you.* ^{7}*Greet Andron'icus and Ju'nias, my kinsmen and my fellow prisoners; they are men of note among the apostles, and they were in Christ before me.* ^{8}*Greet Amplia'tus, my beloved in the Lord.* ^{9}*Greet Urba'nus, our fellow worker in Christ, and my beloved Stachys.* ^{10}*Greet Apel'les, who is approved in Christ. Greet those who belong to the family of Aristob'ulus.* ^{11}*Greet my kinsman Hero'dion. Greet those in the Lord who belong to the family of Narcis'sus.* ^{12}*Greet those workers in the Lord, Tryphae'na and Trypho'sa. Greet the beloved Persis, who has worked hard in the Lord.* ^{13}*Greet Rufus, eminent in the Lord, also his mother and mine.* ^{14}*Greet Asyn'critus, Phlegon, Hermes, Pat'robas, Hermas, and the brethren who are with them.* ^{15}*Greet Philol'ogus, Julia, Nereus and his sister, and Olym'pas, and all the saints who are with them.* ^{16}*Greet one another with a holy kiss. All the churches of Christ greet you.*

w So Dunn, *Unity and Diversity*, pp. 256f. On the whole issue see Wilckens III, pp. 129–31: the acceptability of the collection was bound up with the acceptability of the Pauline gospel and the Pauline churches.

x After v. 33 the MS 𝔓^{46} adds the doxology found only at 16$^{25-27}$ in RSV, before going on to Ch. 16. On the whole question see Introduction 4, especially (*b*) (ii).

¹⁷*I appeal to you, brethren, to take note of those who create dissensions and difficulties, in opposition to the doctrine which you have been taught; avoid them.* ¹⁸*For such persons do not serve our Lord Christ, but their own appetites, and by fair and flattering words they deceive the hearts of the simple-minded.* ¹⁹*For while your obedience is known to all, so that I rejoice over you, I would have you wise as to what is good and guileless as to what is evil;* ²⁰*then the God of peace will soon crush Satan under your feet. The grace of our Lord Jesus Christ be with you.*

²¹*Timothy, my fellow worker, greets you; so do Lucius and Jason and Sosip'ater, my kinsmen.*

²²*I Tertius, the writer of this letter, greet you in the Lord.*

²³*Ga'ius, who is host to me and to the whole church, greets you. Eras'tus, the city treasurer, and our brother Quartus, greet you.*

²⁵*Now to him who is able to strengthen you according to my gospel and the preaching of Jesus Christ, according to the revelation of the mystery which was kept secret for long ages* ²⁶*but is now disclosed and through the prophetic writings is made known to all nations, according to the command of the eternal God, to bring about the obedience of faith –* ²⁷*to the only wise God be glory for evermore through Jesus Christ! Amen.*

Apart from a puzzling warning against false teachers (vv. 17–20), and a long and florid doxology of disputed provenance (vv. 25–27), this chapter consists of an exceptionally long series of greetings. Since we have taken it that this chapter was written by Paul to the church in Rome, we are faced with the questions why he greeted so many people, and why they are so often greeted in groups. It seems very unlikely that he could have known so many people in a church he had not visited, though he clearly knew some of them from their participation in his churches elsewhere. As there are references to the church in someone's house, and also to some people 'and the brethren who are with them', it looks as if Paul is addressing the chief members of a series of house churches, some of whom he knows and who probably support his kind of Christianity. Some of them may not. The chapter certainly reads like an attempt to be as comprehensive as possible. If so, it is presumably because there is a problem of disunity which may arise from more than one cause. The issue dealt with in Ch. 14, for a start, may easily have resulted in house churches which were not in fruitful communion with each other. Again, the fact that so much of the letter is devoted to the relationship between Jews and Gentiles in the people of God suggests that there were strained relations between them in Rome. At all events, as in no other letter, he appears to be including as many groups and individuals as possible.

At this stage in its history, the church in any city could only meet as one group when it was very small. House churches were therefore inevitable, which made it the more vital that they should be in active fellowship with one another. The practicalities of space created enough divisions without more being added as a consequence of theological or ethical disputes. At the same time it is clear that, as in Paul's churches generally,[y] there was in the Roman church pretty much of a cross-section of society, with the exception that there are no signs of the presence of either the truly upper class or the really destitute.

In vv. 17–20 we have a denunciatory passage unlike anything else in the letter. Elsewhere, differences of opinion are tackled discursively, by reasoned argument and persuasion. Here there is simply a brief and unexplained tirade. Therefore, either Paul did not address this chapter to the Romans, but to some other church to which vv. 17–20 were appropriate, or we have here an echo of a problem in Rome which otherwise goes without mention (see the Introduction 4 (*a*) (iv).)

Apart from the doxology, the letter closes with greetings from Paul's present associates, including Tertius who was its scribe.

ॐ

1

Phoebe, a deaconess of the church at Cenchreae: Cenchreae was the port of Corinth, from which Paul is usually assumed to have written to the Romans. In view of her pagan name, she is probably a Gentile, and it looks as if she is the bearer of the letter. We learn from v. 2 that she is a woman of some means; it is therefore reasonable to infer that, accompanied no doubt by servants, she is travelling to Rome on business and so is entrusted with the letter.

---

y See Meeks, *Urban Christians*, especially pp. 51–73, who also provides a most useful analysis of the persons named in this chapter in terms of their social and economic status.

The suggestion that she is a deaconess is misleading, for the word is *diakonos*, elsewhere translated 'deacon', cf. Phil. 1[1]; I Tim. 3[8, 12]. If the word is used of an office at all, then the office is that of deacon; she happens to be a woman, but that is no reason to suppose the nature of the office is changed. It is possible, however, that no formal office is implied, and that *diakonos* is a functional term, telling us that she gave service to the needy (perhaps it is necessary to add that the same could be true of men who are called *diakonoi*).

2

she has been a helper: the Greek is *prostatis*, which can indeed mean one who gives (unspecified) help. It can also mean 'president', but such a meaning is unlikely here: it is hard to imagine Paul regarding her or anyone else except Christ as presiding over him! More to the point, it could mean 'patron',[z] in which case she was something more than a generally helpful person. She was a woman of influence and wealth who was able to give protection to the struggling community of Christians in Cenchreae.

3

Prisca and Aquila: in Acts, the diminutive form Priscilla is used for the former, 18[2, 18, 26], but in the epistles she is always called Prisca. It is unusual that her name is mentioned before that of her husband here, as well as in II Tim. 4[19]; Acts 18[18, 26]. It may be because her social standing was higher than his, or because she was more active as a Christian, or because she became a Christian first. Both names are Roman, but according to Acts (18[2f., 18f., 26]) they were Jews who settled in Cenchreae after having been expelled from Rome along with other Jews, under Claudius. They then moved to Ephesus with Paul. In I Cor. 16[19] they send greetings *to* Corinth, and are presumably then in Ephesus, from which Paul is usually taken to have written I Corinthians (see 16[8]). Clearly, they were well acquainted with the Pauline mission, and were doubtless among those on whose support Paul could count in Rome.[a] They are thus Jewish Christians who are also supporters of Paul; they

---

z On this see Meeks, *Urban Christians*, p. 60, following the suggestion of E. A. Judge.

a If II Timothy, like I Timothy, is addressed to Ephesus, and if it is written by Paul, then II Tim. 4[19] shows that they have moved back to Ephesus. Both assumptions, however, are vulnerable.

are presumably well-to-do, as they have been able to offer hospitality to the church both in Ephesus and in Rome (cf. I Cor. 16⁹; Acts 18²ᶠ·).

4

they risked their necks for my life: we do not know how, when, or where. It may be an oblique reference to the serious trouble Paul faced in Ephesus: see I Cor. 15³², and the long list of troubles in II Cor. 11²³⁻²⁷, most of which are otherwise without mention in the NT. Acts 19³²⁻⁴⁰ may partly recount it.

5

the church in their house: for house churches see also I Cor. 16¹⁹; Col. 4¹⁵; Philemon 2. Church buildings were not usual before the fourth century, and were probably rare before the third, and even when they did exist they were at first ordinary houses given over entirely to church purposes. All this explains why hospitality was not a fringe virtue, but a basic necessity (see also on 12¹³). It also means that Christian gatherings were for a long time no larger than could be accommodated in an ordinary house, or especially in Rome, in the ancient equivalent of a flat (apartment). This limitation on size may well be reflected in the number of different groups mentioned in this chapter, and would make the more urgent all efforts to prevent further fragmentation of the community.

Epaenetus, who was the first convert in Asia for Christ: literally, 'who was the first fruits of Asia'. In view of his being called Paul's beloved, he also was probably a Pauline Christian, whom Paul had known in Asia. There is no reason to suppose he was anything but a Gentile, who had the means to travel.

6

Mary: of her we know nothing, and her name does not enable us to determine whether she was a Jew or a Gentile.

7

Andronicus and Junias: throughout the verse RSV assumes that these were both men. Increasingly this is being seen as unlikely: they were probably a married couple, Andronicus and Junia, the latter being a common Roman name for a woman. Junias as a man's name appears to be unsupported anywhere.[b]

---

[b] See Wilckens III, p. 135 and n. 647; Cranfield II, p. 788; R. R. Schulz, 'Romans 16:7: Junia or Jnias?', *Exp T* 98. 4, 1987, pp. 108–10.

my kinsmen: this almost certainly means they were fellow-Jews, not Paul's blood relations. If we accept that they were a married couple, then we should render *sungeneis* as 'my kins*folk*'. Like Prisca and Aquila, they were Jewish Christians who somewhere had participated in the Pauline mission (see below).

my fellow prisoners: there is no reason to avoid taking this literally. Somewhere they and Paul had been in prison together. It is less probable that they had shared the experience of imprisonment, but not at the same time in the same place.

men of note among the apostles: we should rather translate, 'people of note among the apostles'. 'Among' renders *en*, for which it is a natural translation; *en* would be an unusual word to choose if Paul wanted to say that they were well-known *to* the apostles. Andronicus and Junia were themselves well known apostles, one male and one female. Clearly they were not among the Twelve, nor even among that inner group expanded so as to include Paul (I Cor. 15⁹), from which it follows that this is an instance of the word *apostolos* used in a wider sense, cf. above on 1¹, and Acts 14⁴, ¹⁴; II Cor. 11⁵, ¹³⁻¹⁵; 12¹¹ᶠ·; *Did.* 11⁴.

they were in Christ before me: 'they were Christians before I was', and thus were very early Jewish Christians. 'In Christ' and 'in the Lord' are frequent expressions in this chapter, and the immediate reference is plain: to be in Christ is to be a Christian. Nevertheless behind the terms lies the conviction that was prominent earlier in the letter (most notably in 5¹²⁻²¹ and 8¹⁻¹¹) that Christians exist within the power and under the authority of Christ and his Spirit, cf. on 6¹¹.

8
Ampliatus: a slave name. If his being beloved by Paul implies that Paul knows him already, that may mean he is free to travel about, and so is an ex-slave, a freedman.

9
Urbanus: another slave name.

10
those who belong to the family of Aristobulus: this may well be the grandson of Herod the Great and friend of the Emperor Claudius. It is not he him-

self who is greeted, but his household, which almost certainly means his slaves. [c]

11

my kinsman Herodion: see on v. 7. He is a fellow-Jew.

who belong to the family of Narcissus: cf. on v. 10. As Narcissus himself is not greeted, he is presumably a pagan.

13

Rufus: a common enough name, and there is no particular reason to identify him as the son of Simon of Cyrene (Mark 15[21]), though Cranfield (II, pp. 793f.) thinks it is reasonable to do so.

his mother and mine: this is hardly to be taken literally so that Rufus was the brother of Paul. All it need mean is that somewhere she had been Paul's benefactress.

16

Greet one another with a holy kiss: the holy kiss is mentioned also in I Cor. 16[20]; II Cor. 13[12]; I Thess. 5[26]; I Peter 5[14]. It became a regular part of Christian worship, cf. Justin Martyr's *First Apology* 65[2], [d] and may already have been a normal practice when Paul wrote. We need to remember that this letter would almost certainly be read to the Roman Christians as they gathered together.

17

those who create dissensions and difficulties: at the end of enumerating people to be greeted, and before listing the people who join him in sending greetings, he breaks off. Perhaps the mention of the kiss, with its associations of peace in the church, has prompted the digression, though such sudden polemic near the end of a letter has parallels, see Gal. 6[12f.]; I Cor. 16[22]; even perhaps Phil. 3[18f.].

The most unexpected thing about vv. 17–20 is not the abrupt way in which they appear, but the fact that in them Paul does not argue. He simply denounces. It could hardly be farther from the mutual acceptance of differences of 14[1-12] and 15[7]. Unless we are to suppose that this

[c] On the extended household of the time see the useful summary in Meeks, *Urban Christians*, pp. 29f.

[d] For further early church evidence see Cranfield II, p. 796.

is a clumsily placed interpolation,[e] there seem to be three possible explanations.

(*a*) This chapter was not addressed to Rome at all, and the problem reflected in vv. 17–20 was a problem in another church, perhaps Ephesus, a problem for which such denunciatory terms were appropriate. However, for arguments against detaching this chapter from the rest of the letter and having it directed to another church see Introduction, 4(*a*).

(*b*) The passage is directed to Rome, but refers to some issue not otherwise mentioned in the letter. In that case it has nothing to do with the issue of the weak and the strong in Ch. 14. It may be a warning against a new group in Rome, or one about to visit Rome.[f] Paul cannot be expected to write in detail about everything in one letter, even in one as long as this, and here we have the adumbration of a further issue.

(*c*) This is addressed to those who will not accept the reconciling position Paul has argued for in Ch. 14, and in particular to those among the weak who will not concede that the view of the strong is legitimate, and so will not join in worship with them.[g]

If we reject the first solution, there is no coercive reason for choosing either the second or the third, in preference to the other. However, the second has an edge of inherent probability: despite the disadvantage that it invokes an unknown quantity, it is slightly preferable to supposing that Paul now reverts to an earlier issue but in dramatically different terms.

in opposition to the doctrine which you have been taught: on explanation (*c*) above, this would have to mean the position set out in 14[1]–15[6]. On the second explanation, 'the doctrine' would be quite generally the Christian gospel as they had received it, including its ethical aspect, cf. Rom. 6[17]; I Cor. 15[1ff.]; I Thess. 4[1ff.]; II Thess. 2[15]; perhaps especially Gal. 1[6–9]. 'Doctrine' is *tēn didachēn.*

e See O'Neill, pp. 252f.; against such a theory, see Wilckens III, p. 140. There is no MS evidence that it is an interpolation.

f See Wilckens III, p. 143. He suspects they were Judaizers, cf. Phil. 3[18f.]; Gal. 1[16f.]; 6[12ff.], rather than libertines. They could also be some form of early Gnostic group, but the absence of any attack on them for their speculations rather tells against this. See the whole of Wilckens III, pp. 141–5.

g So Watson, *PJG*, p. 102. Paul knows there will be some such recalcitrant people, and pre-empts their objections by denouncing them.

avoid them: if this is held to imply that they are not, or not yet, within the church, then we have reinforcement for the view that we have here a problem not hitherto discussed in Romans.

18

such persons do not serve our Lord Christ, but their own appetites: literally, they serve 'their own belly' (*koilia*). Since Paul is warning against their teaching, it is improbable that he is here talking about their gluttony. There could be a reference to Jewish food laws, or back to the discussion about idol-meat in Ch. 14 (though in that case the troublemakers would most plausibly be the strong who insisted on eating no matter what harm it did, not the weak who persisted in condemning those who ate). It is most likely that the reference to their appetites is figurative, especially in the light of their being servants of Satan (v. 20) and not real servants of God. They are then simply being accused of serving their own ends, whatever those may be. This is the rhetoric of denunciation, not the language of judicious assessment, compare II Cor. 11$^{13-15}$.

by fair and flattering words they deceive the hearts of the simple-minded: this may be held to imply a group trying to impose Jewish legal requirements (cf. Gal. 4^{17}; 6$^{12f.}$) rather than one of Gnostic tendency. The latter would not wish to be bothered with the simple-minded, nor would they expect to be understood by them. On the other hand, 'simple-minded' (*akakōn*) may just mean the godly, those who are sometimes all too ready to listen to what purports to be a divine message. It must be confessed that the whole passage is too vague and too allusive to enable us to draw firm conclusions about the identity of the threatening group.

20

the God of peace will soon crush Satan: as in II Cor. 11$^{14f.}$, the false teachers are not merely mistaken; they are missionaries of the Devil. Nevertheless, the End is not far away (cf. 13$^{11ff.}$), and with it will come the final defeat of the power of evil.

The grace of our Lord Jesus Christ be with you: in some MSS this occurs instead as v. 24. See Introduction, 4(*b*)(iii).

21

Timothy, my fellow worker: Paul's own greetings are now supplemented by some from his present companions. According to Acts 16$^{1-3}$

Timothy was half-Jewish. He was a regular fellow worker and messenger of Paul, cf. I Cor. 16[10f.]; II Cor. 1[9]; Phil. 2[19-24]; I Thess. 3[2, 6] (and see also Acts 16[1-4]; 17[14f.]; 18[5]; 19[22]; 20[4f.]). He is named with Paul as addressing and greeting churches in II Cor. 1[1]; Phil. 1[1]; Col. 1[1]; I Thess. 1[1]; II Thess. 1[1]; Philemon 1. Moreover, whatever view is taken of the authorship of the Pastoral Epistles, it cannot be insignificant that two of them are addressed to him. His association with Paul was obviously a particularly close one.

Lucius and Jason and Sosipater, my kinsmen: once again, this means that they were Jewish, like Paul. Lucius is a possible variant of Luke, but this is not sufficient reason to conclude that this is the Luke of Philemon 24, etc.

22
I Tertius, the writer of this letter: see Introduction, 5. We find similar indications that a scribe has done the actual writing of the letter in I Cor. 16[21]; Gal. 6[11]; Philemon 19.

23
Gaius, who is host to me and to the whole church: this seems to say, not only that Paul is staying in his house, but also that he can have the whole church meeting in it at one time. If so, he must have been a man of substantial wealth. His name is Roman.[h]

Erastus, the city treasurer: although it is possible he was a freedman, he is obviously now a person of considerable wealth and importance. Clearly not by any means all members of the Pauline churches were poor or socially insignificant. This man may be the Erastus named on a first-century stone discovered in Corinth.[i]

25
Now to him . . .: vv. 25–27 are commonly held not to be authentically Pauline, see Introduction 4, especially (*b*)(ii) and (*c*)(i)–(iii). The language is not typical of Paul, though there is nothing in the passage that is at odds with his thought, or indeed that he might not have adapted from

h See Meeks, *Urban Christians*, p. 57. Meeks has something illuminating to say about very many of the names in this chapter.

i On the issues involved in determining this, see Cranfield II, pp. 807f.; Meeks, *Urban Christians*, pp. 58f.

liturgical tradition. If it is a pious addition, it was made by someone who understood and agreed with the Pauline gospel.[j]

the revelation of the mystery which was kept secret for long ages: for 'mystery' (*mustērion*) see on 11[25]. What has always been part of the divine plan for the world is now at last openly visible. It is not the sort of thing reserved for an élite. See also I Cor. 2[6–10]; Col. 1[26f.]; Eph. 1[9f.]; 3[9–11]; II Tim. 1[9f.]; Titus 1[2f.]; I Peter 1[20].

26

through the prophetic writings is made known to all nations: this is a little unexpected. We should have anticipated that Paul would say that it is made known to all nations through the preaching of the gospel, per-haps with judicious but subsidiary reference to the OT (as in 1[17]; 4[3]; 9[33], for example). The strangeness is a little mitigated if we observe that it is the dissemination, but not the disclosure itself, that is through the prophetic writings.

27

to the only wise God . . .: whether Paul himself wrote this or not, the letter now ends appropriately with praise of God through Jesus Christ.

j So Wilckens III, p. 148; Gamble, *Textual History*, pp. 107–10.

Index of References

THE BIBLE
Old Testament

GENESIS

1	132, 144
1^2	202, 209
1^{26}	110
1^{27}	78, 227
2	144
2^7	202
$2^{16f.}$	187
2^{17}	145, 167
3	144, 182
3^{1-5}	220
3^{15-16}	220
3^{17-18}	219, 220
3^{19}	79, 145, 150, 167, 187
4^{21}	243
$6^{2,\,4}$	62
7^3	243
9^{12}	243
9^{16}	242
$10^{20,\,27}$	243
11^{10}	243
12^1	129
12^2	129, 216
12^5	129
12^7	129, 238
13^{14-17}	129, 238
13^{16}	129
$14^{4,\,8}$	243
14^{17}	242, 243
$15-18$	132
15^5	129, 131, 240
15^6	45, 60, 96, 109, 120, 121, 123, 125, 128, 129, 131, 132
$15^{17ff.}$	237
$17^{1ff.}$	237

17^{4-8}	216
17^{4-6}	96
17^5	131
17^8	129, 216
17^{10-14}	93, 128
$17^{16ff.}$	129, 238
17^{22-7}	129
18^3	121
18^{10}	240
18^{18}	129, 216
18^{19}	226
18^{25}	98
21^{12}	240
22	228
22^{12}	228
22^{16-18}	216, 238
22^{16}	228
22^{17-18}	96, 129
$25^{21ff.}$	240
25^{23}	241
$32^{24ff.}$	346

EXODUS

$4^{22f.}$	236
6^6	111
14^{13}	69
15^2	69
$15^{13,\,16}$	111
16^{10}	237
19^5	237
20^7	66
20^{16}	317
20^{17}	185
23^7	126
$24^{1ff.}$	237
24^{16}	237
$32^{31f.}$	236

33^{19}	242
33^{22}	237
$40^{34f.}$	237

LEVITICUS

9^2	204
14^{31}	204
16	113
16^{14}	114
17^{11}	114
18^5	187, 258–9
18^{22}	78
19^{18}	315, 317
19^{23-5}	277
20^{13}	78
20^{24-6}	59

NUMBERS

3^3	58
$6^{1ff.}$	323
8^{11}	59
11^{15}	236
$11^{24ff.}$	202
11^{34}	182
15^{17-21}	277
35^{30}	235

DEUTERONOMY

5^{20}	317
5^{21}	185
6^4	119
6^5	226, 317
$7^{6ff.}$	270
7^8	111
7^9	96, 226
$7^{25f.}$	91
9^4	260

Apocrypha

New Testament

NON-BIBLICAL JEWISH WRITINGS

EARLY CHRISTIAN WRITINGS

OTHER ANCIENT WRITINGS

Index of Authors

Index of Subjects

Abraham, 12, 15, 36, 38, 39, 45–6, 83, 96, 120–5, 127–9, 130–4, 203, 213, 216, 226, 228, 233–4, 237–9, 240–1, 251–5, 269, 277–8, 286–7, 339

Acceptance/Acceptability with God, 6, 40, 72–3, 118–19, 133, 152, 155, 319, 327, 338

Adam, 36, 75, 78, 131, 138, 144–53, 155–6, 159–60, 167, 180–5, 187–9, 191, 203, 210, 220, 227, 297

Adam, Christ as new/last, 39–40, 144–5, 147–9

Adoption, 214–15, 221, 222, 236, 240

Adoptionist christology, 62–3

Ages, old and new, 51, 61, 63, 69, 82, 108, 114, 144, 148–9, 152, 155, 157–8, 160, 162, 192, 201–2, 208, 211, 218, 222, 293–4, 311, 314, 316, 319–20; see also Eschatology, End

Akedah, 228; see also Isaac

Angels, 231

Apostle, apostleship, 57, 58–9, 275, 295, 340, 352

Apostolic Council, 9–10, 345

Aquila and Prisca, 13, 22, 350–1

Astrology, 52, 68, 154, 231, 329

Atonement, Day of, 113–14

Augustine, 139, 146, 149

Baptism, 154, 156–9, 168, 175, 194, 227, 262, 320

Blood (of Christ), 110, 114–15, 141

Boasting, 41–3, 46, 90, 116–18, 123–4, 143, 280, 282, 295–6

Body (sōma), 159–60, 164–5, 198–9, 211–13, 222, 292

Body of Christ, 172, 175, 236, 291, 296–8

Call of God, 50, 58–9, 64–5, 95, 225, 227, 233–5, 240–1, 248–9, 267, 274

Calling on God, 264

Catechesis, 29–31, 168, 299, 303, 320; see also Parenesis

Charismata; see Gifts, charismatic, and Powers, charismatic

Chrestus, 13

Christ; see Jesus Christ
  in Christ, 111–12, 142, 146, 162–4, 171, 175, 178, 201–2, 211, 232–3, 296–8, 321, 352

Church, 15, 175, 239, 278, 282, 287, 291, 296–8, 300, 303–4, 338

Cicero, 33

Circumcision, 9, 15, 43, 45–6, 48–9, 61–2, 65, 92–4, 95, 118–19, 121, 128–9, 178, 206–7, 316–18, 329, 339

Claudius, 13, 230, 350, 352

Clean and unclean foods, 331–4

Collection, the, 10–11, 18, 248–9, 275, 303, 341–2, 344–7

Coming again of Jesus, 261, 276

Command against eating, 180, 182, 184–7

Commandments, 48–9, 187, 206–7, 261, 315, 317

Condemnation, 136, 149, 152, 154, 201, 205, 249

Conscience, 88, 235, 313–14, 327, 334–5

Corporate personality, 163

Covenant, 11, 43, 67, 70–1, 92–5, 96–8, 105, 113, 138, 237, 240–1, 251–2, 270, 285

375